THE LEGAL DIMENSIONS
OF PRIVATE INCARCERATION

by

Ira P. Robbins

Barnard T. Welsh Scholar and Professor of Law & Justice
The American University
Washington College of Law

AMERICAN BAR ASSOCIATION
Criminal Justice Section
1800 M Street, NW
Washington, DC 20036
202/331-2260

Cite as:

I. Robbins, The Legal Dimensions of Private Incarceration
(American Bar Association, 1988).

This project was supported by grants to the American Bar Association Fund for Justice and Education from the John D. and
Catherine T. MacArthur Foundation and the National Institute of
Justice. The analyses, conclusions, and points of view expressed
in this study have not been approved by and do not necessarily
represent the official positions of the American Bar Association,
the MacArthur Foundation, or the National Institute of Justice.

PREFACE

The costs and frustrations of running the nation's prisons and jails have escalated in recent years. It is not surprising, therefore, that all levels of government have desperately been seeking new ways to respond to what appears to many to be an uncontrollable crisis.

One approach that gained adherents during this decade was to turn to private enterprise for solutions. It has long been assumed that the private sector, with far more flexibility than governmental bureaucracies have, can provide a range of services more efficiently and economically. Thus, it was inevitable that the concept of private prisons and jails would emerge at some point. In fact, private companies have administered individual programs such as vocational training and health-care services in some jurisdictions for many years.

When proposals for privatization of single institutions or entire prison systems first emerged, little thought had been given to the complex legal issues that they created. It was not all that clear, for example, whether government could delegate a function such as corrections to private industry, what the implications of such a delegation would be for liability if negligence or constitutional deprivation occurred, what the standards of performance should be, how performance should be monitored, and what would happen if there were breaches of contract or if a private correctional entity declared bankruptcy.

Given the potential importance of privatization and the legal uncertainties, the Prison and Jail Problems Committee of the ABA Criminal Justice Section agreed to review these issues. The Committee determined after an initial assessment that jurisdictions should not move precipitously into privatization arrangements until more careful analysis of the legal issues could be made. It recommended, therefore, that the ABA adopt the following Resolution:

> Be It Resolved, That the American Bar Association urges that jurisdictions that are considering the privatization of prisons and jails not proceed to so contract until the complex constitutional, statutory, and contractual issues are satisfactorily developed and resolved. "Privatization" refers to contracting for total operational responsibility for a prison or jail; it does not encompass construction or leasing physical facilities or contracting for institutional services, such as food preparation, medical care, and vocational training, in full security institutions or for operation of non-secure facilities such as half-way houses.

This Resolution was formally adopted in February 1986.

The Criminal Justice Section next applied for and received grant funds from the John D. and Catherine T. MacArthur Foundation and the National Institute of Justice to do the comprehensive study and to prepare a Model Contract and Model Statute as guidance for all jurisdictions considering delegating correctional functions to private enterprise. The Section selected Professor Ira P. Robbins, a nationally recognized correctional-law scholar from American University's Washington College of Law, to undertake the necessary research and report preparation. An Advisory Committee met on two separate occasions and was asked to comment on the Report while it was in draft form.

Professor Robbins has now completed this major project, which cuts across a large number of legal fields. Professor Robbins takes no position on privatization in his Report. Instead, Professor Robbins addresses the myriad legal issues in neutral terms. In my view, the Report will be an invaluable resource document.

The decision has been made to distribute the Report immediately, even though it has not yet been reviewed by the ABA Committees nor formally endorsed by the ABA. That process will take some time. In the interim, it was felt that interested jurisdictions should have access to this comprehensive work by an eminent correctional-law scholar.

Sheldon Krantz, Chair
Privatization of Prisons
  Advisory Board
ABA Section of Criminal Justice

August 1988

ACKNOWLEDGEMENTS

The author is pleased to acknowledge the contributions of the Privatization of Prisons Advisory Board:

Chairperson:

Sheldon Krantz
Dean
University of San Diego
School of Law

Members:

Alvin J. Bronstein
Executive Director
National Prison Project
    of the ACLU
Washington, D.C.

Paul Cascarano
Director
Office of Communication and
    Research Utilization
National Institute of Justice
Washington, D.C.

Tom Foley
Ramsey County Attorney
St. Paul, Minnesota
        Washington, D.C.

David Kozlowski
Senior Counsel
Legal Services of South Central
    Tennessee, Inc.
Tullahoma, Tennessee

Sidney I. Lezak
Newcomb, Sabin, Schwartz &
    Landsverk
Portland, Oregon
        Washington, D.C.

Thomas J. Madden
Venable, Baetjer, Howard
    & Civiletti
Washington, D.C.

Arthur McDonald
President
Eclectic Communications, Inc.
Ventura, California

J. Michael Quinlan
Director
Federal Bureau of Prisons

Anthony P. Travisono
Executive Director
American Correctional
    Association
College Park, Maryland

Penny Wakefield
Associate General Counsel
National Criminal Justice
    Association

National Sheriffs'
   Association Liaison:

H. Jerome Miron
Director of Research and
    Special Projects
National Sheriffs' Association
Alexandria, Virginia

ABA Staff Coordinator:

Elizabeth M. Harth
American Bar Association
Washington, D.C.

The author also acknowledges the following individuals who provided invaluable advice or assistance during the course of the project:

Wayne T. Ault
Thomas E. Baker
John B. Corr
Janice L. Gardner
Evelynn M. Gentemann
Karen Goxem
John Q. Heywood
Richard G. Higgins
David Jerome
Kirk S. Jordan
Charles H. Logan
Graciela Maldonado
Dan Messina
Louis Miron
Anne Palmer
Bernard H. Ross
Thomas O. Sargentich
Leslie A. Stout
Elisabeth A. Viar
Burton D. Wechsler
Maureen Williams

Sharyl Van Bogart deserves special recognition for meticulously typing the countless drafts of the manuscript.

Finally, the author acknowledges the correctional administrators and private-industry personnel who responded to his many inquiries.

IPR
August 1988

EXECUTIVE SUMMARY

Although the policy aspects of private-prison and private-jail operation have received a great deal of recent attention, there is a dearth of literature on the legal aspects of private incarceration. Not surprisingly, therefore, discussions to date have largely been uninformed, ill informed, or misinformed, since many of the policy questions have important constitutional, statutory, or contractual dimensions. This project was undertaken to present a comprehensive analysis of these dimensions and to provide practical guidance in the form of a Model Contract and Model Statute.[*]

An important feature of this study is the relationship between these model documents, on the one hand, and the constitutional-delegation doctrine, on the other hand. That doctrine has the potential to invalidate delegations of governmental functions that affect the liberty interests of individuals. The Model Contract and Model Statute, therefore, attempt to safeguard these interests, while at the same time accommodating the interests of the public, the government, and the private contractors.

---

[*] Formulation of these documents, however, should not be taken as an indication that either the American Bar Association or the author supports private incarceration. Rather, the documents have been drafted to balance the interests of the respective parties _if_ privatization is undertaken.

Other significant issues that are addressed in this study include:

- state-action liability;

- indemnification, immunity, and insurance;

- standards of operation;

- monitoring;

- inmate management; and

- statutory authority to privatize federal facilities.

The privatization of incarceration may be neither constitutional nor wise. Therefore, this study concludes that, if this critical governmental function is to be contracted out, it must be accomplished with total accountability. With incarceration, as with all areas of the justice system, we must remain eternally vigilant.

CONTENTS

I. INTRODUCTION

Few people would contend that the state of our nation's prisons and jails is ideal. Apart from whatever other ills plague these institutions, overcrowding is pervasive. Populations have doubled in a decade, and -- with preventive detention, mandatory minimum sentences, habitual-offender statutes, and the abolition of parole in some jurisdictions -- there is no relief in sight. Some states are even leasing or purchasing prison space in other states. And it is costing the taxpayers more than seventeen-million dollars a day to operate the facilities, with estimates ranging up to sixty dollars a day per inmate. Several commentators have not so facetiously noted that we could finance college educations at less cost for all of the inmates in the country.[1]

To reduce some of this stress on the system, a new concept has emerged: the privatization of incarceration facilities, sometimes known as "prisons for profit" or "punishment for profit."[2] The idea is to remove the operation (and sometimes the ownership) of an institution from the local, state, or federal government and turn it over to a private corporation.[3]

---

[1] See, e.g., Burger, The High Cost of Prison Tuition, 40 U. Miami L. Rev. 903, 909 (1986) (article by Chief Justice Warren E. Burger).

[2] See, e.g., Bacas, When Prisons and Profits Go Together, Nation's Bus., Oct. 1984, at 62; Castro, Public Service, Private Profits, Time, Feb. 10, 1986, at 64; Kroll, Prisons for Profit, Progressive, Sept. 1984, at 18; Logan & Rausch, Punish and Profit: The Emergence of Private Enterprise Prisons, 2 Just. Q. 303 (1985).

At the outset, it should be emphasized that private prisons are different from private <u>industries</u> in prison. The latter concept refers to Chief Justice Burger's "factories with fences" proposal, which seeks to turn prisoners into productive members of society by having them work at a decent wage and produce or perform services that can be sold in the marketplace.[4] In the process, the prisoners would be able to pay off some of the costs of their incarceration and, one would hope, gain some self-esteem. Privatization is also different from the situation in which <u>some</u> of the services of a facility -- such as medical, food, educational, or vocational services -- are contracted out to private industry. Rather, the developing idea, which may turn out to be a lasting force or just a passing fancy, is to have the government contract with a private company to run the <u>total</u> institution.

The privatization concept has sparked a major debate.[5] Its

---

[3] Privatization, of course, is not unique to incarceration. One writer has noted, for example, that experiments in privatization literally run the gamut of the alphabet, from adoption and airport services to zoning control. E. Savas, Privatization: The Key to Better Government 73-74 (1987) (listing 157 city and county services contracted out to private firms).

[4] Keynote address by Warren E. Burger, National Conference on "Factories with Fences": The Prison Industries Approach to Correctional Dilemmas (June 18, 1984), <u>reprinted</u> <u>in</u> Prisoners and the Law ch. 21 (I. Robbins ed. 1987).

[5] This debate has not been peculiar to the United States. Other countries have been looking to us for guidance, giving our early experience mixed reviews. <u>See</u>, <u>e.g.</u>, Home Affairs Comm. (U.K.), <u>Fourth Report: Contract Provision of Prisons</u>, 1986-87 Sess. (May 6, 1987); Home Affairs Comm. (U.K.), <u>Third Report: State and Use of Prisons</u>, 1986-87 Sess. (Apr. 23, 1987); Sénat Rapport No. 102 (France), Première Session Ordinaire de 1986-87

proponents, who include not only some corrections professionals, but also major financial brokers who advise investors to consider putting their money into private prisons and jails, argue that the government has been doing a dismal job of administering its correctional institutions and detention facilities. Costs have soared, prisoners are coming out worse off than when they went in, and while they are in they are kept in conditions that shock the conscience, if not the stomach.

The private sector, advocates claim, can save the taxpayers money. It can build facilities faster and cheaper, and it can operate them more economically and more efficiently. With maximum flexibility and little or no bureaucracy, new ideas (like testing new philosophies) and routine matters (like hiring new staff) can be implemented quickly. Overcrowding -- perhaps the

---

(Dec. 10, 1986); H. Friel, Operational and Resource Management, Review No. 7: Privatization, Phase 1 (1985) (Canada); P. Young, The Prison Cell 39 (1987) (recommending "wide-ranging [privatization] experiment in Britain"); Ballantyne, US Private Gaols 'Shock' UK Officers, Guardian, Feb. 12, 1987, at 6; Ballantyne, MPs Say Private US Gaols Show Way for Britain, Guardian, Oct. 28, 1986, at 5; Le Gendre, Prisons Privées: Les "Pour" et les "Contre", Le Monde, Dec. 19, 1986; Le Gendre, Une Seule Solution, la Privatisation des Prisons, Le Monde, Nov. 20, 1986 (noting argument that incarceration is an essential duty of government, but also noting expectation of reduced costs from privatization); Prison Officers' Association (U.K.), America's Private Prisons: "Penal Institutions as Potential Moneyspinners", Jericho, Fall 1987, at 10, 11 (warning of "loss leader" concern from private company "establish[ing] the respective state's dependence on the private sector and then . . . substantially increas[ing] charges"); PROP, Private Prisons -- By Appointment to H.M. The Queen: Purveyors of Incarceration, Solitary Confinement and Body Belts, Abolitionist, No. 23, at 23 (1987) [hereinafter Purveyors of Incarceration] ("[t]he model, as is so often the case with penal policies, is an American one -- a fact which, in itself, should be sufficient to counsel extreme caution"); M. Ryan & T. Ward, Politics and Prison Privatization in Britain (1988) (unpublished manuscript).

major systemic problem facing corrections today -- can be reduced. A further anticipated benefit of privatization is decreased liability of the government in suits that are brought by inmates and prison employees.

The critics respond on many fronts. They claim, for example, that it is inappropriate to operate incarceration facilities with a profit motive, which provides no incentive to reduce inmate populations (especially if the company is paid on a per-prisoner basis), nor to consider alternatives to incarceration, nor to deal with the broader problems of criminal justice. On the contrary, critics claim that the incentive would be to build more prisons and jails. And if they are built, we will fill them. This is a fact of correctional life: the number of incarcerated criminals has always risen to fill whatever space is available.

Moreover, opponents argue that private-prison corporations will be drawn to cost-cutting measures that will have adverse effects on the prison system. As a reporter for Barron's has written, "the brokers, architects, builders and banks . . . will make out like bandits."[6] But questions concerning people's freedom should not be contracted out to the lowest bidder. In short, privatization is not a panacea; the private sector is more interested in doing well than in doing good.[7]

_____

[6] Duffy, Breaking Into Jail, Barron's, May 14, 1984, at 20, 22.

[7] This idea was succinctly expressed by the director of program development of Triad America Corporation, a multimillion-dollar Utah-based company that was considering

-4-

These _policy_ aspects of private incarceration have gotten a great deal of attention.[8] Unfortunately, however, there is scant _legal_ literature on private-prison and private-jail operation.[9] Not surprisingly, therefore, discussions to date have largely been uninformed, ill informed, or misinformed, since many of the policy questions have important constitutional, statutory, or contractual dimensions. Such questions include the following:

- Is it constitutional to contract out the operation of an entire prison or jail facility?

- Will privatization reduce or eliminate the government's state-action liability?

- What standards will govern the operation of a private institution?

- Who will monitor implementation of the standards?

- Will the public still have access to the facility?

- What recourse will members of the public have if they do not approve of how the institution is operated?

- Who will be responsible for maintaining security and

---

proposing a privately run county jail in Missoula, Montana: "We'll hopefully make a buck at it. I'm not going to kid any of you and say we are in this for humanitarian reasons." _Triad Studies Possibility of Building, Operating Jail in Missoula County_, Deseret News, June 20-21, 1985, at B7 (statement of Jack Lyman); _see_ also _Privatizing Prisons Has Become a Ripe Market for Entrepreneurs Despite Public Sector, Union Opposition and Risks_, Privatization, July 21, 1988, at 4.

[8] _See infra_ Selected Bibliography.

[9] Some of the literature is excellent. _See_, _e.g._, Note, _Inmates' Rights and the Privatization of Prisons_, 86 Colum. L. Rev. 1475 (1986) (analyzing theoretical and practical legal aspects of privatization). Some is superficial and naive. _See_, _e.g._, Report of the President's Commission on Privatization, _Privatization: Toward More Effective Government_ 146-59 (1988) (providing thinly supported and poorly reasoned recommendation for contracting out entire facilities).

using force at the institution?

- Who will be responsible for maintaining security and controlling the institution if the private personnel go on strike?

- Where will the responsibility lie for making quasi-judicial decisions -- such as classification, transfer, discipline, and parole?

- Will the private company be able to refuse to accept certain inmates -- such as those who have contracted AIDS?

- What options will be available to the government if the private company substantially raises its fees?

- What safeguards will prevent a private contractor from making a low initial bid to obtain a contract, then raising the price after the government is no longer able to reassume the task of operating the facility (e.g., due to a lack of adequately trained personnel)?

- What will happen if the company declares bankruptcy (e.g., because of liability arising from a prison riot), or simply goes out of business because there is not enough profit?

- What safeguards will prevent private vendors, after gaining a foothold in the incarceration field, from lobbying for philosophical changes for their greater profit?

Because of these and other weighty and difficult questions, the House of Delegates of the American Bar Association passed a Resolution in February 1986 recommending that "jurisdictions that are considering the privatization of prisons and jails not proceed . . . until the complex constitutional, statutory, and contractual issues are satisfactorily developed and resolved." This study picks up where the Resolution left off. Its goals are twofold: to present a comprehensive analysis of the numerous legal dimensions of private incarceration; and to provide practical guidance in the form of model contractual and statutory provisions, with accompanying commentary, for those jurisdictions that wish to privatize.

A word of caution is in order regarding these provisions. The Model Contract and Model Statute contained in this paper do not presuppose the desirability of private incarceration. That question was not the subject of this study. Plainly stated, therefore, formulation of these documents should not be taken as an indication that either the American Bar Association or the author supports the private operation of prisons and jails. Rather, the documents have been drafted to accommodate the interests of the respective parties *if* privatization is undertaken.[10] The theme of the documents -- and, indeed, of this entire study -- is that, if jurisdictions seek to privatize their incarceration facilities, they must ensure accountability -- to the public, to the government, to the inmates, and to the contractor's own promises.

---

[10] More than one individual has already missed the significance of this distinction. *See*, *e.g.*, Report of the President's Commission on Privatization, *supra* note 9, at 154 (seeming to infer support for privatization from ABA's grant to develop model statutes and contracts); Letter from Richard Crane, Vice President, Legal Affairs, Corrections Corporation of America (Jan. 1987) ("[The grant to work] on model contractual provisions . . . obviously implies something more than a simple 'don't do it' position.").

II. CONSTITUTIONAL DIMENSIONS

All of the issues and concerns that are mentioned in the
Introduction are significant. Before any of them come into play,
however, three constitutional dimensions of private incarceration
must be addressed: the delegation doctrine, the state-action
requirement, and the thirteenth amendment. The most important of
these subjects -- the delegation doctrine -- raises the threshold
question for private incarceration: Is it constitutional, under
both federal and state constitutions, to delegate the
incarceration function to private corporations? This question
alone is the subject of this section of the paper.

A. The Delegation Doctrine

1. Introduction

Since prison privatization is an issue at both the federal
and state levels, it is necessary to discuss the development of
the delegation doctrine at both levels. This discussion,
however, necessarily involves different approaches because
development of the doctrine itself has differed markedly in
federal and state courts. The doctrine has suffered from lack of
attention and use at the federal level, while state courts
continue actively to review private delegation. At the federal
level, the Supreme Court has not invalidated legislation on
delegation grounds since 1936, in <u>Carter v. Carter Coal Co.</u>[11]

Federal courts have accepted, often without comment, delegation of federal power to private actors.[12] In 1974, Justice Marshall wrote that the doctrine "has been virtually abandoned by the Court for all practical purposes."[13] Although several recent concurring and dissenting opinions may prove this comment to have been a bit premature, it is clear that doctrinal development at the federal level has been hampered by disuse.

In addition, fundamental differences between federal and state due process approaches, the constitutional source for limitations on private delegation, account for differences in the development and application of the doctrine. Federal courts face considerations of judicial economy, federalism, and institutional constraints that do not present particular concern to many state courts.[14]

The first part of this portion of the paper discusses the likely impact that the federal delegation doctrine would have on an attempt to privatize federal prisons. The second part discusses similar issues under state delegation doctrines. These parts explain the oversight and review functions that the governmental entity must perform over private-prison companies. Moreover, they note the activities that the government cannot

---

[11]   298 U.S. 238 (1936).

[12]   Lawrence, Private Exercise of Governmental Power, 61 Ind. L.J. 647, 648 (1986).

[13]   FPC v. New England Power Co., 415 U.S. 345, 352-53 (1974) (Marshall, J., concurring).

[14]   See Lawrence, supra note 12, at 672-75.

delegate to the private-prison company and conclude that the principles announced in current delegation law may allow government to delegate prison management to a private company if the government properly oversees, reviews, and circumscribes the private company's authority. This section of the paper notes, however, that, because incarceration implicates the life and liberty interests of the persons who are detained, courts might not apply the delegation principles announced in extant delegation cases, since only property interests generally were at issue in those cases. Thus, the question is an extremely close one, and it would not be surprising if a court were to rule against constitutionality.

2. Federal Delegation

a. Brief History

Although the Constitution does not explicitly state that Congress may not delegate its powers to others, the United States Supreme Court has asserted the principle that Congress may not delegate its powers to other branches of the government[15] or to private parties.[16] Roots of the doctrine are found both in article I of the Constitution, which states that "[a]ll legislative Powers herein granted shall be vested in a Congress

---

[15] Field v. Clark, 143 U.S. 649, 692 (1892) (dictum).

[16] Carter v. Carter Coal Co., 298 U.S. 238, 311 (1936).

of the United States,"[17] and the due process clauses of the fifth and fourteenth amendments.[18] As Justice Brandeis pointed out, the two concepts are related: "The doctrine of the separation of powers was adopted by the Convention of 1787, not to promote efficiency but to preclude the exercise of arbitrary power."[19] The constitutional limits on executive power serve to prevent arbitrary executive action under the conviction that the people must look to representative bodies and courts to protect their liberties. Protection of the individual from the arbitrary and capricious exercise of power, by an official body or a private party acting under delegated authority, is an essential element of free government. Thus, the underlying purpose of the delegation doctrine should be to provide needed protection against uncontrolled discretionary power.[20] The Supreme Court generally has used an article I separation-of-powers argument when considering delegation to an agency or other public body. When considering delegations to private parties, however, the Court has employed a due process analysis.

---

[17] U.S. Const. art. I, § 1.

[18] See Dreyer v. Illinois, 187 U.S. 71, 83-84 (1902) (rejecting argument that state government improperly delegated judicial power to executive parole board and upholding delegation on fourteenth amendment due process grounds).

[19] Myers v. United States, 272 U.S. 52, 293 (1926) (Brandeis, J., dissenting).

[20] 1 K. Davis, Administrative Law Treatise § 3.2, at 150 (2d ed. 1978).

(1) Delegation to Public Bodies

Although it frequently asserts the nondelegation principle,
the Supreme Court almost always sustains the constitutionality of
challenged delegations.[21] In doing so, the Court has taken
various approaches to accommodate increasingly broad
congressional delegations.[22] Although in its early stages the
delegation doctrine required Congress to legislate "as far as was
reasonably practicable,"[23] the doctrine now requires only that
Congress state an "intelligible principle"[24] when it delegates
legislative power.

Field v. Clark[25] was one of the early Supreme Court cases to
discuss the delegation doctrine. Congress had empowered the
President to raise tariff schedules and suspend trade with a
foreign country if he determined that a duty imposed by the
foreign country on American products was "reciprocally unequal
and unreasonable."[26] This delegation was challenged on the
ground that it delegated the power to tax; it was upheld,
however, on the theory that the President "was the mere agent of

---

[21] Freedman, Delegation of Power and Institutional
Competence, 43 U. Chi. L. Rev. 307, 307 (1976).

[22] Comment, The Fourth Branch: Reviving the Nondelegation
Doctrine, 1984 B.Y.U. L. Rev. 619, 621-30.

[23] Buttfield v. Stranahan, 192 U.S. 470, 496 (1904).

[24] J.W. Hampton, Jr. & Co. v. United States, 276 U.S. 394,
409 (1928).

[25] 143 U.S. 649 (1892).

[26] Id. at 693.

the law-making department" and his only role was to ascertain a fact.[27]

The principle announced in Field, that Congress constitutionally may delegate a fact-finding function, was reiterated in Buttfield v. Stranahan.[28] In Buttfield, Congress delegated authority to the Secretary of the Treasury to prohibit the importation of impure and unwholesome tea.[29] The Supreme Court observed that the duty of the government experts who examined the tea was to ascertain whether such conditions existed that conferred a right to import.[30] Citing Field, the Court held that the statute did not confer legislative power on administrative officials, and added that "Congress legislated on the subject as far as was reasonably practicable."[31]

Within twenty-five years, the Court retreated to a less stringent standard. In United States v. Grimaud,[32] the Court cited Field's prohibitory language against delegation, but deflated its meaning by stating that "the authority to make administrative rules is not a delegation of legislative power."[33] A further retreat in the Grimaud case involved the

---

[27] Id.

[28] 192 U.S. 470 (1904).

[29] Id. at 471-72 n.1.

[30] Id. at 497.

[31] Id. at 496.

[32] 220 U.S. 506 (1911).

[33] Id. at 521.

shift to permitting delegation if it was accompanied by an "adequate standard."[34]

In J.W. Hampton, Jr. & Co. v. United States,[35] the Supreme Court changed its "adequate standard" test to require Congress to establish "intelligible principles."[36] The Court upheld a delegation of authority to the President to audit tariffs to equalize differences between costs of goods produced domestically and those produced by foreign competitors.[37] The Act also established certain guidelines for determining trade imbalances and fixing limits of exchange, and made investigation by the Tariff Commission a prerequisite to changing duties.[38] The Court stated that, "[i]f Congress shall lay down by legislative act an intelligible principle to which the person or body authorized to fix such rates is directed to conform, such legislative action is not a forbidden delegation of legislative power."[39]

---

[34] Id. at 515-16; see also Union Bridge Co. v. United States, 204 U.S. 364, 384-85 (1907) (holding that Congress cannot delegate any part of its legislative power except under the limitation of a prescribed standard); cf. United States v. Chicago, M., St. P. & Pac. R.R., 282 U.S. 311, 324 (1931) (asserting that an Interstate Commerce Commission rule was a proper exercise of delegated authority only if it was warranted by statutory standards that defined the delegated authority).

[35] 276 U.S. 394 (1928).

[36] Id. at 409.

[37] Id.

[38] Id. at 400-02.

[39] Id. at 409; see Yakus v. United States, 321 U.S. 414, 426 (1944) (applying intelligible-principle test to uphold constitutionality of Emergency Price Control Act of 1942); Amalgamated Meat Cutters v. Connally, 337 F. Supp. 737, 745-46 (D.D.C. 1971) (upholding Economic Stabilization Act of 1971

The Supreme Court has invalidated Congress's delegation of authority on article I grounds on only two occasions, both occurring during the New Deal era of the 1930s. Although the Court has never expressly overruled either case, the cases are probably aberrations, because the Court has never relied seriously on either case to analyze delegation issues. In A.L.A. Schechter Poultry Corp. v. United States,[40] the Court struck down a section of the National Industrial Recovery Act (NIRA) authorizing the President to establish "codes of fair competition" for a virtually unlimited number of industries and trades.[41] Section 3 of the Act gave the President power to approve detailed codes on his own initiative or on application by the industries or trade associations that were affected.[42] The Court focused on the absence of standards or restrictions as well as on the scope of the delegated powers and the discretion granted to the President. Justice Cardozo termed the statute

---

against delegation challenge) (citing Yakus, 321 U.S. at 424).

[40] 295 U.S. 495 (1935).

[41] Id. at 521-22.

[42] Id. at 521-23. The Court summarized its discussion of Section 3 by stating:

> It supplies no standards for any trade, industry or activity. It does not undertake to prescribe rules of conduct to be applied to particular states of fact determined by appropriate administrative procedure. Instead of prescribing rules of conduct, it authorizes the making of codes to prescribe them. For that legislative undertaking, § 3 sets up no standards, aside from the statement of the general aims of rehabilitation, correction and expansion described in section one.

Id. at 541.

"delegation running riot," amounting to a complete transfer of Congress's power under the commerce clause.[43]

In contrast, the Court in <u>Panama Refining Co. v. Ryan</u>[44] dealt with a different section of NIRA that seemed more in line with legislation that the Court had previously upheld. It authorized the President to restrict the interstate transportation of petroleum produced in excess of the amount permitted by state law.[45] The Court found no adequate criteria to control the President's authority. General policy statements admonishing the President "to remove obstructions to the free flow of interstate and foreign commerce which tend to diminish the amount thereof," "eliminate unfair competitive practices," and "conserve natural resources" were declared to be inadequate principles.[46]

(2) Delegation to Private Parties

Although the Supreme Court has held delegations to private parties to be unconstitutional on delegation grounds several times during this century,[47] the vast majority of Court cases

---

[43] <u>Id</u>. at 553 (Cardozo, J., concurring).

[44] 293 U.S. 388 (1935).

[45] <u>Id</u>. at 406-07.

[46] <u>Id</u>. at 417.

[47] <u>See</u> Washington <u>ex rel</u>. Seattle Title Trust Co. v. Roberge, 278 U.S. 116, 122 (1928) (invalidating ordinance that prohibited philanthropic home for the aged in zoning district without consent of designated portion of neighbors); Eubank v.

have upheld such delegations as constitutionally valid.[48] In fact, the Supreme Court has not invalidated a private delegation since the New Deal era case of Carter v. Carter Coal Co.,[49] in which a federal statute making maximum hours and minimum wages agreed on by a majority of miners and producers binding on the remainder was held invalid. The Court in Carter Coal stated:

City of Richmond, 226 U.S. 137, 144 (1912) (invalidating statute that delegated to two-thirds of certain property owners the power to determine how far buildings were to be set back from the street).

[48] See, e.g., Sunshine Anthracite Coal Co. v. Adkins, 310 U.S. 381, 397-98 (1940) (holding that Bituminous Coal Act did not unconstitutionally delegate to National Bituminous Coal Commission the power to fix prices because statutory standard that guided Commission was sufficiently specific); United States v. Rock Royal Coop., 307 U.S. 533, 577-78 (1939) (upholding against delegation challenge statute providing that administrative determination concerning milk price was not effective unless two-thirds of area milk producers approved price); Currin v. Wallace, 306 U.S. 1, 15-16 (1939) (reasoning that statute conditioning tobacco-inspection requirements on votes of two-thirds of affected tobacco producers did not unlawfully delegate legislative power to those producers, but rather was a condition that Congress permissibly could place on operation of its own statute); Old Dearborn Distrib. Co. v. Seagram-Distillers Corp., 299 U.S. 183, 193-94 (1936) (holding that Illinois fair-trade law forbidding retailers to sell product below resale price, fixed in contract with other producers, did not unconstitutionally delegate legislative power to those other retailers because producer's interest in protecting value of its good will in trademark or brand name was itself a property interest that the state could legitimately protect); Thomas Cusack Co. v. City of Chicago, 242 U.S. 526, 531 (1917) (reasoning that statute permitting one-half of property owners to remove zoning restriction on property was not unconstitutional delegation because statute merely allowed property owners to remove existing restrictions rather than impose new ones); Butte City Water Co. v. Baker, 196 U.S. 119, 126-27 (1905) (upholding against delegation challenge statute giving legal effect to rules that miners had developed concerning whether and in what circumstances property rights in mining claim vest).

[49] 298 U.S. 238 (1936).

This is legislative delegation in its most obnoxious
form; for it is not even delegation to an official
or an official body, presumptively disinterested,
but to private persons whose interests may be and
often are adverse to the interests of others in the
same business. . . . And a statute which attempts
to confer such power undertakes an intolerable and
unconstitutional interference with personal liberty
and private property.[50]

The ban on delegation was based on fifth amendment due
process grounds. The choice of due process grounds rather than
separation-of-powers notions might suggest that article I imposes
no per se ban on federal delegations to private parties[51] and
that they are to be judged by more flexible due process criteria.
Carter also may suggest that whatever constitutional restrictions
do exist may apply equally to the states by virtue of the
fourteenth amendment, a result that would not be reached if the

_____

[50] Id. at 311.

[51] See Lawrence, supra note 12, at 665-66. Lawrence
explained that

[s]eparation of powers may have some relevance to
delegations of legislative power to executive
agencies, in that one department might then in fact
be exercising the power of another, but a private
delegation does not cross the lines between
departments. It has been argued that the purpose of
the separation-of-powers requirement is to protect
individual liberty, in that dispersing power among
several agents prevents a liberty-endangering
concentration of power in one or a few hands. If
that view is correct, then private delegations serve
the same goal because power is spread still
further. One need not carry the argument that far,
however, to see that the separation-of-powers
principle is a weak foundation for limiting private
delegations.

Id. (footnote omitted).

prohibition found its source in article I.[52] (It is important to note, however, that, whatever the federal practice, state courts continue actively to review private delegations.[53]) The delegation cases that followed Carter all upheld increasingly broad private delegations without ever questioning Carter's holding that Congress could not delegate legislative power to private parties.[54]

Commentators generally agree that the Supreme Court has not stated a satisfactory theory of the principles governing the delegation doctrine and has failed to articulate a precise test to distinguish between statutes that properly delegate and those that do not.[55] Although there is some indication of renewed interest in the doctrine in dissenting and concurring opinions,[56]

---

[52] Liebmann, Delegation to Private Parties in American Constitutional Law, 50 Ind. L.J. 650, 664 (1975).

[53] See Lawrence, supra note 12, at 675. Lawrence stated that

> the doctrinal development of federal due process may
> be affected by considerations of judicial economy,
> federalism, and institutional constraints that do
> not so strongly affect the state courts. In
> addition, the election of state courts, the nature
> of state constitutions, and the methods of state
> legislatures combine to make it more tenable for a
> state court to overturn legislative decisions.

Id.

[54] See supra note 48 (listing, inter alia, post-Carter delegation cases upheld by the Supreme Court).

[55] For commentary criticizing the Court's failure to develop and consistently apply rational principles to delegation cases, see, e.g., 1 K. Davis, supra note 20, § 3.12, at 193; Liebmann, supra note 52, at 664; Schoenbrod, The Delegation Doctrine: Could the Court Give It Substance?, 83 Mich. L. Rev. 1223, 1289 (1985); Comment, supra note 22, at 620.

not since 1948 has any opinion for the Court's majority even attempted to deal in a substantial manner with the delegation doctrine. Consequently, it is difficult to predict how the Court would treat delegation in the private-incarceration context. The Supreme Court has often decided cases that could have turned on delegation issues on other grounds and avoided the issue altogether, or has treated it only in passing.[57] For example, the Court chose to decide several cases on state-action grounds even though it could have ruled on delegation grounds.[58]

---

[56] See infra notes 89-104 and accompanying text.

[57] See Schoenbrod, supra note 55, at 1232-33 (arguing that recent Supreme Court cases that have narrowed or invalidated statutes on vagueness or due process grounds have avoided explication of delegation doctrine); cf. Liebmann, supra note 52, at 653-54 (observing that the distinction between deprivation of due process and equal protection, on the one hand, and unlawful delegation, on the other hand, is often obscure).

[58] See Liebmann, supra note 52, at 654 n.16 (citing Fuentes v. Shevin, 407 U.S. 67 (1972) and Sniadach v. Family Fin. Corp., 395 U.S. 337 (1969)). Liebmann argued that,

> if courts are willing to find state action under such circumstances, definite parallels to the former abuses of the delegation doctrine exist. It may not be too much to say that the due process and equal protection clauses have in recent years been doing some of the work formerly done by the delegation doctrine.

Id. But see Schneider, The 1982 State Action Trilogy: Doctrinal Contraction, Confusion, and a Proposal for Change, 60 Notre Dame L. Rev. 1150, 1152 (1985) (observing that in recent years the Supreme Court has been moving toward a restrictive state-action doctrine). See generally infra notes 115 & 214-395 and accompanying text (discussing state-action doctrine in private-incarceration context).

b. Current Federal Law

.Because there are no recent Supreme Court cases that have
turned on the delegation doctrine, current federal law that is
most analogous to the private-prison context is found in opinions
upholding the Maloney Act,[59] which authorizes self-regulation of
the securities industry, against challenges that the Act
unconstitutionally delegated legislative power to a private
institution. The Act provides for promulgation of rules by a
dealer association and disciplinary proceedings against its
members.[60] Under the statute, disciplinary rules must require
specific charges, a hearing of record, and a statement of the
findings.[61] In addition, if an association member is
disciplined, it has the right to appeal to the Securities and
Exchange Commission (SEC), which in turn decides whether the
petitioner committed the charged acts and whether those acts
violated the association's rules.[62] The SEC may then reduce,
cancel, or leave undisturbed the penalty that was imposed.[63]

In R.H. Johnson & Co. v. SEC,[64] the United States Court of
Appeals for the Second Circuit found no merit in a constitutional

---

[59] 15 U.S.C. § 78o-3 (1982).

[60] Id. § 78o-3(b).

[61] Id. § 78o-3(h).

[62] Id. § 78o-3(h)(3).

[63] Id.

[64] 198 F.2d 690 (2d Cir. 1952).

challenge to the delegation. The court summarily dismissed the challenge, noting that the SEC, a fully public body, has the power, according to reasonably fixed statutory standards, to approve or disapprove of the association's rules and to review any disciplinary action.[65]

(1) The Todd Test

The test for measuring the constitutionality of the delegation was stated more specifically in Todd and Co. v. SEC.[66] The United States Court of Appeals for the Third Circuit held that the Maloney Act did not unconstitutionally delegate governmental power to private securities associations.[67] In so holding, the court articulated a three-pronged test.[68] First, following R.H. Johnson & Co., the SEC must have the power to approve or disapprove of the association's rules.[69] Second, in any disciplinary proceeding, the SEC must make de novo findings aided by additional evidence, if necessary.[70] Third, the SEC must make an independent decision on the violation and the

---

[65] Id. at 695.

[66] 557 F.2d 1008 (3d Cir. 1977).

[67] Id. at 1012.

[68] Id.

[69] Id.

[70] Id. But cf. First Jersey Sec. v. Bergen, 605 F.2d 690, 697 (3d Cir. 1979) (holding that amendment to Maloney Act was constitutional even though it restricted the SEC's ability to receive additional evidence), cert. denied, 444 U.S. 1074 (1980).

penalty.[71] Another part of the _Todd_ opinion held that the Board of Governors of the National Association of Securities Dealers (N.A.S.D.) erred in reinstating a dropped charge without notice of its intention to do so.[72] The court chastised the SEC for failing to insist on meticulous compliance with N.A.S.D. appellate procedure.[73] As a consequence, the SEC order was vacated and remanded with instructions that the proper procedure be followed.[74] The decision thus emphasized the close link between the delegation doctrine and due process concerns.[75]

The _Todd_ test suggests that the constitutionality of the delegation in the private-prison context would turn on the structure under which the delegation occurred. If a corrections agency promulgated rules of prison administration in the first instance, then the delegation would satisfy the first prong of

---

[71]   557 F.2d at 1012.

[72]   _Id_. at 1014.

[73]   _Id_.

[74]   _Id_. at 1015.

[75]   The court reasoned that, because the SEC was

[c]harged with making independent decisions and its own interpretations of the N.A.S.D.'s rules, the Commission must insure fair treatment of those disciplined by the Association. . . . Since it is a departure from the traditional governmental exercise of enforcement power in the first instance, confidence in the impartiality and fairness of the Association's procedures must be maintained. The S.E.C., therefore, should not cavalierly dismiss procedural errors affecting the rights of those subjected to sanctions but should insist upon meticulous compliance by the private organization.

_Id_. at 1014.

the Todd test because the public body, not the private party, is responsible for the rule-making process. If the private company had rule-making power, however, then the corrections agency, an independent public body, must have authority to approve or disapprove of those rules according to reasonably fixed standards. The second and third prongs of the Todd test concern disciplinary proceedings. This aspect is of particular concern in the private-prison context because these proceedings may affect the length of a prisoner's confinement, his eligibility for parole, or his loss of good-time credits. Under the second prong of the test, the corrections agency must make de novo findings. Under the third prong, the agency must make an independent decision on the violation and the penalty. Whether a delegation would satisfy the second and third prongs depends initially on who has control over disciplinary proceedings. If the private company maintained control over such proceedings, then the corrections agency must make de novo findings and an independent decision on the violation and the penalty.

A recent article suggests that, to avoid legal challenge, it might be preferable for the state to maintain control over all disciplinary proceedings.[76] In this situation, where the private company is confined to a primarily administrative role, the United States Court of Appeals for the Ninth Circuit, in Crain v. First National Bank,[77] suggested a minimal delegation problem.

---

[76] Mayer, Legal Issues Surrounding Private Operation of Prisons, 22 Crim. L. Bull. 309, 320 (1986).

[77] 324 F.2d 532 (9th Cir. 1963).

Crain dealt with provisions of the Klamath Termination Act, which provides that Indians who are determined to be in need of assistance may place their funds in private trusts.[78] Pursuant to provisions of the Act, the Secretary of the Interior made individual determinations that certain members of the Klamath Indian tribe were in need of assistance in conducting their affairs and placed appellants' funds in private trusts that the bank administered. The court held that the Act did not unconstitutionally delegate legislative power to a private corporation. In support of its holding, the court cited Berman v. Parker,[79] a 1954 Supreme Court case that distinguished between the power to enact laws and authority or discretion concerning their execution.[80] The court stated: "While Congress cannot delegate to private corporations or anyone else the power to enact laws, it may employ them in an administrative capacity to carry them into effect."[81] Additionally, the court observed that Congress had detailed the proper objectives, goals, and methods of carrying out such management.[82]

Again, when applied in the private-prison context, Berman suggests that courts would uphold delegations to private-prison

---

[78] Id. at 533.

[79] 348 U.S. 26 (1954).

[80] Crain, 324 F.2d at 537.

[81] Id.

[82] Id. But see Republic Indus., Inc. v. Central Pa. Teamsters Pension Fund, 693 F.2d 290 (3d Cir. 1982) (striking delegation to private arbitrator of power to adjudicate rights of employers in multi-employer pension fund).

companies because the private corporation was employed not to enact laws but to carry them into effect in an administrative capacity. The extent to which this case is fully analogous to the private-prison context, however, depends on who makes the initial determination to discipline the prisoner. In Crain, the Secretary of the Interior had made the initial determination. An employee of the private company, however, might make the initial determination to discipline a prisoner.

(2) Possible Inapplicability of the Todd Test

It is important to note that all of the aforementioned cases dealt with property interests. Therefore, courts might not apply the reasoning of these cases to the private-prison context because a private prison affects the prisoner's liberty interests. In Kent v. Dulles,[83] the Supreme Court suggested that it would apply a more stringent standard when it analyzed the constitutionality of delegations in cases affecting a liberty interest.[84] The Court in Kent construed a statute that granted broad discretion to deny passports.[85] The Court held that, if "activities or enjoyment, natural and often necessary to the well-being of an American citizen, such as travel, are involved, we will construe narrowly all delegated powers that curtail or

---

83   357 U.S. 116 (1958).

84   Id. at 129.

85   Id.

dilute them."[86] The opinion did not identify these rights, but commentators generally have understood these standards to apply to statutes involving "protected freedoms," as opposed to statutes that regulate property.[87]

c. Possible Trend to Revive the Delegation Doctrine

As stated earlier, no Supreme Court majority opinion since 1948 has even attempted to deal in a substantial manner with the delegation doctrine.[88] A number of dissents and concurrences, however, have argued forcefully for one side or the other.[89] Moreover, two opinions by Justice Rehnquist may signify that the doctrine is not entirely dead, although their line of reasoning

---

[86] Id.; cf. United States v. Robel, 389 U.S. 258, 275 (1967) (Brennan, J., concurring) (asserting that "numerous deficiencies connected with vague legislative directives . . . are far more serious when liberty and the exercise of fundamental rights are at stake").

[87] Schoenbrod, supra note 55, at 1232. The property/ liberty distinction has been used to invalidate the federal sentencing guidelines on delegation grounds. See, e.g., United States v. Williams, No. 3-88-00014, slip op. (M.D. Tenn. June 23, 1988) (en banc). The Williams court stated: "In our view, . . . the property interests in [economic] regulations, which fall at one end of the delegation continuum, are readily distinguishable from the liberty interest implicated in being incarcerated or subject to other criminal sanctions." Id. The Supreme Court has recently granted certiorari on this issue in another case. See United States v. Mistretta, 56 U.S.L.W. 3848 (U.S. June 13, 1988) (Nos. 87-1904, 87-7028).

[88] See FPC v. New England Power Co., 415 U.S. 345, 352-53 (1974) (Marshall, J., concurring) (the delegation doctrine "has been virtually abandoned by the Court for all practical purposes," except where personal liberties are involved).

[89] Schoenbrod, supra note 55, at 1233.

is not directly applicable to private delegations.[90]

Justice Brennan wrote a well-considered analysis of the delegation doctrine in a dissenting opinion in the 1971 case, McGautha v. California,[91] which upheld a California statute allowing the jury to fix the death penalty without guidelines. Three Justices would have invalidated the statute on delegation grounds. After sketching the history of the delegation doctrine, Justice Brennan outlined three legislative techniques that Congress has used to "assure that policy is set in accordance with congressional desires and that individuals are treated according to uniform principles rather than administrative whim."[92] He noted, first, that Congress has undertaken to regulate even rather complex questions by the prescription of relatively specific standards.[93] Second, Justice Brennan noted that Congress has at times granted to others the power to prescribe fixed rules to govern future activity and adjudication.[94] Third, he noted that the most common legislative technique for dealing with complex questions has been delegation to another group of lawmaking power that the group may exercise either through rule-making or the adjudication of individual

---

[90]   See infra notes 97-104 and accompanying text (discussing recent Supreme Court opinions in which Justice Rehnquist wrote separately on delegation grounds).

[91]   402 U.S. 183 (1971).

[92]   Id. at 275 (Brennan, J., dissenting).

[93]   Id.

[94]   Id. at 276.

cases, with choice between the two methods left to the agency's judgment.[95] Justice Brennan then concluded that there was nothing inherent in the nature of capital punishment that made impossible the application of any or all of these means to check arbitrary action, but that the two state procedures under review failed to provide the necessary safeguards.[96]

Justice Brennan's opinion in McGautha involved a delegation of judicial sentencing power to a private group, the jury. A 1980 opinion by Justice Rehnquist, however, discussed the delegation doctrine in a case involving a delegation to a governmental agency. In Industrial Union Department v. American Petroleum Institute (the Benzene case),[97] five Justices voted to overturn an action taken under the Occupational Safety and Health Act. Four Justices reached this result by narrowly construing

---

[95] Id. at 278.

[96] Id. at 280, 287. For other cases that discussed the delegation doctrine, see National Cable Television Ass'n v. United States, 415 U.S. 336, 340-42 (1974) (construing narrowly a statute that authorized the FCC to set licensing fees to avoid the possibility that the statute unconstitutionally delegated the power to tax); Arizona v. California, 373 U.S. 546, 625-26 (1963) (Harlan, J., dissenting in part) (arguing that a statute that delegated power to Secretary of Interior to allocate waters from the Colorado River system was unconstitutional because the statute lacked standards to guide the Secretary's discretion).

Justice Harlan's dissent in Arizona discussed two purposes for the delegation doctrine that he believed were not furthered by the statute at issue. First, he stated that the delegation doctrine ensures that the elected body that is immediately responsible to the people will make fundamental policy decisions. Id. at 626. Second, Justice Harlan asserted that the delegation doctrine provides a statutory standard against which the courts can review a challenged official action. Id.

[97] 448 U.S. 607 (1980).

the Act to avoid an unconstitutionally broad delegation.[98]
Justice Rehnquist, the fifth vote, asserted that the
congressional delegation itself was unconstitutional because it
was ambiguous and violated the delegation doctrine.[99] He argued
that the delegation doctrine serves three important
functions.[100] First, "it ensures to the extent consistent with
orderly governmental administration that important [social policy
choices] are made by Congress."[101] Second, it guarantees that
the recipient of the authority is provided "with an 'intelligible
principle' to guide the exercise of the delegated
discretion."[102] Third, the doctrine enables "courts charged with
reviewing the exercise of delegated legislative discretion . . .
to test that exercise against ascertainable standards."[103]
Justice Rehnquist believed that the legislation at issue failed
on all three counts.[104]

---

[98] Id. at 607-71 (Stevens, J., joined by Burger, C.J.,
Stewart & Powell, JJ.).

[99] Id. at 685-86 (Rehnquist, J., concurring).

[100] Id.

[101] Id. at 685.

[102] Id. at 685-86.

[103] Id. at 686.

[104] Id.; see also American Textile Mfrs. Inst. v. Donovan,
452 U.S. 490, 543, 547-48 (1981) (Rehnquist, J., dissenting)
(arguing that Occupational Safety and Health Act of 1970 at issue
in Industrial Union Department unconstitutionally delegated to
Secretary of Labor the policy choice of whether and to what
extent cost-benefit analysis should determine industrial-safety
standards) (citing Industrial Union Dep't, 448 U.S. at 671
(Rehnquist, J., concurring)).

Justice Rehnquist's logic in the Benzene case is not directly applicable to the private-prison context, because the case dealt with a congressional delegation to a public agency rather than to a private party. Justice Rehnquist's concern centered on delegation of congressional responsibility for deciding major social policy. A delegation to a private-prison company that had adequate statutory guidelines does not involve the same issues.

At least one commentator[105] has viewed Justice Rehnquist's opinion in Benzene as consistent with the Court's decision in Immigration and Naturalization Service v. Chadha.[106] The Court in Chadha invalidated the legislative-veto provision in an immigration statute on the theory that the provision improperly delegated legislative power because it violated article I separation-of-powers requirements.[107] The Court approved the delegation to the Attorney General of authority to waive deportation because the Attorney General was bound by an articulated principle that could be applied in a consistent manner.[108] The Court, however, rejected the further delegation of uncontrolled decisionmaking discretion to one house of the legislature.[109]

---

105 See Schoenbrod, supra note 55, at 1235.

106 462 U.S. 919 (1983).

107 Id. at 954.

108 Id.

109 Id. at 958-59.

The Supreme Court used a formalistic and structural argument, turning on express constitutional requirements of bicameral passage and congressional presentment of the legislation to the President for signature into law. In striking down the legislation, the Court demanded that each branch of government exercise its constitutional responsibilities. The Court's focus, however, was abdication of constitutional functions to another branch of government, and not to a private party.

Justice White's dissent suggested that delegation to a private group contingent on some fixed statutory standard was not overruled and that previous doctrine survived.[110] But commentators have suggested that Chadha will effect "a significant judicial tightening of the limits within which Congress may entrust anyone with lawmaking power,"[111] and that Chadha will encourage Congress to delegate less with better policy standards when it does delegate.[112] Thus, although the analysis in Chadha does not apply directly to delegations to private-prison companies, Chadha may encourage Congress to make delegations under stricter statutory standards.

In summary, although no Supreme Court majority has attempted to deal in a substantial manner with the delegation doctrine

---

[110]   Id. at 967-1013 (White, J., dissenting); see also supra note 48.

[111]   Tribe, The Legislative Veto Decision: A Law by Any Other Name?, 21 Harv. J. on Legis. 1, 17 (1984) (emphasis in original).

[112]   Comment, supra note 22, at 621.

since 1948, there have been several important dissenting and concurring opinions. A consideration of these opinions leads one to conclude that courts might apply a more stringent standard of review to delegations that affect liberty interests than they do to those that affect property interests.

3. State Delegation

Although some commentators regard state delegation cases as unprincipled,[113] for the purpose of analysis this section of the paper divides state delegation cases into three parts. The first part discusses cases upholding statutes that delegate the management of government programs to private persons. The

---

[113] See, e.g., 1 K. Davis, supra note 20, § 3.12, at 196 ("The first edition of the Treatise and the 1970 Supplement elaborately presented the state law concerning delegation to private parties, but retention of that material in the present edition, along with the updating of it, seems undesirable, because identifiable principles do not emerge."); Lawrence, supra note 12, at 647 (noting that cases on delegation are inconsistent both within and among the states); see also D. Mandelker, D. Netsch & P. Salsich, State and Local Government in a Federal System 598 (2d ed. 1983). Mandelker, Netsch, and Salsich concluded that

> [t]he nondelegation doctrine is alive and well in the state courts. Delegation of power objections are frequently made to state and local legislation, although a review of the state cases indicates that most delegations are upheld. State delegation cases are common but the decisions are unprincipled. Except for the conclusion that some state courts more frequently invalidate delegations of power than others, a principled basis for the application of the delegation of power doctrine is difficult to find.

Id.

private parties in these cases had neither rule-making nor adjudicative powers, but merely managed government programs within the parameters established by either the legislature or an administrative agency. The second part discusses the issue of whether and in what circumstances states may delegate rule-making functions to private parties. The third part discusses the circumstances in which a state may allow a private party to adjudicate the rights of others and whether judicial review of private adjudication is necessary.

As each of these classes of cases is discussed, this section compares the factual differences between the cases discussed and the private-prison context. This section then explores the issue of whether a court would actually apply the principles announced in these cases to the private-prison context. The section concludes that the principles announced in existing case law may permit states to contract with private companies for the incarceration of its prisoners. The state, though, must retain certain rule-making and adjudicative functions.

It is crucial to note, however, that the factual and philosophical differences between the private-prison context and the cases discussed may well motivate a court to hold that a statute authorizing a state to contract with a private company to incarcerate its prisoners is unconstitutional.

a. Delegation of Management Functions

The constitutionality of privatization focuses, in the first
instance, on whether a particular activity in which the
government is involved is a governmental power, rather than a
governmental function. If the privatization at issue involves
the former, a delegation issue arises.[114] A private entity

_____

[114] See Lawrence, supra note 12, at 647. Professor
Lawrence stated:

> Much of the debate over privatization has been
> political in nature, rather than legal; and indeed
> when privatization involves governmental functions,
> the legal issues are largely secondary, involving
> only details. But if privatization proposals should
> involve governmental powers, the legal problems
> become considerably more formidable. The transfer
> of governmental powers raises the issue of to what
> extent it is constitutionally permissible to
> delegate those powers to private actors.

Id. (emphasis in original). An early New York Court of Appeals
case explained this distinction between governmental functions
and powers differently. In Fox v. Mohawk & Hudson River Humane
Soc'y, 165 N.Y. 517, 59 N.E. 353 (1901), Judge Cullen wrote:

> I certainly should deny the right of the legislature
> to vest in private associations or corporations
> authority and power affecting the life, liberty, and
> property of the citizens . . . . Of course, the
> state . . . may employ individuals or corporations
> to do work or render service for it, but the
> distinction between a public officer and a public
> employee or contractor is plain and well recognized.

Id. at 525, 59 N.E. at 355. Thus, if the government gives a
private party power to affect a person's life, liberty, or
property interest, it is delegating governmental power. If,
however, the government merely contracts with a private party to
confer a benefit on members of the public that does not affect
any person's existing life, liberty, or property interest, it has
not delegated its governmental power. Therefore, a contract to
provide food or medical care to prisoners in an institution that
the state owns and controls does not in itself raise a
constitutional issue. A prisoner has no interest in receiving

exercises governmental power when it deprives a person of life, liberty, or property at the behest of government.[115]   Thus, a

his food or medical care directly from the government rather than from an independent contractor. But, if the government leaves the entire operation of the prison in private hands, it is the private company, and not the government, that is immediately responsible for the prisoner's day-to-day deprivation of liberty.

For a critique of the "government functions" approach in a different context, see Garcia v. San Antonio Metro. Transit Auth., 469 U.S. 528, 538-47 (1985) (holding that transit authority was not immune from minimum-wage and overtime requirements of the Fair Labor Standards Act).

[115]   If the government gives a private party the authority to deprive another of life, liberty, or property, the issue of state action arises. If a private actor exercises governmental power, the state nevertheless retains the responsibility to protect the constitutional rights of those persons over whom the private company exercises control. Schneider, supra note 58, at 1169-70. Thus, "[a]lthough the state may have a private actor performing the service . . . , the nondelegable nature of the service means that the state must remain responsible for the performance of that service." Id. at 1170. Stated another way, the government can delegate the function, but not the duty to perform that function. Compare Ancata v. Prison Health Servs., 769 F.2d 700, 703 (11th Cir. 1985) ("Although Prison Health Services and its employees are not strictly speaking public employees, state action is clearly present. Where a function which is traditionally the exclusive prerogative of the state . . . is performed by a private entity, state action is present.") with West v. Atkins, 815 F.2d 993, 994-96 (4th Cir.) (7-3) (en banc) (declining to overrule Calvert v. Sharp, 748 F.2d 861 (4th Cir. 1984), cert. denied, 471 U.S. 1132 (1985), in which the court held that a physician who had contracted with the state to furnish medical services in prison was not acting under color of state law when he allegedly provided inadequate medical treatment to prisoner), rev'd, 56 U.S.L.W. 4664 (U.S. June 20, 1988). See generally infra notes 381-392 and accompanying text (discussing West v. Atkins). Noting the overlap between the state-action and delegation analyses, the court in Ancata stated:

The federal courts have consistently ruled that governments, state and local, have an obligation to provide medical care to incarcerated individuals. . . . This duty is not absolved by contracting with an entity such as Prison Health Services. Although Prison Health Services has contracted to perform an obligation owed by the county, the county itself remains liable for any constitutional deprivations caused by the policies or customs of the Health

delegation can occur even though the private party exercises neither rule-making nor adjudicative powers but merely manages a government program that is already in place.

The first category of delegations, therefore, is the delegation of the management of government property and programs. In People v. Chicago Railroad Terminal Authority,[116] for example, the validity of a statute permitting railroad-terminal authorities to contract with private companies to maintain and operate the authorities' terminals was attacked on delegation grounds.[117] The statute reserved ultimate power over the terminal's management to the Authority[118] and authorized the railroad-terminal authorities to delegate administrative duties to railroad companies.[119] The court held that this delegation was constitutional.[120]

Service. In that sense, the county's duty is non-delegable.

769 F.2d at 705 (footnote omitted).

Even if a state-action problem does not exist under current law, the validity of the delegation still depends, in part, on whether the private actor performs its duty in a constitutional manner. See Lawrence, supra note 12, at 693 (even if state action is not present, if the private party makes decisions regarding the life, liberty, or property of citizens at the behest of the government, courts may find delegation improper unless the private actor creates and follows a program that satisfies principles of procedural due process).

[116] 14 Ill. 2d 230, 151 N.E.2d 311 (1958).

[117] Id. at 238-40, 151 N.E.2d at 316-17.

[118] Id.

[119] Id. at 239-40, 151 N.E.2d at 317.

[120] Id. at 242, 151 N.E.2d at 318.

Chicago Railroad established the proposition that, under the Illinois Constitution, a governmental body can constitutionally delegate the management of a government enterprise to a private company if the governmental body retains ultimate control over the program. Significantly, the statute challenged in _Chicago Railroad_ did not permit private railroad companies to choose the terminal sites or acquire the land for the terminals.[121] Thus, the Terminal Authority, not the railroad company, made the policy decision concerning terminal location and design, including the issue of whether and how many shops to construct and lease. The statute at issue permitted the Terminal Authority to vest the power to supervise and control the construction, maintenance, and operation of the terminal in a committee that was composed, in part, of railroad-company officials.[122] Noting that the Terminal Authority retained ultimate control over the terminal, the court held that the statute did not unconstitutionally allow the Authority to delegate its powers to private parties.[123]

The statute did not, however, permit the Terminal Authority to delegate either rule-making or adjudicative powers to private railroad companies. Rather, it reserved the adjudicative power of condemning land for terminal use to the Terminal Authority itself. Although the statute permitted the prerogative to

---

121 See _id._ at 234, 240-41, 151 N.E.2d at 314, 317 (noting that the statute required the Authority to select and the city council to approve the terminal site and, once approved, the Authority had the power to acquire designated land).

122 _Id._ at 239-40, 151 N.E.2d at 316.

123 _Id._ at 238-40, 151 N.E.2d at 316-17.

delegate the authority to establish terminal management policy to a board consisting of private-company appointees, the Authority retained ultimate control over the board. Thus, because the Authority could accept, reject, or modify the rules that the management committee established, the rules were advisory. The board, therefore, did not have rule-making power. Instead, the statute limited the private delegate's power to the function of administering a program that a governmental body established.

Nevertheless, because the statute permitted the Terminal Authority to yield physical control of terminal property to a private company, a private delegate potentially could affect the property rights of terminal lessees. Therefore, the statute in fact permitted a true delegation of governmental power to affect private property interests for a public purpose.

Statutes that permit private security guards to detain suspected shoplifters present another example of administrative delegation. Although the statutes and relevant cases do not expressly discuss the delegation doctrine, they effectively authorize private persons to deprive people of their liberty for the public purpose of enforcing criminal laws. An Indiana statute, for example, authorizes private security guards to detain suspected shoplifters if the guards have probable cause to believe that the detainee has stolen any item belonging to the store.[124] But this statute does not authorize store security

---

[124] See Ind. Code Ann. §§ 35-33-6-1 to -5 (Burns 1985) (outlining circumstances in which store employee may detain suspected shoplifter). An Indiana appellate court has upheld the constitutionality of the predecessor statute sub silentio. Crase

guards to make arrests;[125] their power is investigatory only.

Humane-society officers perform law-enforcement functions analogous to those of store security guards. In ASPCA v. City of New York,[126] for example, a Humane Society officer directed a police officer to a person whom the Society suspected had been cruel to a horse.[127] The police officer, however, actually arrested the suspect and prosecuted him before a magistrate.[128] The Humane Society officers wore special uniforms, patrolled the streets, and reported any suspected violations of the state's humane laws.[129] The New York appellate court characterized the Humane Society's law-enforcement activities as "purely administrative,"[130] and held that the state government constitutionally could delegate the law-enforcement functions at issue to the Humane Society.[131]

In both the store security guard and Humane Society

---

v. Highland Village Value Plus Pharmacy, 176 Ind. App. 47, 52, 374 N.E.2d 58, 62 (1978) (remanding case to determine whether "statutory defense" to false-imprisonment action applied, without discussing Act's constitutionality).

[125] See Ind. Code Ann. § 35-33-6-2(b) (Burns 1985) (limiting store security guards' authority to temporarily detaining suspected shoplifter until police can come to make arrest).

[126] 205 A.D. 335, 199 N.Y.S. 728 (1923).

[127] Id. at 336, 199 N.Y.S. at 729.

[128] Id.

[129] Id. at 338, 199 N.Y.S. at 730.

[130] Id. at 341, 199 N.Y.S. at 733.

[131] Id. (citing Fox v. Mohawk & Hudson River Humane Soc'y, 165 N.Y. 517, 59 N.E. 353 (1901)).

examples, the private officers had no authority either to arrest suspects or to adjudicate crimes. The private officers' only authority was to identify suspected lawbreakers and facilitate their ultimate arrest and prosecution by government officials. In both instances, independent, governmental decisionmakers ultimately decided whether to arrest, prosecute, and sentence the wrongdoer. Thus, the private entities performed only administrative, not adjudicative functions.[132]

Moreover, in each of these examples of administrative delegation, the private party had neither rule-making nor adjudicative powers, but merely assisted a government agency in implementing its policy decisions. The principles announced in these cases, therefore, might allow private prison management under rules that the state established. A state agency with authority to accept, reject, or modify administrative rules that the private-prison company proposed, however, would have to review any proposed rule that would affect the prisoners. Additionally, a state judicial or administrative officer would have to determine whether an individual prisoner had violated an administrative rule. This would be necessary if the prisoner's incarceration were prolonged as a result of such a determination.[133]

_____

[132] See also Hogan v. State Bar, 36 Cal. 2d 807, 811, 228 P.2d 554, 556 (1951) (rejecting challenge on delegation grounds to state bar association's authority to recommend disciplinary action against attorney because recommendation was advisory and subject to de novo review in state supreme court).

[133] This would occur, for example, if an administrative infraction resulted in a loss of the prisoner's good-time credits

Courts might not apply the principles established in the cases discussed in this section to the private-prison context, however. The private delegates in these cases performed functions that states commonly permit private parties to perform. Private citizens typically have the right to identify and even arrest suspected lawbreakers.[134] Private railroads certainly may construct and operate railroad terminals without first seeking state approval. Hence, none of the delegates in the cases discussed performed functions that were unique to government.

Incarcerating prisoners, however, unlike identifying lawbreakers or managing railroad terminals, is a power that the states traditionally have had to themselves. Thus, because this function is "intrinsically governmental in nature," the courts may distinguish the administrative-delegation cases and enjoin private-prison operations on delegation grounds.[135]

---

or affected his chance for parole. Mayer, supra note 76, at 320-21 (suggesting that the state might maintain ultimate control over disciplinary proceedings because they potentially could increase the length of a prisoner's incarceration by reducing his chance for parole or good-time credits). Similar to store security guards or humane-society officers, however, the private-prison company could perform an accusatory function in which its agents acted as complaining witnesses at disciplinary proceedings. See id. at 320 (suggesting this role for private-prison company).

[134] See id. at 317-19 (discussing private citizens' common-law right to arrest felons).

[135] See Melcher v. Federal Open Mkt. Comm'n, No. 84-1335, slip op. at 16 (D.D.C. Sept. 25, 1986) (dictum) (noting, in case upholding private delegation, that "many responsibilities may be so intrinsically governmental in nature that they may not be entrusted to a non-governmental entity"). The court suggested "the powers to conduct foreign affairs or to establish military and naval forces" as examples of nondelegable powers that are intrinsically governmental. Id. at n.24; cf. Brief for Appellee at 32, Bowsher v. Synar, 478 U.S. 714 (1986) (arguing that

b. Delegation of Rule-Making Authority

Administrative delegations raise the policy concern of whether government should allow a private company to manage a program rather than have the government manage the program itself. A related concern is whether routine administrative decisions would contravene the goals of the program. These concerns become more pronounced when the legislature grants power to a private company to make administrative rules that are binding on private persons.

The problem with this practice is that a private company can exercise governmental power affecting a citizen's liberty or property interest outside of any legislative or administrative control. This practice is constitutionally suspect for two reasons: first, only the legislature has express constitutional authority to exercise rule-making governmental power in the public interest; and, second, a private company might make rules that are repugnant to the public interest for its own pecuniary or political gain.

Two common types of rule-making delegations are prevailing-wage laws and statutes that adopt technical codes not yet in existence. The prevailing-wage laws typically provide that private contractors who perform municipal contracts must pay the prevailing wage established by a labor commissioner. They also

---

Congress's power to spend government revenues was nondelegable because it was Congress's core function).

typically provide that the labor commissioner must adopt a union wage rate established by collective bargaining.

Industrial Commission v. C & D Pipeline[136] is representative of the cases holding prevailing-wage laws unconstitutional on delegation grounds.[137] The Arizona Court of Appeals noted that the statute granted no discretion "to the Commission to do anything other than ascertain and record the union rate."[138]

---

[136] 125 Ariz. 64, 607 P.2d 383 (Ct. App. 1979).

[137] The statute provided:

For the purpose of determining the general prevailing rate of per diem wages, the industrial commission of Arizona shall ascertain and keep on record the rates or scale of per diem wages required to be paid to each craft or type of workman belonging to or affiliated with the American Federation of Labor, the Arizona State Federation of Labor, or any other state or national labor organization similarly constituted, prevailing in the locality in which the public work is to be performed. If such method of arriving at the general prevailing rate of per diem wages cannot reasonably and fairly be applied in any political subdivision of the state for the reason that no such organization is maintained in the political subdivision, the industrial commission shall determine the prevailing rate to be the rate required to be paid to each craft or type of workman of the same or most similar class, working in the same or most similar employment in the nearest and most similar neighboring locality, and affiliated with any such labor organization.

Ariz. Rev. Stat. Ann. § 34-324(A) (1974) (emphasis omitted in part); see 125 Ariz. at 65-66, 607 P.2d at 384-85.

[138] 125 Ariz. at 67, 607 P.2d at 386. The court distinguished Baughn v. Gorell & Riley, 311 Ky. 537, 224 S.W.2d 436 (1949), a case cited by the Industrial Commission that upheld a prevailing-wage law. 125 Ariz. at 66, 607 P.2d at 385-86. The statute challenged in Baughn provided:

The wages paid for a legal day's work to laborers, workmen, mechanics, helpers, assistants and

Accordingly, the court held, under the Arizona Constitution, that the prevailing-wage law unconstitutionally granted the power to determine the prevailing wage to private unions and management.[139]

Statutes adopting technical codes that a private trade association drafts and periodically revises raise delegation issues that are similar to those found in the prevailing-wage cases. If a state legislature were to adopt prospectively an extant technical code, no delegation problem would exist. In such a case, the legislature would merely be exercising its right to adopt one political option over another.[140] A delegation problem would arise, however, if a statute were to adopt

----

apprentices upon public works shall not be less than the prevailing wages paid in the same trade or occupation in the locality. The public authority shall establish prevailing wages at the same rate that prevails in the locality under collective agreements or understandings between bona fide organizations of labor and their employers at the date the contract for public works is made if there are such agreements or understandings in the locality applying to a sufficient number of employees to furnish a reasonable basis for considering those rates to be the prevailing rates in the locality.

311 Ky. at 540, 224 S.W.2d at 438 (emphasis omitted). The court in Industrial Commission noted that, unlike the statute in Baughn, the Arizona statute granted no discretion to the Commission to consider factors other than the union wage rate to determine the prevailing wage rate. 125 Ariz. at 67, 607 P.2d at 385-86. The court concluded that the Arizona statute was unconstitutional because it did not grant any discretion to the Commission to question the union rate. Id. at 68, 607 P.2d at 386.

[139] 125 Ariz. at 68, 607 P.2d at 386. For another case that held a prevailing-wage law unconstitutional, see Schryver v. Schirmer, 84 S.D. 352, 357-58, 171 N.W.2d 634, 637 (1969).

[140] Liebmann, supra note 52, at 680.

prospectively any changes that the technical trade association might make in the future. This type of statute would grant the trade association power to make legally binding rules that affect the property interest of private tradesmen.

Hillman v. Northern Wasco County People's Utility District[141] is typical of the cases that hold such statutes unconstitutional. In Hillman, a contractor injured himself after receiving an electrical shock from exposed wiring in an old building while he was removing some beams.[142] Hillman fell from the wall after his shoe brushed against the exposed wire.[143] He later brought a tort action against the electric company that had originally installed the wiring.[144]

In his complaint, Hillman alleged that the Northern Wasco County People's Utility District had violated the National Electric Code.[145] Oregon's adoption of the Code included revisions and additions "as they are published from time to time."[146] After the trial court instructed the jurors that violation of the Code would be negligence per se,[147] the jury

---

141 213 Or. 264, 323 P.2d 664 (1958), overruled on other grounds, Maulding v. Clackamas County, 278 Or. 359, 563 P.2d 731 (1977).

142 Id. at 273-74, 323 P.2d at 669.

143 Id.

144 Id. at 270-72, 323 P.2d at 668.

145 Id. at 275-76, 323 P.2d at 670.

146 Id.

147 Id.

returned a verdict for the plaintiff.[148] Both plaintiff and
defendant cross-appealed from the trial court's order granting
the defendant's motion for a new trial but denying its motion for
a judgment notwithstanding the verdict.[149]

The issue that the defendant raised in support of its motion
for a new trial was whether the statute that adopted the Code,
including revisions and additions not yet in existence,
unconstitutionally delegated legislative rule-making power to the
American Standards Association, the private party that had
drafted the Code.[150] The court stated that the Oregon
Constitution vested lawmaking power exclusively in the
legislature[151] and noted that neither the legislature nor any
other department of government had any control over the
Association.[152] As a result, the court held that the Oregon
statute unconstitutionally delegated legislative rule-making
power to the Association.[153]

---

[148]   Id. at 270-71, 323 P.2d at 668.

[149]   Id.   The Oregon Supreme Court affirmed the trial
court's decision.   Id. at 314-15, 323 P.2d at 688.

[150]   Id. at 275-83, 323 P.2d at 670-73.

[151]   Id. at 277-78, 323 P.2d at 671.

[152]   Id. at 278-81, 323 P.2d at 671-72.

[153]   Id. at 281, 323 P.2d at 673.   Because the statute
adopting the Code was unconstitutional, any Code provision
adopted pursuant to the statute did not have any legal effect.
Thus, the defendant achieved its objective of overcoming a
finding of negligence per se solely because it did not comply
with the Code.   For other cases that held statutes that adopted
future technical codes unconstitutional on delegation grounds,
see, e.g., Agnew v. City of Culver City, 147 Cal. App. 2d 144,
156-57, 304 P.2d 788, 797 (1956); State v. Crawford, 104 Kan.

Hillman also involved a similar private-delegation issue concerning the National Electric Safety Code, issued and periodically revised by the Bureau of Standards of the Department of Commerce.[154] The court pointed out that the Bureau adopted some of the Safety Code's provisions even though it did not agree with them.[155] These provisions were proposed by private committees composed of representatives of various private groups that the Safety Code affected.[156] The Bureau followed this

_____

141, 143, 177 P. 360, 361 (1919).

[154] 213 Or. at 281-87, 323 P.2d at 673-75.

[155] Id. at 284-85, 323 P.2d at 674.

[156] Id. In support of its observation, the court quoted the following passage from the preface of the Bureau's handbook:

> In preparation of the first few editions of the code, the Bureau held meetings in many parts of the country and welcomed suggestions from everyone concerned. It, however, reserved to itself the final decision on all contested points. The procedure followed in later revisions subsequent to the establishment of the American Standards Association differs essentially from the former practice in that final decisions as to all details are made by the sectional committees formally approved by the American Standards Association and operating under their rules of procedure. The Bureau, as sponsor for the work under this procedure, has given up its prerogative of determining details in return for the implied understanding that the many parties concerned will accept such a code as they can agree upon among themselves. All such codes of practice necessarily include compromises between conflicting aims. The Bureau has felt that decisions made by practically unanimous agreement among the interests affected would, in general, be wiser than those at which it might arrive after weighing the arguments of advocates for different views. It has, therefore, welcomed this procedure in spite of the fact that this involves the acceptance of some details of which it might not itself approve.

procedure because it placed a higher priority on promoting broad-based acceptance of the Safety Code in the private sector than on agreeing with all of its provisions.[157]

Oregon's Public Service Commission was statutorily authorized to make safety rules for employers and common carriers concerning the use of electrical equipment.[158] The Commission, in turn, adopted the Safety Code as it existed at the time of its order, as well as all of the Bureau's subsequent revisions and additions to the Safety Code.[159]

The court distinguished the enabling statute from the Commission's order that adopted the Safety Code. The enabling statute was constitutional, the court noted, because an administrative agency such as the Commission may adopt an extant edition of the Code after a hearing and a proper exercise of its discretion.[160] If the Commission did not do so, the court observed, it would not perform its duty to determine whether the Safety Code provisions that the Bureau adopted were "necessary and proper for the protection of the health and safety of the citizens of this state."[161] The court asserted, however, that the Commission abdicated its legislative power when it adopted future Safety Code provisions without further consideration.[162]

Id.

157   Id.

158   Id. at 281-83, 323 P.2d at 673.

159   Id. at 282-85, 323 P.2d at 673-74.

160   Id. at 284-85, 323 P.2d at 674.

161   Id. at 285-86, 323 P.2d at 674-75.

The court in _Hillman_, as most state courts do, spoke in conclusory terms of the unconstitutionality of private delegations, without specifically indicating the policy concerns that inspired the doctrine. But it did make three assertions that evinced its real policy concerns. First, the court explained that no department of government had any control over a private organization.[163] Second, the court stated that, through the Constitution, the people vested the lawmaking power in the legislature.[164] Thus, the people effectively prohibited any group except the legislature from exercising lawmaking powers.[165] Third, the court noted that, when private parties adopt rules that further their own interests, the rules may not reflect the best judgment of an agency that is concerned only with the public interest.[166] Thus, the court's underlying policy concern apparently was that a private party, not subject to any political control, could impose rules to further its own interest at the expense of the public interest.[167]

Industrial Commission and _Hillman_ are examples of the state

---

162 _Id._ at 286-87, 323 P.2d at 675.

163 _Id._ at 277-79, 323 P.2d at 671.

164 _Id._ at 279-80, 323 P.2d at 671 (quoting Marr v. Fisher, 182 Or. 383, 187 P.2d 966 (1947)).

165 _Id._

166 _Id._ at 285-86, 323 P.2d at 674-75.

167 _But see_ Liebmann, _supra_ note 52, at 682-84 (arguing that, because private rule-making affects the community at large, any abuses are visible and likely to be corrected by the political process).

courts' almost uniform condemnation of statutes delegating rule-making power to private parties. Both cases addressed similar concerns about whether private organizations would make rules that placed personal gain ahead of public welfare and whether the absence of neutral administrative-agency review of the private parties' determination would encourage self-serving policies. This latter aspect was particularly troublesome, the cases noted, because the private parties themselves were not subject to any political control. Both cases indicated, however, that a rule that a private party proposes is not constitutionally suspect if it is adopted by an administrative-agency that has power to accept, reject, or modify the rule.[168]

In the private-prison context, the principles that these cases establish would not permit a legislature to authorize a private-prison company to make rules governing the conduct of the prisoners who are committed to its care. The prison company could propose rules to an administrative agency, however, if the agency had authority to accept, reject, or modify them. The agency would then have a constitutional duty to exercise discretion concerning whether and in what form it should adopt the rules.

It must be emphasized that the rules at issue in Industrial Commission and Hillman only affected the property interests of private tradesmen. Any rules governing a private prison,

----

[168] Cf. id. at 680 (noting that the Supreme Court has held that "freedom for private groups to seek their legislative ends is itself constitutionally protected").

however, likely would affect the prisoners' life and liberty interests as well as other fundamental constitutional rights. Because of these differences in the constitutional importance of the interests affected, a court might require the legislature or an administrative agency to take a more active role in determining the rules by which private prisons governed the prisoners under the company's control. A court might hold, for example, that a statute authorizing a private prison or jail is unconstitutional on delegation grounds unless it specifies in detail the rules governing the relationship between the private-prison company and the prisoners under the company's control.[169] Alternatively, a court might require an administrative agency to create the necessary rules. Neither of these holdings would prevent private-prison companies from proposing their own rules. The legislature or administrative agency merely would draft the rules itself, instead of passively reviewing the private party's proposals. Because of the life and liberty interests involved, however, a court might bar the delegation altogether.

c. Delegation of Adjudicative Powers

When a private party exercises delegated administrative and rule-making power, its actions generally affect a large number of persons and entities. If a private party exercises delegated

_____

[169] Of course, a rule itself may be unconstitutional on other grounds, even though the delegation is proper.

adjudicative power, however, its actions usually affect a single person or entity. Because of the disproportionate effect of an exercise of adjudicative power, an arbitrary or unreasonable exercise of such power is not as easily corrected through the political process. Therefore, courts should scrutinize delegations of such power more carefully.[170]

State courts generally invalidate statutes and administrative regulations that delegate adjudicative power to private parties when there is no provision for judicial review of the private adjudications. When there is provision for such review, however, the delegation generally is upheld. DiLoreto v. Fireman's Fund Insurance Co.[171] is an example of the latter type of case. At issue in DiLoreto was a private insurer's authority pursuant to a Massachusetts statute and implementing regulations of the Board of Appeal on Motor Vehicle Liability Policies and Bonds.[172] The statute allowed a private insurer to determine, in the first instance, whether an insured was at fault in an accident, in order to assess a premium surcharge.[173] The insured

---

[170] Liebmann, supra note 52, at 682-83. Liebmann explained several differences between rule-making and adjudicative power that suggest a greater need for judicial scrutiny of the latter type of power. He noted that "abuses of rule making power are more visible, fall on and thus give rise to reaction by the community at large, and may more readily be redressed after the event." Id. at 682. Liebmann contrasted this with adjudicative powers because they "bear more heavily on individuals, while abuses of them are less likely to be brought to public view or be susceptible of easy correction." Id. at 682-83. Liebmann concluded that courts should scrutinize carefully and, in most cases, invalidate delegations of adjudicative power. Id.

[171] 383 Mass. 243, 418 N.E.2d 612 (1981).

[172] Id. at 244, 418 N.E.2d at 613.

retained the right, however, to both administrative[174] and judicial[175] review.

DiLoreto argued that the delegation of adjudicative authority to a private insurer violated the Massachusetts Constitution.[176] The Massachusetts Supreme Judicial Court first explained that the merit-rating program was based on a detailed and comprehensive plan established by the Board pursuant to

_____

[173] Id. at 245-46, 418 N.E.2d at 614. The insurer's determination is binding on the insured unless the insured appeals the insurer's decision to the Board of Appeal on Motor Vehicle Liability Policies and Bonds. See Mass. Ann. Laws ch. 175, § 113P (Law. Co-op. 1977) (insured may appeal any determination of insurer within 30 days). Thus, the insurer's authority in this situation is greater than the authority granted to store security guards, because the insurer's decision is a binding, albeit appealable, determination of the insured's rights and the onus of challenging that decision is on the insured. See supra notes 124-125 and accompanying text (noting that store security guards in Indiana have no authority to arrest or charge suspected shoplifters but rather have authority only to hold suspected shoplifters until police can come to make arrest).

[174] See Mass. Ann. Laws ch. 175, § 113P (Law. Co-op. 1977) (insured may appeal insurer's determination to Board within 30 days of adverse decision).

[175] See id. (insured may appeal Board's decision to superior court).

[176] 383 Mass. at 245, 418 N.E.2d at 614. The stipulated facts on which the insurer based its decision to surcharge were as follows. DiLoreto parked his automobile along the right-hand side of a street and opened the left front door to exit his automobile. After opening the door and starting to get out of the automobile, DiLoreto noticed another automobile headed toward his vehicle at an unsafe speed of approximately 30 miles an hour. The driver was not paying attention to her driving, but instead was talking to a passenger. After observing the approaching vehicle, DiLoreto got back into his automobile. At that point, the vehicle struck his door. The insurer assessed a surcharge on DiLoreto pursuant to a regulatory presumption that a person whose doors are opened at the time of a collision is at fault in excess of 50 percent. Id. at 244 & n.3, 418 N.E.2d at 613-14 & n.3.

statutory mandate.[177] It then noted that Board regulations narrowly channeled the insurer's determination.[178] Additionally, the insurer's determination was subject to administrative and judicial review.[179] Thus, the court asserted that the statutory scheme prevented the insurer from benefiting from its decision to assess a surcharge in a particular case.[180] The court concluded, therefore, that the statute did not unconstitutionally delegate adjudicative power to private insurers.[181]

In upholding the DiLoreto statute, the court distinguished its earlier holding in Corning Glass Works v. Ann & Hope, Inc.[182] The nonsigner provision of the fair-trade law[183] in

---

[177] Id. at 246-47, 418 N.E.2d at 614-15.

[178] Id. at 247, 418 N.E.2d at 615.

[179] Id.

[180] Id. The statute created a system by which the insurer must offset all of its surcharges with good-driver credits in an amount equal to its income from the surcharges, including the insurer's income from investing the proceeds of the surcharge prior to distribution. Mass. Ann. Laws ch. 175, § 113P (Law. Co-op. 1977).

[181] 383 Mass. at 247-48, 418 N.E.2d at 615.

[182] 363 Mass. 409, 294 N.E.2d 354 (1973).

[183] See 1 K. Davis, supra note 20, § 3.12, at 196. Davis explained the history and effect of nonsigner provisions of fair-trade laws as follows:

> The history of non-signer provisions of the so-called fair trade laws may have some value. Such laws were enacted by 46 states. A non-signer provision of such a law provides that a minimum resale price fixed in an agreement between a manufacturer (or other distributor) and a retailer is binding upon other retailers. The effect is that parties to such an agreement have the legislative power to fix the minimum resale price at which

Corning Glass was constitutionally defective because there was no standard to limit the contracting parties' discretion to set the retail price that others must charge.[184] Furthermore, the statute at issue in Corning Glass did not provide for administrative or judicial review of the private decision.[185] Therefore, the DiLoreto court concluded that, because the insurance statute provided an effective standard to channel the private insurer's discretion and adequate review of private-party determinations, the delegation was constitutional.[186]

The court in DiLoreto upheld a delegation of adjudicative power because of the availability of judicial review. If review of a private adjudication is not available, however, state courts generally invalidate such delegations. International Service Agencies v. O'Shea[187] is typical of those cases. International Service Agencies (ISA) had requested the right to participate in the annual solicitation of charitable contributions from New York state employees through the State Employees Federated Appeals (SEFA).[188] The statute in question provided that the Commissioner of General Services must select one "federated

---

nonparties may sell; any seller who sells at a price lower than the price fixed in such an agreement is subject to suit by any person damaged.

Id.

184 DiLoreto, 383 Mass. at 246-47, 418 N.E.2d at 615.

185 Id.

186 Id.

187 104 Misc. 2d 1071, 430 N.Y.S.2d 224 (Sup. Ct. 1980).

188 Id. at 1072, 430 N.Y.S.2d at 225.

community campaign"[189] for each county or area in which a solicitation took place.[190] The Commissioner, in turn, delegated to the United Way and the National Health Agencies his authority to select the charitable nonprofit organization that would have the right to participate in a local campaign.[191] ISA had applied to both the Commissioner and the United Way for permission to participate in a local charitable drive.[192] Both entities rejected ISA's applications.[193]

ISA argued that the Commissioner unconstitutionally delegated the power to select local federated community campaigns to private charities.[194] The New York Supreme Court observed that the Commissioner admitted that he had no role in the decision concerning ISA's participation in the federated campaign.[195] The court charged that, although the Commissioner

_____

189   See id. at 1073, 430 N.Y.S.2d at 226. The statute defined a federated community campaign as "a charitable non-profit organization which solicits funds for distribution among a substantial number of charitable non-profit organizations, which has been approved as such by the Commissioner of General Services." Id. ISA solicited funds for seven different charities. Id. at 1072, 430 N.Y.S.2d at 225. Thus, ISA would have qualified under the statutory definition if the Commissioner of General Services had approved its program.

190   Id. at 1073, 430 N.Y.S.2d at 226.

191   Id. at 1074, 430 N.Y.S.2d at 226-27.

192   Id. at 1076-77, 430 N.Y.S.2d at 228. The Commissioner referred ISA to the United Way which, in turn, referred ISA back to the Commissioner. The court described this process as a "Ring around the Rosey." Id.

193   Id.

194   Id. at 1073, 430 N.Y.S.2d at 226.

195   Id. at 1074, 430 N.Y.S.2d at 226.

was empowered to do so, he failed to promulgate regulations
establishing a procedure to determine inclusion in a SEFA.[196] As
a result, the statutory delegation unconstitutionally deprived
ISA of a valuable interest in soliciting funds directly from
state employees' paychecks.[197]

The court's primary policy concern became apparent when it
noted three times in the opinion the likelihood that the United
Way's self-interest motivated ISA's exclusion from participating
in a SEFA.[198] On one such occasion, for example, the court
observed that "[o]ne can readily understand the reluctance of
United Way to permit ISA to join in. Their own self-interest
would dictate a policy of exclusion in order to maximize the
amount of their own contributions."[199]

A case that raised similar issues was Group Health Insurance
v. Howell.[200] In that case, Group Health Insurance of New Jersey

---

196 Id.

197 Id. at 1076-78, 430 N.Y.S.2d at 228-29. In so holding,
the court rejected the argument that state employees remained
free to make donations to ISA if they chose to do so. Id. at
1076, 430 N.Y.S.2d at 228. Instead, the court held that ISA had
a due process interest in a fair opportunity for inclusion in a
SEFA. Id. at 1077, 430 N.Y.S.2d at 228.

198 Id. at 1074, 430 N.Y.S.2d at 227 ("It is clear that
delegations of public authority must be carefully circumscribed
to insure that self-interest does not become the overriding
consideration."); id. at 1077, 430 N.Y.S.2d at 228 ("Fortunately,
the reins of government cannot be turned over to private interest
groups to be utilized to preserve self-interests."); see infra
text accompanying note 199 (noting United Way's pecuniary
interest in excluding ISA).

199 Id. at 1076-77, 430 N.Y.S.2d at 228.

200 40 N.J. 436, 193 A.2d 103 (1963).

(GHI), a nonprofit corporation, proposed to offer a medical-services plan[201] similar to the then-existing plan that Blue Shield offered.[202] A New Jersey statute provided, however, that before a company could offer such a program it had to obtain prior approval from the Medical Society.[203] The Commissioner of

---

[201] See id. at 439-41, 193 A.2d at 105-06. The statute at issue defined a medical-services plan as

> any plan or arrangement operated by such a corporation under the provisions of the Law whereby the expense of medical services to subscribers and covered dependents is paid in whole or in part by such corporation to participating physicians of such plans or arrangements and to others as provided in the Law. A subscriber is one to whom a subscription certificate is issued by the corporation which sets forth the kinds and extent of the medical services for which the corporation is liable to make payment. A participating physician is any physician licensed to practice medicine and surgery in New Jersey, who agrees in writing with the corporation to perform the medical services specified in the subscription certificates issued by the corporation, at such rates of compensation as shall be determined by its board of trustees, and who agrees to abide by the corporation's rules. Medical service includes all general and special medical and surgical services ordinarily provided by such licensed physicians in accordance with accepted practices in the community. No subscriber or his covered dependents shall be liable for any payment to any participating physician for medical services specified in the subscriber's certificate to be paid to the participating physician by the corporation.

Id. at 441-42, 193 A.2d at 106 (quoting N.J. Stat. Ann. § 17:48A-1 (West 1939 & Supp. 1962)).

[202] Id. at 443, 193 A.2d at 107.

[203] Id. at 444-45, 193 A.2d at 108. The statute did not, in so many words, require Blue Shield's approval. Instead, it required approval of a recognized medical society with at least 2,000 members that was incorporated for at least 10 years. The court noted, however, that the parties did not dispute that Blue Shield, a private organization, was the only organization that met the statutory requirements. Thus, although the statute did

Banking and Insurance was powerless under the statute to certify a corporation's proposed medical-services plan without the approval of Blue Shield.[204] Because the statute in effect delegated to Blue Shield the power to deny licenses to corporations proposing medical-service plans,[205] the court held that the delegation violated the New Jersey Constitution.[206]

The New Jersey Supreme Court specifically noted two policy concerns with the delegation at issue. First, the statute contained no standards or safeguards to guide Blue Shield's discretion.[207] Second, the court declared that this deficiency was exacerbated because "the Medical Society's self-interest might tend to color its determination whether to approve . . . an applicant which may become a competitor of Blue Shield."[208]

---

not provide expressly that Blue Shield's approval was a necessary prerequisite to having the state license a medical-services plan, its effect was identical. Id.

[204] Id. at 446, 193 A.2d at 109. Technically, the organization from which approval was necessary was the "Medical Society." Although legally separate from Blue Shield, the Medical Society formed Blue Shield, had four interlocking directors, and approved nominees to Blue Shield's board of directors before they were elected. Thus, the court noted that, in practical effect, the Medical Society represented Blue Shield's interests in licensing matters. Id. at 445, 193 A.2d at 107. Therefore, the terms "Medical Society" and "Blue Shield" are interchangeable when discussing this case.

[205] Id. at 446-47, 193 A.2d at 109.

[206] Id. at 447, 193 A.2d at 109.

[207] Id.

[208] Id. As in International Service Agencies, the court in Howell noted its concern about the self-interest of the licensor, Blue Shield, on several different occasions. See id. at 445, 193 A.2d at 108 (legislature may not empower private party to determine who has a right to engage in an otherwise lawful enterprise if "exercise of such power is not accompanied by

The state cases discussing delegation of adjudicative power to private parties have established several principles. If judicial review of a private adjudication is available, as in DiLoreto, courts are more likely to uphold the delegation even though the private determination is binding until reversed on appeal, and the onus of appealing the action is on the affected party. Such a result is still more likely if, as in DiLoreto, the statute limits the delegate's discretion so as to preclude any pecuniary interest in adjudicative outcomes. If judicial review were not available, however, state courts would not uphold the delegation.

---

adequate legislative standards or safeguards whereby an applicant may be protected against arbitrary or self-motivated action on the part of such private body"); id. at 447, 193 A.2d at 109 (the "Medical Society . . . has an interest in promoting the welfare of the only existing medical service corporation in this State"). For other cases that held delegations of licensing power unconstitutional, see, e.g., Gumbhir v. Kansas State Bd. of Pharmacy, 228 Kan. 579, 588, 618 P.2d 837, 842 (1980) (invalidating a statute that excluded graduates of pharmacy schools not approved by private accrediting agency from taking the entrance examination necessary to register as a pharmacist); Fink v. Cole, 302 N.Y. 216, 225, 97 N.E.2d 873, 876 (1951) (holding unconstitutional an act that allowed a private jockey club to license participants in horse races); Farias v. City of New York, 101 Misc. 2d 598, 604-05, 421 N.Y.S.2d 753, 757 (Sup. Ct. 1979) (invalidating statutory requirement that private Society for Prevention of Cruelty to Children must approve any permit allowing children to perform); Union Trust Co. v. Simmons, 116 Utah 422, 429-30, 211 P.2d 190, 192-93 (1949) (charging that a statute requiring approval of existing banks in a community before a new branch bank could operate unconstitutionally delegated power to a competitor whose private interest in excluding competition may not coincide with the public interest).

d. Application of State Law to Private Incarceration

Because prison privatization is in its infancy, no reported cases have ruled on a delegation challenge to a private prison's or jail's operations. Therefore, the courts have not explicated the standards that they would use to judge the constitutionality of such a delegation. The principles announced in delegation cases in other contexts, however, provide some evidence of the delegation standards that courts might apply.

First, the courts might uphold the constitutionality of delegations of management functions to private-prison companies. This would include activities such as cell assignment, scheduling, record-keeping, and counting the prisoners. The courts might uphold such activities even though they incidentally affected the liberty of the prisoners. To avoid constitutional defect, however, the management activities at the least would have to apply uniformly to all prisoners and could not unreasonably restrict constitutional freedoms, such as religious freedoms, of any inmate.

Second, the courts might uphold the right of private-prison companies to propose internal disciplinary rules. The rules could not form the basis for disciplining inmates, however, unless they were adopted by the state legislature or an administrative agency with authority to accept, reject, or modify the proposed rules. The rules would also be unconstitutional if they were so vague that they granted too much power to the private companies to single out an inmate for punishment arbitrarily.

Finally, the courts would not allow a private-prison company to make a binding factual determination that an inmate had violated a prison rule and was therefore subject to discipline. This is true because the private-prison company is not a neutral decisionmaker. If the prison company's compensation were based on the number of inmates it housed each day, for example, a decision to revoke an inmate's good-time credits would inure to the company's financial benefit. Even if the private prison's compensation were based on a flat rate or were otherwise unrelated to the length of an inmate's incarceration, however, the company nevertheless would have an institutional bias toward disciplining prisoners. A decision to deny certain privileges or services, for example, would reduce the operating costs of the company and would promote its administrative convenience. Thus, a private-prison company may decide to discipline a prisoner to further its own interests at the expense of the interests of both the inmate and the public.[209] Moreover, any exercise of

----

[209] In DiLoreto v. Fireman's Fund Ins. Co., 383 Mass. 243, 418 N.E.2d 612 (1981), the insurer was required totally to offset any income from surcharges it had assessed with good-driving credits to other customers that it insured. Thus, the insurer had no financial incentive to assess a surcharge in any particular case. Indeed, the regulation requiring the insurer to assess a surcharge was necessary, as the court pointed out, because the absence of any financial incentive to do so created a natural bias against assessing surcharges due to the insurer's desire to promote good customer relations. Id. at 247-48, 418 N.E.2d at 615. In the private-prison context, contrastingly, there is a natural bias in favor of disciplining inmates. Thus, the opinion in DiLoreto does not support the proposition that a private-prison company can constitutionally perform the adjudicative function of determining whether an inmate has violated a rule.

nonreviewable discretion by the company would be cheaper than complying with due process constraints. Therefore, the only input that a private-prison company constitutionally might have concerning the decision whether a prisoner had violated a disciplinary rule is that of a complaining witness before a judicial officer.[210]

4.   Conclusion

The delegation doctrine has developed differently at the federal and state levels. At the federal level, the constitutionality of a delegation to a private-prison company would likely turn on the structure under which the delegation occurred. If the corrections agency both formulated disciplinary procedures and maintained control of disciplinary proceedings, the courts might uphold the delegation on the theory that the private corporation was employed in an administrative capacity to carry the law into effect. If a private-prison company formulated disciplinary rules, however, or if it had control over disciplinary proceedings, the courts might then apply the three-pronged Todd test to determine whether or not the

---

[210]   See Model Contract § 5(A)(3) (Discipline); cf. Mayer, supra note 76, at 320 (suggesting this and other approaches). In practice, the system could operate in much the same manner as the mental-commitment process in Fairfax County, Virginia. There, private mental hospitals contract to detain temporarily persons alleged to be dangerous to themselves or others as a result of mental illness. The private hospital's only role in the actual commitment, however, is that of a complaining witness before a judicial officer who travels to the hospital to conduct the commitment hearing.

delegation was constitutional. But, even if the delegation were held to be constitutional, the principles announced in Todd would require the private company to comply meticulously with appellate procedure in all of its disciplinary proceedings. Finally, federal courts nevertheless might not apply the reasoning in these cases to the private-prison context because the courts have indicated that a different analysis may apply to delegations affecting liberty, rather than property, interests.

At the state level, legislatures might constitutionally adopt an extant disciplinary code proposed by a private company. If the private party regularly amended the code, however, those amendments could not constitutionally bind prisoners until the legislature or an administrative agency specifically adopted them. Further, state courts generally invalidate statutes and administrative regulations that delegate adjudicative power to private parties when there is no provision for judicial review of the private determinations. When there is provision for such review, however, the delegation generally is upheld.

If a private-prison contract were structured so that the company did not financially benefit from its decision to revoke a prisoner's good-time credits, the principles announced in DiLoreto might permit the prison company to adjudicate the prisoner's rights in the first instance if judicial review were available. Even in such a case, however, statutory or administrative rules would have to channel the prison's discretion concerning its procedure for adjudicating a prisoner's rights. However, because any adjudication by a private-prison company would directly affect a prisoner's liberty rather than merely his property, courts may distinguish cases such as DiLoreto and hold that a private-prison company is not empowered at all to decide whether a prisoner has violated a disciplinary rule.

Finally, any prison-privatization plan must take special account of the policy concern that the delegate's private interests will prevail over the interests of both the affected party and the public. When such a conflict of interest exists, the courts may invalidate the delegations whether or not judicial review is available.

Absent clear precedent, of course, good predictions about the direction and application of the law are difficult to make. There are no clear precedents regarding delegation of the incarceration function to private corporations. In an important sense, though, the delegation question is also a question of symbolism.

The American Correctional Association, in its 1985 policy statement on prison privatization, began: "Government has the ultimate authority and responsibility for corrections."[211] This should be undeniable. When a court enters a judgment of conviction and imposes a sentence, it exercises its authority, both actually and symbolically. Does it weaken that authority, however -- as well as the integrity of a system of justice --

---

[211] American Correctional Association, National Correctional Policy on Private Sector Involvement in Corrections 1 (1985).

when an inmate looks at his keeper's uniform and sees an emblem that reads "Acme Corrections Company," for example, instead of "Federal Bureau of Prisons," or "State Department of Corrections"?[212]

In other words, apart from questions of cost, apart from questions of efficiency, apart from questions of liability, and assuming that inmates will retain no fewer rights and privileges than they had before the transfer to private management, who should operate our nation's prisons and jails? It could certainly be argued that virtually anything that is done in a total, secure institution by the government or its designee is an important expression of government policy, and therefore should not be delegated. Just as we would not likely privatize our criminal courts, perhaps too we should not privatize our prisons. And just as the inmate should perhaps be obliged to know -- day by day, minute by minute -- that he is in the custody of the government, perhaps too the government should be obliged to know -- also day by day, minute by minute -- that it is its brother's keeper, even with all of its flaws. One cannot help but wonder what Dostoevsky -- who wrote that "[t]he degree of civilization in a society is revealed by entering its prisons"[213] -- would have thought about privatization of corrections.

But, while prison privatization arguably may be profoundly

---

212 See Purveyors of Incarceration, supra note 5, at 23-24.

213 F. Dostoevsky, The House of the Dead 76 (C. Garnett trans. 1957).

unwise as a matter of public policy, this does not mean that delegating the incarceration function to a private company would necessarily be unconstitutional. In deciding the constitutional question, therefore, the courts ultimately will be determining how we wish to be perceived as a civilization.

B. The State-Action Requirement of the Fourteenth Amendment and 42 U.S.C. § 1983

1. Introduction

The privatization of prisons and jails raises important issues with respect to liability in suits brought by inmates. If a private company operates a prison, for example, the state likely will be directly involved in some aspects of prison life, such as using force when necessary or making quasi-judicial decisions, but it may not be directly involved in the day-to-day operation of the institution. This dichotomy of involvement may lead to confusion over responsibility and accountability when a violation of rights is alleged to have occurred.

When a private party, as opposed to a government employee, is charged with abridging rights guaranteed by the Constitution or laws of the United States, the plaintiff, in order to prevail under 42 U.S.C. § 1983,[214] must show that the private party was acting "under color of state law" -- that is, that there was

---

[214] Section 1983 provides in pertinent part:

Every person who, under the color of any statute, ordinance, regulation, custom, or usage, of any State or Territory or the District of Columbia, subjects, or causes to be subjected, any citizen of the United States or other person within the jurisdiction thereof to the deprivation of any rights, privileges, or immunities secured by the Constitution and laws, shall be liable to the party injured . . . .

42 U.S.C. § 1983 (1982).

state action.[215] The reason for this is fundamental. The fifth

and fourteenth amendments, which prohibit the government from

denying federal constitutional rights and which guarantee due

process of law, apply to the acts of state and federal

governments, and not to the acts of private parties or

entities.[216]

The ultimate issue in determining whether a person is

subject to suit for violation of an individual's constitutional

rights is whether "the alleged infringement of federal rights

[is] 'fairly attributable to the State.'"[217] A person acts under

color of state law "only when exercising power 'possessed by

virtue of state law and made possible only because the wrongdoer

is clothed with the authority of state law.'"[218]

---

[215] The constitutional standard for finding state action is
closely related, if not identical, to the statutory standard for
determining "color of state law." See Lugar v. Edmondson Oil
Co., 457 U.S. 922, 928-29 (1982).

[216] See Shelley v. Kraemer, 334 U.S. 1, 13 (1948); Civil
Rights Cases, 109 U.S. 3, 11 (1883). Throughout this paper, the
term "state action" refers to action at any level of
government. See, e.g., 4 Encyclopedia of the American
Constitution 1729 (L. Levy, K. Karst & D. Mahoney eds. 1986)
(explaining that the term "state action" denotes action of any
"unit or element of government"); 2 R. Rotunda, J. Nowak & J.
Young, Treatise on Constitutional Law § 16.1, at 157 (1986)
("[A]ll problems relating to the existence of government action
-- local, state or federal -- which would subject an individual
to constitutional restriction come under the heading of 'state
action.'"); L. Tribe, American Constitutional Law § 18-1, at 1688
& n.2 (2d ed. 1988) (utilizing the term "state action" when
denoting "action by any level of government, from local to
national") (emphasis in original).

[217] Rendell-Baker v. Kohn, 457 U.S. 830, 838 (1982)
(quoting Lugar, 457 U.S. at 937).

[218] Polk County v. Dodson, 454 U.S. 312, 317-18 (1981)
(quoting United States v. Classic, 313 U.S. 299, 326 (1941)); see

-71-

These concepts are crucial to prison and jail privatization. One argument in favor of privatization is that it will reduce or eliminate government liability. Yet an examination of the state-action issue indicates that this will not happen. If the state-action requirement is _not_ met, then the private company will not be liable under the Civil Rights Act. If the requirement _is_ met, however, leading to the private company's liability, then the company's costs will increase, resulting in higher rates charged to the government. Privatization thus will be less attractive, both to the government (due to increased prices) and to investors (due to greater risk on their investment).

The thesis of this section of the paper is that, in the privatization situation in which the operation of an entire institution is contracted out to private hands, there is no doubt that state action is present. If the answer to the delegation question is uncertain, the answer to the state-action question is not: Privatization will neither eliminate nor reduce the liability of the government or the private company for violations of an individual's rights.

----

also Evans v. Newton, 382 U.S. 296, 299 (1966) ("[W]hen private individuals or groups are endowed by the State with powers or functions governmental in nature, they become agencies or instrumentalities of the State . . . .").

2. Overview of State-Action Doctrine

The progenitors of the fourteenth amendment[219] established the state-action requirement as a constitutional limit on the government, in order to protect individual rights.[220] Despite the framers' efforts, however, the courts over the past half

---

[219] The fourteenth amendment provides in part:

No State shall make or enforce any law which shall abridge the privileges or immunities of citizens of the United States; nor shall any State deprive any person of life, liberty, or property, without due process of law; nor deny to any person within its jurisdiction the equal protection of the laws.

U.S. Const. Amend XIV, § 1.

[220] See The Federalist No. 28, at 178 (A. Hamilton) (C. Russiter ed. 1961) (stating that federal and state governmental scheme is in place to check possible misdeeds); id. No. 46, at 294 (J. Madison) (positing that the rights reserved by the state governments were designed to keep encroachment of federal government in check); id. No. 51, at 201 (J. Madison) (arguing that rights of citizens are protected by double security system of separate federal and state governments and three distinct governmental branches on both federal and state levels); id. No. 47, at 300 (J. Madison) (arguing that absence of separation of powers is equal to tyranny); see also Comment, Section 1983 and the Independent Contractor, 74 Geo. L.J. 457, 468 (1985) (examining constitutional limits on government and individual rights). The fourteenth amendment is also the vehicle through which constitutional limitations restrain the states. U.S. Const. amend XIV (mandating certain limitations on government interference); see also Schneider, supra note 58, at 1153 (describing fourteenth amendment as limiting); Comment, supra, at 468 (arguing that fourteenth amendment serves to restrain state governments as well as federal government). In addition to the protection of federalism, state-action cases also concern the competing constitutional claims of the actors. See Note, State Action After Jackson v. Metropolitan Edison Co.: Analytical Framework for a Restrictive Doctrine, 81 Dick. L. Rev. 315, 343 (1977) (discussing conflict between the right to be free from governmental interference and the fourteenth amendment).

century have muddled the meaning of state action, failing to apply a consistent analysis for determining whether it is present.[221] Perhaps not surprisingly, the development of the state-action doctrine has depended on the composition of the United States Supreme Court and the interests that were involved in a particular claim.[222] These interests included the public expectation of equality and due process and, conversely, the right to act without federal or state interference.[223] Because these factors have caused inconsistencies in the doctrine, the state-action inquiry has been labelled a "paragon of unclarity," a "protean concept," an "impossible task,"[224] and a "conceptual

---

[221] See, e.g., Schneider, State Action -- Making Sense Out of Chaos -- A Historical Approach, 37 U. Fla. L. Rev. 737, 737 (1985) (stating that Supreme Court has not been able to articulate consistent state-action doctrine).

[222] See, e.g., Rendell-Baker v. Kohn, 457 U.S. 830, 840-43 (1982) (no state action found for due process claims of vocational counselor who was terminated by private school that received more than 90 percent of its operating budget from the state); Burton v. Wilmington Parking Auth., 365 U.S. 715, 721-26 (1961) (finding state action where restaurant, which operated in premises leased from an agency of the State of Delaware, refused to serve blacks during civil-rights era); Marsh v. Alabama, 326 U.S. 501, 505 (1946) (state action found because of preferred position of first amendment where company-owned town completely barred the distribution of religious literature on its sidewalk).

[223] See Note, supra note 220, at 343 (discussing conflict between the right to be free from governmental interference and the fourteenth amendment); see also supra note 220 and accompanying text (positing question of whether due process or individual freedom ought to be held as most important right or fundamental right).

[224] See Frazier v. Board of Trustees, 765 F.2d 1278, 1283 n.8 (5th Cir. 1985) (citing Black, The Supreme Court, 1966 Term -- Foreword: "State Action," Equal Protection, and California's Proposition 14, 81 Harv. L. Rev. 69, 89 (1967) (stating that "eight decades of metaphysical writhing around the 'state action' doctrine have made it the paragon of unclarity"); Lewis, The

disaster area."[225]

a. Historical Approaches to State Action: Four Traditional Tests

In the earlier cases, courts used several analyses to determine the existence of state action. In Burton v. Wilmington Parking Authority,[226] for example, the Supreme Court articulated a symbiosis test, declaring that "[o]nly by sifting facts and weighing circumstances can the nonobvious involvement of the State in private conduct be attributed its true significance."[227] It found that state action was present because a symbiotic relationship existed between the private entity and the state.[228] The Court emphasized that the entity -- a

_____

Meaning of State Action, 60 Colum. L. Rev. 1083, 1085 (1960) (describing state action as a "protean concept"); Reitman v. Mulkey, 387 U.S. 369, 378 (1967) (noting that the Supreme Court has never attempted the "impossible task" of formulating an infallible test for determining what constitutes state action)), cert. denied, 476 U.S. 1142 (1986).

[225] Black, supra note 224, at 95.

[226] 365 U.S. 715 (1961). In Burton, the plaintiff brought suit against a restaurant that was located in a publicly owned and operated building and that refused to serve him solely due to his race. Id. at 716. The plaintiff claimed that the restaurant violated his rights under the equal protection clause of the fourteenth amendment. Id.

[227] Id. at 722.

[228] Id. at 722-26. The Court used the least restrictive state-action test, finding state action where a racially discriminatory restaurant leased space in a public parking garage. The Court reasoned that the state and restaurant were in a position of interdependence. Id. at 725. This interdependence theory became known as the symbiosis analysis, and was employed frequently in state-action arguments. See, e.g., Holodnak v. Avco Corp., 514 F.2d 285, 289 (2d Cir.) (applying the "symbiotic

restaurant in a building complex that included a public parking garage -- was physically and financially integrated with the public activity such that it was an indispensable part of the state's operation of the public facility.[229]

In <u>Jackson v. Metropolitan Edison Co.</u>,[230] the Court

_____

relationship" analysis enunciated in <u>Burton</u>), <u>cert. denied</u>, 423 U.S. 892 (1975); Howard Univ. v. NCAA, 510 F.2d 213, 217 (D.C. Cir. 1975) (stating that, if the government so far insinuates itself into a position of interdependence, it must be recognized as a joint participant in the challenged activity); Braden v. University of Pittsburgh, 392 F. Supp. 118, 125 (W.D. Pa. 1975) (concluding that the government insinuated itself into a position of interdependence with the university and that this was comparable to the symbiotic relationship present in <u>Burton</u>), <u>aff'd</u>, 552 F.2d 948 (3d Cir. 1977). The symbiosis analysis became so expanded that several commentators considered <u>Burton</u> to be an abandonment of the state-action doctrine altogether. <u>See</u> Hemphill, <u>State Action and Civil Rights</u>, 23 Mercer L. Rev. 519, 533-34 (1972) (stating that several recent decisions of the Supreme Court indicate the "judicial burial" of the state-action doctrine); Williams, <u>The Twilight of State Action</u>, 41 Tex. L. Rev. 347, 382 (1963) (noting that the Court in <u>Burton</u> "for the first time opened the door to the abandonment of the state-action concept"). For the symbiosis analysis to support a state-action finding, there must be a nexus between the plaintiff's injury and the government's gain. <u>Holodnak</u>, 514 F.2d at 289-90. The symbiosis analysis has not been used in recent decisions, however, as the Supreme Court has moved in other directions for state-action analysis. <u>But</u> <u>see</u> <u>infra</u> note 373.

[229] 365 U.S. at 723-24 (concluding that state was involved in and participated in discriminatory action because state had obligations with respect to restaurant, benefits were mutually conferred, and restaurant was integrated into building).

[230] 419 U.S. 345 (1974). In <u>Jackson</u>, the petitioner brought a section 1983 claim against a utility that had terminated her service without providing notice, a hearing, or an opportunity to pay amounts allegedly due. <u>Id.</u> at 347. The petitioner claimed that the utility's conduct constituted state action because state law granted an entitlement to continuous electrical service and because the termination was permitted by a provision in the utility's tariff that had been filed with the Pennsylvania Public Utility Commission. <u>Id.</u> at 347-48. The petitioner also argued that the state granted the utility a monopoly status, which therefore supported a finding of state action. <u>Id.</u> at 351. She further urged that state action was present because the utility provided an essential public service

discussed two tests -- the close-nexus test and the public-function test. The Court stated that the inquiry under the close-nexus test was whether the connection between the state and the challenged action was sufficiently close for the action to be treated as that of the state.[231] Among the factors considered important to this analysis were state funding and state regulation.[232] Alternatively, under the public-function test, the Court required "the exercise by a private entity of powers traditionally exclusively reserved to the State."[233] In Flagg Bros., Inc. v. Brooks,[234] the Court reiterated this test and noted that, although the government traditionally performed many functions, few functions were exclusively reserved to the state.[235]

_____

or public function. Id. at 352. Finally, the petitioner argued that there was a symbiotic relationship between the utility and state. Id. at 357. The Court rejected all of these arguments and concluded that state action was not present. Id. at 358-59.

[231] Id. at 351.

[232] Id. at 350. The Court discussed only the state-regulation element of the close-nexus test; other cases, however, have considered the importance of state funding to the nexus analysis. See Rendell-Baker v. Kohn, 457 U.S. 830, 840-41 (1982) (analyzing state funding and regulation to determine existence of state action). The Jackson Court noted that mere regulation was insufficient state involvement to create a close nexus. 419 U.S. at 350.

[233] 419 U.S. at 352. The Court observed that the performance of a public service or public function was not enough; the function had to be traditionally the exclusive prerogative of the state. Id. at 352-53.

[234] 436 U.S. 149 (1978).

[235] Id. at 158. The Court concluded that the holding of elections is one function that traditionally has been reserved exclusively for states. The other circumstance that indicated a traditional and exclusive function was when a private corporation

A fourth test that the Supreme Court applied in its early decisions involved state compulsion or significant encouragement. In Adickes v. S.H. Kress & Co.,[236] for example, the Court found that the state's compulsion of the challenged conduct by a statutory provision or custom having the force of law warranted a finding of state action.[237] Similarly, in Flagg Bros., the Court found no state action because the state merely permitted the challenged conduct but did not compel it.[238] The compulsion test has rarely been applied alone; it is usually applied in conjunction with another test.[239]

b.   The 1982 Trilogy: An Attempt at Clarification

In 1982, the Supreme Court reevaluated the state-action analyses in Lugar v. Edmondson Oil Co.,[240] Blum v. Yaretsky,[241] and Rendell-Baker v. Kohn,[242] and attempted to articulate a clearer standard.   In Lugar, the Court found state action under

---

controlled a town and provided necessary municipal functions. Id. at 158-59 (citing Marsh v. Alabama, 326 U.S. 501 (1946)).

[236]   398 U.S. 144 (1970).

[237]   Id. at 171.

[238]   436 U.S. at 164-66.

[239]   See Lombard v. Eunice Kennedy Shriver Center, 556 F. Supp. 677, 680 (D. Mass. 1983) (combining state-compulsion analysis with public-function analysis), discussed infra at notes 359-364 and accompanying text.

[240]   457 U.S. 922 (1982).

[241]   457 U.S. 991 (1982).

[242]   457 U.S. 830 (1982).

an analysis that required the challenged conduct to be fairly

attributable to the state.[243] The Court specified that conduct

will be fairly attributable if it is "caused by the exercise of

some right or privilege created by the State or by a rule of

conduct imposed by the State or by a person for whom the State is

responsible" and if the acting party is "a person who may fairly

be said to be a state actor."[244]

In Blum and Rendell-Baker, the Court used some of the

"fairly attributable" language,[245] but concentrated on the four

traditional analyses for determining state action, concluding

that satisfaction of any one of these analyses could lead to a

---

[243] Lugar, 457 U.S. at 937. The Court stated that in its previous decisions it "insisted that the conduct allegedly causing the deprivation of a federal right be fairly attributable to the State." Id.

[244] Id. The Court further explained that a state actor is "a state official," a person who either "acted together with or has obtained significant aid from state officials," or a person whose "conduct is otherwise chargeable to the State." Id. According to the Court, the inquiries involving whether the deprivation was caused by a right or privilege emanating from state authority and whether the party charged with the deprivation was a state actor are separate issues when the constitutional claim is directed against a party without apparent state authority. Id.

[245] Blum, 457 U.S. at 1004 (noting the fair-attribution test but stating that the facts did not support the use of this inquiry because the case did not involve the "enforcement of state laws or regulations by state officials who are themselves parties in the lawsuit"); Rendell-Baker, 457 U.S. at 838 (stating that ultimate issue of whether person is subject to suit under section 1983 is whether infringement is fairly attributable to state). The Rendell-Baker Court, however, believed that the Blum Court used the fairly-attributable analysis, id. at 839-40, and stated that, in Blum, "[t]he Court considered whether certain nursing homes were state actors for the purpose of determining whether decisions regarding transfers of patients could be fairly attributed to the State, and hence be subjected to Fourteenth Amendment due process requirements." Id.

finding of state action.[246] The Blum Court discussed the close-nexus test and noted that the relationship between the challenged conduct and the state must be such that the state was responsible for the conduct -- that the state's exercise of coercive power or significant encouragement would warrant a finding that the state was responsible for a private decision.[247] In addition, if the private entity performed a function that was traditionally the exclusive prerogative of the state, a sufficient nexus would exist.[248]

The Rendell-Baker Court concluded that neither the receipt of substantial public funds nor extensive state regulation was sufficient to establish a close nexus.[249] The Court also stated that a fiscal relationship with the state, similar to the relationship that exists between the state and a contractor performing services for it, was not enough to establish state action by a symbiotic relationship, as in Burton.[250] Finally,

_____

[246] Blum, 457 U.S. at 1003-05; Rendell-Baker, 457 U.S. at 839-43.

[247] Blum, 457 U.S. at 1004-05.

[248] Id. at 1005.

[249] Rendell-Baker, 457 U.S. at 840-41. The Court expressed that "[a]cts of such private contractors do not become acts of the government by reason of their significant or even total engagement in performing public contracts." Id. at 841. The Court also stated that, unless the extensive state regulation compelled or influenced the private party's decision, the decision would not be state action. Id. But see Schneider, supra note 58, at 1164 (stating that the nexus analysis of Rendell-Baker is inappropriate where a state delegates a task that it is statutorily required to provide).

[250] Rendell-Baker, 457 U.S. at 842-43; see also Schneider, supra note 58, at 1160 (noting that in Rendell-Baker the Court

the Court applied the public-function analysis and concluded that the function must belong to the state traditionally and that legislation providing for the state's performance of services does not render those services within the exclusive prerogative of the state.[251] Instead, such legislation must explicitly state that the function may only be performed by the state in order for the "exclusive" requirement to be satisfied.[252]

Despite the Court's attempt to clarify the state-action doctrine in this trilogy of cases, it remains unclear what set of facts will establish state action and which analysis will be most persuasive.[253] One point is clear, however: The 1982 trilogy established a restrictive standard for state action.[254]

---

summarily concluded that the state and the school did not share a symbiotic relationship). At least one court has construed Rendell-Baker's discussion of the symbiotic-relationship test as seriously impairing this test. See Frazier v. Board of Trustees, 765 F.2d 1278, 1287 (5th Cir. 1985), cert. denied, 476 U.S. 1142 (1986).

[251] Rendell-Baker, 457 U.S. at 842. The Court noted that, while the State of Massachusetts had made a legislative policy choice to provide education to maladjusted high-school students at the public's expense, this decision in no way made these services the exclusive province of the state. The services in question had not been traditionally provided by the state, as evidenced by the fact that the state had only recently undertaken the service. Id.

[252] Id. (the question is whether the function performed has been "traditionally the exclusive prerogative of the State") (emphasis in original).

[253] See Schneider, supra note 58, at 1177 (opining that it is unclear whether all analyses must now be satisfied).

[254] But see id. at 1166-70 (proposing new analyses for state action, shifting focus from nexus approach to examination of the particular nature of the challenged conduct).

3.   **Development of the State-Action Doctrine: The Application to Prison and Jail Privatization**

Federal and state cases shed light on three of the state action analyses[255] -- public function, close nexus, and state compulsion -- and suggest the possibility of combining all of these analyses into a fourth test for state action. In addition, the more recent cases illustrate how the courts have applied the holdings of the 1982 trilogy. Most important, the recent case law can help to determine the factors that will be important to the application of the state-action requirement in a private-prison or private-jail context.

a.   **Public-Function Test**

The broadest application of the public-function test came in 1946, in Marsh v. Alabama.[256] In Marsh, the Supreme Court held the state to be in violation of the first and fourteenth amendments when the state enforced a privately owned town's regulation against the distribution of religious literature on the streets of its business block.[257] In making its decision, the Court found that the private town served a public function, as if it were a municipality.[258] The public's expectation

---

[255]   See supra note 228 (noting demise of symbiosis analysis).

[256]   326 U.S. 501 (1946).

[257]   Id. at 509.

regarding the constitutional protection of its first amendment rights was an important factor in the Court's decision.[259] Simply because it was a privately owned town did not decrease the public expectation that the first amendment would be protected.[260]

This expansive analysis was restricted by the Court's 1974 opinion in Jackson v. Metropolitan Edison Co.[261] In Jackson, the Court held that a private utility can only be characterized as performing a public-function if the activity traditionally is reserved exclusively to the state.[262] Four years later, the Court in Flagg Bros. used the traditionally exclusive notion with the public-function analysis.[263] The plaintiff in Flagg Bros. had been evicted and had her belongings placed in a private warehouse for storage.[264] Because the plaintiff did not pay the

---

[258] Id. at 508.

[259] Id. at 507. Thus, the Court's holding in Marsh illustrates both the public-expectation and federalism concerns that are inherent in state-action litigation. Id. at 508 (the corporation "cannot curtail the liberty of . . . these people consistently with the purposes of the Constitutional guarantees, and a state statute . . . which enforces such action by criminally punishing those who attempt to distribute religious literature clearly violates the First and Fourteenth Amendments to the Constitution").

[260] Id. at 507. The Court stated that, "whether a corporation or a municipality owns or possesses the town, the public in either case has an identical interest in the functioning of the community in such a manner that the channels of communication are free." Id.

[261] 419 U.S. 345 (1974).

[262] Id. at 352; see Comment, supra note 220, at 469 (stating that public-function test was limited in Jackson).

[263] 436 U.S. at 157-61.

storage costs, the warehouse threatened to sell the stored goods to satisfy the debt.[265] This sale was permitted pursuant to state statute.[266] The plaintiff brought a section 1983 action against the private warehouse, alleging violation of her fourteenth amendment rights.[267] Employing the traditionally exclusive language in conjunction with the public-function test, the Court found that the settlement of disputes between debtors and creditors was outside the arena of state action.[268]

The Court utilized a similar analysis in Lugar, one of the three salient public-function cases decided by the Court on the same day in 1982.[269] In Lugar, a debtor filed a section 1983 action against a private creditor who had invoked a state statute permitting prejudgment attachment.[270] Pursuant to this statute, the state-court clerk issued a writ of attachment and the sheriff sequestered plaintiff debtor's property.[271] Reversing the lower courts, the Supreme Court held that the creditor, Edmondson Oil, acted under color of state law by using the state-created attachment process.[272] The Court posited that Flagg Bros. did

---

[264] Id. at 153.

[265] Id.

[266] Id. at 151.

[267] Id. at 153.

[268] Id. at 161.

[269] See supra notes 240-254 and accompanying text; see also Schneider, supra note 58, at 1153 (characterizing the three 1982 state-action cases as a trilogy).

[270] Lugar, 457 U.S. at 924.

[271] Id. at 924-25.

not apply, as the court of appeals had concluded, because both the state statute and the state's direct action through its officials denoted state action.[273] This analysis was similar to that used in Flagg Bros., although there was no direct state action through a state official in that case.[274]

Unlike Lugar and Flagg Bros., which permitted a state-action finding under a compulsion or public-function characterization, the Court in Blum v. Yaretsky demanded satisfaction of the state-compulsion, public-function, and close-nexus analyses before a

_____

[272] Id. Justice Powell dissented, arguing that, when a state is not responsible for a private decision, the private action ought not to be considered state action. Id. at 949 (Powell, J., dissenting).

[273] Id. at 942.

[274] 436 U.S. at 164-65. The Court in Lugar developed a two-pronged test to determine state action: "First, the deprivation must be caused by the exercise of some right or privilege created by the state or by a rule of conduct imposed by the state or by a person for whom the state is responsible"; and "[s]econd, the party charged with the deprivation must be a person who may fairly be said to be a state actor." 457 U.S. at 937. The Lugar test was developed by comparing Moose Lodge No. 107 v. Irvis, 407 U.S. 163 (1972) with Flagg Bros., 457 U.S. at 937. In Moose Lodge, a private club licensed by the Commonwealth of Pennsylvania to serve alcohol practiced a racially discriminatory serving policy. 407 U.S. at 171. The Court found that the government did not in any way effect this discrimination. Id. at 175-76. Hence, regarding the first prong, the Court in Lugar stated that government regulation does not necessarily make all private entities' conduct state action. Lugar, 457 U.S. at 938.

The Court then turned to Flagg Bros. to develop the second prong of its test. Id. at 938. To be characterized as a state actor, according to Flagg Bros., one must have done something more than act pursuant to a state statute. 436 U.S. at 164. The second prong focuses on the question of whether a section 1983 defendant can correctly be classified as a state actor. Lugar, 457 U.S. at 941. The Lugar Court held this element to be met because the defendant received the aid of state officials. Id. at 942.

claim for state action could prevail.[275] Blum considered whether

a private nursing home's transfer decisions denoted state action

when the nursing home operated under a state contract.[276] In

Blum, the plaintiffs had been transferred to a unit rendering a

lower level of care.[277] They claimed that these transfers were

in violation of their fourteenth amendment rights.[278]

The Court in Blum established a three-part test to analyze

whether state action existed: There must be a close nexus

between the state and the regulated nursing home; the state must

compel the private nursing home's transfer decision; and the

private nursing home must function in a manner that was

traditionally the exclusive prerogative of the state.[279] Using

this tripartite test, the Court held that the transfer decisions

did not constitute actions under color of state law because the

transfers were premised on independent medical standards that the

state did not establish.[280]

---

[275] The Court referred to the three state-action tests as "requirements." 457 U.S. at 1004-05.

[276] Id. at 1003.

[277] Id. at 995. The Court did not permit the challenge of transfers to a higher level of care. Id. at 1002.

[278] Among other things, the plaintiffs claimed that they had not been afforded adequate notice of the transfer decisions and the reasons supporting them or of their right to an administrative hearing to challenge those decisions. Id. at 996.

[279] Id. at 1004-05.

[280] Id. at 1012. The Court in Blum compared the independent professional standards relevant to its holding to the adverse relationship that the lawyer has with the state due to the lawyer-client relationship. Id. at 1008-09. The Court addressed the adverse lawyer-state relationship in Polk County v.

Neither Blum nor Lugar involved the delegation of activities that the state is normally obliged to perform. Because Rendell-Baker, however, did involve such a delegation, and because its outcome is at odds with the public expectation of the state's responsibility,[281] it has an impact on state-action analysis with respect to the privatization of state functions -- the privatization of prisons, for example.[282] In fact, until recently Rendell-Baker was the most relevant Supreme Court privatization case that involved state action.[283] This case concerned a privately owned, legislatively established institution for maladjusted high-school students.[284] A

Dodson, 454 U.S. 312 (1981). In Polk County, the Court held that a public defender's activities or functions did not constitute state action because the state had not developed the professional standards that govern a lawyer's conduct. Id. at 321-22. The Court's reference to Polk County in Blum is interesting, because the Court in Polk County contrasted the functions of the legal and medical professions. Id. at 320. The legal profession, as described in Polk County, is in place to ensure protection from harmful state action, whereas the medical profession, when institutional, assumes the same obligation and mission as does the state. Id.; see infra notes 381-392 and accompanying text (discussing West v. Atkins).

[281] See Schneider, supra note 58, at 1167-69 (delineating role of public expectation for finding of state action in privatization cases).

[282] Privatization cases involve at least two sets of interests: the aggrieved party's civil rights and the private defendant's interest in freedom from governmental intervention.

[283] See West v. Atkins, 56 U.S.L.W. 4664 (U.S. June 20, 1988), discussed infra at notes 381-392 and accompanying text. Rendell-Baker presented two cases that were consolidated on appeal. The United States Court of Appeals for the First Circuit consolidated the cases after interlocutory appeal had been granted to the defendant under 28 U.S.C. § 1292(b). Rendell-Baker v. Kohn, 641 F.2d 14 (1st Cir. 1981), aff'd, 457 U.S 830 (1982).

[284] 457 U.S. at 834-35. Massachusetts law imposed

vocational counselor at the school filed a claim under section 1983 after being dismissed for supporting a student petition.[285] In a consolidated appeal of differing district-court judgments, the United States Court of Appeals for the First Circuit ordered dismissal of the claim because the school did not act pursuant to color of state law in its termination decision.[286] The United States Supreme Court affirmed, using the public-function and close-nexus tests together for the first time.[287]

The Court conceded that special education was a public function that state law delegated to a private entity, but the

_____

responsibility on the state to provide special education. Mass. Gen. Laws Ann. ch. 71B, §§ 3, 4 (West Supp. 1981). This same statute permitted the delegation of special education to private schools. Id. § 3. The delegation statute also required extensive regulation, including periodic reviews of each student's progress, specific education programs for each student, and reviews of the original placement decision. Id. The New Perspectives School that was involved in Rendell-Baker received 90 to 99 percent of its budget from public funds because of the large number of students placed there pursuant to the Massachusetts delegation statute. Rendell-Baker, 457 U.S. at 832. But the Court concluded that dependence on public funding did not make the private acts public. Id. at 840.

[285] Rendell-Baker, 457 U.S. at 834. The counselor, Rendell-Baker, requested a hearing or reinstatement. The school decided to appoint a grievance committee to consider her claims. Id. Several months later, five other teachers were dismissed due to their public statements regarding New Perspectives' educational environment and the students' rights to free speech. Id. at 835. The five teachers also brought suit pursuant to section 1983. Id.

[286] Rendell-Baker v. Kohn, 641 F.2d 14, 26-27 (1st Cir. 1981), aff'd, 457 U.S. 830 (1982).

[287] 457 U.S. at 840-43. The Court in Rendell-Baker found that the fourteenth amendment and section 1983 were functionally similar. Id. at 838. This finding is to be distinguished from Lugar, in which the Court cautiously stated the differences between the two. Lugar, 457 U.S. at 927-28 & n.8.

question remained whether special education was the traditional and exclusive prerogative of the state.[288] The Court held that the state delegation statute, as well as the school's public function, were not enough to prove that special education was an exclusive state prerogative.[289]

The requirement of an exclusive state prerogative was first applied to the public-function test in Jackson v. Metropolitan Edison Co.,[290] reflecting the concern of increasing litigation under section 1983.[291] In Jackson, the plaintiff brought a section 1983 action against a monopolistic private utility, claiming a violation of due process because service to her home had been terminated for failure to pay.[292] Under the test formulated by the Court, the plaintiff could prevail if the utility functioned in a fashion traditionally and exclusively reserved for the state.[293] Plaintiff's claim failed because the Court held the utility provision to be neither the traditional nor the exclusive function of the government.[294]

---

[288] Rendell-Baker, 457 U.S. at 842.

[289] Id. at 841-42. Using the exclusivity clause imposed in Jackson v. Metropolitan Edison Co., 419 U.S. 345, 352 (1974), the Court thus limited the public-function doctrine.

[290] 419 U.S. at 352.

[291] Compare Administrative Office of the United States Courts, 1983 Annual Report of the Director 135, at table 15 (reporting 19,735 civil-rights cases) with Administrative Office of the United States Courts, 1960 Annual Report of the Director 232, at table C2 (reporting only 280 civil-rights cases), cited in Comment, supra note 220, at 457.

[292] 419 U.S. at 347-48.

[293] Id. at 353.

Given its reliance on the _Jackson_ holding, _Rendell-Baker_ built upon the _Jackson_ exclusivity test, which required that the delegated function be traditionally provided by the state.[295] Yet the Massachusetts delegation statute, as well as the huge public school system, tended to show that the provision of education _was_ a traditional state function. Nevertheless, the requirement of exclusivity in _Rendell-Baker_ was said to follow from the _Jackson_ decision.

Ignoring _Jackson_'s requirement that a delegation of a traditional government function be found before applying the exclusive state-action test, the _Rendell-Baker_ Court couched the issue as whether a private school with public funding and regulation, when terminating employees, acts under color of state law.[296] Given the statutory duty to provide special education, if the state had provided the service itself it would not be permitted to act outside the limits of the Constitution. The state should not be permitted to distance itself from its traditional and statutory duties through privatization.

Although cases in state courts and lower federal courts have addressed state action and the public-function analysis,[297] the

---

[294] _Id._ Still, it is clear that _Jackson_ did not intend the exclusivity limitation to apply whenever the public-function test is used. _Id._

[295] _Id._

[296] _Rendell-Baker_, 457 U.S. at 840.

[297] Compare Ancata v. Prison Health Servs., Inc., 769 F.2d 700, 703 (11th Cir. 1985) (holding that private health-care provider to county jail may be liable under section 1983 for inadequate medical services to prisoners) _and_ Ort v. Pinchback,

number of these cases diminishes considerably when limited to the privatization issue involved in Rendell-Baker. The most pertinent post-Rendell-Baker federal case regarding privatization, especially of prisons, is Medina v. O'Neill.[298] The federal district court in Medina considered the issue of whether the Immigration and Naturalization Service (INS) was liable under state-action theory after it had contracted for the incarceration of undocumented workers with a private-detention corporation.[299] Prior to deportation, sixteen Colombian inmates were incarcerated by that corporation for the INS.[300] After recapturing the prisoners following an escape attempt, a private guard, untrained in the proper use of firearms, was using his

---

786 F.2d 1105, 1107 (11th Cir. 1986) (physician who contracts with state to provide medical care to inmates acts under color of state law) with Calvert v. Sharp, 748 F.2d 861 (4th Cir. 1984) (finding no state action where doctor merely cared for patients without a supervisory function or dependence on state funds), cert. denied, 471 U.S 1132 (1985).

In a 1987 en banc decision, the United States Court of Appeals for the Fourth Circuit declined to overrule Calvert. West v. Atkins, 815 F.2d 993, 994-96 (4th Cir. 1987) (en banc) (7-to-3 vote) (holding that physician who was under contract to provide orthopedic services to inmates at a state prison hospital did not act under color of state law for purposes of section 1983 when he allegedly provided inadequate medical treatment to prisoner). The United State Supreme Court reversed. West v. Atkins, 56 U.S.L.W. 4664 (U.S. June 20, 1988); see infra notes 381-392 and accompanying text (discussing West).

298 589 F. Supp. 1028 (S.D. Tex. 1984), vacated in part & rev'd in part on other grounds, 838 F.2d 800 (5th Cir. 1988). Because the government in Medina had control over the prison conditions, a close-nexus analysis could also have been employed despite the fact that the detention facility was privately operated.

299 Id. at 1038; see supra note 216 (indicating that state-action analysis applies to actions of federal government).

300 589 F. Supp. at 1031 n.6.

shotgun as a prod when it discharged, killing one of the detained aliens and wounding another.[301] The plaintiffs claimed, pursuant to section 1983, that they had been unconstitutionally deprived of due process and subjected to cruel and unusual punishment.[302] They argued that state action existed because the INS had a duty to monitor their detention and had failed in this duty. The INS responded that there was no state action because the detained aliens were at all times in the custody of the private-detention corporation.[303]

The court held for the plaintiffs, finding "obvious state action" on the part of both the INS and the private company.[304] The court noted that, although there was no precise formula for finding state action,[305] the Supreme Court has recognized that the public-function concept includes whether the function performed has been traditionally the exclusive prerogative of the state.[306] The court in Medina then stated: "[D]etention is a power reserved to the government, and is an exclusive prerogative of the state . . . . [Thus,] it is evident that the actions of all the defendants were state action within the purview of the

---

[301] Id. at 1032 n.8.

[302] Id. at 1038.

[303] Id.

[304] Id.

[305] Id. (citing Burton v. Wilmington Parking Auth., 365 U.S. 715, 722 (1961)).

[306] Id. (citing Blum, 457 U.S. at 1011; Rendell-Baker, 457 U.S. at 842; and Jackson, 419 U.S. at 353).

public function doctrine."[307]

Indicative of most state cases involving state action is
Rathbun v. Starr Commonwealth for Boys.[308] Like Rendell-Baker
and Medina, Rathbun is a privatization case.[309] In Rathbun, the
plaintiff was an employee of a private institution that housed
boys in the custody of the Michigan Department of Social
Services.[310] Because the plaintiff had been raped by one of the
detained residents, she brought suit against the Department of
Social Services under section 1983.[311] The Michigan Court of
Appeals stated that a private entity acted under color of state
law pursuant to section 1983 when it performed a function that is
essentially and traditionally public.[312]

This standard is obviously similar to the public-function
analysis that was employed in Rendell-Baker and Medina. Unlike
Rendell-Baker, but just as in Medina, the Rathbun court found
state action. The Rathbun holding is bothersome, however,
because its fact pattern is much closer to Rendell-Baker than it
is to Medina. But Rathbun and Rendell-Baker can be distinguished
in that the facility in Rendell-Baker was used principally for
education. Education under Rendell-Baker was not an exclusive

---

307 Id. at 1038-39.

308 145 Mich. App. 303, 377 N.W.2d 872 (1985).

309 Id. at 312, 377 N.W.2d at 877.

310 Id. at 307, 377 N.W.2d at 874.

311 Id. at 308, 377 N.W.2d at 875.

312 Id. at 312, 377 N.W.2d at 877.

public function, whereas the Rathbun facility was concerned only with detention, a traditional and exclusive public function.

A distillation of these cases thus leads to the conclusion that the conduct of those who operate private prisons or jails will be held to constitute state action under the public-function test.

b. Close-Nexus Test

The Burger Court primarily applied the close-nexus test during its earlier years, perpetuating the prior Court's expansive view of the state-action doctrine; the Court now uses this test much less frequently.[313] State action is found under this test if a substantial connection or nexus is established between the state and the private entity's challenged actions.[314] The critical question is whether the private party's

---

[313] Schneider, supra note 221, at 760. The close-nexus test is an "expansive approach to state action, which was acceptable in the context of racial discrimination, [but] was not as desirable in subsequent cases where race was not a factor." Id. at 741. The decrease in racial-discrimination litigation explains the Burger Court's shift from reliance on this test to more restrictive tests.

[314] Id. at 760 n.152. This source further states that the Burger Court used the nexus test to "replace the cumulative totality approach of Burton." Id. It may be argued, however, that the Burger Court, and recent federal district and appellate courts, have returned to the use of a totality approach to state action, combining the exclusive-public-function test, the state-compulsion test, and the close-nexus test. See, e.g., Blum, 457 U.S. at 1004-05 (stating that the required nexus is present if the state is responsible for conduct because the conduct has a sufficiently close nexus with the state, if there is evidence of the state's exercise of coercive power or significant encouragement, or if a private party exercises power that

challenged action can be treated as that of the state.[315] Courts usually examine the extent of the state's funding and regulation of the private entity to determine if the required nexus is present.[316] Although the determination of state action in a private-incarceration context will turn on the facts of each case, the trend in the courts may shed light on what is required.

Recently, state action has not been found under a pure close-nexus test based on factors such as state funding and regulation; courts have considered other factors important and have used the nexus language in connection with other tests.[317] The best example of the use of the close-nexus test is in Milonas v. Williams.[318] In this case, former students brought a section 1983 claim against a private residential school for youths with behavioral problems, alleging that the school's behavior-modification program violated their constitutional rights.[319] Specifically, the plaintiffs claimed that the school administrators, acting under color of state law, had caused them

---

traditionally and exclusively has been that of state); Frazier v. Board of Trustees, 765 F.2d 1278, 1284-88 (5th Cir. 1985) (discussing nexus, public-function, and encouragement analyses), cert. denied, 476 U.S. 1142 (1986); Thorn v. County of Monroe, 586 F. Supp. 1085, 1090-93 (M.D. Pa.) (analyzing facts under various tests for state action), aff'd, 745 F.2d 48 (3d Cir. 1984).

315   Jackson v. Metropolitan Edison Co., 419 U.S. at 351.

316   Id.

317   See, e.g., Woodall v. Partilla, 581 F. Supp. 1066, 1076 (N.D. Ill. 1984) (using nexus language but public-function test).

318   691 F.2d 931 (10th Cir. 1982), cert. denied, 460 U.S. 1069 (1983).

319   Id. at 934.

to be subjected to antitherapeutic and inhumane treatment, resulting in violations of the cruel and unusual punishment clause of the eighth amendment and the due process clause of the fourteenth amendment.[320] The court found that there was significant state regulation of the school's educational program and substantial state funding of its students' tuition.[321] According to the court, however, the critical factor was that the state, through juvenile courts and other state agencies, placed the students at the school without the students' consent.[322] The court therefore concluded that state action was present because the facts established a close nexus between the state and the conduct of the school and school officials.[323]

Similarly, state action was found in Woodall v. Partilla,[324]

----

[320] Id.

[321] Id. at 940.

[322] Id. It was on this ground that the court distinguished Rendell-Baker. Rendell-Baker involved a private school's allegedly wrongful termination of an employee. 457 U.S. at 834. The United States Supreme Court found no state action sufficient to support a section 1983 claim, although there was state funding and regulation. Id. at 840-43. The involuntary nature of the placement of students at the school in Milonas and the fact that Milonas involved students, and not employees, allowed the court in Milonas to find that Rendell-Baker was not controlling. 691 F.2d at 940; see also Schneider, supra note 221, at 742 n.27 (discussing Milonas and distinguishing it from Rendell-Baker).

[323] 691 F.2d at 939 ("[T]he state ha[d] so insinuated itself with the [school] as to be considered a joint participant in the offending actions."); see also Kentucky Ass'n for Retarded Citizens v. Conn, 510 F. Supp. 1233, 1250 (W.D. Ky. 1980) (upholding mentally retarded citizens' class action under section 1983 against privately operated residential facility and concluding that sufficient relationship existed between state and facility because state substantially funded facility and facility undertook duties traditionally within province of state), aff'd, 674 F.2d 582 (6th Cir.), cert. denied, 459 U.S. 1041 (1982).

a case that involved a former inmate's labor claims against a private corporation that provided food service at a prison.[325] The Illinois Department of Corrections had contracted with a private food-service corporation to prepare food for the prison using inmate labor.[326] The plaintiff alleged that his federal and state constitutional rights had been violated because he worked for the food service in excess of the number of hours and

_____

[324]   581 F. Supp. 1066, 1076 (N.D. Ill. 1984).

[325]   Id. at 1069. The plaintiff joined another claim against the private corporation, one of its employees, and certain prison officials, alleging that disciplinary proceedings that had been brought against the inmate by an employee of the private corporation violated his constitutional rights. Id. at 1070. The court concluded that the private corporation's employee did not act under color of state law for the purpose of that claim, and that, as to the other defendants, no cause of action was stated concerning authorization of the disciplinary action. Id. at 1072-73. Therefore, state action did not exist with respect to any party's conduct regarding the disciplinary claim. Id.

This part of the holding in Woodall may be incorrect. The inmate complained about the conduct of an employee of the private corporation, or, as the court suggested, "a non-employee of the state," whose conduct was "analogous to that of a private citizen who acts as complainant in a criminal prosecution." Id. at 1071. Thus, the court's conclusion would serve to immunize the conduct of all employees of private corporations that contract with the state to provide a state function. The employee in this case was not acting as a private citizen. Her conduct instead was the product of work-related circumstances, and the work that was to be done -- supplying food service -- was a function that the state was obligated to provide. If the state had not contracted out its obligation, the employee would have been an employee of the state, and the conduct would have been state action. The state does not shed its responsibility for such conduct just because it contracts with a private party. See Frazier v. Board of Trustees, 765 F.2d 1278, 1287 n.20 (5th Cir. 1985) (noting that states cannot avoid constitutional obligations by delegating to private entities), cert. denied, 476 U.S 1142 (1986); see also infra text accompanying note 392; infra note 395 and accompanying text.

[326]   581 F. Supp. at 1076.

below the wage level required by law.[327] The court analyzed the question of whether the private food service acted under color of state law in order to support the plaintiff's section 1983 claim.[328] It concluded that the requisite close nexus did exist between the state and the private corporation because the corporation paid the inmate's wages, directed the inmate's work, and compelled the inmate to work allegedly excessive hours.[329] Therefore, the corporation exercised a typically state power and state action was established because there was a sufficient nexus alleged in the complaint.[330]

In the event that such a claim is brought against a private prison that contracted with the state for the operation of an entire institution, and not just for the provision of a single service, these cases strongly suggest that state action would be found under a close-nexus analysis. A privately operated prison would be significantly funded and regulated by the state or federal government. In addition, state and federal courts would place prisoners at such prisons. Moreover, courts using the nexus language, but applying the public-function test, may find a close nexus because the private entity, in operating the prison, would wield a typically state power, as in Woodall.

---

327 Id.

328 Id.

329 Id.

330 Id. Although the court believed that the allegations gave rise to a finding of state action, the labor claims were determined to be without merit. Id. at 1077-78.

Several recent cases, however, have not found state action under a close-nexus test, even when the governmental involvement was almost as apparent as it would be in the private-prison or private-jail context. In Graves v. Narcotics Service Counsel, Inc.,[331] for example, an inmate brought a section 1983 claim against a halfway house for improper treatment of his drug addiction. A private nonprofit corporation operated the halfway house, which served as a drug- and alcohol-rehabilitation center and employment facilitator for federal and state inmates.[332] The federal district court determined that the halfway house was subject to state regulation because it was required to have the certification of the Department of Mental Health before it was entitled to receive state referrals.[333] The halfway house also received substantial funding from both the state and federal governments: the federal government reimbursed the halfway house for all of the costs incurred in treating federal inmates and the state paid ninety percent of the costs for state inmates.[334] Nevertheless, the court held that the plaintiff did not allege sufficient facts to establish state action and support a claim under section 1983.[335]

---

[331] 605 F. Supp. 1285 (E.D. Mo. 1985).

[332] Id. at 1286.

[333] Id.

[334] Id. In addition, the state reimbursed the halfway house for 60 percent of the costs of treating non-inmate patients. Id.

[335] Id. at 1287.

In a short opinion, the court examined the analyses in
Rendell-Baker and Blum and concluded that public funding and
regulation were insufficient factors to establish a close
nexus.[336] The court interpreted the two cases to mean that the
close nexus must exist between the state and the challenged
activity, and not just the actor.[337] Since there were no facts
in Graves alleging that the government was involved in the
treatment policy or detoxification program, there was thus no
nexus between the state and the challenged activity.[338]

Other courts have reached a similar result under equally
compelling facts. In Gilmore v. Salt Lake Community Action
Program,[339] the United States Court of Appeals for the Tenth
Circuit found no state action under the close-nexus standard. In
this case, a former director of a community-action agency,
organized as a private nonprofit corporation, brought a section
1983 claim against the agency, challenging his termination.[340]

---

[336] Id. The Graves court compared the halfway house to the
private school in Rendell-Baker and the nursing home in Blum,
both of which had been publicly funded and regulated. Id.

[337] Id.

[338] Id.

[339] 710 F.2d 632 (10th Cir. 1983).

[340] Id. at 632-35. Gilmore also alleged that he was
deprived of a property interest without due process of law and
that the termination constituted government action. Id. at 633.
He asserted that government action was established because of
significant federal funding and regulation. Id. at 636. The
court analyzed this issue separately from the state-action issue
and concluded that these factors, in the absence of others, were
insufficient to establish government action. Id. The court
found particularly important the fact that the federal government
did not exercise influence or control over the agency's

The plaintiff claimed that the termination decision constituted state action because there was extensive state involvement in creating, funding, operating, and regulating the agency.[341] The court noted that, in light of recent United States Supreme Court decisions, state funding and regulation were not enough to establish state action.[342]

The plaintiff, however, stated that other factors supported a finding of state action. For example, state officials substantially participated in the creation of the agency and the state chose to designate the agency as a private organization rather than as a public organization or a political subdivision.[343] More significantly, one-third of the agency's governing board was composed of local public officials who were extensively involved in operating the agency and who had veto power over the agency's programs.[344] These facts, according to the court, warranted a finding that the agency was a state actor but did not necessarily mean that the conduct was state action.[345]

The court applied the two-part test established in Lugar,

_____

employment decisions. Id.

[341] Id. at 635.

[342] Id. at 637. The court reviewed Rendell-Baker and Blum before reaching its conclusion. Id. at 636.

[343] Id. at 637.

[344] Id. (indicating that the board members who were public officials offered services and assisted the agency and were not merely acting in an "honorary or figurehead capacity").

[345] Id. at 638-39. The Gilmore court recognized that not all of the actions of state actors are state actions. Id.

requiring that there be a state actor and that the challenged activity be state action.[346] Although the agency was a state actor, the court concluded that the termination decision did not result from "the exercise of a right, privilege, or rule of conduct having its source in state authority."[347] The court determined that no facts established that the agency's personnel decisions were a product of state policy or decision, even though members of the governing board were public officials.[348]

Gilmore represents a trend in the courts that sets an extremely high standard for state action. Not only must the state fund and regulate an entity, but it must also have a policy governing the challenged decision or conduct; state action will not be established if the state merely has officials participating in the decisionmaking process.[349]

---

[346] _Id_. at 637. See _Lugar_, 457 U.S. at 937, for the appropriate analytical framework for assessing the relevance of involvement by public officials in nominally private activities.

[347] 710 F.2d at 638.

[348] _Id_. at 638-39; _see also_ Krieger v. Bethesda-Chevy Chase Rescue Squad, 599 F. Supp. 770, 774 (D. Md. 1984) (noting that a public official's mere participation in private affairs does not make entity the state; rather, there must be a nexus between one's capacity as an official and the challenged activity), _aff'd_, 792 F.2d 139 (4th Cir. 1986).

[349] This case may not be representative of the courts' position on state action, but rather may indicate the direction in which the courts are moving. _See_ Thorn v. County of Monroe, 586 F. Supp. 1085, 1090-91 (M.D. Pa.) (holding no state action for private corporation operating nursing home that terminated nurses, despite facts that public officials were on nursing home board, state regulation existed, and county previously owned home), _aff'd_, 745 F.2d 48 (3d Cir. 1984). _But see_ Milonas v. Williams, 691 F.2d 931, 940 (10th Cir. 1982) (finding state action based on state funding, regulation, and placement of students at private schools), _cert. denied_, 460 U.S. 1069 (1983).

Furthermore, the strict standards established by the holdings in _Graves_ and _Gilmore_ imply that it may be difficult to establish state action in a private-prison or private-jail context. This is probably a false implication, however, because a claim that is brought in such a context can be distinguished from both _Graves_ and _Gilmore_ in several ways. First, the funding and regulation for a private prison or jail will exceed the funding and regulation that were present in either _Graves_ or _Gilmore_. The state or federal government will substantially, if not totally, fund a privately operated facility. The government will retain its responsibility for the treatment, physical environment, and duration of confinement of the inmates; therefore, the government will extensively regulate the private facility. Second, unlike the situations in _Graves_ and _Gilmore_, the government will have policies that address various aspects of the facility's operations, conditions, and treatment of inmates because it is the state that is ultimately obligated to protect these aspects of institutional life. Third, also unlike the situations in _Graves_ and _Gilmore_, the defendant entity will be a for-profit company, thus raising important questions of accountability. Fourth, the government will retain exclusive control over the placement of inmates in private facilities. These factors, taken together, signify that _Graves_ and _Gilmore_ are not controlling. Even if they were, however, a private-prison or private-jail case will be strong enough to establish state action under a stricter test.

Therefore, under the traditional two-factor close-nexus

test, the private company will be a state actor and its operations will constitute state action. The two-factor test, however, probably will not be used frequently in the future. Additional factors will be required, such as the state's placement of inmates at the institution and a significant state role in overseeing certain policies and management of the facility.

c.   State-Compulsion Test

In addition to using the public-function and close-nexus tests, many courts have recognized that state compulsion or significant encouragement is an important factor in state-action analysis.[350] Few courts, however, have applied the state-compulsion test as the sole determinant.[351] In fact, the infrequency of the use of this analysis indicates that state compulsion is difficult to establish and that only in a rare case will this analysis alone support a finding of state action.

Adickes v. S.H. Kress & Co.[352] is one such case. In

---

[350]   The United States Supreme Court has articulated that "a State normally can be held responsible for a private decision only when it has exercised coercive power or has provided such significant encouragement, either overt or covert, that the choice must in law be deemed to be that of the State." Blum, 457 U.S. at 1004; see also supra notes 236-238 & 247 and accompanying text.

[351]   See Adickes v. S.H. Kress & Co., 398 U.S. 144, 171 (1970) (indicating that state action is present when state compels act); see also supra note 239 and accompanying text.

[352]   398 U.S. 144 (1970).

Adickes, a white woman brought a section 1983 claim against a private party for refusing to serve her in its lunchroom, allegedly because she was accompanied by blacks, and for conspiring with local police who arrested her for vagrancy on the private party's premises after the incident.[353] The United States Supreme Court determined that the fourteenth amendment, while clearly prohibiting the state from discriminating, did not prohibit a private party from discriminating on the basis of race unless that party acted "against a backdrop of state compulsion or involvement."[354] The Court believed, however, that the fourteenth amendment was offended if the state, by its law, compelled the private party to discriminate on the basis of race.[355] The state-action requirement was satisfied whether the state compelled a private party's racially discriminatory act by statute or "by a custom having the force of law."[356] The Court concluded that state action was present because the police, as state officials, gave the discriminatory custom the force of law when they arrested the claimant.[357]

---

[353] Id. at 146.

[354] Id. at 169.

[355] Id. at 171 (state may not discriminate on the basis of race "'by direct action or through the medium of others who are under State compulsion to do so'") (quoting with emphasis Baldwin v. Morgan, 287 F.2d 750, 755-56 (5th Cir. 1961)).

[356] Id.

[357] Id. at 172. The Court hypothesized that it could be established that the police gave the discriminatory act the force of law because they made a false arrest of the claimant to harass her for attempting to eat with blacks or because they tolerated the threats of violence against those who violated the

A state-compulsion analysis may readily be applied in the private-prison context as well. For example, if the private entity engages in conduct that may be challenged as cruel and unusual punishment as a result of the state setting unreasonably high standards to govern how the entity may treat prisoners,[358] it may be argued that the state has significantly encouraged or compelled the activity. If the facts are sufficiently persuasive, this may be all that is necessary to establish state action.

Recent case law, however, indicates that state compulsion will be considered in conjunction with other factors. In Lombard v. Eunice Kennedy Shriver Center,[359] for example, the federal district court discussed the state-compulsion analysis but ultimately relied on the public-function test. In this case, the plaintiff, an involuntary resident at a state mental institution, brought a section 1983 claim alleging that he had received inadequate medical care from a private organization that had contracted with the institution to provide medical services.[360] In determining whether state action was present to support the claim, the court recognized that the state must compel the act

---

segregation custom. Id.

[358] It is unlikely, of course, that the state's standards would be impossible to meet. But they might be set at a higher level for private incarceration facilities than for public ones to assure accountability and to hold private companies to their word that they can do a better job than the government can at managing prisons and jails.

[359] 556 F. Supp. 677 (D. Mass. 1983).

[360] Id. at 678.

and that "[a] private party's action or decision must be required by a rule of decision imposed by the state before that action or decision will be deemed state action."[361]   Yet the court also noted that state compulsion would not be required for a finding of state action if the private party performed a traditional and exclusive public function.[362]   Here, the court considered it decisive that the state had an affirmative duty to provide adequate medical services for involuntarily committed residents of a state institution.[363]   Since the state delegated this duty,

---

[361]   Id. at 679.

[362]   Id. at 680.

[363]   Id.   "The critical factor in our decision is the duty of the state to provide adequate medical services to those whose personal freedom is restricted because they reside in state institutions."   Id. at 678.   In a statement that virtually summarizes the experiences of the courts on the question of whether the acts of private entities performing functions that are delegated by the state constitute state action, the court added:

> [I]t would be empty formalism to treat the [private entity] as anything but the equivalent of a governmental agency for the purposes of 42 U.S.C. § 1983.   Whether a physician is directly on the state payroll . . . or paid indirectly by contract, the dispositive issue concerns the trilateral relationship among the state, the private defendant, and the plaintiff.   Because the state bore an affirmative obligation to provide adequate medical care to plaintiff, because the state delegated that function to the [private corporation], and because [that corporation] voluntarily assumed that obligation by contract, [the private entity] must be considered to have acted under color of law, and its acts and omissions must be considered actions of the state.   For if [the private entity] were not held so responsible, the state could avoid its constitutional obligations simply by delegating governmental functions to private entities.

Id. at 680.   See generally infra notes 381-392 and accompanying

the private organization assumed a public function; thus the court found that its acts constituted state action.[364]

Lombard indicates that, in the state-action determination, evidence of state compulsion carries equal, if not greater, weight than that which is accorded to the performance of a public function. Although state compulsion or encouragement may be difficult to prove if the state does not exercise it through a written law, the courts have left open the possibility that the coercion or encouragement of a decision may be exercised overtly or covertly. This analysis can have major importance in the privatization area, in which the state will likely retain a significant oversight function.

d. Multi-Characterization Analysis

The current state-action analysis, which combines the several tests, has been most clearly articulated by the United States Court of Appeals for the Fifth Circuit in Frazier v. Board of Trustees.[365] No state action was found in this case, in which a discharged employee of a private corporation that provided respiratory-therapy services for a county hospital brought a section 1983 claim against the hospital for violating her free speech, due process, and equal protection rights.[366] Although

---

text (discussing West v. Atkins).

[364]   556 F. Supp. at 678, 680.

[365]   765 F.2d 1278 (5th Cir. 1985), cert. denied, 476 U.S. 1142 (1986).

the court described the state-action question as a "paragon of unclarity," a "protean concept," and an "impossible task,"[367] it believed that its path was "relatively well-marked" based on the instruction of Rendell-Baker and Blum.[368] The court stated that the critical inquiry was whether "the alleged infringement of federal rights [was] 'fairly attributable to the state . . . .'"[369]

The court reviewed the case law and found several factors to be important to a state-action analysis. It first recognized that the state's financial involvement and regulation, although significant, were not enough to create a sufficiently close relationship between the hospital's conduct and the state.[370] The court also found that the performance of a traditional and exclusive state function and the joint participation or symbiosis between the state and the hospital were important, but dismissed both factors with respect to the facts of the case.[371] According

---

[366] Id. at 1288.

[367] Id. at 1283 & n.8; see also supra notes 224-225 and accompanying text.

[368] 765 F.2d at 1283-84.

[369] Id. at 1283. This test originated in Lugar, 457 U.S. at 937; see supra notes 243-244 and accompanying text.

[370] 765 F.2d at 1285. The Court examined Rendell-Baker and Blum for this result. It concluded that state funding did not make a private personnel decision state action and that general regulation was not enough -- the regulation must control the challenged decision before state action can be found. Id.

[371] Id. at 1286-87. The court discussed the public-function theory and inferred that the Rendell-Baker Court required the delegation of a function before state action could be found. Id. at 1285. Applying the test to its own facts, the Frazier court concluded that respiratory therapy was not "an

to the court, "only when the state has had some affirmative role, albeit one of encouragement short of compulsion, in the particular conduct underlying a claimant's civil rights grievance," will private conduct be fairly attributable to the state.[372] The state in this case played no such role.[373]

Frazier indicates that the state's funding, regulation, delegation of a public function, and symbiosis will be factors that warrant consideration in the state-action analysis, but that the crucial factor is whether the state was involved in,

---

activity that has traditionally been the exclusive prerogative of the state." _Id._ at 1286.

The court considered the joint-participation/symbiosis theory to be the best argument for state action in this case. In light of _Rendell-Baker_ and _Blum_, however, the court did not feel that this theory, as developed in Burton v. Wilmington Parking Auth., 365 U.S. 715 (1961), had as much weight as it once had. In fact, it stated that "[t]he 'joint' of 1961 does not the 'symbiosis' of today make." 765 F.2d at 1287; _see_ _also_ _supra_ note 228 and accompanying text. Nevertheless, the court used the joint-participation analysis and found that the private corporation was located on the hospital's premises, that the hospital paid for the utilities and supplied equipment, and that it profited from the services that the private corporation provided. 765 F.2d at 1287. The court concluded that the core of the relationship was missing -- the state did not play "some meaningful role in the mechanism leading to the disputed act." _Id._ at 1288 (footnote omitted). Therefore, there was no symbiotic relationship. _Id._

[372] 765 F.2d at 1286 (citing Moose Lodge No. 107 v. Irvis, 407 U.S. 163, 173, 176-77 (1972)).

[373] _Id._ at 1288. The Supreme Court recently used a similar, albeit cursory, analysis in San Francisco Arts & Athletics, Inc. v. United States Olympic Comm., 107 S. Ct. 2971, 2984-87 (1987). The plaintiff argued, _inter_ _alia_, that the Olympic Committee's enforcement of the use of the word "Olympic," under a charter granted to it by Congress, was discriminatory in violation of the fifth amendment. _Id._ at 2984. Rejecting this challenge, a majority of the Court (5-to-4 vote on this issue) utilized the close-nexus test, the public-function test, the state-compulsion test, and the symbiosis test. _Id._ at 2984-87.

encouraged, or compelled the challenged conduct or decision.[374] Under this analysis, the claim against a private prison will be supported by state action. To determine whether a nexus exists, a court should consider that the private prison or jail would be substantially, if not totally, funded and regulated by the government. It should also analyze the government's policies or regulations, if any, that address the challenged conduct. In addition, the operation of a prison or jail is traditionally and exclusively a function of the government, and thus the delegation of this task to a private entity would satisfy a public-function analysis.[375] Furthermore, in the event that the government

---

[374] See Comment, supra note 220, at 479 ("All of these traditional factors converge on the common goal of discovering when private exercise of power presents the unique danger to individual liberty posed by the exercise of governmental power."); see also Watkins v. Reed, 557 F. Supp. 278, 281 & n.9 (E.D. Ky. 1983) (suggesting that the factors that Blum and Rendell-Baker deemed important included state regulation, state financial assistance, symbiotic relationship, performance of traditional and exclusive public function, and state coercion or encouragement), aff'd, 734 F.2d 17 (6th Cir. 1984).

[375] The court in Frazier noted that, if the state delegated its obligations in an attempt to avoid its constitutional responsibilities, such a "sham delegation of state tasks would clearly implicate both the state action and the under-color-of-law requirements of section 1983." 765 F.2d at 1287 n.20. Furthermore, "[i]f the state is allowed to delegate its responsibility, . . . those persons who exercise governmental power are shielded, at least partially, from political safeguards and political accountability." Comment, supra note 220, at 477 (footnote omitted). This point is particularly significant with respect to the development of private prisons and jails, because one argument is that states can avoid liability by delegating their obligation to maintain and operate the facilities. Privatization of Corrections: Hearings Before the Subcomm. on Courts, Civil Liberties, and the Administration of Justice of the House Comm. on the Judiciary, 99th Cong., 1st & 2d Sess. 24 (1985 & 1986) [hereinafter Hearings] (statement of the American Federation of State, County and Municipal Employees).

furnishes the facilities for the private entity and retains ownership over the land and equipment, thereby remaining integrated with the facility, a court should find a symbiotic relationship. The establishment of any of these factors will be considered significant to the state-action determination.

State action will not be found under a multi-characterization analysis unless the government specifically participated in the challenged conduct. Although direct participation may not be a frequent occurrence in the privatization context, this point will probably not be difficult to establish. The claims that inmates typically bring against the government involve infringement of rights that the government plays a major role in protecting; consequently, the government controls or at least participates in the challenged conduct.[376] The conditions of the prison or jail[377] and the treatment of inmates,[378] for example, are obligations that belong to the

---

[376] This statement is too obvious to require extensive citation. See generally Robbins & Buser, Punitive Conditions of Prison Confinement: An Analysis of Pugh v. Locke and Federal Court Supervision of State Penal Administration Under the Eighth Amendment, 29 Stan. L. Rev. 893 (1977).

[377] See Medina v. O'Neill, 589 F. Supp. 1028, 1031 n.7 (S.D. Tex. 1984) (challenging confinement conditions where 16 detainees had been confined in windowless cell designed to hold six), vacated in part & rev'd in part on other grounds, 838 F.2d 800 (5th Cir. 1988). In Medina, state action was established under a public-function theory; a close-nexus theory could have been used, however, because the government would have significant influence over the conditions of the facility even though a private entity operated it.

[378] See Ancata v. Prison Health Servs., Inc., 769 F.2d 700, 702 (11th Cir. 1985) (challenging improper medical diagnosis and treatment). The court in Ancata used a public-function analysis to find state action and believed that the state's involvement in

government, in spite of the delegation of operation to a private entity.[379] State action will thus be found for conduct in these areas and others affecting the inmates under a multi-characterization analysis, even if it is the private party that engages in the conduct.[380]

Unlike the claims of inmates, the claims of a private entity's employees against the government may not fit easily within a Frazier analysis. Although the government may fund and regulate the private entity, it is not responsible for and does not control or influence decisions or conduct regarding the entity's employees to the same extent that it regulates and is responsible for the treatment of inmates and the conditions of their confinement.

---

this area of prisoners' rights was well settled. Id. at 703. State action also could have been found under a close-nexus test, because the treatment of inmates is the state's obligation and because the state has control over the policies and regulations governing this area and therefore the challenged conduct.

[379] See supra note 363 (recognizing that state cannot sidestep its constitutional obligations through delegation); see also supra notes 11-213 and accompanying text (discussing constitutionality of delegating incarceration function).

[380] Under the eighth and fourteenth amendments to the United States Constitution, respectively, the states must protect against cruel and unusual punishment and must protect a prisoner's due process and equal protection rights. U.S. Const. amends. VIII & XIV. In addition, the state controls parole decisions and sets standards for review. Conduct in these areas will be considered state action. See, e.g., Mayer, supra note 76, at 319-20 (suggesting that, to avoid potential legal consequences, state might retain control over prison disciplinary proceedings and decisions). See generally Note, supra note 9, at 1484-99.

4. The Latest Word: West v. Atkins

On June 20, 1988, the United States Supreme Court decided West v. Atkins,[381] the closest case to prison or jail privatization that the Supreme Court has yet addressed. The Court considered the question of "whether a physician who is under contract with the State to provide medical services to inmates at a state-prison hospital on a part-time basis acts 'under color of state law,' within the meaning of 42 U.S.C. § 1983, when he treats an inmate"[382] -- that is, whether state action is present when the state contracts out one facet of its prison operation, in this case medical services. Presenting no major surprises for state-action jurisprudence, the Court answered the question in the affirmative, concluding that "respondent's delivery of medical treatment to West was state action fairly attributable to the State."[383]

Justice Blackmun, writing for a unanimous Court on the state-action question,[384] found "unpersuasive"[385] the Fourth

---

[381] 56 U.S.L.W. 4664 (U.S. June 20, 1988); see supra note 297 (citing cases creating split among the circuits).

[382] 56 U.S.L.W. at 4665.

[383] Id. at 4668.

[384] Justice Scalia wrote a one-paragraph concurring opinion, noting that the lower courts had construed West's pro se allegation of inadequate medical attention as claiming an eighth amendment violation. Justice Scalia instead saw a due process claim:

> I agree with the opinion of the Court that respondent acted under color of state law for purposes of § 1983. I do not believe that a doctor

Circuit's reliance on Polk County v. Dodson,[386] in which the Supreme Court held in 1981 that a public defender's activities or functions did not constitute state action because public defenders were in an adversarial relationship with the state and because the state had not developed the professional standards that govern a lawyer's conduct. "In contrast to the public defender," Justice Blackmun wrote, "Doctor Atkins' professional and ethical obligation to make independent medical judgments, did not set him in conflict with the State and other prison authorities. Indeed, his relationship with other prison authorities was cooperative."[387] Justice Blackmun stressed that the Fourth Circuit had "misread Polk County as establishing the general principle that professionals do not act under color of state law when they act in their professional capacities":[388]

385   Id. at 4667.

386   454 U.S. 312 (1981); see supra note 280 (discussing Polk County).

387   56 U.S.L.W. at 4666-67.

388   Id. at 4667.

The [Fourth Circuit] considered a professional
not to be subject to suit under § 1983 unless he
was exercising "custodial or supervisory" authority.
. . . To the extent this Court in Polk County
relied on the fact that the public defender is a
"professional" in concluding that he was not engaged
in state action, the case turned on the particular
professional obligation of the criminal defense
attorney to be an adversary of the State, not on the
independence and integrity generally applicable to
professionals as a class.[389]

This distinction leaves little, if any, room for applying

Polk County's restrictive state-action holding to providers of

other services, such as prison or jail management. Concluding on

this point, Justice Blackmun stated: "Defendants are not removed

from the purview of § 1983 simply because they are professionals

acting in accordance with professional discretion and

judgment."[390] Further, the Court attached no importance to the

fact that Dr. Atkins was a contractor, rather than an employee of

the state prison system:

---

[389] Id.

[390] Id. The Court did suggest, however, that professional
discretion and judgment were not "entirely irrelevant to the
state-action inquiry. Where the issue is whether a private party
is engaged in activity that constitutes state action, it may be
relevant that the challenged activity turned on judgments
controlled by professional standards, where those standards are
not established by the State." Id. at 4667 n.10 (emphasis in
original). Citing Blum v. Yaretsky, 457 U.S. 991 (1982), and
Rendell-Baker v. Kohn, 457 U.S. 830 (1982), Justice Blackmun
indicated that the requisite "nexus" with the state must be
present for state action to exist. 56 U.S.L.W. at 4667 n.10; see
supra notes 313-349 and accompanying text (discussing close-nexus
test in private-incarceration context); see also supra notes 350-
364 and accompanying text (discussing state-compulsion test in
private-incarceration context).

It is the physician's function within the state
system, not the precise terms of his employment,
that determines whether his actions can be fairly
attributable to the State. Whether a physician is
on the state payroll or is paid by contract, the
dispositive issue concerns the relationship among
the State, the physician, and the prisoner.[391]

Thus, if there was any ambiguity concerning the application
of state-action doctrine to privatization of corrections and
detention before West, the Supreme Court has now eliminated it:
State action will clearly exist in the prison- or jail-
privatization context. Although West v. Atkins provides little
insight into the precise test to be used in state-action
analysis, the case is significant in the way in which it
distinguishes and restricts Polk County v. Dodson. West is also
significant because some of its language, albeit in the medical
context, summarizes well this paper's position on the state-
action requirement:

Contracting out prison medical care does not relieve
the State of its constitutional duty to provide
adequate medical treatment to those in its custody,
and it does not deprive the State's prisoners of the
means to vindicate their Eighth Amendment rights.
The State bore an affirmative obligation to provide
adequate medical care to West; the State delegated
that function to respondent Atkins; and respondent
voluntarily assumed that obligation by contract.[392]

---

391   56 U.S.L.W. at 4668.

392   Id.; see also supra note 363 (quoting nearly identical
language from Lombard v. Eunice Kennedy Shriver Center).

If state action is present when the state contracts out its obligation to perform _one_ _service_, then state action is certainly present when the government contracts out the _entire_ _operation_ of a prison or jail facility.

5. Conclusion

One argument in favor of private incarceration has been that it will eliminate, or at least reduce, government liability. This argument does not withstand examination. State action can be found in the private-prison or private-jail context under any of the various tests -- public function, close nexus, state compulsion, and multi-characterization. Although the Supreme Court has increasingly restricted the application of the state-action doctrine, with many lower federal courts following suit, the doctrine is certainly flexible enough to be used with vigor in the "right" case, such as one involving the management of a private prison or jail. Indeed, to lessen liability in that context would be to curtail accountability. Common sense tells us that, if we delegate the incarceration function to private hands, we would want just the opposite to occur. As Justice Brennan has written in a different context,[393] in language similar to that used in West v. Atkins,[394] "[t]he Government is

_____

[393] San Francisco Arts & Athletics, Inc. v. United States Olympic Comm., 107 S. Ct. 2971, 2984-87 (1987) (holding that the fact that Congress granted a corporate charter to the United States Olympic Committee does not render that Committee a government actor to whom the fifth amendment applies).

free . . . to 'privatize' some functions it would otherwise perform. But such privatization ought not automatically release those who perform government functions from constitutional obligations."[395] If there is a benefit to be gained from prison or jail privatization, therefore, it will have to come in some other form.

394 _See supra_ text accompanying note 392.

395 107 S. Ct. at 2993 (Brennan, J., dissenting); _see also_ Report of the President's Commission on Privatization, _supra_ note 9, at 149 ("Prisons remain subject to the supervision and regulation of the government -- and, most important, subject to the rule of law -- whether they are run by government employees or by a private agency."); _supra_ note 375.

C. The Thirteenth Amendment

1.   Introduction

Some interesting questions that are not addressed in the
private-incarceration literature concern the application of the
thirteenth amendment. In particular: Does the thirteenth
amendment's prohibition against involuntary servitude preclude
the confinement of prisoners in private-prison facilities? If
not, does the thirteenth amendment bar such facilities from
compelling prisoners to perform labor? Are there federal or
state laws that prohibit such an arrangement?

2.   Analysis

No thirteenth amendment[396] issue arises when a person is

---

[396] The thirteenth amendment provides:

> Section 1. Neither slavery nor involuntary
> servitude, except as a punishment for crime whereof
> the party shall have been duly convicted, shall
> exist within the United States, or any place subject
> to their jurisdiction.

> Section 2. Congress shall have power to
> enforce this article by appropriate legislation.

U.S. Const. amend. XIII. 18 U.S.C. § 1584 is the criminal
statute that prohibits involuntary servitude. Section 1584
provides:

> Whoever knowingly and willfully holds to
> involuntary servitude or sells into any condition of
> involuntary servitude, any other person for any
> term, or brings within the United States any person
> so held, shall be fined not more than $5,000 or

confined to prison after being duly convicted of a crime.[397] The

thirteenth amendment expressly permits involuntary servitude as

"punishment for crime whereof the party shall have been duly

convicted."[398] Thus, once a prisoner is convicted, it appears

---

imprisoned not more than five years, or both.

18 U.S.C. § 1584 (1982). In the earlier cases interpreting "involuntary servitude" under section 1584, courts applied the provision primarily to slavery and peonage. United States v. Garrone, 36 U.S. 73 (1837); United States v. Shackney, 333 F.2d 475 (2d Cir. 1964). In Shackney, the Second Circuit narrowly interpreted "involuntary servitude" to include the use or threat of physical punishment to enforce work and the use of state-imposed legal coercion to make a debtor work for his creditor. Id. at 485-87. The applicability of section 1584 was gradually expanded to cover cases involving migrant laborers and child labor. United States v. Mussry, 726 F.2d 1448 (9th Cir. 1984) (permitting proof of psychological coercion as evidence of "involuntary servitude"); United States v. Ancarola, 1 F. 676 (S.D.N.Y. 1880) (finding that service can be involuntary when one is incapable of giving valid legal consent).

The most recent word concerning the definition of "involuntary servitude" under the thirteenth amendment and section 1584 came from the United States Supreme Court on June 29, 1988. In United States v. Kozminski, 56 U.S.L.W. 4910 (U.S. June 29, 1988), the Court for the first time considered the reach of the statute, holding that "the term 'involuntary servitude' necessarily means a condition of servitude in which the victim is forced to work for the defendant by the use or threat of physical restraint or physical injury, or by the use or threat of coercion through law or the legal process." Id. at 4915. The Court rejected the government's broad interpretation of the term to include "compulsion through psychological coercion as well as almost any other type of speech or conduct intentionally employed to persuade a reluctant person to work." Id. at 4914.

[397] E.g., Omasta v. Wainwright, 696 F.2d 1304, 1305 (11th Cir. 1983) (finding that, when a prisoner is "incarcerated pursuant to a presumptively valid judgment and commitment order issued by a court of competent jurisdiction and is forced to work pursuant to prison regulations or state statutes, the thirteenth amendment's prohibition against involuntary servitude is not implicated"); Draper v. Rhay, 315 F.2d 193, 197 (9th Cir.) (holding that, when a person is "duly tried, convicted, sentenced and imprisoned for crime in accordance with law, no issue of . . . involuntary servitude arises"), cert. denied, 375 U.S. 915 (1963).

that the "convict labor exception" applies without regard to the type of facility in which the confinement shall take place, whether public or private. In fact, courts have rarely taken the thirteenth amendment inside the prison gates.[399] Specifically, courts have uniformly rejected claims that the prison-labor system imposes involuntary servitude in violation of the thirteenth amendment.[400] Likewise, courts have unanimously

_____

[398] U.S. Const. amend. XIII, § 1.

[399] The thirteenth amendment has been successfully employed in the prison context in only a few instances. E.g., Bailey v. Alabama, 219 U.S. 219, 244 (1911) (striking down peonage laws allowing state to "compel one man to labor for another in payment of a debt, by punishing him as criminal if he does not perform the service or pay the debt"); Jobson v. Henne, 355 F.2d 129 (2d Cir. 1966) (finding that persons committed to mental institutions cannot be forced to work unless the tasks meet certain requirements); Ex parte Lloyd, 13 F. Supp. 1005 (E.D. Ky. 1936) (holding that prisoner's thirteenth amendment rights would be violated if he were held at federal narcotic facility after expiration of period within which Surgeon General had estimated that a cure would take place).

[400] In United States v. Reynolds, 235 U.S. 133 (1914), the Court explained that

> there can be no doubt that the State has authority
> to impose involuntary servitude as a punishment for
> crime. This fact is recognized in the Thirteenth
> Amendment, and such punishment expressly excepted
> from its terms. Of course, the State may impose
> fines and penalties which must be worked out for the
> benefit of the State, and in such manner as the
> State may legitimately prescribe.

Id. at 149. Shortly thereafter, in Butler v. Perry, 240 U.S. 328 (1916), the Court found that the thirteenth amendment did not prohibit a state from requiring all of its male citizens to work on public roads because the amendment was

> adopted with reference to conditions existing since
> the foundation of our government, and the term
> "involuntary servitude" was intended to cover those
> forms of compulsory labor akin to African slavery
> which, in practical operation, would tend to produce
> like undesirable results . . . and certainly was not

upheld laws requiring prisoners to work, finding no

intended to interdict enforcement of those duties
which individuals owe to the state.

Id. at 332-33; see also Bailey v. Alabama, 219 U.S. 219, 244
(1911) (concluding that the "state may impose involuntary
servitude as a punishment for crime"); Glick v. Lockhart, 759
F.2d 675, 676 (8th Cir. 1985) (upholding general rule that
thirteenth amendment does not prohibit state law requiring
prisoners to work); Mosby v. Mabry, 697 F.2d 213, 215 (8th Cir.
1982) (holding that prisoners may be required to work without
violating the thirteenth amendment); Omasta v. Wainwright, 696
F.2d 1304, 1305 (11th Cir. 1983) (finding that, when prisoner is
"incarcerated pursuant to a presumptively valid judgment and
commitment order issued by court of competent jurisdiction and is
forced to work pursuant to prison regulations or state statutes,
the thirteenth amendment's prohibition against involuntary
servitude is not implicated"); Ray v. Mabry, 556 F.2d 881, 882
(8th Cir. 1977) (finding that "[c]ompelling prison inmates to
work does not contravene the Thirteenth Amendment"); Marchese v.
United States, 445 F.2d 1268, 1271 (Ct.Cl. 1972) (explaining that
"involuntary servitude is the essence of incarceration and the
Thirteenth Amendment by its very language excepts the convicted
prisoner from its reach"); Draper v. Rhay, 315 F.2d 193, 197 (9th
Cir.) (finding that "[t]here is no federally protected right of a
state prisoner not to work while imprisoned after conviction
. . . [and that] prison rules may require [prisoners] to work but
this is not the sort of involuntary servitude which violates
Thirteenth Amendment rights"), cert. denied, 375 U.S. 915 (1963);
Lindsey v. Leavy, 149 F.2d 899 (9th Cir. 1945) (invoking
thirteenth amendment exception because defendant had been duly
"tried, convicted, sentenced and imprisoned as a punishment for a
crime in accordance with law"), cert. denied, 326 U.S. 783
(1946); Woodall v. Partilla, 581 F. Supp. 1066, 1077 (N.D. Ill.
1984) (noting that requiring prisoners to work is permissible
under the thirteenth amendment); Sims v. Parke Davis & Co., 334
F. Supp. 774, 792-93 (E.D. Mich. 1973) (holding that "[l]awfully
convicted criminals may be required to work by prison
authorities"); Holt v. Sarver, 309 F. Supp. 362, 369-72 (E.D.
Ark. 1970) (concluding that state convict-labor system is not
prohibited by the thirteenth amendment, since, when "Congress
submitted the Thirteenth Amendment to the States, it must have
been aware of generally accepted convict labor policies and
practices, and the Court is persuaded that the Amendment's
exception manifested a Congressional intent not to reach such
policies and practices"), aff'd, 442 F.2d 304 (8th Cir. 1971);
Wilson v. Kelly, 294 F. Supp. 1005, 1012 (N.D. Ga.) (concluding
that "it has long been held that hard labor as a penalty for
crime is expressly permitted by the Thirteenth Amendment"), aff'd
mem., 393 U.S. 266 (1968); Kent v. Prasse, 265 F. Supp. 673 (W.D.
Pa.), aff'd, 385 F.2d 406 (3d Cir. 1967); Blass v. Weigel, 85 F.
Supp. 775, 781 (D.N.J. 1949) (holding thirteenth amendment

constitutionally protected right not to work.[401]

Courts have interpreted the thirteenth amendment as neither proscribing the use of prison labor nor restricting how that labor may be used, as long as it is imposed as punishment for a crime of which the prisoner has been duly convicted. Thus, it would seem irrelevant whether prisoners worked for publicly or privately owned facilities. Historically, this appears to be the case. Judicial treatment of the thirteenth amendment with respect to prison labor has remained unaltered despite the private sector's presence or absence within the prison-labor system. For example, the private sector participated extensively in the nineteenth-century prison-labor system unhampered by the thirteenth amendment.[402] When private-sector involvement was

---

inapplicable when a person is held to answer for a violation of a penal statute). See generally Comment, Involuntary Servitude: An Eighteenth-Century Concept in Search of a Twentieth-Century Definition, 19 Pac. L.J. 873 (1988); Note, Minimum Wages for Prisoners: Legal Obstacles and Suggested Reform, 7 U. Mich. J.L. Ref. 193, 204, 208-09 (1973) (stating that "[a]ll allegations that the prison labor system imposes involuntary servitude in violation of the thirteenth amendment have been uniformly rejected").

[401] See supra note 400 (collecting cases).

[402] In the nineteenth century, prison labor was organized under four systems: (1) the lease system, under which prisoners were placed in the custody of businessmen who paid the state for the prisoners' services; (2) the contract system, under which the state retained custody and control of the prisoners and businesses contracted with the state for labor on a daily basis, providing the prison with materials and supervisors and distributing the finished product; (3) the piece-price system, which was similar to the contract system, except that employers paid a price based on completed items rather than paying daily wages; and (4) the state-use system, under which the state controlled the manufacture and sale of goods. Note, Prisoners as Entrepreneurs: Developing a Model for Prisoner-Run Industry, 62 B.U.L. Rev. 1163, 1168-70 (1982); Note, supra note 400, at 196-97; see also National Institute of Justice, Private Sector

eliminated in the early twentieth century it was not due to the thirteenth amendment, but rather to strong public pressure from trade unions and free laborers who feared unfair wage competition and businessmen who feared unfair price competition.[403] Obviously, this does not mean that the thirteenth amendment could not now be employed to bar a private prison facility from requiring its prisoners to work. A strong policy argument could be made that such an arrangement would act as an incentive for abusing and exploiting prisoners.[404]

Although the thirteenth amendment does not appear to prohibit privately operated prison facilities from requiring prisoners to work, there is both federal and state law that may place restrictions and prohibitions on such arrangements. In the 1930s and 1940s, Congress passed a wave of restrictive legislation that totally prohibited prisoner-made goods from entry into interstate commerce, thus severely limiting possible

---

Involvement in Prison Based Businesses: A National Assessment 11 (1985) [hereinafter Private Sector Report]. See generally Cody & Bennett, The Privatization of Correctional Institutions: The Tennessee Experience, 40 Vand. L. Rev. 829 (1987) (examining Tennessee's convict-labor leasing practices of 19th century); McAfee, Tennessee's Private Prison Act of 1986: An Historical Perspective with Special Attention to California's Experience, 40 Vand. L. Rev. 851, 861-63 (1987) (discussing need for state control over convict labor because of historically high rate of security breaks under profit-motivated system).

403 See supra note 402 (collecting sources). In addition to labor and business concerns, there was also concern that the contract and lease systems abused and exploited prisoners in order to make a profit. See Note, supra note 400, at 196.

404 Such an argument would be supported by prisoners' experiences at the hands of private employers in the nineteenth century. Note, supra note 402, at 1168-70; Note, supra note 400, at 196-97; see also Private Sector Report, supra note 402, at 11.

markets for these goods.[405] Significantly, 18 U.S.C. § 436[406] expressly prohibits the "contracting out" of federal prison labor to individuals or corporations.[407] This statute arguably would

---

[405]   E.g., 18 U.S.C. § 1761 (1982) (making it a federal offense to transport prisoner-made goods in interstate commerce, and preempting state law permitting the transportation of prisoner-made goods for private use); 41 U.S.C. §§ 35-45 (1982) (prohibiting use of prison labor to fulfill government contracts in excess of $10,000); 49 U.S.C. § 11507 (1982) (providing that prisoner-made goods that move from one state to another are subject to the laws of the importing state once the goods cross its borders). But see infra notes 414-415 and accompanying text (discussing Justice Improvement Act and current legislative trend revealing willingness to experiment with prison industry).

[406]   18 U.S.C. § 436 (1982).

[407]   The statute provides:

    Whoever, being an officer, employee, or agent of the United States or any department or agency thereof, contracts with any person or corporation, or permits any warden, agent, or official of any penal or correctional institution, to hire out the labor of any prisoners confined for violation of any laws of the United States, shall be fined not more than $1,000 or imprisoned not more than three years, or both.

Id. Free-market and free-labor concerns prompted the passage of section 436, as well as other restrictive prison-labor measures of the early twentieth century. Senate Report 1691 noted that section 436 was

    designed to relieve the law-abiding laborers and producers of this country from the burden of competition with the production now thrown upon the market by combination between private capital, assisted by the State, and cheap labor, made so by its involuntary servitude for crime. It is not aimed at production which may be placed upon the market by virtue of the employment on behalf of the State of criminals whose support would otherwise be wholly charged upon the honest industry of the country.

    It is not meant to relieve criminals from hard labor, but to substitute employment by the State itself, with its common interest, for all and its

have to be confronted directly if the federal government

delegated its authority to operate and manage a prison facility

to a private corporation. It would then be necessary either to

repeal or to amend section 436, or to include in the contract

establishing such a relationship specific language that would

dispel, in both form and substance, any suggestion that the

government was "contracting out" its prisoners.[408]

Other pertinent restrictions include legislation that

administers Federal Prison Industries, Inc., the organization

charged with providing meaningful employment opportunities and

training for federal prisoners.[409] Federal Prison Industries is

authorized to

> determine in what manner and to what extent
> industrial operations shall be carried on in Federal
> penal and correctional institutions for the
> production of commodities for consumption in such

> responsibility for the humane and reformatory policy
> toward the criminal classes for the abuses which are
> invited, and which too often arise from the contract
> system of which there is such general complaint.

S. Rep. No. 1691, 49th Cong., 2d Sess. 1 (1887).

[408] For instance, the contract could clearly spell out that
the private corporation receive no profit from the prisoner's
labor. This would be no simple matter, however, as the
government would have to devise a system to monitor the use of
prisoner labor effectively and efficiently, as well as account
for the profits from such labor. In this respect, one
commentator offered an interesting discussion of the problems
presented by the monitoring of private prisons. Note, The
Panopticon Revisited: The Problem of Monitoring Private Prisons,
96 Yale L.J. 353 (1986). The author's proposed solutions (fines
and bonuses, public access, and monitoring by prisoners),
however, would be of questionable help in monitoring the
financial activities of the private corporation.

[409] 18 U.S.C. § 4122 (1982).

institutions or for sale to the departments or agencies of the United States, but not for sale to the public in competition with private enterprise.[410]

Furthermore, Federal Prison Industries must provide

employment

for all physically fit inmates in the United States penal or correctional institutions, diversify, so far as practicable, prison industry operations and so operate the prison shops that no single private industry shall be forced to bear an undue burden of competition from the products of the prison workshops, and to reduce to a minimum competition with private industry or free labor.[411]

These laws emphasize Congress's intent to promote fair wage

and price competition in conjunction with prison industry. As

---

[410] Id. § 4122(a) (emphasis added).

[411] Id. § 4122(b) (emphasis added). The text provides a general overview of relevant federal prison-labor laws. To be sure, there are many other laws that affect federal prison labor. Under 18 U.S.C. § 4125, for example, the Attorney General of the United States may

make available to the heads of the several departments the services of United States prisoners under terms, conditions, and rates mutually agreed upon, for constructing or repairing roads, clearing, maintaining and reforesting public lands, building levees, and constructing or repairing any other public ways or works financed wholly or in major part by funds appropriated by Congress.

18 U.S.C. § 4125 (1982). With respect to federal prisoners confined in state institutions, 18 U.S.C. § 4002 provides that they may be employed "only in the manufacture of public works for, the production of supplies for, the construction of public works for and the maintenance and care of the institutions of, the State or political subdivision in which they are imprisoned." 18 U.S.C. § 4002 (1982).

noted above, the elimination of private-sector involvement in prison labor during the early twentieth century was motivated primarily by economic considerations. The focus of such legislation does not appear to be the prohibition of private profit or prisoner exploitation. This explains, in part, why Congress began promoting private-sector involvement in the prison-labor system in the 1970s following changing perceptions that prison labor does not pose a threat to labor and business interests.[412] Thus, for example, Congress enacted 18 U.S.C. § 4082(c)[413] providing for a federal work-release program that permits participating prisoners to work during the day for local businesses.

Congress also enacted the Justice Improvement Act of 1979 to test the feasibility of private-sector involvement in prison industry.[414] The law exempted seven pilot programs from the interstate-commerce restrictions that have severely curtailed the economic advantages of using prison labor. Due to the program's

---

[412] See Note, supra note 400, at 224; see also Private Sector Report, supra note 402, at 12 (adding that inmate idleness and the potential of raising state revenues were also factors in changing views on private-sector involvement); National Institute of Justice, A Study of Prison Industry: History, Components, and Goals 7 (1986) (noting that changes in correctional theory -- related to D. Glaser's 1963 study, The Effectiveness of a Prison and Parole System, showing correlation between pre-release preparation, post-release employment, and recidivism -- also spurred interest in private-sector involvement); Burger, supra note 4.

[413] 18 U.S.C. § 4082(c) (1982).

[414] Pub. L. No. 96-157, § 2, 93 Stat. 1215 (amending 18 U.S.C. § 1761 and 41 U.S.C. § 35) (amended by Pub. L. No. 98-473, § 819).

success, Congress increased the number of exempt projects to twenty in 1984.[415]

State laws regarding private-sector involvement in prison labor vary considerably. In many respects, state laws have paralleled federal legislative efforts both in form and in rationale.[416] Many states, for example, followed the federal lead during the 1930s and 1940s and enacted laws prohibiting the open-market sale or importation of prisoner-made goods within their borders, effectively barring the private sector from prison industry.[417] The current trend toward increased integration of the private sector in prison industry, however, is more evident in state laws than in federal laws.[418] The status of state laws

---

[415] Justice Assistance Act of 1984, 42 U.S.C. §§ 3701-5601 (1982).

[416] See Private Sector Report, supra note 402, at 11-12; Note, supra note 402, at 1171 n.40.

[417] Private Sector Report, supra note 402, at 11.

[418] The Private Sector Report found that "[m]ore than twenty states have revised their statutes over the last ten years to authorize and encourage private sector prison-based businesses." Id. at 105.

The following example of statutory language shows how one state legislature has addressed the issue of private-sector employment of prisoners:

> The commissioner may establish programs for the employment of offenders by private persons. In establishing these programs, the commissioner may enter into agreements with any private person under which that person establishes, by construction, lease, or otherwise, facilities within the exterior boundary of any state adult correctional facility, for the manufacture and processing of goods or any other business, commercial, or agricultural enterprise.

is summarized in the National Institute of Justice's Report, Private Sector Involvement in Prison-Based Businesses:[419]

      Twenty-one states have statutes specifically authorizing the private sector employment of prisoners or the contracting of prisoner labor by

---

Ind. Code Ann. § 11-10-7-2 (Burns 1981). Minnesota addressed the issue of private-sector contracting for goods and services with the following legislation:

      No contracts for leasing the labor of prisoners confined in any such institution, at a certain rate per diem, giving the contractor full control of the labor of the prisoners, shall be made; but such prisoners shall be employed, under rules established by the commissioner of corrections, in such industries as shall, from time to time, be fixed upon by the officers in charge and the commissioner, or in the manufacture of articles by the piece, under the so-called "piece price system," by contracts with persons furnishing the materials. The chief officer, under the direction of the commissioner, shall purchase such tools, implements, and machinery as the officer shall deem necessary for the work.

Minn. Stat. Ann. § 243.61 (West 1972 & Supp. 1988); see Private Sector Report, supra note 402, at 52-55. Tennessee permits convict labor to be used to manufacture goods on the open market, provided that free labor is not detrimentally affected. Tenn. Code Ann. § 41-22-116(c) (Cum. Supp. 1987).

      The following statute is an example of how one state addressed the issue of open-market sales:

      Except as prohibited by applicable provisions of the United States Code, inmates of state correctional institutions may be employed in the manufacture and processing of goods, wares and merchandise for introduction into interstate commerce, provided that they are paid no less than the prevailing minimum wages for work of a similar nature performed by employees with similar skills in the locality in which the work is being performed.

Minn. Stat. Ann. § 243.88 (West Supp. 1988); see Private Sector Report, supra note 402, at 55-58.

[419] Private Sector Report, supra note 402.

the private sector, or both. A majority of the
remaining states have no statutes that specifically
authorize or prohibit one or both of these
activities. Eight states specifically prohibit
private sector employment of prisoners, and 14
prohibit either the contracting of prisoner labor or
contracting with private firms for the production of
goods or services. Six prohibit all three forms of
private sector involvement.

Open market sales of prisoner-made goods are
prohibited in 25 states and authorized in 20, with
only five states silent on the issue. In some of
the latter, silence can be interpreted as
prohibition, while in others it probably should not
be.

Only two states specifically authorize the use
of incentives to encourage private sector
participation. Six have statutes designed to
protect the jobs of non-prison labor.[420]

This Report makes it clear that state law must be examined

on an individual basis to determine whether the private sector

may become involved, and to what degree, in that jurisdiction's

prison-labor system.

3. Conclusion

The thirteenth amendment does not bar the confinement of

prisoners in private-prison facilities, nor does it prohibit such

facilities from compelling prisoners to work. There are,

however, state and federal laws that may prohibit or deter such

arrangements. To be sure, these laws appear to be changing in

favor of private-sector involvement. Nevertheless, in many

---

[420]   Id. at 73.

instances "[s]tatutory authorization of private sector involvement [will be] a fundamental prerequisite" to further development in this direction.[421] Although these laws are viewed by many as promoting the goal of prisoner rehabilitation, it will nevertheless be important to keep concerns regarding prisoner exploitation in such a profit-motivated environment at the forefront of the privatization debate.[422]

---

[421] Id. at 12.

[422] See generally Model Contract § 5(D) (Inmate Labor).

III. CONTRACTUAL DIMENSIONS

The Model Contract presented in this section responds directly to the concerns raised in the constitutional-delegation section of the paper.[423] Indeed, the relationship between the delegation doctrine, on the one hand, and the Model Contract and Model Statute, on the other hand, may well be the most important feature of this study. If privatization of prisons and jails cannot be insulated from a judicial finding of unconstitutionality, then no other questions need to be asked; private incarceration will have no future. The Model Contract, therefore, is founded on the premise that the interests of the respective parties -- the contracting agency, the contractor,[424] the public, and the inmates -- must be appropriately balanced with a view toward preserving accountability in the private-incarceration process.

To this end, the best provisions from existing contracts and requests for proposals (RFP's) were incorporated or adapted, and other provisions were formulated. The Model Contract is not intended to be exhaustive, however, for particular contracts will have to be tailored to the needs of the particular contracting

---

[423] See supra notes 11-213 and accompanying text (analyzing constitutionality of delegating incarceration function).

[424] Throughout the Model Contract and Model Statute, the term "contracting agency" refers to a jurisdiction's supervising body for corrections and detention, whether it be the Department of Corrections, the Department of Social Services, or some other agency. The term "contractor" refers to any private entity that enters the process of contracting with the contracting agency.

agency. Some contracts, for example, may include the responsibility for construction of a facility, while others may include only the responsibility for operation and management. The contracting parties should therefore negotiate for other provisions, within the parameters set by the letter of the Model Contract and the spirit of its commentary.[425]

Due to the agency-specific nature of government procurement, this section of the paper focuses more on the substance of the contractual provisions than on the RFP and contracting process. Nevertheless, a word about that process is important. Most contracting agencies solicit proposals from prospective contractors through an RFP. The RFP describes the work being contracted out and, in some cases, sets forth minimum requirements governing various aspects of a contractor's proposal. RFP's in the private-incarceration context vary greatly in length and detail. One is as short as five pages;[426] others are quite lengthy and address with some specificity most or all of the contractual issues.[427]

A short, general RFP may reduce the complexity of the RFP process and give prospective contractors more freedom in

_____

[425] Even if some of the Model Contract's provisions are not used, they should prompt the parties to consider other ways of addressing the issues to their mutual satisfaction -- without neglecting the interests of the public and the inmates.

[426] See Texas RFP.

[427] See Federal Bureau of Prisons RFP (177 pages); INS RFP (98 pages); 1985 Kentucky RFP (41 pages). Oklahoma's statute prescribes a detailed process for soliciting bids. See Okla. Stat. Ann. tit. 57, §§ 561(C)-(J) (West Cum. Supp. 1988).

developing their proposals. There are serious drawbacks to this approach, however. An RFP that does not address all of the major contractual issues may not provide sufficient guidance for companies that are preparing proposals. The substance of proposals submitted may vary widely, may not address key issues adequately, and may concentrate unduly on the interests of the contractor. The failure to draft an RFP that is specific enough may therefore result either in a more prolonged and expensive solicitation and evaluation process or in a contract that does not include significant provisions.

Ideally, an RFP should address every contractual issue, stating minimum requirements when appropriate, but in general or open-ended language that encourages the contractor to develop its own innovative concepts in response to the RFP. The contracting agency may, for example, establish a minimum staffing requirement in the RFP and ask prospective contractors to submit a projected staffing schedule. Structuring the RFP in this manner ensures that the proposals will meet the contracting agency's needs, putting the responsibility on the private contractor to address the details.

The process of evaluating proposals is at least as important as the formulation of the RFP itself. Proposals should not be evaluated solely on the basis of cost -- i.e., awarding the contract to the lowest bidder.[428] Rather, they should be

_____

[428] Indeed, at least one state so provides by statute. See Mont. Code Ann. § 7-32-2233(3) (1987) ("In selecting a proposal and awarding a contract, a county need not accept the proposal with the lowest cost.").

evaluated on the basis of other factors that may be critical to the contracting agency, such as the contractor's experience in operating correctional or detention facilities, the contractor's financial stability, and the quality of the services offered by the contractor.[429] Legislation may be needed to require a contracting agency to evaluate proposals with such criteria in mind.[430]

The following contracts and RFP's were considered in drafting the Model Contract:[431]

Contracts:

- Agreement Between County of Ramsey, St. Paul, Minn. and Reentry Services, Inc., for the period of Jan. 1, 1987 through Dec. 31, 1987.

- Management and Service Contract and Lease Between Santa Fe Board of County Commissioners and Corrections Corporation of America, dated Aug. 6, 1986.

- Minnesota Department of Corrections Contract with Best, Inc. for the provision of specialized services, for the period of July 1, 1986 through June 30, 1987.

- State of Rhode Island and Providence Plantations Department for Children and Their Families

---

[429] See INS RFP § I(M) (listing weight given to various factors in evaluation of proposals).

[430] Several states that have enacted statutes authorizing privatization of correctional facilities have included language specifying the factors that should be weighed in the evaluation process. See, e.g., Okla. Stat. Ann. tit. 57, § 561(F) (West Cum. Supp. 1988); Tex. Rev. Civ. Stat. Ann. art. 6166g-2, §§ 3(b), (c) (Vernon Supp. 1988).

[431] The titles of these contracts and RFP's were taken directly from the cover sheets of the documents. Many other contracts and RFP's were requested but were not sent.

("Department") Contract for Residential Care Services
Between Department and RCA Service Co., a division of
RCA Corp., dated July 1, 1986.

- General Revenue/Federal Funds Contract Between State of
  Florida Department of Health & Rehabilitative Services
  and Eckerd Family Youth Alternatives, Inc., dated June
  26, 1986.

- Agreement Between County of Ramsey, St. Paul, Minn. and
  Volunteers of America, dated June 16, 1986.

- Agreement Between the Commonwealth of Pennsylvania,
  Department of Public Welfare and RCA Service Company,
  dated Apr. 25, 1986, for operation of Weaversville
  Intensive Treatment Unit.

- Agreement Between County of Allegheny, Pa. and 268
  Center, Inc., dated Sept. 10, 1985.

- Bay County Detention Facilities Contract Between
  Corrections Corporation of America and Bay County,
  Florida, dated Sept. 3, 1985.

- Contract Documents & Specifications for Three-Party
  Contract Among New Jersey Department of Corrections,
  County of Atlantic, and RCA Service Co., Cherry Hill,
  N.J., dated Sept. 1, 1985.

- Agreement Between State of Washington Department of
  Corrections and Social Treatment Opportunity Programs,
  dated June 28, 1985.

- Agreement Between Florida Department of Corrections and
  Prisoner Transport Service, Inc., for the period of
  Oct. 1, 1984 through Sept. 30, 1985.

- Hamilton County, Tennessee Corrections Facilities
  Agreement, by and among Hamilton County, Tenn., Dalton
  Roberts, County Executive, and Corrections Corporation
  of America, dated Sept. 20, 1984, as amended by
  Hamilton County Board of Commissioners Resolution No.
  886-62, dated Aug. 18, 1986.

- Agreement for Professional Services Between RCA Service
  Co., Division of RCA Corp., and the Department of
  Public Welfare for Penn., dated Dec. 9, 1983.

RFP's:

- Federal Bureau of Prisons RFP No. 100-134-7 NC, dated Mar. 26, 1987, for residential halfway-house services for federal offenders.

- State of California Department of Corrections, Parole & Community Services Divisions RFP No. CCC 8/86.

- Immigration and Naturalization Service RFP, dated June 16, 1986.

- Santa Fe County RFP, dated Apr. 7, 1986.

- Texas Department of Corrections RFP for 500-Bed Pre-Release Center, dated 1986.

- Kentucky RFP, dated Apr. 12, 1985, for 200-Inmate Correctional Facility.

- Kentucky RFP, dated Oct. 23, 1984, for 200-Inmate Correctional Facility.[432]

- 1985 State of New Mexico Corrections Department RFP for Adult Inmates in the State Correctional Institutions of New Mexico.

---

[432] This RFP is similar in many, but not all, respects to the 1985 Kentucky RFP.

A. Model Contract and Commentary

Section 1: Policy Statement --
Goals and Responsibilities of the Parties

Commentary:

Advocates of privatization posit that its merits include cost savings to the public and the provision of proper inmate treatment.[433] The private sector's assertion that private prisons will provide better, less expensive corrections than will prisons operated by the contracting agency is untested.[434] Nevertheless, the contracting agency should require that these assertions be incorporated in the contract to ensure that the private contractor is obligated to fulfill its promises. The contractor's failure to meet its contractual obligations could make it liable to the contracting agency for breach of contract

---

[433] See, e.g., Crane, Should Prisons Be Privately Run?: A Business Like Any Other, A.B.A. J., Apr. 1, 1987, at 39; Nightline: Who Should Run Our Prisons? (ABC television broadcast, July 11, 1986) (transcript on file with author). Corrections Corporation of America (CCA), for example, promises that "CCA will do the job of running a prison or jail more cheaply and so 'save the taxpayers money,'" and that "every prison CCA runs will be of such high standards as to be certified by the American Correctional Association." Davis, 2 "Model" Prisons Cast Doubt on CCA Claims, Tennessean, May 15, 1988, at 1D, col. 1 [hereinafter 2 "Model" Prisons].

[434] Although contracting for private-prison operations began more than three years ago, information concerning the short- and long-term benefits of privatization has yet to be collected and analyzed thoroughly. See, e.g., Durham, Evaluating Privatized Correctional Institutions: Obstacles to Effective Assessment, Fed. Probation, June 1988, at 65.

and, under the language of the Model Contract, to the public and inmates as third-party beneficiaries. Although the possibility of third-party-beneficiary claims increases the economic risk for the contractor, the opportunity for such claims provides the contracting agency with the necessary assurance that its risks -- legal, social, and economic -- in handing over the prison or jail are justified.

Although it is obvious that the contracting agency should have rights to sue under the contract to which it is a party, it is not as obvious that either the public or inmates, as third-party beneficiaries, should have rights to sue as well.[435] Indeed, there is no requirement that the contracting parties create such rights in these third-party beneficiaries. In fact, it would be difficult to prove that the public or inmates were third-party beneficiaries with the right to enforce the contract unless it could be shown that (1) the contracting parties intended to grant them legally enforceable rights, or (2) there was a law mandating that certain persons be considered third-party beneficiaries.[436] For the reasons discussed above, it is

---

[435] Under the Model Contract language, for example, third-party-beneficiary rights would include public standing to sue the private contractor for failure to remain below a specific maximum contract rate and inmate standing to sue for failure to provide the type of care that the company contractually promised.

[436] An inmate, for example, may be made a third-party beneficiary without regard to the principal contracting parties' intentions by merely making third-party-beneficiary status for inmates an overriding statutory policy. See Restatement (Second) of Contracts § 303 comment d (1981). This policy could be expressly stated in a statute or implied from the case law. See Owens v. Haas, 601 F.2d 1242, 1247-51 (2d Cir.) (holding that inmate who had been beaten and injured while housed in county

in the contracting agency's best interest (and thus the public's best interest as well) that it secure an intention to create third-party-beneficiary rights. While such an intention need not be expressly stated in the contract in order to find such rights, the Model Contract recommends that this intention unambiguously be stated in the contract to put all parties on notice of their rights and obligations. Because of the importance of third-party-beneficiary rights under privatization contracts, a discussion of these rights follows. In addition, contracting parties should make a careful study of third-party-beneficiary law in their jurisdictions.

Contracts that benefit third parties may create legally enforceable rights in those parties. A third party whose benefit is merely "incidental" to the performance of the contract has no contractual rights.[437] An "intended" beneficiary, on the other

_____

jail had third-party-beneficiary claim on contract between federal and county government because federal government had statutory and constitutional duty to provide safe care), cert. denied, 444 U.S. 980 (1979). Failure to provide the statutorily mandated care may also give rise to damage actions in state court. See, e.g., Blair v. Anderson, 325 A.2d 94 (Del. 1974) (holding that federal inmate had third-party-beneficiary claim against state for its failure to provide safe care, as it was contractually bound to do); Farmer v. State, 224 Miss. 96, 104, 79 So. 2d 528, 531 (1955) (involving claim that inadequate medical care led to inmate's death); Smith v. Slack, 125 W. Va. 812, 813-14, 26 S.E.2d 387, 388 (1943) (holding valid inmate's complaint alleging that prison failed to provide adequate food service).

437 An "incidental beneficiary" is one to whom the promisee neither owed money or services, nor contracted for his direct benefit. See Restatement (Second) of Contracts §§ 302(1), (2) (1981); Note, Third Party Beneficiary and Implied Right of Action Analysis: The Fiction of One Governmental Intent, 94 Yale L.J. 875, 877-78 (1985) (noting that, although not all jurisdictions have adopted the Restatement (Second) of Contracts, it is the "generally accepted text for beneficiary rights"). See generally

hand, is one to whom "recognition of a right to performance . . . is appropriate to effectuate the intention of the parties."[438] Significantly, an intended third-party beneficiary need not be named specifically in the contract,[439] but instead can be determined from the circumstances surrounding the contract.[440] Thus, when the contract does not expressly name a third-party beneficiary, a court may have to spend considerable time deciding whether the parties intended to confer contractual rights on that third party. Further, "[w]hen a third party may enforce the contract, the scope of the promisor's duty is greater than if the promise was enforceable only by the promisee. It would be helpful to have some indication that the promisee bargained for this greater undertaking."[441] For this reason, express language such as that used in the Model Contract's Policy Statement is advisable.

Under the Restatement (Second) of Contracts, "[a] promise in a contract creates a duty in the promisor to any intended beneficiary to perform the promise, and the intended beneficiary may enforce the duty."[442] Thus, when the promisor _intends_ to

---

Note, supra note 9, at 1502-03 (discussing other sources of liability for contractor).

[438] Restatement (Second) of Contracts § 302(1) (1981).

[439] Id. § 308; see, e.g., Owens v. Haas, 601 F.2d 1242, 1250 (2d Cir.), cert. denied, 444 U.S. 980 (1979).

[440] Restatement (Second) of Contracts § 302(1)(b) (1981).

[441] S. Burnham, Drafting Contracts 163 (1987).

[442] Restatement (Second) of Contracts § 145 comment e (1981) (emphasis added).

confer on the beneficiary a right to enforce the contract, recognition of this right rests on the same ground as the promisee's right to enforce.[443] In cases of doubt, the question of whether such an intention is attributed to the promisee is influenced by whether recognition of the right "will further the legitimate expectations of the promisee, make available a simple and convenient procedure for enforcement, or protect the [beneficiary's] reasonable reliance on the promise."[444]

Government contracts pose unique problems in the area of third-party-beneficiary rights because to some extent every member of the public is intended to benefit from the contract.[445] Consequently, both courts and legislatures have taken a more narrow view of third-party-beneficiary status in this context and have applied a stricter test to determine whether the third party qualifies for beneficiary status. Not only must the contracting parties have intended to benefit the third party, but they must also have intended to confer a right to enforce the benefit on the third party.[446]

---

[443] Id.

[444] Id.; see also id. § 145 comment e, Illustrations (providing example of application of rule). The case involves A, a common carrier that is required as a condition of its license to maintain liability insurance covering claims for bodily injury arising out of A's operations. A files a policy written by B. C claims to have been injured in circumstances covered by the policy. C may maintain a direct action against B. Id.

[445] Note, supra note 437, at 878.

[446] Restatement (Second) of Contracts § 313(2) (1981). In Shell v. National Flood Insurers Ass'n, 520 F. Supp. 150 (D. Colo. 1981), the court relied on section 145 of the 1932 Restatement of Contracts that a promisor

In the context of prison or jail privatization, part of the promised performance of the private contractor should include the provision of proper treatment for inmates and less expensive corrections for the public. Providing the public with third-party-beneficiary rights in this fashion is not unusual. In Ratzlaff v. Franz Foods,[447] for example, the court had to determine whether a downstream landowner was an intended beneficiary under a contract that controlled a fertilizer plant's use of the municipality's sewage system.[448] In finding that the

---

> bound to the United States . . . by contract to do an act or render a service to some or all members of the public, is subject to no duty under the contract to such members to give compensation for the injurious consequences of performing or attempting to perform it, or failing to do so, unless
>
> > (1) an intention is manifested in the contract, as interpreted in the light of the circumstances surrounding its formation, that the promisor shall compensate members of the public for such injurious consequences . . . .

Id. at 157. Section 145 of the Restatement (Second) of Contracts also makes reference to the concept of third-party beneficiaries. Section 145(1) provides that "[t]he rules stated in this chapter apply to contracts with a government or governmental agency except to the extent that the application would contravene the policy of the law authorizing the contract or prescribing remedies for its breach." Section 145(1) applies to cases in which the government enters a contract to secure advantages for the public, such as lower-cost services. Such contracts tend to specify maximum rates and are enforceable by individual members of the public. Thus, for example, some courts have recognized that public contracts with utilities and common carriers with maximum rates create third-party-beneficiary rights in individual members of the public. See J. Calamari & J. Perillo, Contracts Handbook § 17-7 (3d ed. 1987) (citing Bush v. Upper Valley Telecable Co., 96 Idaho 83, 524 P.2d 1055 (1974)).

[447]   250 Ark. 1003, 468 S.W.2d 239 (1971).

[448]   Id. at 1005, 468 S.W.2d at 241.

landowner was an intended beneficiary, the court noted that "a party who owes no obligation to third persons or the public in general may by contract assume an obligation to use due care towards such persons or the public in general."[449] Likewise, in Bush v. Upper Valley Telecable Co.,[450] the court found that a city resident was an intended third-party beneficiary under a franchise contract between the city and the cable company because "[e]ven a cursory examination of the [evidence] reveals the city's intent to benefit a limited well defined class of people."[451]

Just as members of the public are third-party beneficiaries of the private-prison contract, so too are members of the inmate population. The rehabilitation of inmates, for example -- including job training, counseling, chemical abuse programs, medical treatment, and education -- should be one of the major concerns and goals of a correctional facility. In addition, private contractors must address the serious problem of overcrowding and safety in the prisons. Certain standards and

---

449 Id.

450 96 Idaho 83, 524 P.2d 1055 (1974).

451 Id. at 85, 524 P.2d at 1057. But see Schell v. National Flood Insurers Ass'n, 520 F. Supp. 150, 157 (D. Colo. 1981) (finding that flood victims were only incidental beneficiaries under contract between Department of Housing and Urban Development and flood insurer and were therefore unable to recover damages for insurer's failure to perform under contract); Feldman v. United States Dep't of Housing and Urban Dev., 430 F. Supp. 1324, 1328 (E.D. Pa. 1977) (holding that tenants of federally financed apartment project could not claim third-party-beneficiary status under regulatory agreement between HUD and private company because parties did not intend to confer rights on the tenants).

conditions of confinement are constitutional or statutory rights of the prisoners that simply cannot be contracted away. In Owens v. Haas,[452] for instance, a federal prisoner housed in a county jail pursuant to a contract between the county and the United States government brought an action under a third-party-beneficiary theory, claiming that he had received an injury while he was in the custody of county corrections officers.[453] The United States Court of Appeals for the Second Circuit held that the prisoner could bring a third-party-beneficiary claim because of a policy statement in the contract that provided for the safekeeping and protection of prisoners.[454] The statement read: "[P]risoners shall be placed in contract facilities which provide a secure, humane and orderly environment, and in which adequate attention is given to the maintenance of each inmate's health, safety, and general welfare."[455]

All of the above-mentioned factors taken together show that a member of the public or an inmate in a private facility may bring a third-party-beneficiary claim against the company for damages attributable to a breach of the contract to provide the correctional services. Whether the right to bring such a claim will be express or implied from the contract will depend on many factors, including the existence of: statutory language creating

---

[452] 601 F.2d 1242 (2d Cir.), cert. denied, 444 U.S. 980 (1979).

[453] Id. at 1244-45.

[454] Id. at 1250.

[455] Id. at 1250 n.9.

such a right; legislative history supporting a finding that such a right was intended; case law concerning third-party claims; contractual language creating such a right; and evidence indicating that the parties intended to grant such a right. To avoid the problem of determining contractual intent, it is recommended that the legislature create such third-party-beneficiary status[456] and that the parties include the Model Contract's language.

Model Contract Provision:

This contract between the contracting agency and the contractor for the operation and maintenance of incarceration facilities, entered for the benefit of the public and inmates, is premised on the following goals of privatization:

(A) to provide the public with prison or jail services that are cost efficient and effective with respect to the purposes and goals of incarceration;

(B) to provide inmates with proper care, treatment, rehabilitation, and reformation; and

(C) to provide the public and inmates with prison or jail services that meet the requirements of the American Correctional Association and other such minimum standards that may be promulgated by the contracting agency.

This contract is entered in consideration of these goals of privatization.

---

456 See Model Statute § 1 (Enabling Legislation).

Section 2: Private Financing and Physical Plant

Section 2(A): Private Financing

Commentary:

The issues concerning the financing of a correctional or detention facility are distinct from the issues concerning the operation and management of a facility.[457] Many jurisdictions, under pressure to expand their prison and jail capacities,[458] have found themselves unable to finance the needed facilities through traditional means, such as current appropriations or general-obligation bonds.[459] Some of these contracting agencies have turned to private financing to avoid the initial fiscal burdens of construction,[460] and a few agencies have combined this arrangement with a contract for the private operation and management of the facilities.[461]

---

[457] See, e.g., DeWitt, Ohio's New Approach to Prison and Jail Financing, NIJ Construction Bulletin 10 (Nov. 1986) (advising that issues that involve financing should be examined separately from issues that involve operations and management).

[458] See National Prison Project, Status Report: The Courts and Prisons, reprinted in Prisoners and the Law app. B (I. Robbins ed. 1987) (listing jurisdictions that are under court order to remedy overcrowding in correctional facilities).

[459] See infra notes 465-466 and accompanying text (explaining reasons that some contracting agencies might not be able to use traditional methods of financing).

[460] See National Institute of Justice, The Privatization of Corrections 38 (1985) [hereinafter Privatization of Corrections] (describing private-sector involvement in leasing correctional facilities to government agencies).

The decision whether to use private financing rather than the various methods of public financing necessarily depends on the financial and political circumstances of each individual jurisdiction.[462] Thus, the discussion and contract provisions presented in this section address the issues concerning private financing in general terms, highlighting matters that every jurisdiction should consider when determining how to finance a facility. The discussion considers why some jurisdictions have used private financing instead of the traditional methods of public financing. It then outlines several types of private financing arrangements, the advantages of each arrangement relative to the more traditional means of public financing, and in what circumstances each type of private financing might prove to be advantageous to a jurisdiction.

1.   Private Financing Generally

   a.   Advantages and Disadvantages

The decision to use private financing for the construction

---

461   See, e.g., INS RFP at 9, § I(C)(2) (requiring prospective contractors to provide "necessary physical structure, equipment, facilities, personnel and services"); 1985 Kentucky RFP at 10-1, § 10.000 (requesting bids for "provision and operation" of facility); Texas RFP at 1 (soliciting bids for contract to "construct, operate and manage" four pre-release centers).

462   See Privatization of Corrections, supra note 460, at 48 (noting that the most appropriate method of financing for a particular contracting agency may vary according to circumstances).

of a new correctional or detention facility, for an addition to or renovation of an existing correctional facility, or for the conversion of an existing structure to a correctional or detention facility will be based on those factors that are most important to a particular contracting agency. One factor is cost. In most cases, a contracting agency should not consider private financing if its primary goal is to use the least expensive means of financing. Traditional public-sector financing is generally less expensive than private-sector methods due to the lower costs of governmental borrowing[463] and the

_____

463 National Institute of Justice, Corrections and the Private Sector: A National Forum 11-14 (1985) [hereinafter Corrections and the Private Sector]. The lower cost of public financing is due mainly to the fact that interest rates on the various methods of traditional public financing are lower than those that are incurred by private contractors. A contracting agency can avoid interest costs altogether by financing through current appropriations, or the "pay as you go" approach. See Privatization of Corrections, supra note 460, at 33-36 (explaining mechanics of pay-as-you-go approach and when it is most advantageous for a jurisdiction to use this method of financing). If the contracting agency must borrow, it can take advantage of interest rates that are lower than those that are available to private investors. General-obligation bonds are considered to be the least expensive and most secure type of governmental borrowing, and are the most often used form of public debt financing for correctional facilities. Id. at 36. Assuming that the jurisdiction has a strong bond rating, general-obligation bonds can be issued at a lower rate of interest for two reasons. First, because they are full-faith-and-credit bonds secured by the taxing authority of the jurisdiction, they are considered to be a more secure type of investment than are other forms of lending. DeWitt, supra note 457, at 2-3; see M. Gelfand, State and Local Government Debt Financing §§ 2:01, 2:03 (1986) (defining general-obligation bond and assurance of full-faith-and-credit). Second, because the interest that taxpayers receive from the bonds is exempt from taxation, the jurisdiction can pay lower interest rates and still provide the investor with a return that remains competitive with other forms of taxable investments.
This second advantage, however, has been lessened slightly by the Tax Reform Act of 1986, which lowered individual tax rates. See

recent reductions in tax benefits for private investors.[464]

_____

I.R.C. § 1 (1986) (reducing maximum individual rate to 28%, with certain qualifications).

Although general-obligation bonds may provide savings on interest costs, there are also some hidden costs that are associated with these bonds. There may be significant costs that are connected with the issuance of the bonds, for example, including underwriter fees, legal fees, and printing and distribution fees. See DeWitt, supra note 457, at 3 (noting that issuance costs may require the amount of the issue to be raised by 1.5% to 3%). In addition, delays that are associated with the voter approval required for most bond issues often raise the cost of construction. See Privatization of Corrections, supra note 460, at 37 (citing California study finding that referendum requirements delay prison construction by eight to ten months).

Revenue bonds are another, less frequently used, method of financing incarceration facilities. They are less secure investments because they are not backed by the full faith and credit of the jurisdiction. Rather, they are repaid through revenues that are generated from the project that they financed. In the case of a private prison or jail, the revenue would be the rent payments made on the facility. As less secure investments, they may require a higher interest rate. Thus, savings to the contracting agency may not be as great. They may still be a desirable method of raising revenue, however, because they are not subject to debt ceilings or referenda requirements. Privatization of Corrections, supra note 460, at 36. Again, this apparent benefit raises other policy costs, such as eliminating the voters from the direct decisionmaking process.

[464] Under previous tax laws, when a facility was privately owned the investors received tax benefits through depreciation and various forms of investment tax credits, such as the rehabilitation tax credit. These savings were in part passed on to the jurisdiction in the form of lower lease payments for the facility. The Deficit Reduction Act of 1984, however, restricted the ability of private investors to take advantage of accelerated-depreciation deductions and eliminated the rehabilitation tax credit for property leased to a governmental contracting agency. See Staff of the Joint Committee on Taxation, 98th Cong., 2d Sess., Description of S. 2933 Relating to Leasing of Qualified Correctional Facilities to State and Local Government Units (Comm. Print 1984) [hereinafter Staff Description]; Corrections and the Private Sector, supra note 463, at 11 (statement of John Peterson, Municipal Finance Officers Ass'n). The Tax Reform Act of 1986 repealed the investment tax credit entirely and instituted more restrictive rules on depreciation. See Uhlfelder & Hanlon, The New Face of Privatization Under Tax Reform, 33 Tax Notes 135 (Oct. 1986). These changes are expected to force the restructuring of some

Considerations other than cost may be more important, however, and lead the contracting agency to prefer private financing over traditional public methods of financing. In some instances, a shortage of current revenues, inability to obtain voter approval for bond issuances, or debt ceilings may prevent a contracting agency from financing a facility through current revenues or bonds.[465] In other cases, a contracting agency may find that the public financing process does not allow it to construct a facility as quickly as one is needed.[466] In such

_____

current private-sector transactions and lead to the complete demise of others. Id.

[465] There are several reasons that a contracting agency may not be able to utilize traditional public-financing methods. Rising construction costs have made it impossible for many contracting agencies to fund new facilities on a pay-as-you-go basis. See DeWitt, supra note 457, at 2 (observing that most state and local governments do not have the resources that are necessary to fund a major capital expenditure, such as a prison or jail, on a cash basis). A contracting agency's ability to issue general-obligation bonds may be limited by constitutional or statutory debt ceilings or voter-referenda requirements. M. Gelfand, supra note 464, at § 2:04; see National Criminal Justice Ass'n, Special Report: Private Sector Involvement in Financing and Managing Correctional Facilities 3 (1987) (noting that many jurisdictions have experienced difficulties in winning approval for bond issuance to support prison and jail construction).

[466] See Corrections and the Private Sector, supra note 463, at 14 (statement of John Gillespie, Correctional Facilities Finance Specialist, Shearson Lehman/American Express) (stating that one benefit of private financing is the speed of planning and construction). This reduction in construction time is due to several factors. Private financing provides a contracting agency with a large amount of capital that might otherwise take several appropriations periods to raise. Interview with Robert Schmidt, Supervisory Detention and Deportation Officer, INS (Feb. 10, 1987) (noting that privatization allowed INS to complete Houston facility in matter of months, instead of the two to three fiscal years that are normally required to obtain necessary appropriations). It also eliminates the time that is typically required for voter referenda and bond issuance and distribution. Time may be an important factor to a contracting agency whose overcrowding problem has reached crisis proportions

circumstances, a contracting agency may decide that privatization provides an attractive alternative means of financing.

Contracting agencies should also consider, however, the negative public-policy implications of privatization. Using private financing to build a facility that voters have rejected or that does not fall within constitutional or statutory debt limits thwarts the will of citizens who still ultimately pay for the facility, albeit through a different type of transaction.[467] Private financing may provide a short-term

_____

or that is under court order to improve prison or jail conditions. It can also reduce both the impact of inflation on the cost of the facility and the time for conflicts, such as labor or zoning disputes, to arise. Corrections and the Private Sector, supra note 463, at 11.

Some private firms are now offering what are termed "turnkey" packages, which further enhance the time-saving advantage of private financing. Under such an arrangement, the private company contracts with the government agency to provide the financing, design, and construction of the facility. See DeWitt, supra note 457, at 10 (describing structure of turnkey arrangement); District of Columbia Appropriations for Fiscal Year 1986: Hearings on H.R. 3067 Before a Subcomm. of the Comm. on Appropriations, United States Senate, 99th Cong., 1st Sess. 327 (1986) [hereinafter District of Columbia Appropriations Hearings] (discussing types of private leasing arrangements). The private company then leases the finished facility back to the government agency. Id. Normally, a government agency must go through separate bidding processes for the architectural, underwriting, and construction phases of a project. Such arrangements may be subject to challenge, however, under a jurisdiction's competitive-bidding laws. See id. at 327; Privatization of Prison Construction in New York: Hearings on S. 98-1279 Before the Joint Economic Comm. of the Congress of the United States, 98th Cong., 2d Sess. 20 (1984) [hereinafter Privatization of Prison Construction in New York].

[467] See Privatization of Corrections, supra note 460, at 90 (discussing the possibility that public opposition and new regulations may develop in response to the use of private financing to avoid debt limits and voter referenda). In Jefferson County, Colorado, for example, the voters twice rejected a jail bond issue before E.F. Hutton underwrote a $30-million issue for private jail construction. Rosenberg, Who Says

solution to a jurisdiction's financial difficulties, but it does not solve the long-term problem of funding. Money must still be found to service the private debt. Thus, private financing may not advance the ultimate goal of responsible fiscal management.[468]

b. Tax Aspects

The types of private financing arrangements that are discussed below all involve various forms of lease arrangements between private investors and a governmental contracting agency. Although there is some variance in the tax treatment given to these different types of leasing structures, there are some tax implications that are common to all types of private/governmental leasing arrangements. These factors affect the feasibility and desirability of privately financed

---

Crime Doesn't Pay?, Jericho, Spring 1984, at 1, 4. A more egregious example concerns a proposal by a private firm in Pennsylvania to build a 720-bed medium- and maximum-security interstate protective-custody facility on a toxic-waste site, which it had purchased for $1. The spokesperson for the Pennsylvania Department of Corrections is reported to have said: "If it were a state facility, we certainly would be concerned about the grounds where the facility is located. [As for a private prison, however, there] is nothing in our legislation which gives anyone authority on what to do." Levine, Private Prison Planned on Toxic Waste Site, Nat'l Prison Project J., Fall 1985, at 10, 11. In the face of proposed legislation in Pennsylvania to place a one-year moratorium on the construction or operation of private prisons, the company reportedly abandoned its plan, attempted to sell the waste site for $790,000, and sought to open the facility in Idaho. Elvin, Private Prison Plans Dropped by Buckingham, Nat'l Prison Project J., Winter 1985, at 11.

[468] District of Columbia Appropriations Hearings, supra note 466, at 294 (statement of Sen. Specter).

-156-

correctional facilities.

In a purely private leasing arrangement, the lessor enjoys the tax benefits of ownership -- depreciation and, until recently, the investment tax credit.[469] In a leasing arrangement between a private lessor and a governmental lessee, however, there are restrictions that significantly reduce the tax benefits accruing to the private lessor.[470] The most significant of these is the limitation imposed on depreciation deductions.[471] The Deficit Reduction Act of 1984 imposed special limitations on property that is leased to tax-exempt entities, including government contracting agencies.[472] This property, termed "tax-

---

[469] The investment tax credit was repealed by the Tax Reform Act of 1986, Pub. L. No. 99-0514, 100 Stat. 2085 (codified as amended in scattered sections of 26 U.S.C.). See Prentice-Hall Information Services, A Complete Guide to the Tax Reform Act of 1986 201 (1986) (explaining changes in tax law affecting depreciation and investment tax credit).

[470] The private lessor must first qualify as the tax owner of the facility to receive the tax benefits of ownership. For the purposes of the tax law, the Internal Revenue Service will look to the facts and circumstances of each transaction in determining whether it is a lease or a conditional sale. See Warren, Leases and Service Contracts with Tax-Exempt Entities After the DRA, 7 Tax Advisor 230, 232 n.4 (1985) (including cases defining what constitutes a lease or conditional sale). Factors that the IRS will consider include: whether the lessor retains an interest in the property at the end of the lease term; whether the lease term exceeds the useful life of the property; whether the lessor retains the risks and benefits of appreciation or depreciation in the value of the property; and the cost to the lessee of any option to purchase. M. Gelfand, supra note 463, at § 3:32.

[471] Under 26 U.S.C. § 48(a)(5) (1982), property leased to governmental entities for their use was not entitled to an investment tax credit. This distinction is no longer significant, as the Tax Reform Act of 1986 repealed the investment tax credit. See supra note 469.

[472] Pub. L. No. 98-369, 98 Stat. 494 (1986) (now codified

exempt use" property,[473] is not eligible for accelerated methods of depreciation. Rather, the lessor must depreciate the property on the straight-line method over a longer cost-recovery period.[474] The Tax Reform Act of 1986 continued these restrictions on tax-exempt-use property. Thus, tax incentives that originally attracted private investors to leasing transactions with governmental units are no longer available, making privatization a less attractive alternative method of financing a correctional facility.

2. Types of Private Financing

The following discussion provides a description of several types of private leasing arrangements that are currently available, along with a synopsis of advantages and disadvantages that are unique to each particular arrangement. Because of the complexity of the issues surrounding private-financing methods, it is strongly suggested that a contracting agency that is contemplating private financing consult a professional who is familiar with the financing of correctional and detention facilities.

---

at I.R.C. § 168(g) (1986)).

[473] 26 U.S.C. § 168(j)(1) (Supp. III 1985) (defining tax-exempt-use property).

[474] Previously, the lessor would pass on to the contracting agency that leased the property a portion of the benefits that had been derived from accelerated methods of depreciation. See supra note 464.

a. Straight Lease

One way of financing a facility privately is through a lease agreement with a private entity.[475] This type of financing is available independent of a contract for the private management and operation of a facility.[476] Under such an arrangement, the private entity finances the construction of the facility and leases it to the contracting agency for a shorter term than its predicted useful life.[477] The lease may contain a provision that the contracting agency has an option to purchase the facility before the end of the lease term.[478] The option to purchase should be set at fair-market value at the time of the exercise of the option, with the option cost realized when it is

---

[475] There are many different types of leasing arrangements that are available. This section deals only with what is sometimes termed a "true lease" or an "operating lease," pursuant to which the lessor retains a residual interest in the property at the end of the lease term and carries the burdens and benefits of ownership. M. Gelfand, supra note 463, at § 3:02. Other sections deal with sale/leaseback and lease-purchase transactions, pursuant to which the government lessee is or will be the owner of the property at the end of the lease term. Id.

[476] See infra notes 494-504 and accompanying text (discussing private ownership combined with private operation of a correctional facility).

[477] A. Vogt & L. Cole, A Guide to Muncipal Leasing 223 (1983). The shorter term is one factor indicating that the transaction is a true lease and not merely a method to finance the purchase of a facility.

[478] See Privatization of Corrections, supra note 460, at 42. In many cases, the option gives the contracting agency an opportunity to buy the facility after each year of the lease term. Id. The option to purchase may also come at the end of the lease term. Id. The option to purchase may be particularly important in the context of private ownership and operation of a facility. See infra notes 494-504 and accompanying text.

exercised.[479] This approach ensures that the transaction will be viewed as a lease and not a long-term purchase, both for tax purposes and for the purposes of calculating the jurisdiction's long-term debt that is subject to a ceiling or referenda.[480] Also important for the purpose of avoiding debt ceilings and voter referenda is a non-appropriation clause providing that lease payments are subject to periodic appropriation by the legislature.[481]

---

[479] M. Gelfand, supra note 463, at § 3:02. The option to purchase adds to the already high cost of leasing, particularly where the government lessee has made a number of lease payments prior to exercising the right to purchase. In some cases, the lease provides that the cost of exercising the option will decrease throughout the term of the lease, but at a slower rate than that at which the rent payments accumulate. In effect, the private entity applies a portion of the rent paid to reduce the cost of the purchase option. See Privatization of Corrections, supra note 460, at 42. The total cost of a lease with an option to purchase remains high. Id.; see also supra notes 463-464 and accompanying text (outlining the reasons that leasing arrangements are generally more expensive than the pay-as-you-go or general-obligation-bond financing methods).

[480] See M. Gelfand, supra note 463, at § 3:02. Tax law looks in part to the price of acquiring ownership of the property in determining whether a transaction is a lease or a financing arrangement. See id. In a financing arrangement, the purchase price would correspond roughly to the amount of payments remaining on the principal. See id.; see also supra notes 469-474 and accompanying text (discussing tax implications of lease transactions with contracting agencies). The price of the option itself is another factor that will be weighed in characterizing the transaction for tax purposes.

It is also important that the lease be viewed as a current expense, and not as a purchase agreement, in order to avoid debt ceilings or voter-referenda requirements. M. Gelfand, supra note 463, at § 3:30.

[481] A non-appropriation clause provides that, if funds have not been appropriated by the end of the fiscal year, the contracting agency may terminate the lease. See Model Contract § 7 (Termination). Such a lease will not be classified as debt. M. Gelfand, supra note 463, at § 3:17.

There are several reasons why a contracting agency might consider leasing a prison facility from a private entity. As with all private financing discussed in this section, a properly structured lease will not be regarded as a long-term obligation of the jurisdiction, but rather as a current expense.[482] Thus, a jurisdiction can lease the facility without impairing its ability to borrow for other needs. It also allows a contracting agency to forego the delay and expense -- not to mention the potential for voter rejection -- that are associated with referenda requirements.[483]

Another perceived benefit that is unique to the leasing alternative is the flexibility without risk that it would provide the contracting agency.[484] If the prison population declined sharply, for example, or the facility became obsolete, the contracting agency would have the option of simply terminating its lease agreement through non-appropriation.[485]

In reality, however, the amount of flexibility that a jurisdiction would gain from a private-lease arrangement will in most cases be minimal.[486] Although the private contractor would

---

[482] See supra notes 475-481 and accompanying text (describing structure of lease agreement).

[483] See supra note 463 (observing, inter alia, that referenda requirement may delay construction of facility from eight to ten months).

[484] C. Ring, Contracting for the Operation of Private Prisons: Pros and Cons 23 (1987).

[485] Id. at 22-23. The threat of non-appropriation may also put pressure on the private contractor to perform well or risk losing its investment in the facility. See Privatization of Corrections, supra note 460, at 40.

retain the remedy of foreclosure, it would certainly be reluctant to enter an agreement that is subject to non-appropriation without some assurance of a return on its investment.[487] Such protection may come in the form of a non-substitution clause, which restricts the contracting agency's ability to replace the leased property with property performing the same function for a stated period of time.[488] Other means of protection may include higher lease payments[489] or a liquidated-damages provision requiring the contracting agency to reimburse the private contractor for a stated percentage of its capital investment in the event of a non-appropriation.[490] These types of restrictions shift the financial risks of prisoner-population fluctuation and obsolescence back to the contracting agency.

The most serious drawback of the private-lease arrangement

---

[486] C. Ring, _supra_ note 484, at 23-24.

[487] Under such an agreement, the lessor retains the right of foreclosure. In the context of a lease for a correctional or detention facility, however, the risk of non-appropriation for the lessor is minimal because use of the facility will usually be essential to the contracting agency. Cole, _Tax-Exempt Leasing: A Financing Option_, 1985-1986 Current Mun. Probs. 439, 440.

[488] See _Privatization of Corrections_, _supra_ note 460, at 40. Private contractors should be aware, however, that safeguards such as a non-substitution clause may be held unenforceable if they are challenged in court. M. Gelfand, _supra_ note 463, at § 2:15.

[489] See _Privatization of Corrections_, _supra_ note 460, at 40 (noting that private investors will probably consider the threat of non-appropriation in deciding how much rent to charge); C. Ring, _supra_ note 484, at 23 (opining that contractor may seek to protect itself from non-appropriation by demanding higher monthly lease payments).

[490] But _cf._ M. Gelfand, _supra_ note 463, at § 3:17 (observing that such a provision may be unenforceable).

is cost. In addition to the higher cost of private borrowing that would be passed on to the contracting agency,[491] lease payments might also be artificially high if the contractor felt that there was a significant risk of non-appropriation.[492] A contracting agency that plans to obtain a facility through an option to purchase will pay a higher price than if it had obtained the facility through traditional or other alternative methods of financing.[493]

b. Leasing as Part of Contract for Operation and Management of a Correctional or Detention Facility

Contracting agencies have begun to combine private financing with service contracts for the private operation and management of correctional and detention facilities.[494] When a private contractor finances and constructs a facility as part of a contract for operation and management, what would ordinarily be a lease payment is incorporated in the cost reimbursement for the operation and management contract.[495] The reimbursement is

---

[491] See supra note 463 (explaining why private financing may be more expensive than public financing would be).

[492] See supra note 489 (noting that the threat of non-appropriation may affect the amount of rental payments).

[493] See supra note 479 (describing the manner in which an option to purchase adds to the already high cost of private financing).

[494] See Privatization of Corrections, supra note 460, at 45.

[495] For an example of how transactions involving private ownership and operation of correctional facilities can be

structured to ensure that the contractor receives a fair return on its capital investment in the facility.[496] This combination of private financing and management requires further discussion of several issues already discussed in conjunction with lease transactions.

In most cases, the private contractor that provides a facility as part of a service contract is considered to be the tax owner of the property.[497] The major issue that arises in relation to tax treatment is whether payments for use of the property under the contract constitute an integral part of the service contract or instead constitute a lease to a contracting agency.[498] The issue is important with respect to the availability of accelerated-depreciation deductions for the tax owner.[499] On the one hand, if the contract is deemed to be a service contract, rather than a lease, then the restrictions that are applicable to property leased to a contracting agency would

_____

structured, see State of California Dep't of Corrections, Financial Management Handbook for Private Return to Custody Facilities 12-13 (1985) (describing policy for reimbursement of lease/use costs).

[496] Id. at 12; cf. Privatization of Corrections, supra note 460, at 38 (observing that in all private lease transactions it is important to allow the lessor a fair return on its capital investment).

[497] M. Gelfand, supra note 463, at § 3:40.

[498] Id.; see I.R.C. § 7701(e)(1) (1986) (listing factors that determine whether a service contract is actually a lease).

[499] M. Gelfand, supra note 463, at § 3:40. Until recently, the issue was also important in determining the availability of the investment tax credit. The investment tax credit was eliminated, however, by the Tax Reform Act of 1986, Pub. L. No. 99-514, 100 Stat. 2085 (codified as amended in scattered sections of 26 U.S.C.).

not apply and the property would not qualify for accelerated-depreciation deductions.[500] On the other hand, if the contract does not meet the definition of a service contract, then the private owner's tax benefits would be determined in accordance with the rules governing tax-exempt-use property.[501]

The combination of private ownership and operation of a facility may enhance the advantages of private financing. As with the lease transactions discussed in the previous section, payments under service contracts are normally exempt from constitutional and statutory debt ceilings.[502] The cost of private financing is reduced somewhat, as any additional tax benefits should be passed on to the contracting agency in the form of lower lease/use payments.

One important disadvantage that must be addressed, however, is the lack of flexibility that this arrangement affords. A contract that combines the private ownership and operation of a facility could severely limit a contracting agency's ability to replace an inadequate provider if the contract does not provide

---

[500] I.R.C. § 168(a) (1986) (accelerated cost-recovery system). Whether the contract is considered to be a service contract or a lease, the private owner as tax owner still retains deductions for "ordinary and necessary expenses including taxes, maintenance, and insurance." I.R.C. § 162(a) (1986); see M. Gelfand, supra note 463, at § 3:40.

[501] I.R.C. § 168(g) (1986) (alternate depreciation system encompassing tax-exempt-use property).

[502] M. Gelfand, supra note 463, at § 9:17. Such contracts are generally subject to non-appropriations. Therefore, they are not considered long-term debt for the purposes of calculating the debt ceiling. See supra note 481 (describing non-appropriations clause).

the means for the contracting agency to obtain possession or
ownership of the facility on short notice. Thus, the contracting
agency should not enter an agreement that does not include an
option to purchase the facility in the event of default or other
circumstances that are enumerated in the contract.[503]

Another solution may be to contract separately for the
ownership and operation of the facility, either with the same
party or with two separate providers. This would allow the
contracting agency to change operators as frequently as necessary
and still enter a long-term lease with the private owner that
would provide the owner with greater security and thus encourage
lower lease payments. The problem with such an arrangement,
however, is that the facility's owner probably would not qualify
for the same tax benefits as a combined service otherwise
would.[504]

_____

[503] At least one state statute requires that the
contracting agency have the option to purchase a privately owned
and operated facility. See Okla. Stat. Ann. tit. 57, § 561(R)(4)
(West Cum. Supp. 1988).

[504] See supra notes 497-501 and accompanying text (noting
that an important factor in determining whether property will
qualify for special tax treatment is whether payments for use of
the property are an integral part of the service contract).
Third-party ownership of the facility may also raise other issues
that will need to be addressed in the operations contract, such
as right of possession, responsibility for damage or repairs on
the owner's property, and responsibility for property taxes.

c. Sale/Leaseback

Another financing technique that allows a contracting agency to utilize private resources is the sale/leaseback arrangement. In this type of transaction, private investors purchase property from a contracting agency and immediately lease it back to the governmental unit for its use.[505] In the typical sale/leaseback transaction the contracting agency maintains control over the operation and management of the facility being built.[506] It is conceivable, however, that sale/leaseback could be used in conjunction with a contract for operation and management of a correctional or detention facility. But interest in sale/leaseback transactions in general has decreased significantly due to the numerous restrictions on tax benefits that are available to lessors who have obtained property through sale/leaseback transactions.[507]

Sale/leaseback arrangements provide many of the same benefits to a contracting agency that other forms of private lease arrangements provide.[508] For example, they provide a

---

[505] See M. Gelfand, supra note 463, at § 3:37. The lease payments generally correspond to the finance payments that are due on the property. The agreement provides a mechanism whereby the contracting agency becomes the owner of the property at the end of the lease term.

[506] District of Columbia Appropriations Hearings, supra note 466, at 296 (statement of T. Don Hutto, President, American Correctional Association, and Executive Vice-President, Corrections Corporation of America).

[507] See Corrections and the Private Sector, supra note 463, at 15 (statement of John Gillespie, Correctional Facilities Finance Specialist, Shearson Lehman/American Express).

contracting agency with a means to finance a facility that it might not otherwise be able to construct or renovate.[509] Because lease payments are subject to non-appropriation by the legislature, they are not subject to voter-referenda requirements or debt ceilings.[510] Moreover, construction costs may be reduced because the private investors do not need to abide by the same procedural and purchasing requirements as does a governmental unit, thus accelerating the construction process.[511] The contracting agency usually becomes the owner at the end of the lease term, thus allowing it to regain its capital investment.[512]

The major drawback of the sale/leaseback transaction is that, in most cases, it is no longer economically feasible. One of the main attractions of the arrangement to both the private investor and the contracting agency had been the tax benefits that accrued to the private investor and which were passed on to

---

[508] See supra notes 463-468 and accompanying text (describing advantages and disadvantages of private financing generally).

[509] See supra notes 465-466 and accompanying text (explaining why jurisdictions may not be able to construct or renovate needed facilities through traditional methods). In the past, sale/leaseback transactions have been favored by contracting agencies for financing the renovation of older facilities. Privatization of Corrections, supra note 460, at 42.

[510] See supra note 481 and accompanying text.

[511] Tolchin, Companies Easing Crowded Prisons, N.Y. Times, Feb. 17, 1985, at A29, col. 1 (providing examples of sale/leaseback transactions used by various jurisdictions).

[512] Corrections and the Private Sector, supra note 463, at 42. If the sale/leaseback transaction is so structured, then the lessor may also enjoy the benefits of capital appreciation on its property. Id.

the governmental lessee in the form of lower lease payments.[513] In addition to the general restrictions placed on deductions that are available to owners of tax-exempt-use property under the Deficit Reduction Act of 1984 (DRA) and the Tax Reform Act of 1986,[514] these legislative actions impose additional stringent restrictions on tax benefits that may accrue to owners of property acquired through sale/leaseback transactions.[515] For example, the DRA sets forth several technical rules regarding the characterization of property as tax-exempt-use property that make it even more difficult for the purchaser/lessor of sale/leaseback property to take advantage of any of the traditional benefits of property ownership.[516] In 1985, Senator D'Amato introduced the Prison Construction Privatization Act, which would have restored

---

[513] M. Gelfand, supra note 463, at § 3:37. These tax incentives acted as a federal subsidy for state and local prison construction. See Privatization of Prison Construction in New York, supra note 466, at 2 (statement of Sen. D'Amato); Staff Description, supra note 464, at 6.

[514] See supra notes 471-474 and accompanying text.

[515] Congress has also passed several other pieces of legislation that have a negative effect on tax benefits that are associated with sale/leaseback transactions. See Pollack, Sale-Leaseback Transactions Adversely Affected by a Variety of Recent Developments, 64 J. Tax'n 151, 151 (Mar. 1986).

[516] Id. at 151-53. Under the DRA's tax-exempt-use restrictions, there is a provision listing exceptions whereby 19-year real property may be excluded from the definition of tax-exempt-use property. Otherwise qualified property that was acquired by the owner as part of a sale/leaseback transaction, however, must meet further requirements before qualifying for available exemptions. Id. Other examples of especially stringent treatment for sale/leaseback property include rules regarding the computation of imputed interest, I.R.C. § 1274 (1986), and rules regarding stepped rental leases where lease payments at the end of the lease term are substantially higher than those at the beginning of the lease term. Id. § 467 (1986).

many of these tax benefits to investors who purchased correctional facilities in sale/leaseback transactions.[517] Congress never passed the bill; the lessors in these transactions therefore remain subject to restrictions imposed by the 1984 Act.

The Tax Reform Act of 1986 further diminished tax incentives for sale/leaseback investors by placing restrictions on the use of tax-exempt private-activity bonds.[518] Thus, the tax-shelter character of the sale/leaseback transaction that made it a viable private-financing technique has been removed, and there is no longer any economic incentive for the investor or the contracting agency to enter such an arrangement.[519] It is expected that sale/leaseback arrangements will be used less frequently in the future due to the negative impact that recent tax law has had on

---

[517] Staff Description, supra note 464; see Tax Treatment of Property Leased by a Tax Exempt Entity to Certain Correctional Facilities: Hearing on S. 2933 Before the Subcomm. on Taxation & Debt Management of the Comm. on Finance of the United States Senate, 98th Cong., 2d Sess. (1984). Senator D'Amato introduced the bill in an attempt to generate interest in this form of privatization; in effect, he was proposing a federal subsidy to aid state and local governments struggling to raise the capital necessary to meet the demand for prison space. Under the proposed bill, private investors who purchased qualified prisons, jails, or other incarceration facilities through a sale/leaseback transaction would again be eligible for accelerated depreciation and rehabilitation tax credits. In addition, the bill would have assured investors that, if they characterized their transaction as a lease, it would be regarded as such even if, under the tax law, the transaction would otherwise have been regarded as a conditional purchase.

[518] See supra note 464 and accompanying text (discussing in greater detail the impact of the 1986 Act on private-activity bonds).

[519] But see supra notes 511-512 and accompanying text (discussing other ways in which sale/leaseback transactions may save a governmental unit money).

this type of transaction.[520]

The sale/leaseback technique may still be used, however, by jurisdictions that have poor or non-existent bond ratings, or that for other reasons find that this type of financing is the only possible method for providing for a badly needed facility. But it is being replaced with other types of transactions that are structured in a more economically attractive manner.[521]

3.   Other Types of Financing for Incarceration Facilities

In response to the shortage of capital that is available for the construction of additional space for correctional and detention facilities, financial institutions have developed other alternative methods of financing that entail some of the same benefits and drawbacks as privatization, but which do not involve private ownership of a facility. These transactions generally have been utilized by contracting agencies that intend to operate and manage their own facilities, but they can also be used in conjunction with contracts for the private operation and management of a facility.

The lease-purchase agreement is an example of an alternative finance technique that is receiving a great deal of attention from contracting agencies throughout the country.[522] Under the

---

520 Privatization of Prison Construction in New York, supra note 466, at 3 (statement of Sen. D'Amato).

521 Cf. Uhlfelder & Hanlon, supra note 464, at 135-36 (noting that the loss of tax incentives will probably result in the restructuring of some private-financing transactions).

typical lease-purchase agreement, a special legal entity, such as a public building authority or a nonprofit corporation, issues to private investors certificates of participation or revenue bonds on behalf of a contracting agency.[523] Because the bonds are issued on behalf of a governmental entity, investors receive tax-free interest on their investment.[524] The money that is raised from these sales is used by the special entity to finance the needed construction.[525] The special entity is considered the nominal owner of the facility. The entity transfers all of the obligations of ownership to a trustee through whom all subsequent transactions are carried out.[526] The entity then leases the new space to the contracting agency, which agrees to make monthly payments, subject to non-appropriation by the jurisdiction's legislature, until the bond issue is paid. At the end of this period, the contracting agency receives title to the facility.

Lease-purchase agreements provide many of the same benefits as the privatization alternative does. Because lease payments

---

[522] See National Criminal Justice Ass'n, supra note 465, at 3 (noting increasing popularity of various types of lease-purchase arrangements); Privatization of Corrections, supra note 460, at 142-43 (providing examples of jurisdictions that have used or are considering using lease-purchase arrangement to finance correctional or detention facilities).

[523] Privatization of Corrections, supra note 460, at 43.

[524] See E.F. Hutton, Innovative Alternatives to Traditional Jail Financing 6 (undated) (pointing out that, as with municipal bonds, interest on bonds that are used in lease-purchase agreement is tax exempt).

[525] Privatization of Corrections, supra note 460, at 43.

[526] Id. at 45-46.

are subject to non-appropriation by the legislature, they are not classified as long-term debt of the jurisdiction and are not subject to statutory or constitutional debt ceilings. Further, because the bonds are issued as part of a lease-purchase transaction and are not secured by the taxing authority of the jurisdiction, they are not generally subject to voter-referenda requirements. Like privatization, a lease-purchase arrangement may allow a contracting agency to construct necessary space more quickly than is possible using traditional methods of financing.

As with the privatization alternative, however, a fixed-rate lease-purchase arrangement in most circumstances would be more expensive than the traditional general-obligation bond would be. Bonds that are issued pursuant to a lease-purchase arrangement are not considered as secure an investment as general-obligation bonds because they are not backed by the full faith and credit of the jurisdiction on whose behalf they are issued. Therefore, interest on a lease-purchase issue may be as much as a full percentage point higher than interest on general-obligation bonds that are issued at the same time. Some jurisdictions have begun to use variable-rate demand instruments in connection with a lease-purchase transaction. The initial interest rate on such securities may be much lower than on even a comparable issue of general-obligation bonds, but jurisdictions that are considering this option should become fully aware of the potential risks should interest rates rise.

Alternate types of financing allow a contracting agency to construct a facility when it might not otherwise have the funds to do so. As is true of the privatization alternative, however, appropriations must be made from the jurisdiction's current operating budget or a source of revenue other than property taxes must be found to cover monthly lease payments. In essence, most alternative financing techniques are methods of circumventing checks on government spending, and do not actually remedy the shortage of capital that is available to fund needed correctional and detention facilities.

4. Conclusion

Many jurisdictions are under increasing pressure to enlarge prison and jail capacities. They are also under pressure to decrease their spending and balance their budgets. These competing obligations have prompted the development of transactions that utilize private-sector capital to finance incarceration facilities. Privatization may, in some cases, be the only solution for a jurisdiction that must increase space but has insufficient revenue or borrowing capacity to finance the facility. Contracting agencies should be aware, however, that such transactions merely postpone the cost of a new facility. The contracting agency will still need to find the funds that are necessary to service the private debt. Moreover, privatization provides a means to thwart the will of citizens who may have already defeated a voter referendum or supported a constitutional or statutory debt-ceiling requirement.

Additional concerns come into play when a jurisdiction

chooses to contract out for the private ownership and operation of a correctional facility. Perhaps the most important of these concerns is the jurisdiction's ability to regain possession and/or ownership of the facility. A jurisdiction that has relinquished both the ownership and operation of a facility must provide in the contract that it has the right to take possession of and operate the facility. Otherwise, it will risk being unable to replace an inadequate provider because that provider would maintain control of the physical plant.

There are several ways in which a jurisdiction can approach the structuring of a finance plan. It may wish to go to a financial advisor itself and have a financial plan arranged prior to circulating an RFP to potential contractors. The advantage of this approach would be that the jurisdiction would be sure to have a plan that is most favorable to it. It may be more efficient, however, to allow the private contractor to procure its own financing plan, subject to broad outlines that are set forth in the RFP and final approval by the jurisdiction or contracting agency. The jurisdiction will thus save the time and expense of putting together its own financing plan. If a jurisdiction chooses this approach, however, it should make certain that the RFP requires the private contractor to submit a detailed plan that includes information sufficient to allow for a knowledgeable evaluation. The plan should be reviewed by the jurisdiction's own experts, to ensure that its own interest will be well served by the plan.

Model Contract Provision:

     The private contractor will provide financing for the facility under this contract in accordance with the financing plan that has been approved by the contracting agency. Any financial obligation of the contracting agency under this plan is subject to the annual appropriation of funds by the legislature.[527]

     If this contract is terminated at any time under any of the termination clauses provided in Section 7, the contracting agency shall have the right to take possession of the facility immediately for the purpose of operating the facility. It shall also have the option to repurchase the facility within ninety (90) days of the termination of the contract.

----

[527] See Model Contract § 3(A) (Term); Model Statute § 3 (Contract Term and Renewal).

Section 2(B): Physical Plant

Commentary:

Both the RFP and the contract should set forth minimum standards governing the design and construction of the physical plant when the private contractor is responsible for providing a new or additional facility, or plans to renovate or convert an existing facility. The American Correctional Association (ACA) has formulated comprehensive standards governing the physical plant.[528] The ACA Standards address basic questions -- for example, how many inmates should be allowed per unit,[529] what amount of space should be provided for each prisoner,[530] and how many and what types of sanitation facilities should be available for inmate and staff use.[531] These Standards should be incorporated in both the RFP and the contract to ensure that the private contractor provide an acceptable facility.

The RFP and the contract should also require that private contractors comply with state and local building codes. Under the ACA Standards, compliance with state and local codes is not mandatory, only essential.[532] Most contracting agencies,

---

[528] American Correctional Association, Standards for Adult Correctional Institutions, Standards 2-4127 to 2-4161 (2d ed. 1981 & Supp. 1986).

[529] ACA Standards 2-4127 and 2-4128.

[530] ACA Standards 2-4123 to 2-4132, 2-4135, and 2-4157 to 2-4159.

[531] ACA Standards 2-4130 to 2-4132, 2-4135, and 2-4144.

however, require the contractor to comply with all applicable building codes.[533] Additionally, the contracting agency should include any other architectural standards that are essential to ensure that the structure adequately meet the jurisdiction's needs. A contracting agency may include specific requirements relating, for example, to the size of the facility or the type of inmates the facility will house.[534]

In addition to listing standards, the RFP should require potential contractors to submit a detailed description of the physical plant as a part of their proposal, to be incorporated in the contract, preferably including architectural designs as well as plans and specifications.[535] This would enable contracting agencies to evaluate contractor compliance with minimum

---

[532] See Model Contract § 3(F) (Operating Standards and Accreditation) (explaining distinction between mandatory and essential compliance with ACA Standards).

[533] See INS RFP at 21, § I(C)(5)(G); 1985 Kentucky RFP at 30-3, § 30.410. The recent report issued by the Council of State Governments also recommends that private contractors be required to comply with all applicable local and state codes. See The Council of State Governments and the Urban Institute, Issues in Contracting for the Private Operation of Prisons and Jails xiii (1987) [hereinafter CSG Report].

[534] See CSG Report, supra note 533, at 54, 61 (noting that maximum-, medium-, and minimum-security facilities require different types of architectural features, and these features should be spelled out in RFP and contract).

[535] See, e.g., INS RFP at 97, § I(M) (including physical plant in "Evaluation Factors for Award"); 1985 Kentucky RFP at 60-1, § 60.000 (requiring description of physical plant); Texas RFP at 2, § 2 (requiring prospective contractors to submit designs and specifications, including information regarding size of compound, nature of exterior and interior security program, extent of area devoted to programs and services, and type of construction).

standards. It will also encourage prospective contractors to utilize the most efficient and cost-saving design and construction techniques available. Proponents of privatization in the corrections field often argue that private-sector competition will encourage the development and utilization of cost-saving innovations in the field. The design of a facility, particularly a new facility, is one area in which the incorporation of new techniques in a privatization contract may result in savings for the contracting agency.[536] In addition, new construction techniques may save construction time, thereby further reducing the cost of the facility.[537]

Another important issue that will arise regarding the provision of a prison or jail facility is the location of the facility. In some cases, the government may already have acquired or selected the site, in which case the contracting agency will need to provide in the RFP that the facility shall be constructed on that site. Alternatively, a jurisdiction may choose to allow the private contractor to select and acquire the

_____

[536] For example, the cost of operating a facility, particularly a secure facility, depends to a certain extent on how efficiently the design utilizes space. A design that minimizes the use of multiple layers and instead uses configuration to provide security may result in substantial savings for a contracting agency. Privatization of Prison Construction in New York, supra note 466, at 16-17 (statement of Paul Silver, architect, Gruzen Partnership). Use of more efficient materials may also result in overall cost savings. Id.

[537] See generally DeWitt, New Construction Methods for Correctional Facilities, NIJ Construction Bulletin (March 1986) (providing various sources of information on new cost-saving construction techniques available to state and local contracting agencies).

site for the facility, within general guidelines set forth in the RFP.[538] In these situations, site selection requires greater attention. Because this is an issue that affects the interests not only of the contracting parties but also of local communities, however, it is a matter that should be addressed by statute, rather than left to negotiation between the parties. The Model Statute sets forth the criteria for the evaluation of sites for private facilities and approval by the contracting agency and the legislature, including the consideration of community and local-government opinion.[539] The contract should therefore incorporate the site that has been selected through this process.

Model Contract Provision:

> The contractor shall provide a facility in accordance with the final architectural designs and the final plans and specifications that have been [will be] submitted by the contractor [by (date)] and approved by the contracting agency. The facility shall conform to all standards set forth in the contract, including all applicable ACA Standards regarding the physical plant. Compliance with all applicable state and local building codes, including [list, if desired], in accordance with ACA Standard 2-4153, is mandatory. In the event that there is a conflict among state, local, and/or national codes, the more stringent standard(s) shall apply.

---

[538] See, e.g., Texas RFP at 1, § 1.

[539] See Model Statute § 2 (Site Selection).

Section 3: General Contract Terms

Section 3(A): Term

Commentary:

The term of a contract will vary in accordance with a wide variety of factors, including the type and scope of services provided by the private contractor and whether the contractor will build a new prison facility or simply occupy an existing facility. These factors determine whether the contracting parties will choose a short-term (one-to-three-year) or long-term (ten-to-twenty-year) arrangement. Thus, for example, the Bay County Contract has a twenty-year term and provides for the contruction of a new facility.[540] The Santa Fe Contract, on the other hand, has a three-year term and provides for the use of an existing facility.[541]

The term of the contract should be determined in light of several considerations, many of which will be unique to each contract. A uniform concern for all parties, however, should be to maximize competition. More specifically, if privatization is deemed desirable, market forces should be used to create a

---

[540] Bay County Contract at 25, § 7. It appears that this 20-year term has caused many problems for the Bay County community, and even the National Sheriffs' Association has come out against this extended long-term provision. National Sheriffs' Association Position on Privatization of Adult Local Detention Facilities, National Sheriff, June-July 1985, at 38.

[541] Santa Fe Contract at 3, § 2.1.

competitive environment in which private contractors attempt to provide the best <u>and</u> most economical corrections.[542] The term of the contract should therefore be long enough for the private contractor to recoup its front-end capital investment and become economically efficient, and yet short enough to ensure flexibility to deal with new problems, prevent market entrenchment, and encourage other contractors to enter the market on a competitive basis.

These issues will arise in the renewal and bidding contexts as well as in negotiating for term. For example, a private contractor who wins the initial contract will be in a stronger position to compete for future contracts than its competitors will be. This private contractor may own the prison facility and have a lease arrangement as well as a management relationship with the contracting agency, or it may have employed, and created loyalties with, the only experienced corrections labor force in the community.[543] Thus, although there is a real danger that a state-sanctioned monopoly might develop, it need not be inevitable provided that the contracting agency organize its bidding to encourage real competition.[544] The contracting agency, for instance, can reduce the concern that entrenchment

---

[542] <u>See</u> C. Ring, <u>supra</u> note 484, at 24 ("The <u>raison d'etre</u> for virtually all proposals . . . is that the introduction of competitive forces will produce superior services at less cost."); Note, <u>supra</u> note 408, at 368.

[543] <u>See</u> Note, <u>supra</u> note 408, at 357.

[544] <u>See</u> O. Williamson, The Economic Institutions of Capitalism 329 (1985).

will occur and encourage competition even when it leases the facility from a private contractor by executing a lease that is separate from the contract for the management and operation of the facility. Thus, theoretically, a different private contractor could be hired to run the prison at some later time without affecting the underlying lease.[545]

The benefits and drawbacks of both short- and long-term contracts have been discussed at length elsewhere.[546] The advantages of the short-term contract lie primarily in the triggering of competitive bidding on a fairly frequent basis.[547] Arguably, frequent competition creates incentives to provide low-cost, high-quality care in an efficient manner because the contractors will not want to risk losing the contract. Short-term contracts will also help prevent cronyism and market entrenchment as long as the bidding process is conducted properly. In addition, short-term contracts reduce the need for the parties to anticipate all of the issues and problems that might arise in the future. Finally, short-term contracts

---

[545] See Note, supra note 408, at 370 n.102.

[546] See CSG Report, supra note 533, at 98-100; C. Ring, supra note 484, at 44; Hackett, Hatry, Levinson, Allen, Chi & Feigenbaum, Contracting for the Operation of Prisons and Jails, NIJ Research in Brief 5 (June 1987) [hereinafter NIJ Report]; see also Privatization of Corrections, supra note 460, at 37-48; Note, supra note 408, at 368-69.

[547] There are, of course, significant costs that are associated with frequent rebidding. The bidding process requires a commitment of time, money, and personnel from both the contractor and the contracting agency. See NIJ Report, supra note 546, at 5. These costs, as well as the psychological costs related to business uncertainty and instability, must be factored into the decisionmaking process.

may be necessary because many contracting agencies are subject to "availability of funds" restrictions that prohibit contracting beyond a certain budget period.[548]

Nevertheless, short-term contracts may pose many problems. They may increase the contractor's risk in private management -- particularly with respect to private construction and ownership. Specifically, contractors may be concerned that their innovation and investment will not pay for themselves before the contract period is over. They may thus be less inclined to bid for the contract, thereby reducing the benefits of competition. Short-term contracts may also help to hide abuses that would not manifest themselves until after the contract term had elapsed and the private contractor had left the facility.[549] This problem does not necessarily require a longer contract period, however. The contracting agency could, for example, require a hold-over-period performance bond instead, to make sure that funds would be available for such problems.

The negative effects of the short-term contract are less severe when construction of a facility is not an aspect of the privatization project. When construction is a part of the project, however, separate construction and management contracts should be used. Under this arrangement, the operation of the facility can be rebid in the short term without any interference

_____

[548] CSG Report, supra note 533, at 98-100; C. Ring, supra note 484, at 44; see Model Contract § 2(A) (Private Financing); Model Statute § 3 (Contract Term and Renewal).

[549] Cf. Note, supra note 408, at 368-69.

with the underlying lease arrangement.[550] Thus, long-term lease

agreements can still be used in the limited area of construction,

so that innovation and investment in this area are not

sacrificed.

Many problems that are associated with short-term contracts

can be solved with longer terms. Long-term contracts can reduce

bidding costs, increase the likelihood that the private

contractor will recoup its investment, and create market

stability that can affect the contractor's financial prospects

favorably.[551] In addition, continuity in management may benefit

the prison population and the neighboring community that provides

labor and services to the prison. A constant turnover in

management could cause too much flux in the system.[552] Some of

the benefits of a long-term contract can be achieved, however, by

using a short-term contract with a renewal provision that affords

the contractor some of the security and stability that it

_____

[550] It must be considered, however, how well the
privatization arrangement will work with a new third party
managing the prison. At the very least, careful planning will be
required in determining the contracting agency's right as lessor
to sublease the facility to a new contractor.

[551] CSG Report, supra note 533, at 98-100; C. Ring, supra
note 484, at 44.

[552] CSG Report, supra note 533, at 98. Frequent management
changes could also work against solving the prison's problems.
Contractors, faced with a short-term contract and the risk of
nonrenewal, might cut their losses and make minimal efforts to
improve prison conditions, thus continually passing on problems
to new contractors. That is, no contractor will have sufficient
tenure under the contract to be held accountable for solving
problems. Thus, in this example, competition will have worked
results contrary to those sought: high-quality care for inmates
at the lowest reasonable cost.

needs.[553]

Thus, the contracting parties should seek a workable balance between the competing benefits and drawbacks of the long-term and short-term contracts. The three-year term recommended in the Model Contract provision reflects the positions that -- considering the importance of the contractor's accountability -- the short-term contract will more satisfactorily balance the needs and interests of all of the parties.

Model Contract Provision:

> **The term of this contract shall be for a period of three (3) years commencing on [time and date] and terminating on [time and date], subject to the availability of funds and unless earlier terminated in accordance with the relevant provisions of this contract.**

---

[553] See Model Contract § 3(B) (Renewal).

Section 3(B): Renewal

Commentary:

The Renewal provision, like the Term provision, should be closely examined and carefully negotiated by the parties. There is wide variation among renewal provisions in existing contracts.[554] While the terms of a renewal provision will necessarily vary among contracts due to differing individual circumstances, some general recommendations can be made with regard to the issues that should be addressed in this provision and the factors that contracting agencies should consider in addressing these issues.

The renewal provision should address the number and duration of renewal periods allowed under the contract. The parties should consider these issues in light of the discussion regarding length of contract term.[555] With regard to the duration of renewal periods, shorter, rather than longer, periods are most consistent with the overall purpose of the renewal option. Renewal periods of one to two years will serve to maintain incentive for efficient contractor performance and preserve the contracting agency's flexibility in changing contractors, while providing a mechanism whereby a successful contract arrangement

---

[554] See CSG Report, _supra_ note 533, at 99 (describing how various contracting agencies have addressed the issues of term, renewal, and price adjustment in contract provisions).

[555] See Model Contract § 3(A) (Term).

may be extended without incurring the expense associated with the competitive bidding process.[556] The parties should also note that most renewal periods of long duration would be subject to non-appropriation by the legislature.[557]

It is also recommended that the contract limit the number of renewal options and require the contracting agency to open the bidding to all competitors after a specified period of time.[558] Again, the number of options should be determined after the parties have balanced the considerations discussed in reference to shorter or longer terms.[559] The parties should also keep in mind that laws in their jurisdiction may require competitive bidding of government contracts within a specified period of time.[560]

---

[556] Cf. CSG Report, supra note 533, at 98-100 (discussing benefits and drawbacks of shorter versus longer contract terms); C. Ring, supra note 484, at 44 (discussing implications of shorter and longer contract terms in context of statutory provisions). Contracting agencies should also keep in mind, however, the disadvantages of short renewal periods discussed in the earlier section on contract term. See Model Contract § 3(A) (Term).

[557] See CSG Report, supra note 533, at 98 (noting that state/local legislature may not have the authority to appropriate funds for government contracts beyond the biennial budget period); Privatization of Corrections, supra note 460, at 77 (noting that state statutes generally limit government contracts to period of one to three years).

[558] This recommendation is in accordance with the Council of State Governments' recommendation that contracts limit automatic renewals to five years. CSG Report, supra note 533, at 100.

[559] See Model Contract § 3(A) (Term).

[560] See C. Ring, supra note 484, at 44 (citing statutes in New Mexico and Tennessee limiting duration of contracts for private prisons); Model Statute § 3 (Contract Term and Renewal).

The Model Contract provides for renewal at the option of the contracting agency on like terms and conditions, but allows for renegotiation of the contract price upon renewal. Such a provision ensures that the private contractor receives a fair price for the required services throughout the duration of the contract.[561] This benefits both the contractor and the contracting agency.[562] Setting a cap on the maximum price increase allowable under the contract is strongly recommended, however, to ensure that contracting agencies will not be forced to agree to artificially high price increases. In addition, or as an alternative to price renegotiation, the parties may want to include an automatic cost-of-living increase based on an agreed upon measure, such as the Consumer Price Index.[563] This price increase would take effect periodically throughout the duration of the contract, according to the terms negotiated by the parties.

The parties should also agree on a timetable to ensure that the private contractor will have adequate notice of the contracting agency's intent to exercise its renewal option and ample opportunity to respond with a price proposal when appropriate, if it intends to remain under contract. In

---

[561] Many multi-year contracts provide for adjustment of the contract price at some interval throughout the contract term. See CSG Report, supra note 533, at 98 (stating that price of multi-year contracts is usually adjusted annually).

[562] McAfee, supra note 402, at 859 (providing historical background to illustrate that both parties benefit from contract that allows for necessary price adjustments).

[563] See CSG Report, supra note 533, at 98.

negotiating the length of the notice period, the parties will want to ensure that the contracting agency will have enough time to make the transition to another contractor, if that becomes necessary. If the private contractor does not notify the contracting agency of its intent regarding renewal within a reasonable period of time, the contracting agency should be free to rebid the contract and the contractor's retainage account may be forfeited to the contracting agency.

Model Contract Provision:

An option to renew this contract for an additional [number] (___) year term shall be exercisable by the contracting agency on like terms and conditions except with respect to compensation paid to the contractor. The contracting agency may exercise its option to renew the contract [number] (___) times, after which the contracting agency will reopen the contract for competitive bidding.

Compensation shall be negotiated between the parties before each renewal period. The price shall not increase more than [number] (___) percent over any one renewal period, nor shall the price rise more than [number] (___) percent over the entire duration of the contract.

Should the private contractor desire to renew this contract, it shall notify the contracting agency in writing and submit a written price proposal at least [number] (___) days prior to the termination date of this contract. Should the private contractor not desire to renew this contract, it shall notify the contracting agency in writing no later than [number] (___) days prior to the termination date of this contract. Failure to so notify shall be a valid basis for forfeiture of the retainage account balance then held by the contracting agency and subsequent retainage amounts, until the termination of this contract.

Section 3(C): Compensation

Commentary:

Compensation provisions must explicitly set forth the following items: which services are being contracted out (e.g., supervision, medical care, transportation, rehabilitation, education, and training of inmates, construction of a facility, or maintenance of a facility); how much will be paid for these services (e.g., whether the contractor must keep its cost below present cost levels and whether and on what conditions services may be subcontracted out); how payment for those services will be calculated (e.g., under a flat-fee or per-diem arrangement); when payment will be made during the term of the contract; and how payments may be adjusted during the term of the contract.

As several commentators have noted with respect to the first item, for instance, many prison contracts have failed adequately to specify the cost elements of the contract.[564] This failure can result in considerable confusion as well as unanticipated and increased costs to both parties. Therefore, the contract must be quite specific regarding which party is responsible for which services and costs that are associated with operating and maintaining the facility.[565]

_____

[564] See, e.g., CSG Report, supra note 533, at 85-87; NIJ Report, supra note 546, at 5.

[565] The issue of "hidden costs" must also be addressed by the parties. See, e.g., Durham, supra note 434, at 70 (stating that "there are hidden costs [in privatization of corrections]

The contractor's compensation will depend, of course, on the number and types of services that it provides. Undoubtedly, most contract negotiations will begin with the premise that privatization will cost less than the contracting agency currently spends on incarceration. This premise follows from what advocates of privatization have been claiming all along: Competition will produce superior services at less cost.[566] Therefore, to the extent that the provision of services is comparable, the contracting agency's costs should be a starting point for deciding contract price.[567]

An important and complex issue is how payment for services will be calculated. Most existing contracts use some variation of a per-diem (i.e., cost per inmate day) compensation scheme, rather than a flat-fee arrangement.[568] This choice is preferable

that have yet to receive adequate attention"). Hidden costs are all items that are associated with the contracting out of the facility but which are not apparent from the face of the contract between the contracting agency and the private contractor. Such costs may include, but are not limited to: the cost of monitoring compliance with the contract; the cost of attorney, consulting, and other professional fees for developing and executing contracts as well as for securing approval of site selection by the legislature; the costs that are associated with increased liability resulting from the contractor's lack of immunity in situations in which the contracting agency would have been fully protected; and new layers of liability that arise from the contracting-out arrangement, such as liability arising from the agency's failure to monitor the facility adequately or from third-party-beneficiary contract claims that are available to inmates and the public.

[566] See C. Ring, supra note 484, at 24-26, 34-38.

[567] The contractor's promise of higher quality care should also be factored into price negotiations.

[568] CSG Report, supra note 533, at 83; NIJ Report, supra note 546, at 5; C. Ring, supra note 484, at 31.

if the parties want to have the flexibility of using contract
cost fluctuations to keep costs in line with actual
expenses.[569]   That is, contract costs consist of both fixed and
variable costs. Fixed costs do not vary in relation to the
inmate population, and include such items as capital costs (e.g.,
building improvements) and some operating and management costs
(e.g., minimum required labor force). By contrast, variable
costs will increase as the inmate population grows and decrease
as population shrinks. The parties may want to take advantage of
these fluctuations; they will therefore need to choose a
compensation scheme that is sophisticated enough to accommodate
all of the necessary variables.[570]

---

[569]   Because these cost fluctuations can include increases
as well as decreases, the contracting agency must protect itself
by placing a cap on the number of inmates for which it will pay
the private contractor. Unexpected increases in the inmate
population can result in huge cost overruns. See Tolchin,
Privately Operated Prison in Tennessee Reports $200,000 in Cost
Overruns, N.Y. Times, May 21, 1985, at A14, col. 1 (noting that
increase in inmate population in Hamilton County, Tennessee
resulted in 1985 cost overruns of at least $200,000 at CCA's
Silverdale facility); see also 2 "Model" Prisons, supra note 433,
at 4D, col. 4 (reporting in 1988 the finding of Hamilton County
auditor's cost study that CCA operation of the Silverdale
facility not only did not save the taxpayers money, but it also
cost the county more than when the county ran the facility). But
see Morgan, Hamilton Officials, CCA Head Say Author Twisted
Information, Chattanooga Times, May 21, 1988, at B2, col. 1
(stating that auditor denies accuracy of comments in 2 "Model"
Prisons). These persistent difficulties at one facility may
indicate that the problems inherent in private incarceration are
intractable.

[570]   The parties' ability to take advantage of these
variable costs will be determined by the type of cost and the
speed with which the contractor can respond to inmate population
changes. If the population decreases, for example, it will be
much easier to reduce weekly food expenses than it will be to
reduce labor costs.

A variable per-diem arrangement, with established minimum
and maximum inmate population levels, can account for cost
fluctuations. Under this scheme, contractors are paid a
predetermined fee based on the cost per inmate day. A maximum
population level is established to prevent contractors from
increasing the number of inmates and/or the duration of their
confinement in order to receive greater compensation.[571] A
minimum population level is also established to provide the
contractor with a guaranteed income.[572]

The flat-fee arrangement, which sets the price at the outset
of the contract term by predicting cost and adding a profit
margin, is unsuited for taking advantage of cost fluctuations.
This arrangement does, however, offer the contracting parties
security and stability because the negotiated amount cannot be
changed during the course of the contract. In addition, the
flat-fee approach protects the contracting agency from future
cost overruns.[573]

---

[571] See CSG Report, supra note 533, at 84; see also supra
notes 170-210 and accompanying text (discussing constitutionality
of delegating quasi-judicial functions to private contractor);
Model Statute § 11 (Nondelegability of Contracting Agency's
Authority).

[572] But see infra note 850 and accompanying text
(discussing potential danger in parole context arising from
guaranteed minimum income, and suggesting solution that
contractor's employees not participate in parole
recommendations). The CSG Report recommends a hybrid approach,
using a variable daily-rate system. Under this arrangement, the
daily rate paid to the contractor decreases when the inmate
population increases because "certain fixed costs don't change
and . . . some economies of scale [are] available to
contractors." CSG Report, supra note 533, at 90.

[573] Or perhaps it will not. It is arguable that the

The contracting parties must also address the timing and frequency of payments under the contract.[574] Some contracting agencies will be bound by a prompt-payment statute, which will serve as adequate protection for the private contractor who is concerned about prompt and regular payment.[575] Otherwise, the parties will have to negotiate these terms.

Another question concerns provision for adjusting the contract price during the term of the contract. Reopening the contract should be a highly unusual occurrence, limited only to unforeseen circumstances. Thus, with the exception of annual cost-of-living adjustments, the provision should be a strict one.[576] Price-adjustment provisions become increasingly important as the term of the contract increases. Therefore, long-term contracts may require more than an annual-adjustment provision. It may be necessary to provide for price negotiations

---

contracting agency will have to pay cost overruns if the private contractor cannot, such as if the contractor is bankrupt. In that case, the contracting agency will have no choice but to reassume operation of the facility, with its attendant costs.

[574] See CSG Report, supra note 533, at 85; NIJ Report, supra note 546, at 5.

[575] CSG Report, supra note 533, at 88; Privatization of Corrections, supra note 460, at 31.

[576] Annual adjustments are commonly contracted for and permit increases based on some variation of the Consumer Price Index. CSG Report, supra note 533, at 88; C. Ring, supra note 484, at 31. For their mutual protection, the parties might consider including a provision that sets both a floor and a cap on inflation adjustments. See, e.g., Bay County Contract at 21, § 6.7(A) (setting a 2½% floor and a 5% cap); see also Tenn. Code Ann. § 41-24-104(b)(1) (Cum. Supp. 1987) ("If any adjustment is made pursuant to terms of the contract, it shall be applied to total payments made to the contractor for the previous contract year and shall not exceed the percentage of change in the average consumer price index . . . .").

and adjustment at some set point during the term of the contract to allow both parties the opportunity to change price terms to reflect current economic conditions.

Model Contract Provision:

(1) Per-Diem Rate

The contracting agency shall pay the contractor every [number] (___) days (payment period) a per-diem charge of [number] (___) dollars per inmate day (per-diem rate). For purposes of establishing an inmate day, the inmate's arrival and departure days will count as one inmate day. On or before [number] (___) days after the payment period, the contractor shall provide the contracting agency with a statement showing the number of inmate days charged for the prior payment period.

(2) Minimum and Maximum Inmate Population

The contracting agency shall pay the contractor a minimum of [number] (___) dollars per payment period, which shall be determined by multiplying the cost per inmate day times [number] (___) (guaranteed minimum inmate population). In no event shall the contracting agency pay the contractor in excess of [number] (___) dollars, which shall be determined by multiplying the cost per inmate day times [number] (___) (maximum inmate population).

(3) Annual Adjustments to Per-Diem Rate

The per-diem rate shall be adjusted at the beginning of each fiscal year. The adjustment shall be based on increases or decreases in the Consumer Price Index. The adjustments, which are intended to reflect changes in the purchasing power of a given amount of money expressed in dollars, shall not be greater than five percent (5%).[577]

---

[577] This provision is derived from the Bay County Contract at 21, § 6.7(A) (providing minimum and maximum adjustments of $2\frac{1}{2}$% and 5%, respectively).

(4) Unforeseen-Circumstances Adjustment

Although the parties intend to fix the per-diem rate subject to annual adjustments, the parties recognize that unforeseen circumstances may arise during the term of this contract. Therefore, the parties agree that within [number] (___) days after the end of the [ordinal number] full fiscal year of the term of this contract, either party may elect to request in writing a change in the per-diem rate to reflect any change in the cost of operating and maintaining the facility.[578] If there is an irreconcilable breakdown in negotiations, the parties should refer to Section 7 of this contract for termination procedures.

---

[578] This provision is derived from the Bay County Contract at 22-23, § 6.7(C). Such a provision would be necessary only in a long-term contract. The Bay County Contract, for example, provides for a 20-year term.

Section 3(D): Performance Bond

Commentary:

The Model Contract provides for a performance bond to ensure that the private contractor comply with the terms of the contract and that the contracting agency have adequate funds in the event that the contractor is unable to perform. The performance-bond requirement imposes an additional cost on the private contractor that it will undoubtedly pass on to the contracting agency. Thus, the contracting agency will need to assess whether a bond is warranted in its particular situation.[579] With a performance bond, the contracting agency will be protected in the event of bankruptcy, default, strikes, or takeover by or transition to a new firm. The performance-bond provision should specify a dollar amount that will adequately cover the contracting agency's costs if these events occur, including transitional costs related to hiring a new firm to provide services or transportation costs of transferring the prisoners to a different facility.

The formula for determining the amount of the performance bond will vary with the needs of the particular facility. Some contracts impose a flat rate for the duration of the contract,[580]

---

[579]   See CSG Report, supra note 533, at 91-94 (recommending performance bond to protect government when benefit exceeds cost of bond); NIJ Report, supra note 546, at 5 (suggesting use of performance bond if added protection to the government is worth the cost of the bond).

[580]   E.g., Santa Fe Contract at 23, § 7.4 (charging flat fee of $325,000).

while others employ a per-diem formula that multiplies the number of inmates by the rate charged per inmate per day.[581] Whichever method is used, the contracting agency must ensure that the bond be posted for the duration of the contract and, if not, that it be subject to renewal. Furthermore, the contracting agency should require that its approval of the bond term and conditions be obtained before the contract is executed.

Model Contract Provision:

> **A performance bond in the amount of [number] (___) dollars (or [number] (___) percent of the contract price) is required to assure the contractor's faithful performance of the specifications and conditions of this contract. The bond is required throughout the term of this contract. The terms and conditions of the bond must be approved by the contracting agency, and such approval is a condition precedent to this contract taking effect.**

---

[581] See CSG Report, supra note 533, at 92 ("the State of Kentucky contract contains a provision requiring a performance bond 'equal to 70% X 200 (inmates) X 365 (days) X rate per inmate per day'").

Section 3(E): Indemnification, Immunity, and Insurance

1.   Indemnification and Immunity

Commentary:

The goal of the Model Contract's Indemnification section is to hold the private contractor _fully_ accountable for its acts. From the contracting agency's point of view, it is essential that it not be held liable for the actions of the contractor. Indeed, the cost effectiveness of prison and jail privatization would be cast in doubt if this were not the case. Accordingly, the Model Contract provides that the private contractor must indemnify the contracting agency if the agency is held liable for the actions or omissions of the private contractor. This indemnification should encompass liability arising out of tort, contract, or civil-rights actions.[582] To guarantee this indemnification, the

---

[582]   Such actions pose the risk of substantial financial loss. _See_, _e.g._, CSG Report, _supra_ note 533, at 27 (stating that "one of the most serious questions on the agenda of state and local governments today is that of government liability and the inability to adequately insure (at a reasonable price) against massive judgments"); Report of the Private Prison Task Force, General Assembly of the Commonwealth of Pennsylvania, Joint State Government Commission 35 (1987) ("It is not uncommon for [attorneys' fees arising out of civil-rights] litigation to exceed six and occasionally seven figures.") (quoting statement of Stefan Presser, Legal Director, ACLU of Pennsylvania, to the Pennsylvania House Judiciary Committee, Mar. 28, 1985); Woolley, Prisons for Profit: Policy Considerations for Government Officials, 90 Dick. L. Rev. 307, 330 (1985) (stating that section 1983 litigation costs are commonly in excess of six-figure amount) (quoting S. Presser, Legal Director of ACLU of Pennsylvania); C. Thomas & L. Calvert-Hanson, Evaluating Civil Liability Risks in "Privatized" Correctional Facilities 22 (1986)

Model Contract requires the contractor to purchase sufficient

insurance to indemnify the contracting agency fully for any

(unpublished manuscript) ("[T]he litigation costs alone can be substantial -- especially when plaintiff attorney fees are recovered under the fairly liberal interpretations being accorded 42 U.S.C. § 1988."). The need for indemnification of the contracting agency has been generally recognized. Comment, Private Prisons, 36 Emory L.J. 253, 260 (1987) (stating that the "issue of overriding importance to state and local governments considering privatization . . . is whether the government will also be held liable in civil suits brought by inmates against the private prison operators"); see also National Criminal Justice Ass'n, supra note 465, at 12-13 (noting that at least three states have required private contractors to purchase insurance and indemnify the government for liability arising from prison operations, but questioning legality of shifting liability and heavy economic burden it places on contractor which "could inhibit the [contractor's] competitive edge"); C. Ring, supra note 484, at 46 (stating that governments must "make sure that the contractors have adequate insurance to protect themselves and the sponsoring government in the event of a suit or other claims for compensation"); Comment, supra, at 29 (noting that, "[w]hile indemnification is not the perfect answer, it is the best available option to insure against the costs of a negative judgment; the contractor must have adequate self-insurance or outside coverage"). Corrections Corporation of America also recognizes the crucial role that indemnification plays in obtaining contracts. 2 "Model" Prisons, supra note 433. In fact, CCA promises that it "will protect every political figure associated with the prison system by means of a multi-million dollar insurance policy which will be sufficient, [company chairman] Beasley says, to finance all litigation, pay all claims and judgments, and in general insulate those officials from personal liability." Id. Officials involved with both the Hamilton County, Tennessee and Bay County, Florida contracts cite "fear of lawsuits" as the main reason for negotiating and contracting with CCA. Id. (reporting on comments made by Chattanooga, Tenn. County Executive Dalton Roberts and former Bay County, Fla. Commission Chairwoman Helen Ingram). But see Morgan, supra note 569 (reporting that Dalton Roberts now denies having made this statement). One reporter wrote that, within a year of the September 1984 Hamilton County contract date, CCA failed to comply with its promise to supply a $25-million insurance policy. Davis, CCA Falls Short on Accreditation, Insurance Vows, Tennessean, May 16, 1988, at 4E, col. 1 [hereinafter CCA Falls Short]. The reporter stated that, because such a policy was "too expensive," CCA unilaterally decided instead to keep a $5-million escrow account to cover its liability. Id. The Hamilton County Contract was amended on August 18, 1986 to reduce general liability insurance to $5 million.

possible liability arising out of the contractor's operation of the prison or jail.

The Immunity section of the Model Contract raises the question of whether contractors should be extended the same immunity defenses that are available to public actors, and thus presents substantial issues regarding the rights of prisoners and detainees, on the one hand, and the responsibilities of private contractors and the contracting agency, on the other hand, under a private arrangement.

Under the Model Contract, contractors are required to waive any immunity that may extend to them by operation of law. This waiver provision is considered an essential tool to ensure the accountability of the contractor. As one commentator has noted, "[o]ne of the attractions of prison privatization for state and local governments is the belief that contracting prison management to private firms will relieve the government of the burden of defending [actions] and the expense of complying with comprehensive and often financially burdensome court orders."[583] Although this may be true,[584] the emphasis should not be on <u>shifting</u> responsibility, but rather on creating an adequate accountability mechanism to ensure that inmates receive

---

[583] Kay, <u>The Implications of Prison Privatization on the Conduct of Prisoner Litigation Under 42 U.S.C. Section 1983</u>, 40 Vand. L. Rev. 867, 868 (1987).

[584] <u>But see</u> Cody & Bennett, <u>supra</u> note 402, at 848 (stressing that "[p]rivatization will not lessen the burdens on the State's attorneys or reduce the need for them[; indeed], privatization itself may give rise to extremely complicated lawsuits").

proper care and treatment. Because of the provision's importance to both contracting parties, an extended discussion of the immunity issue is presented below.

The immunity issue has arisen in almost all privatization material, including contracts, statutes, and secondary literature. "Immunity" covers a broad array of complex legal issues; therefore, it is important that a clear understanding of its various elements be established at the outset of this discussion. Specifically, the contracting parties must distinguish the various claims giving rise to an immunity defense -- physical-injury or personal-injury claims arising under federal and state tort-claims acts, and civil-rights claims arising under 42 U.S.C. § 1983 -- from the immunities that may be available to them -- sovereign immunity, qualified immunity, and absolute immunity.

a. The Eleventh Amendment, Sovereign Immunity, and Federal/State Tort-Claims Acts

The Supreme Court has interpreted the eleventh amendment to provide that federal courts do not have the authority to hear claims brought against a state by a citizen of that state or any other state.[585] Whereas the eleventh amendment acts as a

_____

585 Edelman v. Jordan, 415 U.S. 651 (1974). This rule applies to suits seeking injunctive relief as well as damages. Id. The eleventh amendment actually provides: "The Judicial power of the United States shall not be construed to extend to any suit in law or equity, commenced or prosecuted against one of the United States by Citizens of another State, or by Citizens or Subjects of any Foreign State." U.S. Const. amend. XI.

-203-

jurisdictional bar to suits against states and their departments

or agencies in federal courts,[586] counties, cities, and other

state subdivisions are not covered by the eleventh amendment, and

therefore are subject to suit in federal courts.[587]

The federal government is protected under the doctrine of

sovereign immunity from suits brought by citizens. The doctrine

prevents suits against the federal government and its agencies

unless the government has consented to be sued under the Federal

Tort Claims Act.[588] Similarly, state governments may not be sued

in state courts unless they have waived their sovereign immunity

in a state tort-claims act, as many states have, or it has been

abolished by case law.[589]

---

[586] Pennhurst State School & Hosp. v. Halderman, 465 U.S. 89 (1984) (applying eleventh amendment to state agency); Hans v. Louisiana, 134 U.S. 1 (1890) (construing eleventh amendment to bar claims against a state).

[587] Edelman v. Jordan, 415 U.S. 651 (1974).

[588] 28 U.S.C. § 1346(b) (1982) (allowing claims against federal government for property loss, personal injury, or death resulting from negligent or wrongful act of government employee acting within scope of his employment when United States, if a private person, would be liable under laws of place where act occurred); see United States v. Testan, 424 U.S. 392, 399 (1976) (stating that, as sovereign, United States is immune from suit unless it has unequivocally waived immunity).

[589] See K. Davis, Administrative Law Treatise § 25.00 (Supp. 1980) (noting that 33 states have abolished several areas of immunity by judicial decision). The New Mexico Supreme Court, for example, abolished sovereign immunity as a defense in tort actions in 1975. Hicks v. New Mexico, 88 N.M. 588, 544 P.2d 1153 (1975). See generally Kovnat, Constitutional Torts and the New Mexico Tort Claims Act, 13 N.M.L. Rev. 1 (1983). During the next legislative session, the legislature enacted the Tort Claims Act, N.M. Stat. Ann. §§ 41-4-1 to -29 (current codification in 1987 Code), to re-establish the defense. The Act immunizes a governmental entity and any public employee acting within the scope of duty from liability, id. § 41-4-4(A), except as waived

The question of whether a private contractor could assert

these defenses or jurisdictional bars has not been addressed by

the courts.[590]   Thus, the contracting parties should be aware

that the availability of defenses is complex, and will depend on

---

by eight enumerated provisions of the Act. Id. §§ 41-4-5 to
-12. Under these exceptions immunity is waived for certain
governmental entities and their employees, including the
statutory waiver of immunity for law-enforcement officers. Id. §
41-4-12. In Methola v. County of Eddy, 95 N.M. 329, 622 P.2d 234
(1980), the court held that section 41-4-12 applies to injuries
caused by the negligence of a sheriff, his deputies, and city
jailers.

The Arizona Supreme Court abolished sovereign immunity in
1963, in Stone v. Arizona Highway Comm'n, 93 Ariz. 384, 381 P.2d
107 (1963). Arizona has no tort-claims act. The court in Stone
stated that "the rule is liability and immunity [is] the
exception." Id. at 392, 381 P.2d at 112. Although the court did
not eliminate judicial or legislative immunity, and did not
subject executive-level, policy-formation activities (i.e.,
discretionary activities) to tort liability, the state courts
have consistently held the state liable for the negligent acts of
its officers, agents, and employees. E.g., Ryan v. State, 134
Ariz. 308, 656 P.2d 597 (1982); Grimm v. Arizona Bd. of Pardons
and Paroles, 115 Ariz. 260, 564 P.2d 1227 (1977). In Grimm, for
example, the court held that members of the Board of Pardons and
Paroles have only partial immunity from suit and can be held
liable for grossly negligent or reckless acts. Id. at 265-68,
564 P.2d at 1233-35. Arizona's approach to questions of immunity
was more recently stated in Ryan v. State:

> Employing the spirit of the Stone decision, we
> propose to endorse the use of governmental immunity
> as a defense only when its application is necessary
> to avoid a severe hampering of a governmental
> function or thwarting of established public
> policy. Otherwise, the state and its agents will be
> subject to the same tort law as private citizens.

134 Ariz. at 311, 656 P.2d at 600. This short discussion on
Arizona and New Mexico immunity law illustrates the diversity and
complexity of states' handling of the immunity question.

[590]   One commentator has concluded that a private contractor
that manages a prison "could not assert the eleventh amendment
defense" because the "eleventh amendment, by its very terms,
protects only the state and those officials whose actions are
considered to be the state's actions." Kay, supra note 582, at
882.

the operation and applicability of federal or state sovereign-immunity laws, which will be based on either a tort-claims act or judicial decision. The law in this area should be carefully examined before contract negotiations begin, so that the parties fully understand their rights and obligations.

b. 42 U.S.C. § 1983

The main source for civil actions brought to remedy violations of prisoners' constitutional rights is 42 U.S.C. § 1983.[591] Section 1983 actions can be brought in either state or federal courts.[592] Section 1983 claims may not be brought against states or their agencies due to their eleventh amendment immunity and because they are not deemed to be "persons" under the statute.[593] Nevertheless, the Supreme Court has permitted claims against state officials in their individual capacities.[594] In addition, section 1983 claims may be made against local governments, counties, cities, and municipalities.[595] There are no section 1983 claims against

---

[591] See id. at 867-68; supra note 214 (providing pertinent text of section 1983). For a thorough and detailed analysis of section 1983 and its ramifications in the prison-privatization context, see C. Thomas & L. Calvert-Hanson, supra note 582; see also Kay, supra note 583, at 881-83 (discussing eleventh amendment immunities available to private contractors).

[592] E.g., Maine v. Thiboutot, 448 U.S. 1 (1980).

[593] Quern v. Jordan, 440 U.S. 332 (1979).

[594] Ex parte Young, 209 U.S. 123, 159-60 (1908).

[595] Monell v. Department of Social Servs., 436 U.S. 658

federal officials because of the statute's "state action" requirement.[596]

In order to maintain a section 1983 action, the plaintiff must be able to prove that: (1) the defendant acted under color of state law, and (2) the interest infringed is secured by the Constitution or laws of the United States.[597] With respect to the state-action requirement, the Supreme Court has held that a finding of state action under the fourteenth amendment will satisfy the same requirement under section 1983.[598] Assuming _arguendo_ that contractors and their employees are found to be state actors, and that the eleventh amendment or common-law immunities do not apply,[599] the contractors could be held liable under section 1983 for monetary damages,[600] injunctive relief,[601]

(1978).

[596] There is an implied right of action for violations of the Constitution by federal officials. See Carlson v. Green, 446 U.S. 14 (1980) (eighth amendment); Bivens v. Six Unknown Named Agents, 403 U.S. 388 (1971) (fourth amendment).

[597] A section 1983 action may be brought even though there is an independent state tort remedy. Monroe v. Pape, 365 U.S. 167 (1961). The federal remedy is supplementary to the state remedy, and the latter need not be first sought and refused before the federal remedy is invoked. Id. In addition, a plaintiff is not required to exhaust its administrative remedies before pursuing section 1983 relief. Patsy v. Board of Regents, 457 U.S. 496 (1982).

[598] Lugar v. Edmondson Oil Co., 457 U.S. 922, 934-35 (1982).

[599] See supra notes 214-395 and accompanying text (concluding that courts will find state action in prison-privatization context). Some advocates of prison privatization have suggested that private corporations are not subject to suit under section 1983, a suggestion that makes privatization attractive, but which is not supported by the law. Woolley, supra note 582, at 327; C. Thomas & L. Calvert-Hanson, supra note 582, at 23.

or declaratory relief for violations of prisoners' constitutional rights.

With respect to the second requirement, local governments may be held liable under section 1983 if it is established that constitutional rights were violated as a result of an officially adopted and promulgated government regulation, policy, or decision.[602] However, evidence of the wrongful actions of a single employee not authorized to make policy will not establish the necessary causal link to hold a government liable.[603] In addition, the mere fact that a government employee commits a constitutional violation would not necessarily make the government liable, because the doctrine of respondeat superior does not apply in this context.[604] Significantly, several courts, including the United States Supreme Court, have held that, if a government entrusts one of its traditional functions to a private contractor, the contractor's actions will be treated as the government's own, thereby subjecting both parties to

_____

[600] United States ex rel. Larkins v. Oswald, 510 F.2d 583 (2d Cir. 1975).

[601] Milonas v. Williams, 691 F.2d 931, 940-43 (10th Cir. 1982).

[602] Monell v. Department of Social Servs., 436 U.S. 658, 690-91 (1978).

[603] City of Oklahoma City v. Tuttle, 471 U.S. 808 (1985).

[604] Parratt v. Taylor, 451 U.S. 527 (1981); Monell v. Department of Social Servs., 436 U.S. 658 (1978). But see Isaac v. Jones, 529 F. Supp. 175 (N.D. Ill. 1981)(holding that doctrine of respondeat superior applies in section 1983 injunctive cases); CSG Report, supra note 533, at 29 (stating that common-law doctrine "can result in considerable civil liability" for the government).

section 1983 liability.[605] Thus, the contracting parties should

be aware that section 1983 poses a significant risk that cannot

be "privatized away"; indeed, the risk should be borne by the

private contractor.

c. Available Immunities

Immunity laws are designed to strike a balance between a

desire to compensate the victim and an interest in protecting

both the public treasuries and the governing process itself.[606]

The contracting parties should recognize how these policy choices

will affect the availability of immunity to either party.

Although governments are protected from suits by the

eleventh amendment and the doctrine of sovereign immunity,

government officials are subject to suit as individuals acting in

their individual and official capacities.[607] Absolute immunity

---

[605] West v. Atkins, 56 U.S.L.W. 4664 (U.S. June 20, 1988)
(holding that a physician who is under contract with the state to
provide medical services to inmates at state-prison hospital on
part-time basis acts "under color of state law," within meaning
of section 1983, when he treats an inmate); Ancata v. Prison
Health Servs., 769 F.2d 700, 703 (11th Cir. 1985) (finding state
action where private entity contracted to provide care to inmates
in county jail); Woodall v. Partilla, 581 F. Supp. 1066, 1076
(N.D. Ill. 1984) (denying dismissal of section 1983 case brought
against private entity involved in scheduling and supervising
inmate laborers); Lombard v. Eunice Kennedy Shriver Center, 556
F. Supp. 677, 680 (D. Mass. 1983) (finding private entity and
government both liable under section 1983 when private entity
assumed state's obligation to provide medical service to state
facility).

[606] The oft-stated policy argument is that subjecting a
government official's decisionmaking process to fear of damage
suits might cause him to make decisions that are in his best
interest and not in the best interest of the public.

from damages liability is generally reserved for those acting in a legislative, judicial, or prosecutorial capacity,[608] and for federal officials exercising discretion within the scope of their official duties.[609] Most government officials and employees (including prison officials) who are sued in their individual capacities are entitled only to qualified immunity in damage suits.[610] Qualified immunity generally extends to actions that are performed in "good faith."[611] As the Supreme Court stated in

---

[607] Carlson v. Green, 446 U.S. 14 (1980); Ex parte Young, 209 U.S. 123, 149-58 (1908). State officials can be sued in their official capacity, but only for injunctive and declaratory relief. Damages are obtained only by suing state officials in their individual capacity.

[608] See, e.g., Supreme Court of Virginia v. Consumers Union, 446 U.S. 719 (1980) (stating that legislators are generally immune for their legislative acts); Stump v. Spark, 435 U.S. 349 (1978) (invoking absolute immunity for acts taken in judicial capacity); Imbler v. Pachtman, 424 U.S. 409, 430-31 (1975) (granting prosecutors absolute immunity for acts taken in "initiating a prosecution and presenting the State's case"). See generally S. Nahmod, Civil Rights and Civil Liberties Litigation 390-449 (2d ed. 1986). Legislators have absolute immunity from both damages liability and injunctive relief, whereas judges and prosecutors only are granted absolute immunity from damages liability. Pulliam v. Allen, 466 U.S. 522, 541-43 (1984); Consumers Union, 446 U.S. at 732-33.

[609] This immunity extends to liability arising from common-law torts. E.g., Granger v. Marek, 583 F.2d 781 (6th Cir. 1978).

[610] Cleavinger v. Saxner, 474 U.S. 193 (1985); Procunier v. Navarette, 434 U.S. 555 (1978). But see Arteaga v. New York, No. 145 (N.Y. Ct. App. June 9, 1988) (LEXIS, States library, NY file) (4-to-3 decision) (concluding that corrections-department employees "commencing and conducting formal disciplinary proceedings" under the "authority of and in full compliance with the governing statutes and regulations" engage in quasi-judicial conduct deserving of absolute immunity from tort liability). Qualified immunity is unavailable in injunctive suits. E.g., Knell v. Bensinger, 522 F.2d 720 (7th Cir. 1975).

[611] See Davis v. Scherer, 468 U.S. 183 (1984); Procunier v. Navarette, 434 U.S. 555 (1978).

Harlow v. Fitzgerald:[612]

> government officials performing discretionary
> functions . . . generally are shielded from
> liability for civil damages insofar as their conduct
> does not violate clearly established statutory or
> constitutional rights of which a reasonable person
> would have known.[613]

Courts have often relied on these common-law tort doctrines

of absolute and qualified immunity to resolve immunity questions

in section 1983 actions.   In Pierson v. Ray,[614] for example, the

Supreme Court extended the common-law qualified-immunity defense

to Jackson, Mississippi police officers who had been sued for

allegedly unconstitutional arrests in violation of section

1983.[615] The Court in Pierson also held that the state judge who

had found the petitioners guilty enjoyed absolute immunity for

actions taken in his judicial role.[616] In Tenney v.

Brandhove,[617] the Supreme Court relied on the common-law

tradition of granting absolute immunity to state legislators

acting within the scope of legislative authority in order to

---

[612]   457 U.S. 800 (1982).

[613]   Id. at 818 (emphasis added). The question is whether
the individual "knew or should have known" that he or she was
violating "clearly established constitutional or statutory rights
of which a reasonable person would have known" at the time of the
act in question. Id.

[614]   386 U.S. 547 (1967).

[615]   Id. at 555-57.

[616]   Id. at 553-55.

[617]   341 U.S, 367 (1951).

support that immunity's extension to section 1983 actions.[618]

d. Immunity For Private-Incarceration Contractors

The principal question that the contracting parties must address is whether contractors and their employees will be able to avail themselves of the qualified-immunity doctrines that public officials enjoy under federal and state tort law and section 1983 case law.[619]

------

[618] Id. at 372-76.

[619] There is precedent for granting qualified immunity to private persons liable under section 1983; to date, however, it has only been granted to individuals who have relied on presumptively valid state laws that were later found to be unconstitutional. Buller v. Buechler, 706 F.2d 844 (8th Cir. 1983) (finding that private party is entitled to qualified immunity if it invoked state garnishment statute prior to declaration of unconstitutionality); Folsom Inv. Co. v. Moore, 681 F.2d 1032 (5th Cir. 1982) (holding that private party who invoked a presumptively valid state attachment statute later held to be unconstitutional is entitled to a good-faith immunity from monetary liability under section 1983); see Alaska Pac. Assurance Co. v. Brown, 687 P.2d 264 (Alaska 1984) (holding that private entity that relies in good faith on validly enacted law cannot be held legally responsible for constitutional defects in the law). See generally S. Nahmod, supra note 608, at 512-14 (reviewing case-law development of qualified immunity for private persons); Kay, supra note 583, at 883-88 (discussing development of case law extending qualified immunity to private persons). Because of the courts' heavy reliance on a policy argument grounded in a desire to protect innocent, law-abiding persons from subsequent judicial determinations, it is unclear whether private persons in different circumstances will also be granted use of a qualified-immunity defense. See Little, McPherson & Healy, Section 1983 Liability of Municipalities and Private Entities Operating Under Color of Municipal Law, 14 Stetson L. Rev. 565, 603-06 (1985) (asserting, without explaining, that "private actors should be treated the same as corresponding state actors"); Note, supra note 9, at 1500 n.176 (opining that "private prison personnel may be able to benefit from the qualified immunity that public corrections officers enjoy").

Although no body of case law has yet developed concerning

immunities for contractors employed by the government,[620] there

---

The Supreme Court, in Lugar v. Edmondson Oil Co., originally suggested that qualified immunity could be extended to private individuals. 457 U.S. 922, 942 n.23 (1982); see also id. at 956 n.14 (Powell, J., dissenting) (concurring with the majority's suggestion that good-faith immunity would solve the problem of holding liable private individuals who "innocently make use of seemingly valid state laws"). The Fifth Circuit relied on Lugar in Folsom Inv. Co., when it held that a private party who invokes a presumptively valid state attachment statute later held to be unconstitutional is entitled to good-faith immunity from monetary and personal liability. 681 F.2d at 1037-38. The court reasoned that

> [t]he private party who invokes a presumptively valid attachment law is not entitled to an immunity because the officer executing it is. Rather, quite independently, the private party is entitled to an immunity because of the important public interest in permitting ordinary citizens to rely on presumptively valid state laws, in shielding citizens from monetary damages when they reasonably resort to a legal process later held to be unconstitutional, and in protecting a private citizen from liability when his role in any unconstitutional action is marginal.

Id. at 1037 (emphasis added). The Eighth Circuit used the same rationale in Buller, when it, too, granted private individuals a qualified-immunity defense after they had relied on a presumptively valid garnishment statute later found to be unconstitutional. 706 F.2d at 850-52. The court noted that

> [t]here is a strong public interest in permitting private individuals to rely on presumptively valid state laws and in shielding those citizens from monetary damages when they resort to a legal process which they neither know, nor reasonably should know, is invalid. . . . Moreover, it would be anomalous to hold that private individuals are state actors within the meaning of section 1983 because they invoke a state garnishment statute and the aid of state officers; but deny those private individuals the qualified immunity possessed by the state officials with whom they dealt because they are not state employees.

Id. at 851 (footnote omitted).

[620] See Little, McPherson & Healy, supra note 619, at 603-

have been attempts to deal with the issue by statute and by

contract.[621] Tennessee, for example, has enacted a statute

---

06 (finding that "no complete 'scenario' of liabilities and
immunities for private entities has been enumerated"); Note,
supra note 9, at 1500 n.176 (concluding that "no body of caselaw
has emerged concerning immunities for contractors employed by the
government"). Recently, however, the United States Supreme
Court, in Boyle v. United Technologies Corp., 56 U.S.L.W. 4792
(U.S. June 27, 1988), upheld the "military contractor defense,"
which immunized military contractors from liability under state
tort law for injury caused by design defects "when (1) the United
States approved reasonably precise specifications; (2) the
equipment conformed to those specifications; and (3) the supplier
warned the United States about the dangers in the use of the
equipment that were known to the supplier but not to the United
States." _Id._ at 4795. This decision is not likely to be
important in the private-incarceration context, for two
reasons: first, _Boyle_ is limited to the issue of federal
immunity, whereas private-prison and private-jail arrangements
typically will involve state immunity law; and, second, _Boyle_
expressly addressed the provision of goods rather than services,
the latter of which is paramount in the context of private
corrections and detention.

[621] The contract between Santa Fe County and Corrections
Corporation of America contains the following language:

> However, nothing herein is intended to deprive
> the County or CCA of the benefits of any law
> limiting exposure to liability and/or setting a
> ceiling on damages, or any laws establishing
> defense(s) for them. By entering this Agreement,
> the County does not waive its sovereign immunity,
> nor does CAA waive any immunity which may extend to
> it by operation of law.

Santa Fe Contract at 22, § 1. It is unclear whether CCA would
fall within the purview of the New Mexico State Tort Claims Act
as a "local public body" which "means all political subdivisions
of the state and their agencies, instrumentalities and
institutions . . . ." N.M. Stat. Ann. § 41-4-3(C) (1987). In
Cole v. City of Las Cruces, 99 N.M. 302, 657 P.2d 629 (1983), a
case that involved a natural-gas association that had entered
into a cooperative-services agreement with the city, the court
held that a private corporation is generally not the type of
"instrumentality" that the legislature had contemplated as coming
within the scope of the Tort Claims Act. The court found,
however, that there may be situations "where a private
corporation may be so organized and controlled, and its affairs
so conducted, as to make it merely an adjunct of a municipality
under the terms of the act." _Id._ at 305, 657 P.2d at 632.

stating that private-prison operators are not entitled to the defense of sovereign immunity.[622] The Arizona legislature, on the other hand, has passed a statute extending qualified immunity to correctional employees;[623] the Governor vetoed the bill twice. With increasing privatization, there are likely to be more such statutes and contractual language. Their exact meaning and parameters will ultimately be decided in the courts.

It is uncertain, for example, whether courts will grant private actors immunities that have been traditionally reserved for public actors. Assuming arguendo that the immunities can flow to the private contractor, the parties must then determine whether it is in the best interest of all of the parties -- i.e., the inmates, the community, the governmental entity, and the private contractor -- to contract for the waiver of the extension of such immunities.[624] For the reasons set out above, it is

_____

It should be noted, however, that, under the New Mexico statute, private-contractor employees are deemed to be law-enforcement officers for purposes of the New Mexico Tort Claims Act, see N.M. Stat. Ann. § 33-3-28 (1987), and immunity for law-enforcement officers is waived under the Act. Id. § 41-4-12; see supra note 589, (discussing New Mexico immunity law).

[622] Tenn. Code Ann. § 41-21-107(c) (Cum. Supp. 1987).

[623] See proposed Arizona S.B. 1039 (1985). As eventually enacted, Arizona made no provision for granting qualified immunity to correctional employees.

[624] See Kay, supra note 583, at 887-88 (discussing policies underlying qualified-immunity defense in context of privatization). Kay suggests that these policies may not apply to the privatization situation because the private contractor is responsible to its shareholders, and such a defense might encourage it "to cut corners to maximize profits." Id. at 887. She notes, on the other hand, that withholding the qualified-immunity defense may "deter good private individuals from providing services to the public." Id. at 888.

recommended that the government should only enter a contract that provides for the waiver of such immunities.

Proponents of prison privatization argue that private prisons would perform better and more economically than public prisons would.[625] As one commentator has noted, however,

> [t]he promised economies [of prison privatization] present powerful temptations to change. In general, as Bentham observed, it is always preferable to have a manager in whom duty and interest are united. Private management does not, however, necessarily unite duty and interest. Two characteristics of prison operation, its inaccessibility to the public and its typical arrangement in monopolistic form, will, in combination with the profit motive, cause the firm's interest to diverge from its duty to implement societal preferences. Unchecked, the very forces that allow private firms to offer pecuniary savings can drive them to sacrifice prison conditions, and even efficiency, in ways that public stewards will not.[626]

---

[625] See, e.g., M. Wolfgang, Prisons: Present and Possible 35-38 (1979) (stating that private contractors will be "far more efficient" than government agencies) (cited in Note, supra note 9, at 1477 n.15); Krajick, Prisons for Profit: The Private Alternative, State Legis., Apr. 1984, at 11-12 (quoting private contractor as saying that his company can reduce prison costs 15-25% because it is free from political considerations and need not hire union labor); Note, supra note 9, at 1477 (stating that companies have promised reduced prison costs by eliminating government red tape and hiring non-civil-service employees, and concluding that some savings have been realized); Comment, supra note 582, at 257-58 (noting that proponents of privatization argue "that private prisons are more insulated from public pressures, and are free from political interference, patronage, and the statutorily mandated high salaries and pensions of public employees"). But see J. Keating, Seeking Profit in Punishment: The Private Management of Correctional Institutions 48 (1984) (suggesting that costs of monitoring contract will affect any cost savings realized by privatization).

[626] Note, supra note 408, at 355-56 (footnotes omitted).

To be sure, if the government is going to contract, it should do so for the highest standard of care and responsibility that it can, to ensure that prisoners are afforded all of their rights and protections, pursuant to both the Constitution and sound policy. Because the state role in privatization will be limited to that of a monitor, however, it will be equally important that it use every means available to ensure that the private contractor comply with its contractual responsibilities, including strict immunity provisions that impose the highest standards of private-actor accountability.[627]

The thrust of the accountability argument is that the contractor will be forced to maintain the requisite levels of care and conduct due to the threat of increased litigation and liability created by the withholding of immunity. Yet contractors might contend that it would be anomalous to charge them with additional liability in their role as state actors and yet deny them the defenses that would be accorded to the government.[628] This contention must fail, however, in light of

---

[627] See Privatization of Corrections, supra note 460, at 75 (stating that government can expect only indirect influence over private prisons through a monitoring system and therefore quality control is made more difficult than in public institutions); Anderson, Davoli & Moriarty, Private Corrections: Feast or Fiasco?, Prison J., Autumn-Winter 1985, at 32, 37 (concluding that meaningful oversight is difficult because private proprietary entities are very protective of their confidentiality and privacy); Note, supra note 408, at 359 (suggesting that "state as monitor will be less reliable than the state as administrator").

[628] See Little, McPherson & Healy, supra note 619, at 604 (stating that private actors should be given the same immunities available to public actors).

the government's primary responsibility and obligation to protect the prisoners' rights and privileges and promote society's correctional goals. The government cannot adequately perform these functions acting solely as a monitor of private business. It must therefore institute these additional accountability measures to further ensure compliance and performance under the contract.[629] Although these measures may impose additional costs and burdens on the contractor and perhaps, therefore, on the government, they are nevertheless a crucial safeguard of the government's, the public's, and the inmates' interests.

Model Contract Provisions:

Section (A) is intended to ensure that the contractor will indemnify the contracting agency for any and all property damage incurred while the contractor operates the prison or jail facility. Both real and personal property are within the scope of Section (A), including structures, buildings, equipment, inventory, and other items that belong to the contracting agency and that the contractor uses in its daily operation of the facility.

---

[629] See Note, _supra_ note 408, at 358-60 (concluding that other measures besides administrative monitoring of private prisons will be necessary for successful privatization); Note, _Breaking the Code of Deference: Judicial Review of Private Prisons_, 96 Yale L.J. 815, 829-31 (1987) (arguing that strict contractual provision alone cannot adequately regulate prison privatization, but must be accompanied by greater judicial willingness to review prison practices).

(A)　The contractor assumes full responsibility for and shall indemnify the contracting agency, its officials, agents, employees, and representatives, including attorneys, other public officials, and the Superintendent/Warden, in their official or individual capacities, and their respective legal representatives, heirs and beneficiaries, and shall pay all judgments rendered against any or all of them for any and all loss or damage of whatever kind and nature to any and all contracting-agency property, real or personal, including but not limited to any buildings, structures, fences, equipment, supplies, accessories, inventory, or parts furnished, while in the contractor's custody and care for use or storage, resulting in whole or in part from the acts, errors, or omissions of the contractor or any officer, agent, representative, employee, or subcontractor thereof for whatever reason.[630]

Section (B) is intended to ensure that the contracting agency is indemnified for any liability that it might incur as a result of the contractor's operation of the facility. The contracting agency should be protected against all liability and claims against it arising out of physical or personal injury to prisoners, prison employees, or other individuals, including claims arising out of civil-rights actions, property-damage actions, and breach-of-contract actions. One of the purposes of having a contractor operate the facility arguably is to relieve the contracting agency of all concerns and responsibilities that are associated with operating these institutions. Consequently, in order to maximize the benefits of privatizing, the contracting agency should be able to leave the complete operation of the facility to the contractor, subject only to the monitoring

---

[630] Section (A) is derived from the Hamilton County Contract at 25-26, § 10(a).

procedures that are set forth elsewhere in the Model Contract. If the private contractor is not held completely responsible for all property damage, personal injury, and damages for breach of contract, the contracting agency will lose one of the most significant benefits of having contracted out the prison operation. The agency will not benefit from using the private contractor if the agency is constantly subject to litigation arising from the private contractor's operation of the facility.

>   **(B)** The company shall save and hold harmless and indemnify the contracting agency, its officials, agents, employees, and representatives, including attorneys, other public officials, and the Superintendent/Warden, in their official or individual capacities, and their respective legal representatives, heirs, and beneficiaries, and shall pay all judgments rendered against any or all of them for any and all loss or damage of whatever kind against any and all liability, claims, and cost, of whatever kind and nature, for physical or personal injury and any other kind of injury, including, specifically, deprivation of civil rights, and for loss or damage to any property or injury resulting from a breach of the terms of this contract occurring in connection with or in any way incident to or arising out of the occupancy, use, service, operation, or performance by the company, its agents, employees, or representatives of any of the provisions or agreements contained in this contract, including any Appendices, for which the contracting agency or any of the hereinabove-mentioned indemnified parties, who may become legally liable resulting in whole or in part from the acts, errors, or omissions of the company, or any officer, agent, representative, employee, or subcontractor thereof for whatever reason.[631]

Section (C) is intended to make the contractor accountable

_____

[631] Section (B) is derived from the Hamilton County Contract at 26-27, § 10(b).

to the public insofar as it requires the contractor to indemnify the contracting agency for any liability arising from a prisoner escape. This Section provides a necessary incentive to ensure that the private contractor will take all possible measures to prevent prisoners from escaping from the facility. One of the main concerns of any prison operation is the security measures that are used to prevent prisoners from escaping. Section (C) attempts to ensure that the prison is at all times properly and adequately staffed, and that the private contractor has established preventive measures for discouraging escapes as well as procedures for handling and coordinating searches in the event of a prisoner escape. These procedures should include steps for involving local and state law-enforcement personnel. Of course, once the local and state governments are brought in to help find the escaped prisoner, there is an increase in the amount of taxpayers' money being used to assist the contractor in its duties under the contract. These costs, plus the potential heightened exposure to liability arising from the escape, must be recognized and accounted for by the contracting parties. Under the Model Contract, Section (C) provides that the private contractor take responsibility for security at the facility and any liability that arises out of the contractor's failure properly to maintain the prisoners in the facility.

(C) The company shall save and hold harmless
and indemnify the contracting agency, its officials,
agents, employees, and representatives, including
attorneys, other public officials, and the
Superintendent/Warden, in their official or
individual capacities, and their respective legal
representatives, heirs, and beneficiaries who may
become legally liable resulting in whole or in part
from any inmate who escapes from the facility.[632]

Section (D) is intended to cover any possible privacy,
copyright, trademark, patent, or trade-secret liability that may
arise out of the operation of the prison. While this is a rather
unique provision with respect to the operation of a prison,
situations may arise that require such protections. For example,
for what purposes may the private contractor use an inmate's
prison record or publish research studies on the basis of their
experience? This Section ensures that the contracting agency
will be held harmless and indemnified for any misconduct by the
private contractor in these areas.

(D) The company shall save and hold harmless
and indemnify the contracting agency, its officials,
agents, employees, and representatives, including
attorneys, other public officials, and the
Superintendent/Warden, in their official or
individual capacities, and their respective legal
representatives, heirs, and beneficiaries who may
become legally liable resulting in whole or in part
from damages to any person or firm injured or
damaged by the company, its officers, agents,
representatives, or employees, by the publication,
translation, reproduction, delivery, performance,
use, or disposition of any data processed under this
contract in a manner not authorized by the contract
or by federal or state statutes, rules, regulations,

---

[632] Section (C) is derived from the 268 Center, Inc.
Contract at 4, § 4(A).

or case law.[633]

Section (E) requires that the private contractor indemnify the contracting agency for any liability arising from the contractor's failure to comply with federal or state laws. With respect to labor-law issues, for example, Section (E) emphasizes that the private contractor's actions vis-à-vis its employees are matters that involve only the contractor and its employees, and that the contracting agency is not an interested party in any dispute that might arise between the two parties nor should it be held liable for the contractor's actions.

> **(E)** The company shall save and hold harmless and indemnify the contracting agency, its officials, agents, employees, and representatives, including attorneys, other public officials, and the Superintendent/Warden, in their official or individual capacities, and their respective legal representatives, heirs, and beneficiaries, for any failure of the company, its officers, agents, representatives, or employees to observe state and federal laws, including but not limited to labor, minimum-wage, and unfair-employment laws.

Section (F)(1) simply requires the private contractor to pay the contracting agency's costs that are associated with enforcing its indemnification rights under the contract.

> **(F)** The company agrees to pay losses, liabilities, and expenses under the following conditions:

---

[633] Section (D) is derived from the 1985 Kentucky RFP at 40-7 to 40-8, § 41.000.

(1) The parties who shall be entitled to enforce this indemnity of the contractor shall be the contracting agency, its officials, agents, employees, and representatives, including attorneys, other public officials, and the Superintendent/Warden, any successor in office to any of the foregoing individuals, and their respective legal representatives, heirs, and beneficiaries.[634]

Section (F)(2) is intended to ensure that the contracting agency is indemnified for any and all costs of litigation in which the contracting agency is a party to the action as the result of the private contractor's conduct.

(F) The company agrees to pay losses, liabilities, and expenses under the following conditions:

(2) The losses, liabilities, and expenses that are indemnified shall include judgments, court costs, legal fees, the costs of expert testimony, amounts paid in settlement, and all other costs of any type whether or not litigation is commenced. Also covered are investigation expenses, including, but not limited to, the costs of utilizing the services of the contracting agency incurred in the defense and handling of said suits, claims, judgments, and the like, and in enforcing and obtaining compliance with the provisions of this paragraph whether or not litigation is commenced.[635]

Section (F)(3) is intended to ensure that any insurance

---

[634] Section (F)(1) is derived from the Hamilton County Contract app. C at 2, § (a).

[635] Section (F)(2) is derived from Hamilton County Contract app. C at 2, § (b); 268 Center, Inc. Contract at 4, § 4(C).

coverage to which the contracting agency may be entitled with respect to actions brought against the contracting agency is not waived or subrogated as a result of its contract with the private contractor.

> (F) The company agrees to pay losses, liabilities, and expenses under the following conditions:
>
> > (3) Nothing in this contract shall be considered to preclude an indemnified party from receiving the benefits of any insurance the contractor may carry that provides for indemnification for any loss, liability, or expense that is described in this contract.[636]

Section (F)(4) is intended to ensure that the private contractor fully cooperates with the contracting agency in any action brought by the agency arising out of the operation of the facility, whether the agency or the contractor operated the facility at the time of the action.

> (F) The company agrees to pay losses, liabilities, and expenses under the following conditions:
>
> > (4) The company shall do nothing to prejudice the contracting agency's right to recover against third parties for any loss, destruction of, or damage to the contracting agency's property. Upon the request of the contracting agency or its officials, the company shall furnish to the contracting agency all reasonable assistance and cooperation, including assistance in the prosecution of suits and the execution of instruments of

---

[636] Section (F)(3) is derived from the Hamilton County Contract app. C at 3, § (e).

assignment in favor of the contracting agency in obtaining recovery.[637]

Section (F)(5) provides that the contracting agency's consent is necessary before any settlement adverse to the government is entered. This provision prevents the contractor from settling a case adverse to the contracting agency's interests that might have negative implications for the government and which the government might prefer to resolve in a different manner. There are times when the contracting agency might find it better to litigate a matter rather than settle a case for economic reasons or admit wrongdoing. This is particularly true when an action involves a prisoner suing the contracting agency. The contracting agency may desire to risk the costs of a lawsuit rather than imply that the contracting agency and/or its employees compromised the prisoner's rights. Thus, Section (F)(5) ensures that the contracting agency's interests in adverse settlement decisions will be protected by requiring that the contracting agency's consent be secured.

(F) The company agrees to pay losses, liabilities, and expenses under the following conditions:

(5) The settlement of any claim or action involving a monetary amount covered by insurance shall require the written consent of each indemnified party to this contract against

_____

[637] Section (F)(4) is derived from the Hamilton County Contract app. C at 3, § (f).

whom a claim is made or action commenced. No
such settlement shall be effective without such
written consent. The indemnified party or
parties shall not unreasonably withhold such
consent.

Section (F)(6) requires the private contractor to obtain the

contracting agency's approval in cases in which the settlement of

a suit will be in excess of insurance limits and will necessitate

that the contracting agency pay from the treasury amounts in

excess of the insurance coverage. In this case, the contracting

agency should be able to determine whether it wants to enter such

a settlement and what the terms of such settlement should be.

This Section is necessary because such relief could be binding on

the contracting agency beyond the term of the contract. Section

(F)(6) also serves an important notice function for the agency.

The need for nonmonetary relief may indicate that the operation

of the facility is not effective or that the contractor is in

breach of the contract.

(F) The company agrees to pay losses,
liabilities, and expenses under the following
conditions:

(6) The settlement of any claim or action
involving a nonmonetary amount, or the
settlement of an amount of damages in excess of
or not otherwise covered by insurance, shall
require the written consent of each indemnified
party to this contract against whom a claim is
made or action commenced. No such indemnified
party shall be liable for any settlement of any
such claim or action effected without his, her,
or its written consent.[638]

---

[638] Section (F)(6) is derived from the Hamilton County

Section (G) enables the legislature to protect the contracting agency from any liability exposure in excess of what the legislature deems appropriate for tort and contract damages. The legislature obviously has a strong concern for the contracting agency's funds. Moreover, the legislature and the courts may establish defenses that may be used by the agency in any actions involving the operation of the facility. These defenses might include qualified immunity and sovereign immunity, as well as other restrictions on the liability of the contracting agency and its employees.

> (G) Nothing herein is intended to deprive the contracting agency of the benefits of any law limiting exposure to liability and/or setting a ceiling on damages, or any laws establishing defense(s) for the contracting agency.[639]

Like Section (G), Section (H) is intended to reiterate that the contracting agency may invoke any immunity to which it is entitled under the law as determined by the legislature or by case law. This includes cases arising out of tort, contract, or civil-rights litigation.

> (H) By entering this contract, the contracting agency does not waive any immunity that may extend to it by operation of law.[640]

Contract app. C at 4, § (h).

[639] Section (G) is derived from the Santa Fe Contract at 22, § 7.1.

Section (I) is discussed in the section of this paper dealing with waiver of immunity, above.

> (I) By entering this agreement, the company expressly waives any immunity that may extend to it by operation of law.

2.   Insurance

Commentary:

The Insurance section of the contract should be very detailed and specific. The contracting parties should attempt to cover all possible liabilities arising from the operation of the facility, including damage to property and injury to persons resulting from fire, escape, and other such incidents.

The amount of insurance should also be an issue of major concern. The private contractor should be required to provide personal-liability insurance in excess of one-million dollars per claim and well in excess of an aggregate amount of twenty-five-million dollars. In class-action cases, the aggregate cost or liability to the private contractor could easily exceed twenty-five-million dollars, particularly when a major overhaul of the facility or system is mandated. It is important that this

---

640 Section (H) is derived from the Santa Fe Contract at 22, § 7.1.

insurance cover both personal-injury claims that are brought under state tort law as well as claims arising out of civil-rights actions that are brought pursuant to 42 U.S.C. § 1983 and the fourteenth amendment.[641]

As a practical matter, the cost of insurance, like other costs of doing business, will factor into the price that the private contractor charges the contracting agency to operate the facility. Because of the difficulty that many private contractors presently face in securing insurance and the high rates that are charged for such insurance,[642] the insurance costs may be a very important element in a cost/benefit analysis of the privatization of prison and jail operations. It is essential, therefore, for the contracting agency to ensure that it is not subject to any _extra_ costs merely because it has chosen to contract out the operation of a facility to a private contractor who either must pay higher insurance rates than the contracting agency did when it operated the facility, or is unable to obtain

---

[641] CCA Chairman Thomas Beasley has stated that "95% of the cases against [CCA] are filed under the Civil Rights Act, and you are only liable if you violate their civil rights. By subscribing to ACA standards we are prima facie not in violation of constitutional issues." CCA Falls Short, supra note 582. This statement is incorrect, and vividly demonstrates why contracting agencies must have a clear understanding of the legal issues surrounding liability in the privatization context. In this example, the misstatement of law operates to reduce the perceived insurance needs of the contractor, and thus increases the contracting agency's risk of liability.

[642] See Corrections Corporation of America Prospectus 5, 19 (Oct. 1, 1986) ("Although the Company maintained $25 million in general liability coverage in 1985, it was able to secure only $5 million in coverage for 1986, despite the fact that it [had] never filed any general liability claims.").

sufficient coverage and consequently places the contracting agency at risk of paying the difference between what the contractor can afford to pay and the amount of money that is due.

Acquiring sufficient "affordable" insurance may be very difficult for the private contractor. Nevertheless, the contracting agency cannot underestimate the importance of requiring this insurance. The taxpayers should not be subjected to additional liability when the contracting agency contracts out to the private sector.

In order for the contracting parties to achieve these goals, some hard negotiations and novel financing arrangements may be required. The parties may consider: using the contracting agency's insurance program and charging the costs to the private contractor;[643] requiring a yearly set-aside of funds, a "reserve fund," to ensure the contractor's performance under the insurance provisions; and, if financing is arranged through a bond issuance, requiring the contractor to set aside a certain percentage of the bond proceeds to create a reserve fund. Allowing self-insurance by the private contractor is not advisable because of the increased risk to the contracting agency that the contractor will be unable to cover its potential liability. Pursuant to the position that the contracting agency should adopt a strategy of limiting its exposure to liability arising from the contractor's conduct to the fullest extent possible, such protection is most appropriately provided by an

_____

643   See infra Proposed Insurance Provision (E).

independent third-party insurance company.[644]

It is important to note that none of the monetary amounts used in the Model Contract are necessarily recommended for any particular contract. These amounts are suggested minimum levels of coverage that are intended to account for any possible claim or liability arising out of the operation of the facility under this contract.

The Model Contract does not address the situations in which the state is self-insured or has operated the facility itself. In these cases, there would be no prior coverage and therefore no amount on which to base the contract amount of required coverage. Thus, the parties would have to use other methods for devising a satisfactory level of coverage.

---

[644] See Model Statute § 9 (Insurance) (providing statutory language prohibiting self-insurance by the contractor). The problems associated with self-insurance are suggested in the facts surrounding CCA's Hamilton County Contract, where, according to one report, CCA, without informing county officials, unilaterally withdrew its promise to provide a $25-million insurance policy and substituted a $5-million escrow account. CCA Falls Short, supra note 582. Not only is this a drastic reduction in the amount of a previously agreed-upon level of necessary insurance funds, but there appears to be a question concerning whether the $5-million account is actually available for such use. See id. (citing account executive in charge of CCA's insurance affairs as stating that "'to say [CCA] stuck some money in a bank is not accurate. They may have $5 million in a general sense, but it's a complex transaction, [CCA pays] something, other companies pay something.'"). In August 1986, the Hamilton County Board of Commissioners passed a resolution amending the contract to require only $5 million in general-liability insurance. Hamilton County Bd. of Comm'rs. Resolution No. 886-62 (Aug. 18, 1986).

Model Contract Provisions:

Section (A) is a logical extension of the Indemnification/ Hold Harmless Section in that it requires that the contracting agency be named as an insured on any and all insurance policies written for the private contractor on the prison or jail facility. The contracting agency must be named as a co-insured, rather than as a third-party or intended beneficiary, to ensure that there will not be any litigation on whether the state will be indemnified for any liability that it may be assessed as the result of the contractor's operation of the facility.

> **(A)** The contracting agency shall be named as an insured on any and all insurance policies taken by the contractor for the construction, operation, or management of a facility or facilities, and the coverage shall extend to its officials, agents, employees, and representatives, including attorneys, other public officials, and the Superintendent/ Warden, in their official or individual capacities, and their respective legal representatives, heirs, and beneficiaries.[645]

It is essential that the contracting agency and its appropriate officials are given adequate notice in the event that an insurance policy is canceled. Cancellation of one or more policies could constitute a breach of the contract and would make this contract voidable by the contracting agency. The potential cost to the contracting agency would clearly be too great if the

_____

[645] Section (A) is derived from the Santa Fe Contract at 23, § 7.2.

contractor were allowed to operate the facility without adequate insurance protection. The parties might consider increasing the thirty days' advance notice so as to enable them to resolve the problem prior to the cancellation of any such insurance.

> (B)(1) All insurance or other certificates required under this contract must provide no less than thirty (30) days' advance notice to the contracting agency of any contemplated cancellation.[646]

Section (B)(2) is intended to prevent the private contractor from canceling any insurance policy or from allowing any insurance policy to be canceled or terminated. As discussed in Section (B)(1), above, the economic risk to the contracting agency if the contractor is allowed to operate the prison without adequate insurance is too great to permit. In no circumstances should the contracting agency allow the contractor to operate the facility without adequate insurance. Section (B)(2) also provides that the contracting agency has the final word concerning whether the contractor has met the requirements set forth in the contract for liability insurance. In effect, then, a condition precedent to the contract going into effect is the requirement that the contractor have insurance that is satisfactory to the contracting agency. The contracting agency should have the last word over whether such insurance is adequate; that decision should not be reviewable by any

---

[646] Section (B)(1) is derived from the Hamilton County Contract at 30, § 11(a).

legislative or judicial body.

> **(B)(2)** The company will not cancel, or allow to be canceled, any policy of insurance without contracting-agency approval. Each policy shall be approved by the contracting agency prior to the effective date of this contract. The contracting agency reserves the right, in its discretion, to reject any policy issued by an insurer that is deemed to be not fully reliable or otherwise deemed to be unsuitable.[647]

Section (B)(3) permits the contracting agency, in its own discretion, to pay any insurance premiums that the private contractor is unable or unwilling to pay, and which are necessary to prevent the insurance coverage from lapsing. The contracting agency is under no requirement to make such advancements of funds, and thus the contractor cannot rely on such advancements of funds, regardless of how often this arrangement is used. In the event that the contracting agency decides to advance the funds for the insurance payments, the contractor must repay the contracting agency such amounts plus interest at the maximum rate allowable by law. Moreover, this total amount due to the contracting agency from the private contractor may be set off and deducted from any amounts due to the private contractor from the contracting agency under the contract. Finally, the contracting agency's election to pay the insurance premium does not operate to cure the contractor's default nor to foreclose the agency's right to take any other action provided under the contract.

_____

[647] Section (B)(2) is derived from the Hamilton County Contract at 31-32, § 11(b)(6).

(B)(3)   The contracting agency shall have the
right, but not the obligation, to advance an amount
of money as required to prevent the insurance
required herein from lapsing for nonpayment of
premiums.   If the contracting agency advances such
amount, then the company shall be obligated to repay
to the contracting agency the amount of any advances
plus interest thereon at the maximum rate allowable
by law, and the contracting agency shall be entitled
to set off and deduct such amount from any amounts
owed to the company pursuant to this contract.   No
election by the contracting agency to advance
insurance premiums shall be deemed to cure a default
by the company of its obligation to provide
insurance.[648]

Section (C) simply reiterates that the private contractor

must fulfill the requisite insurance demands of the contract as a

condition precedent for this contract to go into effect.

Insurance claims should be the sole responsibility of the private

contractor, and not the contracting agency. This insurance

provision will ensure that the contractor has the necessary

resources to pay such claims if they arise.

Section (C)(1) provides that the contractor must have

insurance covering all workers' compensation claims and other

claims that are brought by the contractor's employees. Insurance

must also be maintained for any injuries to employees of

subcontractors or other individuals who are directly or

indirectly employed by the contractor or subcontractor. In

addition, the contractor must have insurance for any personal or

physical injuries to inmates. All insurance under this section

---

[648]   Section (B)(3) is derived from the Bay County Contract
at 29-30, § 9.1.

must cover, at a minimum, personal-injury liability, professional (malpractice) liability, and contract liability claims arising out of the operation of the facility.

> (C)   This contract shall not become effective until the contractor provides the contracting agency with policies of insurance of the following types, for the following purposes, and in the following amounts:
>
> > (1)   Insurance protecting it under workers' compensation acts and from other claims for damages for physical or personal injury, including death, to inmates or prison employees, which may arise from operations performed by the contractor, by a subcontractor, or by a person directly or indirectly employed by either of them. Such insurance will cover, but is not limited to, claims arising out of personal-injury liability, professional liability (malpractice), and contractual liability.[649]

Section (C)(2) requires that the deductible amount for any claims under the private contractor's insurance policies must not be greater than $10,000 and that, in the event of a loss, the contractor shall pay all such deductible amounts. The purpose of this provision is to ensure that the contractor will take full responsibility for all liability arising out of its operation of the facility. This Section also sets forth the requirement that the private contractor maintain insurance on the real and personal property of the facility as discussed elsewhere in the contract. Such coverage must provide for loss by fire, theft, or

---

[649]   Section (C)(1) is derived from Bay County Contract at 30, § 9.2(1); Hamilton County Contract at 30-31, § 11(b)(1); 268 Center, Inc. Contract at 5, § 5.

other hazard whether such property is destroyed in whole or in part.

> (2) Insurance in an amount not less than current coverage as maintained by the contracting agency as of the effective date of this contract with a deductible not greater than ten-thousand dollars ($10,000), protecting the facility, and any other real or personal property described in or used pursuant to this contract, against loss by fire, theft, or any other hazard, including destruction in whole or in part. Future additional coverage shall be determined in accordance with reasonable valuation less the deductible stated above. In the event of a loss, the contractor shall pay all deductible amounts.[650]

Section (C)(3) provides that the private contractor shall maintain general liability insurance in an amount not less than $25,000,000 for each occurrence. This coverage should specifically include liability arising out of civil-rights matters. Each occurrence should be distinguished from an aggregate amount in that the aggregate amount arising out of a single incident should be in excess of the $25,000,000. Thus, if a class-action suit is brought, each of the plaintiffs must be entitled to $25,000,000 rather than limiting the entire class to $25,000,000. This insurance coverage must also provide for the contracting agency's cost of litigation, including coverage for officials who are to be indemnified under this contract.

----

[650] Section (C)(2) is derived from Bay County Contract at 30, § 9.2(2); Hamilton County Contract at 31, § 11(b)(2).

(3) General liability insurance, which
shall specifically include civil-rights
matters, in an amount not less than twenty-
five-million dollars ($25,000,000) for each
occurrence. Such insurance shall also include
coverage for the cost of defense for all
contracting-agency officials and others
indemnified pursuant to this contract.[651]

Section (C)(4) provides that the private contractor must

maintain insurance for any injuries to prisoners or employees who

are injured while traveling to or from the prison facility. This

insurance should include coverage for all possible forms of

transportation, regardless of the type of vehicle used in any

particular instance. The amount of insurance required is large

because the number of inmates and/or officials involved in any

single incident of transportation involving prisoners often

includes more than one prisoner and certainly more than one

prison or jail guard or official.

(4) Automobile and other vehicle
liability insurance in an amount not less than
two-million dollars ($2,000,000) for each
occurrence and ten-million dollars
($10,000,000) for all occurrences.[652]

---

[651] Section (C)(3) is derived from the Hamilton County
Contract at 31, § 11(b)(3). This provision has since been
amended to reduce the amount of general liability insurance to $5
million. See Hamilton County Bd. of Comm'rs. Resolution No. 886-
62 (Aug. 18, 1986).

[652] Section (C)(4) is derived from the Hamilton County
Contract at 31, § 11(b)(4). This provision has since been
amended to reduce automobile and other vehicle liability
insurance to $1 million. See Hamilton County Bd. of Comm'rs.
Resolution No. 886-62 (Aug. 18, 1986).

Section (C)(5) is necessary in the event that an inmate or official or guard is determined to have defrauded, stolen, or absorbed money from the prison facility.

> **(5) Insurance in an amount not less than fifty-thousand dollars ($50,000) relating to instances of dishonesty.**[653]

Section (D) is included to ensure that, if the contracting agency can procure insurance for the facility at a rate better than that which the private contractor can procure on its own, the contracting agency will make its best efforts to help the contractor get such fire- and property-insurance coverage. Because of the great expense in building, developing, and maintaining the facility, this Section provides that the contracting agency must maintain any such insurance on the facility as required by state law. The fact that the contractor must also maintain insurance on the facility does not relieve the contracting agency of its obligations under the law.

> **(D) The contracting agency shall exercise its best efforts to allow the contractor to maintain insurance for the facility at the contractor's expense under the contracting agency's fire and property insurance. The contracting agency shall maintain fire and property insurance in accordance with state law.**[654]

---

[653] Section (C)(5) is derived from the Hamilton County Contract at 31, § 11(b)(5).

[654] Section (D) is derived from Bay County Contract at 31, § 9.2(7); Santa Fe Contract at 24, § 7.5.

Section (E)(1) provides that the private contractor will provide defense counsel for any action brought under this contract that concerns any provision requiring insurance coverage. The contracting agency, however, reserves its power to participate in the defense of any such action as it deems necessary and proper.

> **(E)(1) The contractor shall assume the defense for any action for which there is insurance coverage with counsel selected by the contractor, but the contracting agency may participate in the defense if it chooses to do so.**[655]

Section (E)(2) provides that the contracting agency shall make a good faith effort to notify the private contractor of any action brought against the contracting agency or any employee thereof. The failure to notify the contractor within the fifteen-day period does not relieve the contractor from any liability under the contract unless such failure results in the entry of a judgment against the contractor or the contractor suffers any irreparable injury as a result of the failure to notify the contractor within the notice period. Assuming that the contracting agency and/or its employees notify the private contractor within the notice period (or other reasonable period in the circumstances), the contractor has the right to

----

[655] Section (E)(1) is derived from Hamilton County Contract app. C at 4, § (g); Santa Fe Contract at 24, § 7.6.

participate in and assume the defense of any such action. The contractor also has the right to select counsel for any such defense, subject to the reasonable satisfaction of the contracting agency's counsel.

> (E)(2) Within ten (10) days after receipt by an indemnified party of written notice of the commencement of any action against him, her, or it, such party shall notify the contractor in writing of the commencement thereof. Failure to so notify the contractor within such period shall not relieve the contractor from any liability that it may have to the indemnified party otherwise hereunder unless a judgment shall have been entered against the contractor, or the contractor shall otherwise have suffered irreparable injury, on account of such failure. In case any such action shall be brought against an indemnified party, and if the indemnified party shall notify the contractor of the commencement thereof, the contractor shall be entitled to participate in and assume the defense thereof, with counsel selected by the company who is reasonably satisfactory to the contracting agency's counsel.[656]

Section (F) provides that any action brought as the result of the contracting agency's operation of the facility prior to the effective date of the contract shall remain the sole responsibility of the contracting agency. The agency will be responsible for the losses or costs resulting from any litigation of such matter. The private contractor is obligated to cooperate with the contracting agency in the defense of these actions and must comply with any court orders or settlement agreements that affect the operation of the prison facility.

---

[656] Section (E)(2) is derived from the Santa Fe Contract at 24, § 7.6.

(F) The contracting agency shall remain solely
responsible for any losses or costs resulting from
claims or litigation pending at the time that this
contract first becomes effective or arises
thereafter from an occurrence prior to the time that
this contract first became effective. The
contractor agrees to cooperate with the contracting
agency in the defense of these suits and conform its
operation of the facility or facilities to any court
orders or settlement agreements resulting from such
claims or litigation.[657]

---

[657] Section (F) is derived from the Santa-Fe Contract at
25, § 7.7.

Section 3(F): Operating Standards and Accreditation

Commentary:

1. Operating Standards

In any contract for the private ownership and/or operation of a correctional or detention facility, it is vitally important that there be reasonably specific and objective standards by which the contractor's performance can be measured. The contracting agency will, of course, want to require that the facility be maintained and operated in accordance with the Constitution and all applicable federal, state, and local laws, regulations, and certification requirements.[658] The contractor must also comply with any new laws, regulations, or amendments to existing laws or regulations that become effective during the contract term.[659] A contract provision should also require compliance with any court orders that are rendered after the starting date of the contract that apply to facilities under the

---

[658] See CSG Report, supra note 533, at 95 (recommending that states require contractors to conform to all applicable state laws, regulations, and policies).

[659] The parties may want to negotiate a provision that would allow for cost adjustments where necessary to achieve compliance with the new standards. See Model Contract § 3(C) (Compensation). The Bay County Contract provides that the contractor may apply to the county for an increase in compensation equal to the cost of complying with the change in law or with new standards required by court order. If the parties cannot agree on an amount within 60 days, the contractor may take the matter to arbitration. Bay County Contract at 22, § 6.7(B).

-244-

jurisdiction of the contracting agency.[660]

Moreover, the contract should require that the contractor operate and maintain the facility in accordance with Standards published by the American Correctional Association.[661] The ACA Standards recommend minimum guidelines that govern all aspects of prison life. Adult correctional institutions must meet these Standards in order to receive accreditation. The Standards are characterized as either mandatory, essential, or important. The ACA requires for accreditation compliance with one-hundred percent of the mandatory Standards and ninety percent of the other Standards.[662] The ACA Standards are strict; at present, most public facilities have not met the percentages that are required for accreditation.[663] Thus, incorporating ACA Standards into the contract ensures that the contractor will be held to the

---

[660] Cf. Bay County Contract at 22, § 6.7(B) (providing that the contractor may apply for cost adjustment for increased costs associated with court orders rendered after the commencement of the contract).

[661] For examples of contracts and statutes that require compliance with ACA Standards, see Bay County Contract at 14-15, § 5.1(A); Santa Fe Contract at 7, § 3.5; American Legislative Exchange Council, Nongovernmental Corrections Facilities, Programs and Services Act § 10(B) (proposed 1987).

[662] American Correctional Association, supra note 528, at ii (Supp. 1986). Previously, the ACA had required different levels of compliance for essential and important standards; a facility had to meet 90% of the essential standards and only 80% of the important standards. Id. at xvii (2d ed. 1981).

[663] Some 150 of the more that 700 state and federal prisons in the United States have achieved accreditation. Another 40 to 60 are expected to achieve accreditation within the next year. Telephone interview with John J. Greene, Administrator of Standards and Accreditation, Commission on Accreditation for Corrections (Oct. 9, 1987).

highest industry standards practicable.[664]

Several issues arise in applying the ACA Standards to private prisons. The first question is whether, under the contract, private prisons should be required to comply with the same percentage of nonmandatory standards as is required for accreditation, or whether instead they should be required to meet all ACA Standards, both mandatory and nonmandatory. Requiring private prisons to meet all of the ACA Standards may enhance the quality of the facility. Such a requirement could impose an unreasonable burden on the contractor, however, and make the project financially unattractive.[665] In addition, only the mandatory ACA Standards "address conditions or situations which could become hazardous to the life, health and safety of offenders, employees and/or the public."[666] The "important" and "essential" Standards are not as critical as are the mandatory Standards. In general, therefore, compliance with the current required percentage (90%) of nonmandatory Standards should result in better prisons without deterring contractors from entering the industry.

---

[664] Corrections Corporation of America, although it has promised to back up its claim that it can provide higher quality facilities by attaining compliance with the percentage of ACA Standards required for accreditation, reportedly has yet to obtain accreditation for at least two of its facilities, Bay County and Silverdale -- even though these facilities have been in operation for several years. CCA Falls Short, supra note 582.

[665] Telephone interview, supra note 663 (acknowledging that most existing facilities do not meet the percentage of requirements necessary for accreditation).

[666] American Correctional Association, supra note 528, at xvii (2d ed. 1981).

There are instances, however, when particular Standards may be so important that compliance should be mandatory for purposes of the contract even though the ACA has classified the Standards as nonmandatory. Various provisions of the Model Contract expressly provide that the applicable ACA Standards should be incorporated as mandatory regardless of whether compliance is mandatory for the purposes of accreditation. The contracting agency should also review carefully all nonmandatory Standards and expressly incorporate as mandatory those that it deems to be necessary or desirable.

A related issue is whether, in some instances, private prisons should be held to standards that are higher than those formulated by the ACA. The ACA Standards were intended to provide prison administrators with "a set of reasonable and meaningful guidelines" to operate correctional facilities "in a manner consistent with minimum constitutional and human rights standards."[667] However, some ACA Standards were intended as a minimum that "should be exceeded whenever possible."[668] The contract provides an opportunity to address situations and conditions that demand more stringent standards than those set forth by the ACA. If there is sufficient competition among private contractors, for example, the contracting agency may be

_____

[667] _Id._ at xiii.

[668] _Id._ at xvii. Contrary to claims by some prison-privatization advocates, such as Thomas Beasley, chairman of CCA, see CCA _Falls Short_, _supra_ note 582, compliance with ACA Standards is not necessarily the equivalent of compliance with minimum constitutional standards.

able to negotiate standards that exceed those that are required for accreditation.[669]

In the event that a federal, state, or local law conflicts with an ACA Standard, an issue appears to exist concerning which shall govern. The Bay County Contract states, for example, that, in the event of such a conflict, it should be resolved in favor of the applicable law.[670] The Santa Fe Contract, however, resolves the conflict in favor of the more stringent standard.[671] This issue is illusory if the contractor is held to the higher requirement. Under this approach, the contractor will always be in compliance with the law because the law -- which typically defines only minimum standards for prisons and jails -- will either be more stringent than the ACA Standards, in which case there will be no conflict, or less stringent, in which case adherence to the higher requirement will not violate the law.[672] Thus, the Santa Fe provision is the better one.

---

[669] The Council of State Governments' Report makes a generally positive recommendation with regard to incorporation of ACA Standards in the contract. The Report suggests, however, that those contracting agencies that choose to utilize ACA Standards should strengthen and modify them according to the individual needs of each facility. It also warns contracting agencies to place sufficient emphasis on the implementation and outcome of the policies and procedures embodied in the ACA Standards; the mere existence of written policy and procedure in a given area does not necessarily ensure that those policies and procedures are being satisfactorily implemented. CSG Report, supra note 533, at 97; see Note, supra note 9, at 1494 (criticizing ACA Standards for their emphasis on general written policy and procedure requirements).

[670] Bay County Contract at 14-15, § 5.1(A).

[671] Santa Fe Contract at 7, § 3.5.

[672] One conceivable case that would create a real, and not

There is also an issue regarding whether the contractor will be required to meet ACA Standards immediately, or whether it will be given time under the contract to bring the facility into compliance. It has been argued that, because ACA Standards are so high, it is unrealistic to expect a contractor to be able to meet the percentages required for accreditation upon commencement of the contract.[673] The Model Contract provision requires, however, that the facility be in compliance with all contractual provisions, including ACA Standards, throughout the term of the contract. The only exception is contracts involving the privatization of an existing facility. Because this situation may present special problems,[674] the Model Contract allows an additional ninety days from the starting date of the contract for the contractor to achieve compliance with those ACA Standards relating to physical plant that are not essential to the health and safety of inmates.[675]

---

illusory, conflict between applicable law and ACA Standards would be where, for example, ACA Standards provided that prisoners be paid the prevailing hourly wage for their labor, but applicable law set a cap on prisoner wages that was below the prevailing wage for nonprisoner labor. Although such a situation is highly unlikely, were the contractor to follow ACA Standards it would violate the law.

[673] See CSG Report, supra note 533, at 97 (acknowledging that it may be difficult for contractors to meet ACA Standards unless they are provided adequate time and funding); Santa Fe Contract at 7, § 3.5 (stating that it would be impossible for contractors to meet percentage of ACA Standards necessary for accreditation immediately).

[674] See CSG Report, supra note 533, at 97.

[675] This could include, for example, ACA Standards 2-4127 through 2-4133, 2-4135 through 2-4141, and 2-4143 through 2-4151. The contracting agency should examine these Standards carefully to determine whether, given its particular

A final issue is whether the contractor should be bound only by current ACA Standards or by future Standards as well. The ACA Standards continually evolve as societal interests, prison needs, and technology change. During the contract term, ACA Standards may be modified. The question thus arises whether the contractor will be bound by these modifications. The Bay County Contract states that the contractor must operate in accordance with the "then current" ACA Standards, making clear that future standards are not binding.[676] On the other hand, the proposed Nongovernmental Corrections Facilities, Programs and Services Act demands compliance with the most current ACA Standards.[677] In light of the evolving nature of the ACA Standards and the fact that the term of the contract may extend for a lengthy period, requiring compliance with the most current Standards is the better approach.[678] The application of future Standards to the private facility may, however, impose a burden on the contractor. Therefore, ample time should be afforded the contractor to make the appropriate adjustments. The parties may wish to provide for cost adjustments when the cost of compliance with new ACA Standards is substantial.[679]

---

circumstances, an extension of time is warranted with regard to some or all of them.

[676] Bay County Contract at 14-15, § 5.1(A).

[677] American Legislative Exchange Council, Nongovernmental Corrections Facilities, Programs and Services Act § 10(B) (proposed 1987).

[678] To avoid a possible constitutional problem, the contractor would be bound only by those subsequent Standards that were approved by the contracting agency. See Model Statute § 4 (Standards of Operation).

2.   Accreditation

The accreditation process has been used by correctional and detention facilities as a voluntary, independent, third-party evaluation of performance.[680] While such a process would, in the context of a private facility, provide an additional check on the contractor, given the controversy surrounding the accreditation process,[681] it is unwise to rely on accreditation as a measure of the quality of a private facility, especially when privatization itself is controversial. Therefore, the Model Contract utilizes full-time, on-site monitoring to ensure compliance with ACA Standards[682] and does not include a provision requiring the facility to secure accreditation.[683]

---

[679]   See Model Contract § 3(C) (Compensation).

[680]   American Correctional Association, supra note 528, at xviii (2d ed. 1981). The accreditation process initially requires the facility to evaluate and document its own level of compliance with ACA Standards. Id. at xvii. If the facility's performance falls below ACA Standards in any area, it must also formulate a plan that is designed to bring these areas into compliance. Id. If the Commission on Accreditation for Corrections accepts the self-evaluation it may, upon the request of the facility, conduct an on-site inspection to verify compliance. Id.

[681]   See Prisoners and the Law ch. 18 (I. Robbins ed. 1987) (presenting arguments for and against accreditation process); CSG Report, supra note 533, at 12 (noting that there is disagreement on effectiveness of accreditation process).

[682]   See Model Contract § 6 (Monitoring).

[683]   If the parties have agreed to incorporate ACA Standards and wish to include an additional third-party check on the contractor's performance, requiring the facility to achieve accreditation may provide an effective means for doing so. For

Model Contract Provision:

     The contractor shall [construct,] operate and maintain the facility in accordance with all applicable constitutional standards, federal, state, and local laws, rules, regulations, and ordinances, and certification or licensing requirements that are effective or become effective during the contract term,[684] as well as court orders rendered during the contract term [including, but not limited to, _____ [685]]. The contractor shall also comply with one-hundred percent of the mandatory ACA Standards and ninety percent of the nonmandatory ACA Standards.

     When the contract expressly provides that a Standard is incorporated as mandatory, compliance with that Standard is mandatory for purposes of the contract despite the fact that it may be classified as nonmandatory by the ACA.

     If any provision of this contract is more stringent than the applicable ACA Standard(s), the contract provision shall govern and must be complied with by the contractor.

     If any applicable federal, state, or local law, rule, or regulation is in conflict with the ACA Standards, the more stringent requirement shall govern and must be complied with by the contractor.[686]

     The contractor must maintain compliance with the required percentages of mandatory and nonmandatory ACA Standards, as well as all other contractual provisions and standards, from the date

---

an example of a contractual provision requiring facility accreditation, see Bay County Contract at 15, § 5.1(B). For an example of a statute requiring facility accreditation, see Tex. Rev. Civ. Stat. Ann. art. 6166g-2, § 1(b)(3) (Vernon Supp. 1988).

[684] See County of Ramsey Contract at 5, § IV.

[685] The contracting agency may want to cite directly to the applicable legal standards. This reference will aid both parties in ascertaining exactly what is required of the contractor.

[686] Bay County Contract at 14-15, § 5.1(A).

the contract commences to the date the contract
terminates [except that, when the contractor assumes
operation of an existing facility, it shall have
ninety (90) days from the date the contract
commences to achieve compliance with applicable ACA
Standards relating to the condition of the physical
plant]. In the event that the ACA Standards are
modified during the contract term, including any
renewal period, the contractor shall have [number]
(__) months to bring the facility into compliance
with the new Standards, provided that the new
Standards have been approved by the contracting
agency.

Section 3(G): Subcontracts and Assignments

Commentary:

A contract for the private ownership and operation of a correctional facility requires the contractor to perform a wide range of functions. As a result, the contractor may find it necessary or more efficient to assign or subcontract various portions of the work to other providers.[687] While such agreements may be beneficial to both parties, it is essential that the contracting agency maintain control over the use of such agreements. It must ensure, for example, that the quality and cost of the assigned or subcontracted work meet the same standards as those that were originally agreed on in the contract.

In order to ensure that the contracting agency maintains control over agreements entered by the contractor, the Model Contract includes a general provision prohibiting subcontracts or assignments without the prior express written approval of the

---

[687] It is conceivable that the contractor might want to assign or contract out all of the work under the contract if it is experiencing financial difficulties, or if such an arrangement would prove to be more profitable for the contractor. The Model Contract allows agreements of this scope, as do the Kentucky RFP and the Eckerd Foundation Contract, provided that the contracting agency has given prior approval to the terms and conditions of the agreement. The contracting agency should consider, however, whether its individual needs would be best served by an absolute prohibition of such arrangements. Thus, if the contractor were unable or did not wish to continue work under the contract, its only alternative would be to end the contract according to conditions set forth in the termination provisions. The agency would then be free to rebid the contract.

contracting agency.[688] If the contracting agency grants the contractor permission to subcontract or assign work and all or any portion of the work is contracted out, the Model Contract expressly holds the subcontractor or assignee to the same standards as those that apply to the contractor.[689] In addition, the employees of the subcontractor or assignee are granted the same rights and charged with the same responsibilities as are the employees of the contractor. Finally, the Model Contract expressly affirms that the contractor shall remain responsible for performance of all work under the contract[690] at the contract price[691] regardless of whether all or part of the contract is

---

[688]   See Eckerd Foundation Contract at 2, § J; 1985 Kentucky RFP at 40-7, § 40.850; Weaversville Contract at 1, § 5.   This requirement does not extend to contracts between the contractor and individual consultants or professionals providing services at the facility. See 1985 Kentucky RFP at 40-7, § 40.850. Contract employees are governed by the requirements set forth in Model Contract § 4(C) (Personnel Policy).

In addition to addressing subcontracts and assignments in the contract, the contracting agency may want to state in the RFP that each proposal must include the following: a list of all portions of the contract that the contractor intends to assign or contract out, descriptions of potential subcontractors or assignees that include the same information that the RFP requires the contractor to provide about itself, and copies of the proposed agreements. See 1985 Kentucky RFP at 40-7, § 40.850. The Kentucky RFP also requires the contractor to execute all subcontracting agreements by the contract award date. Id.

[689]   See Eckerd Foundation Contract at 2, § J. The language used in the Eckerd Contract allows the contracting agency to impose any additional conditions that it determines are necessary on the approval of a subcontracting agreement. Id.

[690]   See 1985 Kentucky RFP at 40-7, § 40.850.

[691]   See Eckerd Foundation Contract at 2, § J (stating that the contracting agency shall not be deemed to have approved an agreement that results in an increase in the total contract amount).

contracted out or assigned to others. This provision will ensure that the contractor cannot escape liability for performance of the contract by shifting the responsibility to other providers.

Model Contract Provision:

The contractor shall not subcontract or assign any or all of the services to be performed under this contract without the consent, guidance, and prior express written approval of the contracting agency.[692] In the event that approval is granted and some or all of the services are subcontracted or assigned, the contractor shall guarantee that the subcontractor will comply with all of the provisions of this contract, including the incorporated ACA Standards. Employees of the subcontractor or assignee shall have the same rights and obligations under the contract as do employees of the contractor.

[Optional Paragraph: The contractor shall be required to provide a payment bond with a surety company that is licensed to do business in [the appropriate jurisdiction] and that is acceptable to the contracting agency to insure the payment of all subcontractors, material men, laborers, and taxes, including but not limited to unemployment insurance taxes.][693]

The contractor is ultimately responsible for the performance of all work under the contract at the contract price, regardless of whether some or all of the work is subcontracted or assigned. In the event that the contractor or subcontractor fails to comply with the requirements of this or any other contractual provision, the contracting agency may fine the contractor [number] (___) dollars per violation.[694] Alternately [or in addition], the

_____

[692] 1984 Kentucky RFP at 11, § 26.

[693] 1984 Kentucky RFP at 12, § 26.

[694] The contracting agency may want to set different levels of fines that are appropriate to the seriousness or the degree of the contractual violation. These fines should be specified in

contracting agency may hold the contractor in breach
of the contract and terminate the contract at the
contracting agency's option.

---

the contract.

Section 3(H): Independent-Contractor Status

Commentary:

For purposes of the contract, the private contractor should be an independent contractor vis-à-vis the contracting agency. An express provision in the contract can be used as prima facie evidence that an employer-employee relationship does not exist between the contracting agency and the contractor or its employees and that the contractor and the contracting agency do not have a joint business relationship.

Model Contract Provision:

> Nothing contained in this contract is intended or should be construed as creating the relationship of co-partners, joint-ventures, or an association between the contracting agency and the contractor. The contractor is an independent contractor and neither the contractor nor its employees, agents, or representatives shall be considered employees, agents, or representatives of the contracting agency.[695] These parties shall not, therefore, be entitled to any benefits that accrue to employees, agents, or representatives of the contracting agency.[696]
>
> From any amount due the contractor, there will be no deductions for federal income tax or FICA payments, nor for any state income tax, nor for any other purposes that are associated with any employer-employee relationship, unless required by

---

[695] See County of Ramsey Contract at 8, § VIII.

[696] See Santa Fe Contract at 8, § 3.7. This may include benefits such as insurance, workers' compensation benefits, and disability leave. See id.

law. Payment of federal income tax, FICA, and any
state income tax is the responsibility of the
contractor.[697]

---

697   County of Ramsey Contract at 8, § VIII.

Section 4: Employee Issues

Section 4(A): Hiring Criteria

1.   Employment Discrimination

Commentary:

The Model Contract provision includes standard language prohibiting employment discrimination by the contractor and mandating the implementation of an affirmative-action program.[698] It also incorporates ACA Standards 2-4054,[699] 2-4055,[700] 2-4057,[701] and 2-4059[702] -- which address nondiscrimination and affirmative action -- as mandatory. These requirements ensure that the contract is consistent with

_____

[698] Most RFP's and contracts contain similar requirements. See, e.g., INS RFP at 63, § I(I); 1984 Kentucky RFP at 10, § 21; Santa Fe Contract at 29, § 12.2.

[699] "Written policy and procedure provide for the selection, retention, and promotion of all personnel on the basis of merit and specified qualifications." ACA Standard 2-4054.

[700] "Written policy and procedure provide for lateral entry as well as promotion from within the institution." ACA Standard 2-4055.

[701] "Written policy specifies equal employment opportunities exist for all positions. When deficiencies exist in regard to the utilization of minority groups and women, the institution can document the implementation of an affirmative action program approved by the appropriate government agency, showing annual reviews and necessary changes required to keep it current." ACA Standard 2-4057.

[702] "Written policy and procedure make provision for the employment of qualified ex-offenders." ACA Standard 2-4059.

applicable federal and state regulations. Because of the importance of these provisions, the contracting agency should have the power to cancel the contract or withhold payment under the contract if the contractor fails to comply with them.

Model Contract Provision:

The contractor shall not discriminate against any employee or applicant for employment because of race, color, religion, sex, national origin, age (except as provided by law), marital status, political affiliation, or handicap. The contractor must take affirmative action to ensure that employees, as well as applicants for employment, are treated without discrimination because of their race, color, religion, sex, national origin, age (except as provided by law), marital status, political affiliation, or handicap. Such action shall include, but is not limited to, the following: employment, promotion, demotion or transfer, recruitment or recruitment advertising, layoff or termination, rates of pay or other forms of compensation, and selection for training, including apprenticeship. The contractor agrees to post notices setting forth the provisions of this clause in conspicuous places, available to employees and applicants for employment.

The contractor shall, in all solicitations or advertisements for employees placed by or on behalf of the contractor, state that all qualified applicants will receive consideration for employment without regard to race, color, religion, sex, national origin, age (except as provided by law), marital status, political affiliation, or handicap, except where it relates to a bona fide occupational qualification. The contractor shall comply with the nondiscrimination clause contained in Federal Executive Order 11246, as amended by Federal Executive Order 11375, relative to Equal Employment Opportunity for all persons without regard to race, color, religion, sex, national origin, and the implementation of rules and regulations prescribed by the Secretary of Labor and with Title 41, Code of Federal Regulations, Chapter 60. The contractor shall comply with related [jurisdiction] laws and regulations.

The contractor shall comply with regulations issued by the Secretary of Labor of the United States in Title 20, Code of Federal Regulations, Part 741, pursuant to the provisions of Executive Order 11758 and the Federal Rehabilitation Act of 1973.

The contractor shall comply with the Civil Rights Act of 1964, and any amendments thereto, and the rules and regulations thereunder, and Section 504 of Title V of the Vocational Rehabilitation Act of 1973 as amended.[703] This provision incorporates as mandatory ACA Standards 2-4054, 2-4055, 2-4057, and 2-4059. The contractor has a continuing obligation to comply with the Standards, as well as with revised or additional Standards to the extent that they are approved by the contracting agency.

In the event that the contractor fails to comply with these provisions, including the applicable ACA Standards, or with any other such rules, regulations, or orders, this contract may be cancelled, terminated, or suspended in whole or in part by the contracting agency and the contractor may be declared ineligible for further contracts.[704]

---

[703] This provision is derived from 1985 Kentucky RFP at 40-8, § 41.300.

[704] This provision is derived from Florida Agreement § V.

2. Employment Options for Correctional and Detention Employees
    at Existing Facilities

Commentary:

A contracting agency's decision to contract out the
operation of an existing facilty to a private company raises
difficult issues regarding the possible displacement of public
employees. It is estimated that the costs related to staffing a
correctional facility comprise eighty to ninety percent of the
total operating cost.[705] This is one area, therefore, in which
private contractors must reduce costs if they are to remain
profitable.[706] This fact has raised concern among employees at
existing public facilities. They fear that privatization could
result in the loss of jobs or a reduction in salary and loss of
benefits accrued while they were public employees.[707] The
contracting agency should be sensitive to these concerns when
negotiating contract terms. It also must recognize, however,
that, if the economic benefits of privatization are to be

_____

[705] Note, supra note 9, at 1498 n.158.

[706] Id. at 1477.

[707] See CSG Report, supra note 533, at 106-10 (describing
morale problems experienced by existing employees at various
facilities during transition from public to private operation).
The American Federation of State, County and Municipal Employees
(AFSCME), which represents more than 40,000 correctional
employees, strongly opposes the private management of
correctional facilities. American Federation of State, County
and Municipal Employees, Position on Contracting Out Correctional
Facilities (July 1985); see Privatization of Corrections, supra
note 460, at 74.

realized, the contractor must have some flexibility in choosing and managing its staff.[708]

The Model Contract provision attempts to strike a balance between these two competing interests. It encourages the contractor to retain existing employees without restricting its ability to upgrade the quality and efficiency of the staff. Specifically, the Model Contract provides that the contractor must give priority to qualified existing public employees when filling its initial staff requirements.[709] Former public employees who meet the minimum requirements set forth in the contract, successfully complete the initial training program,[710] and have qualifications that are equivalent to those of new applicants[711] should be hired before new applicants. This hiring preference should continue until all existing employees are placed or staffing requirements under the contract are met.

---

[708] See Note, supra note 9, at 1477 (noting claims of private-prison operators that greater flexibility in hiring and firing employees will lead to cost savings).

[709] The Model Contract restrictions only apply during the initial transition from public to private-sector management. After that time, the contractor is free to hire, retain, and discharge employees according to its needs and subject to other contract provisions regarding employment practices, personnel requirements, and staff/inmate ratios.

[710] See Model Contract § 4(B) (Training Requirements).

[711] The Model Contract language is intended to allow the contractor to consider all appropriate factors, including but not limited to: years of experience in the same or similar position; level of education or training relevant to the position; and quality of previous performance as evidenced by performance evaluations and records, suits against the employee or applicant in his or her individual capacity in which the employee or applicant was held liable, and any other indicia of past job performance.

Under the Model Contract, the contractor is not bound to hire all existing employees. The Model Contract is therefore more permissive than are many existing contracts.[712] Specifically, if the contractor can adequately operate the facility with less staff, it is free to release or not to hire those employees who are no longer needed. This situation should arise rarely, if at all, however, because most existing facilities are currently understaffed.[713] Most contractors, no matter how efficiently they utilize their staff, will have to increase the total number of employees in order to meet staffing requirements under the Model Contract.[714]

Although the contractor is also free to hire a new applicant

----

[712] Many contracts require the contractor to hire all existing employees. See CSG Report, supra note 533, at 106-07 (noting that Bay County and Hamilton County contracts require contractors to hire all existing employees); C. Ring, supra note 484, at 9. The Bay County Contract requires that existing employees complete a 40-hour training course to "be accepted as regular employees of CCA." Bay County Contract at 17, § 5.4. The Hamilton County Contract requires that the contractor hire all existing employees, but gives the contractor discretion to dismiss them as necessary at a later date. Hamilton County Contract at 41, § 16. For a statute that requires that existing employees be hired by the contractor for "any position for which they qualify," see 1988 N.M. Laws § 33-1-17(D). See also Ark. Stat. Ann. § 12-50-110 (Supp. 1987) ("employees whose employment becomes subject to a contract with a private prison contractor shall be given a hiring preference for available positions for which they qualify").

The Council of State Governments' Report recommends that the contract include a provision requiring the contractor to give employment preference to existing employees. CSG Report, supra note 533, at xiv.

[713] Cf. Funke, The Economics of Prison Crowding, 478 Annals 86, 88-89 (discussing high cost of staffing).

[714] See Model Contract § 4(D) (Staff Ratio).

before hiring an existing employee, the contractor must first determine that the new applicant is better qualified for the position.[715] The pool of new applicants who are better qualified than existing employees is likely to be very small. Therefore, only those existing employees who are minimally qualified or unqualified for their positions will face the threat of losing their jobs.

The Model Contract also requires that the contractor offer existing employees salaries and benefits comparable to those that they received as public employees.[716] In addition, the contractor is required to credit each existing employee with the amount of annual leave and compensatory and personal time he or she had accrued while employed by the contracting agency.[717]

---

[715] See supra note 711 (listing factors that contractor should consider in determining qualification levels of employees and new applicants).

[716] In two examples cited by the Council of State Governments' Report, the Bay County and Hamilton County facilities, the contractor agreed to maintain salary and certain benefits at the same or slightly higher levels. CSG Report, supra note 533, at 106-07. In the Bay County Contract, for example, CCA promised that all existing employees would receive at least a $500 increase over the salary they were currently earning with the county. Bay County Contract app. A, attach 1.

[717] Many of the objections raised by employees of existing facilities have centered on the status of accrued-leave time and retirement benefits. See CSG Report, supra note 533, at 106-07 (describing concerns of employees at Bay County, Hamilton County, and Florida School for Boys facilities over loss of accrued benefits). The Model Contract does not expressly address the issue of retirement benefits. It is recommended, however, that the contracting agency take whatever steps are necessary to ensure that accrued employee-retirement benefits are not lost due to the privatization of the facility. This may mean that the contracting agency will have to assume responsibility for payment of benefits already earned.

This requirement is necessary if qualified existing employees are to have the option of keeping their jobs at the newly privatized facility. The practical effect of reducing salaries or eliminating benefits would be to remove this option for many employees.[718]

Model Contract Provision:

> Every correctional employee currently employed by the contracting agency who desires to remain employed at the facility shall be accepted as an employee of the contractor if he or she satisfactorily completes the training requirements detailed in Subsection 4(B) of this contract and meets all other requirements regarding employees set forth in this contract.[719] The contractor shall not be required to hire otherwise qualified employees from the existing facility if the contractor has met the staffing levels required by this contract. The contractor shall also have the discretion to hire a new applicant over an existing employee if the contractor determines that the new applicant is better qualified for the position. Factors to be considered may include, but are not limited to, records and evaluations of the employee's past job performance and his or her years of experience, education, and/or training relevant to the position.
>
> This provision supersedes ACA Standards 2-4054 and 2-4055 during the initial hiring period only.[720]

---

[718] See C. Ring, supra note 484, at 28 (observing that, in general, employees of public corrections facilities remain underpaid). Any further reduction in salary and benefits, therefore, could force many employees to leave the facility.

[719] This requirement does not apply to administrative employees at existing facilities.

[720] These provisions recommend policy for the selection of employees and are incorporated as mandatory in Model Contract § 4(A)(1) (Employment Discrimination).

Existing employees shall be entitled to starting wages and benefits, including [list benefits] that are equal to or greater than the wages and benefits that an employee of comparable qualifications would receive for the same position from the contracting agency. The contractor shall credit to each former contracting-agency employee the amount of annual leave, compensatory leave time, and personal leave time, including sick leave, that the contracting agency certifies the employee has on the day employment terminates with the contracting agency.[721]

_____

[721] This provision is derived from the Santa Fe Contract at 8, § 3.8.

3.   Employee Background Investigations

Commentary:

For security reasons, the Model Contract provides that each prospective employee must be subject to a thorough background investigation before being accepted for employment.[722] This investigation should include examination of an applicant's criminal, medical, and employment history. The applicable ACA Standards are 2-4061 through 2-4063.[723] Included in the ACA Standards are provisions for a criminal record check, a physical examination, and a probationary appointment term of six months to one year. Persons not performing satisfactorily may be terminated during the probationary period.

---

[722] Inadequate background checks on private prison guards may lead to guards with questionable backgrounds being employed at correctional facilities. See Note, supra note 9, at 1498 (citing Pennsylvania Legis. Budget & Finance Comm., Report on a Study of Issues Related to the Potential Operation of Private Prisons in Pennsylvania 30 (1985)).

[723] These Standards provide:

2-4061: "In accordance with state and federal statutes, a criminal record check is conducted on all new employees to ascertain whether there are criminal convictions which have a specific relationship to job performance."

2-4062: "Written policy and procedure require a physical examination of all employees by a physician at the time of employment. Provisions exist for reexamination when indicated."

2-4063: "Written policy and procedure provide that employees are appointed initially for a probationary term of not less than six months or more than one year."

Model Contract Provision:

Prior to and as a condition of employment, a background investigation shall be made of each prospective employee. This investigation shall include criminal (obtaining FBI or NCIC records), medical, and employment histories. A prospective employee may be denied employment if the background investigation reveals information indicating that he or she would not be an appropriate correctional employee. The contractor shall maintain fingerprint charts on every employee.[724]

This provision incorporates as mandatory ACA Standards 2-4061 through 2-4063. The contractor has a continuing obligation to comply with these Standards, as well as with subsequent ACA Standards to the extent that they are approved by the contracting agency.

---

[724] This provision is derived from Santa Fe Contract at 9, § 3.9; 1985 Kentucky RFP at 30-3, § 30.300.

Section 4(B): Employee Training Requirements

Commentary:

It is imperative that all of the private contractor's
employees receive adequate training in order to ensure the safety
and security of the inmates, the staff, and the surrounding
community. Proper training may also enable the contracting
agency to reduce its potential liability.[725] There has already
been some controversy concerning the adequacy of the training
that is currently provided for private corrections employees and
security guards.[726] To avoid problems in this area, the contract
must set forth with sufficient specificity the amount and
substance of the training that the contractor is required to
provide its employees.

The Model Contract requires that all prison and jail
employees receive new-employee orientation training prior to

---

[725] See Note, supra note 629, at 833 n.96 (noting that
insufficient training of staff may lead to prisoner lawsuits
alleging due process violations); W. Collins, Contracting for
Correctional Services: Some Legal Considerations 17-18 (1985)
(unpublished memorandum) (advising that inadequately trained
prison employees may draw contracting agencies into litigation).

[726] See CCA Falls Short, supra note 582 (citing statements
by former CCA employees that CCA has not provided adequate
training for guards at its Silverdale facility); Note, supra note
629, at 833 n.96 (noting inadequate training of prison guards);
Note, supra note 9, at 1498-99 (giving examples of inadequate
training provided for private correctional employees). At least
one contract for a private facility, however, requires training
in accordance with ACA Standards and all applicable statutory
provisions. See Santa Fe Contract at 10, § 3.10 and app. D.
(describing elements of CCA's training program).

their initial assignment with the contractor. It also provides

for regular training and continuing-education programs that are

appropriate for the various types of employment. The contractor

is required to carry out these programs in accordance with the

guidelines set forth in ACA Standards 2-40~~79~~ through 2-4101.[727]

_____

[727] ACA Standards 2-4079 through 2-4101 provide as follows:

2-4079: "Written policy and procedure provide that the institution's training programs for all employees are specifically planned, coordinated, and supervised by a qualified employee at the supervisory level, and reviewed annually. (Essential)." This Standard has been incorporated in the Model Contract as mandatory.

2-4080: "The individual coordinating the training and staff development program has received specialized training for that position. At a minimum, full-time training personnel should have completed a 40 hour training-for-trainers course. (Essential)." This Standard has been incorporated in the Model Contract as mandatory.

2-4080-1 (added Aug. 1985): "The training curriculum is developed, evaluated, and updated based on an annual needs assessment that identifies current job-related training needs." This Standard has been incorporated in the Model Contract as mandatory.

2-4081: (revised Aug. 1983): "There is an advisory training committee composed of the institution's training officer and representatives from various institution departments. The committee develops a training plan for the institution, meets at least quarterly to review progress and resolve problems, maintains a written record of its deliberations, and reports to the warden/superintendent." This Standard has been incorporated in the Model Contract as mandatory.

2-4083: "The institution's training and staff development plan provides for an ongoing formal evaluation of all pre-service, in-service, and specialized training programs, with a written report prepared annually. (Essential)." This Standard has been incorporated in the Model Contract as mandatory.

2-4084: "Library and reference services are available to complement the training and staff development program. (Essential)."

2-4085: "The training and staff development program uses

Standards 2-4079 through 2-4083, 2-4086 through 2-4095, and 2-

the resources of other public and private agencies, private industry, colleges, and libraries. (Important)."

2-4086: "Space and equipment required for the training and staff development program is available. (Essential)." This Standard has been incorporated in the Model Contract as mandatory.

2-4087: "The budget includes funds for reimbursing staff for additional time spent in training or for replacement personnel required when regular personnel are off duty for training purposes. (Essential)." This Standard has been incorporated in the Model Contract as mandatory.

2-4088: "Written policy and procedure provide that all new full-time employees receive 40 hours of orientation/training prior to being independently assigned to a particular job. This orientation/training is to include, at a minimum, orientation to the purpose, goals, policies and procedures of the institution and parent agency; working conditions and regulations; responsibilities and rights of employees; and an overview of the correctional field. Depending upon the employee(s) and the requirements of the particular job, the orientation/training may include some preparatory instruction related to the particular job. There are provisions for acknowledging and giving credit for prior training received. (Essential)." This Standard has been incorporated in the Model Contract as mandatory.

2-4089: "Written policy and procedure provide that all clerical/support employees who have minimal contact with inmates receive an additional 16 hours of training during the first year of employment and 16 hours of training each year thereafter. (Essential)." This Standard has been incorporated in the Model Contract as mandatory.

2-4090: "Written policy and procedure provide that all support employees who have regular or daily inmate contact receive an additional 40 hours of training during their first year of employment and an additional 40 hours of training each subsequent year of employment. (Essential)." This Standard has been incorporated in the Model Contract as mandatory.

2-4091: "Written policy and procedure provide that all professional specialists employees who have inmate contact receive an additional 40 hours of training during their first year of employment, and an additional 40 hours of training each subsequent year of employment. (Essential)." This Standard has been incorporated in the Model Contract as mandatory.

2-4092: "Written policy and procedure provide that all new correctional officers receive an additional 120 hours of training

4098 are incorporated as mandatory provisions in the Model

_____

during their first year of employment and an additional 40 hours of training each subsequent year of employment. At a minimum this training covers the following areas:

        Security procedures
        Supervision of inmates
        Use of force regulations and tactics
        Report writing
        Inmate rules and regulations
        Rights and responsibilities of inmates
        Fire and emergency procedures
        Firearms training
        Key control
        Interpersonal relations
        Social/cultural life styles of the inmate population
        Communication skills
        First aid.

(Essential)." This Standard has been incorporated in the Model Contract as mandatory.

2-4093: "Written policy and procedure provide that all administrative and managerial staff receive 40 hours of training during their first year of employment, and an additional 40 hours of training each subsequent year of employment. This training covers the following areas, at a minimum: general management and related subjects; labor law; employee-management relations; the interaction of elements of the criminal justice system; and relationships with other service agencies. (Essential)." This Standard has been incorporated in the Model Contract as mandatory.

2-4094: "When there is an emergency unit, written policy and procedure provide that all assigned officers have one year of experience as a correctional officer, which includes 160 hours of training, that they receive 40 hours of relevant emergency unit training prior to assignment, which may be part of the first year training (160 hours), and that at least 16 hours of the 40 hours of annual training be specifically related to emergency unit assignment. (Essential)." This Standard has been incorporated in the Model Contract as mandatory.

2-4095: "All part-time staff receive formal orientation appropriate to their assignments and additional training as needed. (Essential)." This Standard has been incorporated in the Model Contract as mandatory.

2-4096: "Prior to assignment to a post involving possible use of a firearm, all personnel authorized to use firearms receive appropriate firearm training; this training covers the use, safety, care, and constraints involved in the use of

Contract.[728]

The contracting agency may also want to strengthen these general ACA guidelines[729] by including more specific training requirements for certain types of employees, or by actually formulating a training program that the contractor would be required to implement.[730] Alternatively, the contracting agency

---

firearms. All authorized personnel are required to demonstrate competency on at least an annual basis. (Mandatory)."

2-4097: "All personnel authorized to use chemical agents are thoroughly trained in their use and in the treatment of individuals exposed to the chemical agent. (Mandatory)."

2-4098: "All security and custodial personnel are trained in approved methods of self-defense and the use of force as a last resort to control inmates. (Essential)." This Standard has been incorporated in the Model Contract as mandatory.

2-4099: "Written policy and procedure encourage employees to continue their education. (Important)."

2-4100: Deleted Mar. 1983.

2-4101 (revised Mar. 1983): "The institution encourages and provides administrative leave and/or reimbursement for employees attending approved professional meetings, seminars, and/or similar work-related activities."

[728] The ACA has classified the majority of these Standards as nonmandatory. Because of the importance of these provisions to the adequate training of correctional employees, however, they are incorporated as mandatory in the Model Contract. Changes from nonmandatory to mandatory status are indicated in supra note 727.

[729] ACA Standards have been criticized for their emphasis on formal policy and procedure rather than actual performance, as well as for the generality of their terms. See Note, supra note 9, at 1475, 1494 (commenting that reliance on ACA Standards, which do not set forth "concrete" requirements, may allow private contractors to cut costs in the area of personnel training).

[730] For example, in addition to requiring the Eckerd Foundation to carry out training of its employees in accordance with ACA Standards, the State of Florida also specifically requires Aggression Control Techniques training for all child-care staff. Eckerd Foundation Contract attach. I, at 4.

may require the contractor to include a detailed training program as a part of its proposal.[731] This program would then be incorporated in the contract, subject to modifications negotiated by the parties.

It has been suggested that adequate training of private correctional employees can be achieved through contractual and statutory provisions that require the contractor's employees to meet the same training standards as do employees of public facilities.[732] While such a requirement is certainly preferable to allowing training levels that are _lower_ than those that are currently achieved by public employees,[733] it nevertheless may not be sufficient. In many cases, statutory and regulatory standards regarding training of prison and jail personnel are minimal and the actual training that is provided to public employees is inadequate.[734] In those cases, however, in which state statutes, local ordinances, or existing contracting-agency

---

Pennsylvania has considered a proposal that provided that its Department of Corrections shall formulate a specific training program for private-prison employees. See H. 307, P.N. 337 (Pa. House of Rep. 1985); Woolley, supra note 582, at 324.

[731] See Texas RFP at 2, § 3(c).

[732] Cf. C. Ring, _supra_ note 484, at 28-30 (arguing that fears that private companies will cut costs in part by spending less on training are unwarranted because the government has authority to and should require that private providers meet the same standards as those that must be met in public facilities).

[733] Florida requires that private providers must meet the same training requirements that the government must meet. Fla. Stat. Ann. § 944.105(6) (West. Cum. Supp. 1988). Other states leave this matter to the contracting parties. See Mont. Code Ann. § 7-32-2232(2)(e) (1987); N.M. Stat. § 33-3-27(C) (1987).

[734] See Note, _supra_ note 629, at 833.

policies set training standards that are _higher_ than those that would be achieved by compliance with ACA Standards, the contract should require the contractor to meet the more stringent public standards.[735]

The parties should also address whether an employee's previous training may be credited to the training hours that are required for new employees under the contract.[736] This issue will arise primarily when the contractor takes over an existing facility and hires employees who are currently working at that facility. The issue may also be relevant, however, when the contractor provides a new facility and hires employees from other facilities (whether in the same or other jurisdictions).[737]

The Model Contract does not include a provision addressing this issue. Should the parties choose to adopt such a provision, they should consider whether to distinguish between employees who have received training under the auspices of the contracting agency and those who have received their training elsewhere. The parties should also consider whether such a provision will adequately assure that the quality of training required by ACA Standards (or more stringent guidelines) will be achieved. Specifically, in deciding whether to credit the employees' previous hours of training, the parties should consider whether to require that the appropriate officials take into account

---

735   Cf. Model Contract § 3(F)(1) (Operating Standards).

736   This issue is addressed by CCA in its training program. See Santa Fe Contract app. D.

737   Id.

factors such as the relative quality of previous training, the similarity between the substance of previous training and that which is provided by the private facility, and the amount of time that has elapsed between the completion of previous training and the date of hire. Finally, all training expenses should be the responsibility of the contractor.[738]

Model Contract Provision:

> All of the contractor's employees shall successfully complete a forty (40) hour new-employee orientation program, as required by ACA Standards, after being hired and prior to regular assignment. Thereafter, the contractor shall comply with all ACA Standards concerning training (or more stringent standards, should the law require) and shall ensure that the contractor's employees receive sufficient training to comply with ACA Standards 2-4079 through 2-4101. Standards 2-4079 through 2-4083, 2-4086 through 2-4095, and 2-4098 are incorporated as mandatory. [In addition, the contractor shall take all reasonable actions to help each correctional or detention employee retain his or her certification from the (appropriate authority and jurisdiction).[739]]

> The contractor shall provide to the contract monitor documentation of all completed employee training as soon as possible after its completion. Upon request, the monitor shall be permitted to review training curriculum and other training-related records that are maintained by the

---

[738] See Fla. Stat. Ann. § 951.062(6) (West Cum. Supp. 1988) (providing that private contractor must pay training expenses of "[p]rivate correctional officers responsible for supervising inmates within the facility"); N.M. Stat. Ann. § 33-3-27(C) (1987) ("All agreements with private independent contractors for the operation, or provision and operation, of jails shall provide for the independent contractor to provide and pay for training for jailers to meet minimum training standards . . . .").

[739] Bay County Contract at 17, § 5.4.

contractor. The monitor shall be permitted to audit training classes at any time.[740]

The contractor shall be responsible for all training expenses.

---

740   Santa Fe Contract at 10, § 3.10(B).

Section 4(C): Personnel Policy

Commentary:

A written personnel policy, approved by the contracting agency, is necessary both to guarantee the rights and privileges of the facility's staff and to delineate their obligations. In addition to requiring compliance with all ACA Standards relating to personnel,[741] the Model Contract requires that the

---

[741] The applicable ACA Standards are 2-4060, 2-4064, 2-4065, 2-4067, 2-4070, 2-4076, 2-4077, and 2-4078, all of which are incorporated in the Model Contract as mandatory. These Standards provide as follows:

2-4060: "The warden/superintendent reviews annually the internal personnel policies of the institution and when indicated, submits recommended changes to the parent agency which are relevant to the parent agency policies."

2-4064: "Compensation and benefit levels for all institution personnel are comparable to similar occupational groups in the state or region."

2-4065: "Written policy and procedure provide for employees to be reimbursed for all approved expenses incurred in the performance of their duties."

2-4067: "There is a personnel policy manual which covers, at a minimum, the following areas: organization; recruitment procedures; equal employment opportunity provisions; job qualifications, descriptions and responsibilities; basis for determining salaries; benefits, holidays, leave and work hours; personnel records; employee evaluation; in-service training; promotion; retirement, resignation and termination; employee-management relations; physical fitness policy; disciplinary procedures; grievance and appeals procedures; statutes relating to political practices and insurance and professional liability requirements. In addition to this information, new staff are informed, in writing, of the hostage policy of the institution as it addresses staff roles and safety. A copy of this manual is available to each employee."

2-4070: "The institution makes available to all employees a

contractor's personnel policy contain all legal standards that
are applicable to private industry, such as the Fair Labor
Standards Act[742] and the Service Contract Act,[743] and any

---

written code of ethics that prohibits employees from using their
official position to secure privileges for themselves or others
and from engaging in activities that constitute a conflict of
interest."

2-4076: "The institution maintains a current, accurate, and
confidential personnel record on each employee."

2-4077: "Written policy and procedure make provision for
employees to challenge information in their personnel file and
have it corrected or removed if it is proven inaccurate."

2-4078: "Written policy and procedure provide for a written
annual performance review of all employees, which is based on
defined criteria and is reviewed and discussed with the
employee."

[742]   29 U.S.C. §§ 201-219 (1982 & Supp. III 1985). The Fair
Labor Standards Act (FLSA) requires covered employers to pay
their employees a minimum hourly wage and overtime compensation
at the rate of one and one-half times their regular hourly wage
for work in excess of 40 hours per work week. 29 U.S.C. § 206
(1982) (minimum wage); 29 U.S.C. § 207 (1982 & Supp. III 1985)
(maximum hours).

The FLSA also applies to certain federal, state, and local-
government employees, including security personnel in
correctional institutions. Congress has enacted several
provisions, however, that somewhat reduce the impact of the FLSA
on these and other public-safety-related activities, particularly
at the state and local levels. See 29 U.S.C. § 203(e)(4)(A)
(Supp. III 1985) (permitting state and local volunteers to
receive nominal compensation for their services without becoming
"employees" subject to the FLSA's wage and overtime
requirements); 29 U.S.C. § 207(k) (1982) (providing federal,
state, and local law-enforcement agencies limited overtime
exception that establishes higher ceilings on the maximum number
of hours that must be worked before overtime compensation is
paid); 29 U.S.C. § 207(o) (Supp. III 1985) (allowing state and
local employees to bargain for compensatory-time plans that allow
them to be compensated for overtime work with time off rather
than with money); id. § 207(p)(1) (exempting from overtime the
hours worked by state and local public-safety employees on
special-detail assignments); id. § 207(p)(2) (providing that
state and local employees may perform part-time work for the same
public employer without hours being counted as overtime if the
work "is in a different capacity from any capacity in which the

additional standards that the contracting agency has included in
the RFP.[744] Examples of specific areas that must be addressed in

_____

employee is regularly employed").

These cost-saving measures are not available to private
safety employees, even if they are under contract with a public
agency. See 29 C.F.R. § 553.1(c) (1987) (expressly limiting
section 207(k) to public agencies).

[743] 41 U.S.C. §§ 351-358 (1982). The Service Contract Act
applies to private independent contractors who perform service
contracts for the federal government or the District of Columbia
and whose contracts are for more than $2,500 and do not fall
within certain statutory exemptions that are provided in the
Act. Id. § 351(a). The Secretary of Labor makes an independent
determination regarding the applicability of the Act, see
Curtiss-Wright Corp. v. McLucas, 364 F. Supp. 750, 769 (1973), so
it is uncertain whether the Act would be found applicable to
contracts for the operation of federal correctional facilities.
At least one RFP for the operation of an INS detention facility,
however, expressly incorporates the Act. INS RFP at 66, § I(I).

The Act requires contractors to pay their employees wages
and provide them benefits that either meet or exceed the levels
that are "prevailing . . . in the locality" as determined by the
Secretary of Labor, or that are determined by a collective-
bargaining agreement. 41 U.S.C. §§ 351(a)(1), (2) (1982). In no
event may compensation fall below levels that are set under the
FLSA. Id. § 351(b)(1). The Act also limits the duration of
service contracts to five years, with provisions for
renegotiation of wage and benefit levels at least once every two
years. Id. § 353(d).

[744] ACA Standards require the contractor to have policies
regarding various personnel issues, but, except for the general
guidelines governing wages and benefits in Standard 2-4064, the
ACA Standards do not address the content of the policies.
Therefore, a contracting agency should require that the
contractor meet more specific contractual guidelines to ensure
that the contractor does not achieve cost savings through
unreasonable personnel practices. These guidelines may be
derived from the contracting agency's existing policies governing
employee relations, or they may be formulated specifically for
private incarceration facilities.

Further, the contracting agency should bear in mind that the
National Labor Relations Board has focused on the amount of
control that is maintained by the contractor over core bargaining
issues, such as salary and benefit levels, in deciding whether
its employees enjoy the protection of the NLRA, including the
right to strike. See Model Contract § 4(E) (Labor Disputes/Right

the personnel policy are: salary and benefit levels; hiring, promotion, and termination procedures; and employee-grievance procedures.

Unlike governmental entities, independent contractors who provide services to contracting agencies are not subject to civil-service requirements.[745] Most federal and state employees, however, as well some local employees, are included in a civil-service system created by constitution or statute.[746] Civil-service regulations address most aspects of personnel policy. Most notable, perhaps, are the guarantees of appointment and promotion on the basis of merit and the prohibition against termination of an employee without cause.[747] Proponents of privatization believe that private industry will be able to operate incarceration facilities at a lower cost than the government will, in part because private management will not be constrained by civil-service regulations.[748] Critics, on the other hand, argue that the civil-service system is necessary to protect employees, particularly if they are not unionized, and to

---

to Strike) (noting that, if an exempt governmental agency maintains extensive control over labor bargaining issues, the employer may not be able to engage in meaningful bargaining with its employees and may therefore not be subject to the NLRA).

[745] R. Kirschner, C. Becker & J. Sullivan, "Punishment for Profit:" The Contracting Out of Corrections 20 (1986) (consultant's report prepared for AFSCME).

[746] Becker, With Whose Hands: Privatization, Public Employment, and Democracy, 6 Yale L. & Pol'y Rev. 88, 94-95 (1988).

[747] Id. at 95-96.

[748] Privatization of Corrections, supra note 460, at 78.

maintain or improve the quality of the labor force.[749]   The Model

Contract provision balances these competing concerns.

---

[749]   See C. Ring, supra note 484, at 28 (citing critics'
argument that correctional employees will not develop the career
orientation that is necessary to improve prison operations if
they do not have the protection of union contracts and civil-
service requirements); Becker, supra note 746, at 108 (arguing
that, when labor's tie to the state is severed, market forces
will drive private companies to employ the cheapest labor
available); Privatizing Prisons Has Become a Ripe Market for
Entrepreneurs Despite Public Sector, Union Opposition and Risks,
Privatization, July 21, 1988, at 4, 6.

A lawsuit challenging privatization as an illegal
infringement on the protections of the state civil-service system
is now pending in California.   The plaintiffs contend that, under
California law,

> the sole justification for contracting out is
> economy.   Such justification has never been accepted
> as a legitimate reason for circumventing the civil
> service system.   [T]he civil service system has been
> constitutionally enacted to ensure that competing
> interests of economy, stability, competency,
> fairness and equality be given shared consideration
> in structuring state government.   The courts have
> never decided that cost-savings should be preeminent
> among these competing interests, and have never
> permitted contracting out solely because it is cost
> efficient to do so.   Consistent with these
> principles, the Agreements must be considered
> constitutionally unsound and cannot be used in lieu
> of retaining civil service employees.

Points and Authorities in Support of Application for Temporary
Restraining Order and Order to Show Cause at 21-22, California
Correctional Peace Officers Ass'n v. California Dep't of
Corrections, No. 356286 (Super. Ct., County of Sacramento, Dec.
22, 1987) (order denying preliminary injunction); cf. Local 2173
of the American Fed'n of State, County, and Municipal Employees
v. McWherter, No. 87-34-II (Tenn. Ct. App. June 5, 1987)
(affirming dismissal for lack of standing because challenge to
proposed private facility was premature).

Model Contract Provision:

        The contractor must implement and at all times
maintain a personnel policy that includes:

        (1) all of the elements and substantive
guidelines that are set forth in ACA Standards 2-
4060, 2-4064, 2-4065, 2-4067, 2-4070, 2-4076, 2-
4077, and 2-4078, which are hereby incorporated as
mandatory;

        (2) all applicable federal, state, and local
statutory and regulatory provisions, including [list
provisions]; and

        (3) the following additional standards: [list
standards].

Section 4(D): Staff Ratio

Commentary:

For security reasons, the facility must be adequately staffed twenty-four hours a day, seven days a week. The parties need not include a specific numerical staff/inmate ratio in the contract.[750] A requirement that the contractor maintain a specific number of employees might reduce the incentive to develop innovative, more efficient staffing methods.[751] Even if the contractor were to develop a system that allowed it to staff the facility adequately with fewer people, it would remain bound by the contractually required number of staff.

More efficient use of personnel is often cited as an anticipated benefit of privatization.[752] Critics of privatization respond that contractors are likely to reduce staff levels in an effort to cut labor costs and realize a greater profit.[753] Private companies contend, however, that the

---

[750]   See, e.g., CSG Report, supra note 533, at 95 (stating that contracting agencies should avoid overly specific requirements in RFP's, such as specific inmate/staff ratios). The parties could certainly decide, however, that a specified staff/inmate ratio is appropriate and necessary for a particular facility.

[751]   See id.

[752]   See, e.g., id.

[753]   See Note, supra note 9, at 1477 (predicting that private-prison industry will have to cut labor-related costs if it is to remain profitable); Taylor, Should Private Firms Build, Run Prisons?, Wash. Post, May 7, 1985, at A15, col. 4 (citing comments of former counsel to Houston ACLU attributing what he

necessary cost savings can be achieved through improvements in compensation and working conditions that boost staff morale and reduce turnover, as well as in efficient staff scheduling to reduce overtime.[754] In order to further ensure that private companies will in fact provide a level of staffing that is adequate, the contracting agency may want to require prospective contractors to include staffing patterns in their proposals, which patterns could later be incorporated in the final contract.[755]

ACA Standards 2-4072 through 2-4075[756] address staff levels

---

viewed as inadequate staffing levels at INS Houston facility to private contractor's need to cut costs).

[754] Corrections Corporation of America Prospectus 14 (Oct. 1, 1986); see C. Ring, supra note 484, at 28 (citing CCA-operated Silverdale facility as example of improvement in staffing levels that can be achieved by privatization). But see CCA Falls Short, supra note 582 (noting critics' claims that Silverdale facility has been plagued by low employee morale and high turnover rates due to poor employee-management relations).

[755] See Federal Bureau of Prisons RFP at 3, §I(C) (requiring that proposals include anticipated staffing patterns). This requirement would also provide a better basis for comparison of proposals on this issue.

[756] "Personnel requirements in all categories of staff are determined on an ongoing basis in order to ensure inmate access to staff and availability of support services." ACA Standard 2-4072.

"There is a formula used to determine the number of persons needed to staff key positions in the institution which considers, at a minimum, regular days off, annual leave, holidays and average sick leave." ACA Standard 2-4073.

"The warden/superintendent can document that the vacancy rate of staff positions that are authorized to be filled and work directly with inmates does not exceed an overall average of 10% during any 18 month period." ACA Standard 2-4074.

"Written policy and procedure provide for provisional appointments to ensure the availability of personnel for short-

at correctional facilities. These Standards should be
incorporated in the contract as mandatory.

Model Contract Provision:

> The facility shall be staffed 24 hours per day,
> 7 days per week. The staffing pattern shall be
> adequate to ensure close inmate surveillance and
> maintenance of security within the facility. The
> contractor shall provide adequate staff to maintain
> an effective patrol of the perimeter of the facility
> during periods of darkness, times of emergency, and
> when inmates are not involved with supervised
> activities and/or programs.[757]

> The staffing pattern shall address
> transportation and security needs. The staffing
> pattern shall also consider the proximity of the
> facility to neighborhoods, schools, etc.[758]

> This provision incorporates as mandatory ACA
> Standards 2-4072 through 2-4075. The contractor has
> a continuing obligation to comply with the existing
> Standards, as well as with subsequent ACA Standards
> to the extent that they are approved by the
> contracting agency.

---

term, full-time, or part-time work in emergency situations." ACA
Standard 2-4075.

[757] This provision is derived from Hamilton County Contract
app. A, at 13, § 5.03(b).

[758] This provision is derived from 1985 Kentucky RFP at 30-
2, § 30.300.

Section 4(E): Labor Disputes/Right to Strike

Commentary:

The Labor Dispute/Right to Strike section of the employee
provisions is a crucial aspect of the Model Contract. The risk
of labor disputes or work stoppages at private correctional or
detention facilities may be increased by the fact that the legal
restraints that apply to strikes by public employees do not apply
to strikes by private employees.[759] The provision that addresses
these problems must be drafted carefully to minimize to the
extent possible the risk of a labor disturbance or work stoppage
that would threaten the security of the facility and the
surrounding community.

1.   Federal Facilities

There are two provisions of federal law that prohibit
strikes by federal employees, including employees of the Federal
Bureau of Prisons. The first, 5 U.S.C. § 7311,[760] prohibits

---

[759] But cf. CSG Report, supra note 533, at 26 (noting
contractors' claims that higher wages and benefits will reduce
risk of labor disturbances).

[760] 5 U.S.C. § 7311 states in relevant part:

An individual may not accept or hold a position
in the Government of the United States or the
government of the District of Columbia if he-- . . .

(3) participates in a strike, or asserts
the right to strike, against the Government of

federal employees from participating in a strike and from

belonging to an organization that participates in or assists in

strikes against the federal government. Federal employers may

seek injunctive relief for violations of this provision.[761] The

second federal anti-strike provision, 18 U.S.C. § 1918,[762]

---

the United States or the government of the
District of Columbia; or

(4) is a member of an organization of
employees of the Government of the United
States or of individuals employed by the
government of the District of Columbia that he
knows asserts the right to strike against the
Government of the United States or the
government of the District of Columbia.

5 U.S.C. § 7311 (1982).

[761] United States v. Professional Air Traffic Controllers
Org. (PATCO), 653 F.2d 1134, 1141 (7th Cir.) (reversing district
court's holding that it lacked subject-matter jurisdiction and
holding injunction to be available remedy against striking
controllers), cert. denied, 454 U.S. 1083 (1981).

[762] 18 U.S.C. § 1918 provides in relevant part:

Whoever violates the provision of section 7311
of title 5 that an individual may not accept or hold
a position in the Government of the United States or
the government of the District of Columbia if he--
. . .

(3) participates in a strike, or asserts
the right to strike, against the Government of
the United States or the government of the
District of Columbia; or

(4) is a member of an organization of
employees of the Government of the United
States or of individuals employed by the
government of the District of Columbia that he
knows asserts the right to strike against the
Government of the United States or the
government of the District of Columbia;

shall be fined not more that $1,000 or imprisoned
not more than one year and a day, or both.

establishes a criminal penalty for violations of section 7311. Based on these provisions, courts have held that strikes by federal employees against the federal government are forbidden.[763]

This prohibition is reflected in 5 U.S.C. § 3333,[764] which requires every federal employee to sign an affidavit that must contain, among other things, a statement to the effect that the employee will not violate the restrictions that are set forth in section 7311 regarding strikes against the federal government. Federal labor unions are also expressly prohibited from

_____

18 U.S.C. § 1918 (1982).

[763] See, e.g., Air Transp. Ass'n (ATA) v. Professional Air Traffic Controllers Org. (PATCO), 516 F. Supp. 1108, 1110 (E.D.N.Y. 1981) ("strikes by federal employees continue to be illegal, 5 U.S.C. § 7311, and indeed criminal, 18 U.S.C. § 1918"); United States v. Professional Air Traffic Controllers Org. (PATCO), 504 F. Supp. 432, 440 (N.D. Ill. 1980) ("it is absolutely clear that a federal employee who strikes . . . may be prosecuted under 18 U.S.C. § 1918"), rev'd on other grounds, 653 F.2d 1134 (7th Cir. 1981); Air Transp. Ass'n v. Professional Air Traffic Controllers Org. (PATCO), 313 F. Supp. 181, 185 (E.D.N.Y.) ("federal law makes it a crime for a government employee to participate in a strike"), vacated in part on other grounds, United States v. Professional Air Traffic Controllers Org. (PATCO), 438 F.2d 79 (2d Cir. 1970), cert. denied, 402 U.S. 915 (1971); Bateman v. South Carolina State Ports Auth., 298 F. Supp. 999, 1001 (D.S.C. 1969) ("[s]trikes by Federal employees against the Federal Government are forbidden").

[764] 5 U.S.C. § 3333 (1982). The relevant portion of section 3333 states:

> (a) [A]n individual who accepts office or employment in the Government of the United States or in the Government of the District of Columbia shall execute an affidavit within 60 days after accepting the office or employment that his acceptance and holding of the office or employment does not or will not violate section 7311 of this title.

Id. § 3333(a).

striking. Executive Order 11491 gives federal employees the right to form, join, and assist labor organizations.[765] It excludes from the definition of "labor organization," however, an organization that assists or participates in strikes against the federal government.[766] It also defines participation in these activities by such an organization as an "unfair labor practice."[767]

The federal courts have upheld the constitutionality of the anti-strike provisions. A leading case on point is United Federation of Postal Clerks v. Blount.[768] The federal court held

---

[765] Exec. Order No. 11491, 3 C.F.R. § 191 (1969).

[766] Id. § 2(e)(2). Specifically, section 2(e)(2) excludes an organization that "asserts the right to strike against the Government of the United States or any agency thereof, or assists or participates in such a strike, or imposes a duty or obligation to conduct, assist, or participate in such a strike." Id.

President Nixon subsequently amended section 2(e)(2) in Executive Order No. 11616, 3 C.F.R. § 202 (1971). The amended version omits the language that prohibits federal-employee labor organizations from asserting the right to strike. Id.; see infra notes 770-772 and accompanying text (discussing district-court decision finding that it is unconstitutional for the federal government to prohibit employees and organizations from asserting the right to strike).

[767] Exec. Order No. 11491, 3 C.F.R. § 191(b)(4) (1969). Under section 191(b)(4), it is an unfair labor practice for a federal-employee labor organization to "call or engage in a strike, work stoppage, or slowdown; picket an agency in a labor-management dispute; or condone any such activity by failing to prevent or stop it . . . ." Id.

[768] 325 F. Supp. 879 (D.D.C. 1971), aff'd, 404 U.S. 802 (1972). The action was brought by a public-employee labor organization, consisting primarily of post-office employees, for declaratory and injunctive relief invalidating the portions of 5 U.S.C. § 7311, 18 U.S.C. § 1918, 5 U.S.C. § 3333, and Exec. Order No. 11491 that prohibit strikes against the federal government or the District of Columbia. Id. at 880.

-292-

constitutional the affidavit requirement of 5 U.S.C. § 3333, as well as those portions of 5 U.S.C. § 7311(3), 18 U.S.C. § 1918(3), and Executive Order 11491 that prohibit federal employees from participating in strikes against the United States government or the government of the District of Columbia.[769]

The court was careful to limit its holding to the constitutionality of the provisions prohibiting actual strikes against the federal government. In an earlier case, National Association of Letter Carriers [NALC] v. Blount,[770] the court had struck down, as an unconstitutional infringement on employees' first amendment rights, portions of 5 U.S.C. §§ 7311(3) and (4) and the portions of the employment-affidavit requirement in 5 U.S.C. § 3333 (since repealed) that prohibited federal employees from asserting the right to strike or from being members of

_____

[769] Id. at 885. The plaintiff had contended that the right to strike was a fundamental right protected by the Constitution. Id. at 881. The court, however, noted that, at common law, neither private nor public employees had a constitutional right to strike. Id. at 882. This right was given to private employees by statute. Id. (citing section 157 of the National Labor Relations Act, which is codified at 29 U.S.C. §§ 141-183 (1982)). In the absence of a statute, therefore, public employees "do not possess the right to strike." Id. The court also disagreed with plaintiff's assertion that the word "strike" and the phrase "participates in a strike" used in the challenged statutes were "so vague that men of common intelligence" would differ on their meaning and application. Id. at 884; see also National Treasury Employees Union v. Fasser, 428 F. Supp. 295, 298 (D.D.C. 1976) (holding that Exec. Order No. 11491 can constitutionally prohibit any picketing -- whether or not peaceful and informational -- that actually interferes or reasonably threatens to interfere with the operation of affected government agency), aff'd without opinion, 103 L.R.R.M. (BNA) 2603 (D.C. Cir. 1979).

[770] 305 F. Supp. 546 (D.D.C. 1969), appeal dismissed, 400 U.S. 801 (1970).

organizations that they knew asserted the right to strike against the federal or District of Columbia governments.[771] The court also found that the provisions of the statute were severable; therefore, the prohibitions against actual striking were viable alone.[772]

The prohibition against strikes by federal employees appears to extend to employees of the Federal Bureau of Prisons. There is no federal statutory language that explicitly defines them as federal employees and, because they have never struck,[773] there are no cases discussing the applicability of the federal anti-strike provisions to federal prison employees. A close reading of several sections of the Federal Code clearly demonstrates, however, that the statutory definition of "federal employee" includes employees of the Bureau of Prisons.

Pursuant to 5 U.S.C. § 2105,[774] a federal-government

---

[771] Id. at 550; see also Police Officers' Guild v. Washington, 369 F. Supp. 543 (D.D.C. 1973) (declaring unconstitutional provision of the D.C. Code, similar to 5 U.S.C. § 7311(4), which prohibited policemen from becoming members of any labor organization that, inter alia, went on strike or claimed the right to strike). Although no court has decided the issue, it is almost certain that identical language in 18 U.S.C. §§ 1918(3) and (4) prohibiting federal employees and their unions from asserting the right to strike would also be held unconstitutional.

[772] 305 F. Supp. at 548, 550; see also United States v. Taylor, 693 F.2d 919 (9th Cir. 1982) (holding that 5 U.S.C. § 7311 is not rendered totally invalid by unconstitutionality of provision prohibiting the holding or accepting of federal employment by one who asserts right to strike, because offending provision may be severed from statute, leaving remainder of section fully operative).

[773] Telephone interview with Marge Harding, Administrator of Affirmative Action Program, Federal Bureau of Prisons (Oct. 30, 1986).

employee is defined as an individual who is appointed to the civil service by the President or other employee of the civil service. Since the President appoints the Attorney General to the executive branch of the United States Government, the Attorney General is an employee of the federal government, as is anyone whom the Attorney General appoints to the civil service.[775] Under 18 U.S.C. § 4041,[776] the Attorney General appoints the Director of the Federal Bureau of Prisons, as well as any other employees that he determines are necessary.[777] Therefore, the Director is an "employee" of the federal government under 5 U.S.C. § 2105,[778] as is anyone whom he has the

---

[774] Section 2105 states in pertinent part:

(a) For the purpose of this title, "employee", except as otherwise provided by this section or when specifically modified, means an officer and an individual who is--

(1) appointed in the civil service by one of the following acting in an official capacity--

(A) the President; . . .
(D) an individual who is an employee under this section . . . .

5 U.S.C. §§ 2105(a)(1)(A), (D) (1982) (emphasis added).

The "civil service" is defined in 5 U.S.C. § 2101(1) (1982). Section 2101 provides that "the 'civil service' consists of all appointive positions in the executive, judicial, and legislative branches of the Government of the United States, except positions in the uniformed services . . . ." Id.

[775] See 5 U.S.C. §§ 2105(a)(1)(A), (D) (1982).

[776] 18 U.S.C. § 4041 (1982).

[777] Id.

[778] 5 U.S.C. § 2105(a)(1)(D) (1982).

authority to appoint.[779]

2.   State Facilities

Most states follow the common-law rule that public employees are denied the right to strike or engage in a work stoppage against a public employer absent express statutory authorization.[780]   A state public employer, when confronted with

_____

[779]   Id.   There are other indications that employees of the Federal Bureau of Prisons are federal employees who are subject to the federal anti-strike provisions. All employees of the Federal Bureau of Prisons must sign a form, supplied by the Civil Service Commission, entitled "Appointments Affidavit." It requires the affiant to sign an "Oath of Office," "Affidavit as to Striking Against the Federal Government," and an "Affidavit as to Purchase and Sale of Office." Appointments Affidavit, U.S. Civil Service Commission, Standard Form 61 (revised Sept. 1970); see supra note 764 and accompanying text (noting that 5 U.S.C. § 3333 requires that every federal employee sign an affidavit swearing to abide by the anti-strike provisions of 5 U.S.C. § 7311).

One other provision of the United States Code supports the conclusion that federal prison employees are federal employees. Entitled "Protection of Officers and Employees of the United States," 18 U.S.C. § 1114 states in relevant part: "Whoever kills or attempts to kill . . . any officer or employee of any United States penal or correctional institution . . . shall be punished . . . ." 18 U.S.C. § 1114 (1982 & Supp. IV 1986). Note that, under 18 U.S.C. § 4042(1) (1982), the Bureau of Prisons is given "charge of the . . . institutions," and that section 1114 equates officers and employees of such institutions with officers of the United States.

[780]   See Hogler, The Common Law of Public Employee Strikes: A New Rule in California, 37 Labor L.J. 94, 94 (1986). Other states have adopted statutes that prohibit public-employee strikes. See Hanslowe & Acierno, The Law and Theory of Strikes by Government Employees, 67 Cornell L. Rev. 1055, 1060 (1983). California is an exception to the general rule that public employees cannot strike. The California Supreme Court has held that it would no longer follow the common-law rule and instead would recognize the legality of a strike by public employees as long as the strike did not endanger the public

an actual or threatened illegal strike by public employees, can

utilize two effective legal weapons to terminate the strike.

First, the public employer, which in the case of the state may be

an agency of a state government or a political subdivision

thereof, can seek injunctive relief against the strike in the

form of a temporary restraining order or a temporary or permanent

injunction. Second, if the party violates the injunction, the

employer may request that the court hold the party in contempt --

either criminal or civil -- and punish the party with a fine or

imprisonment.

Strikes by certain classes of public employees -- such as

police, firefighters, and hospital employees -- can almost always

be enjoined because of the vital and direct role that they play

in preserving public welfare and safety.[781] This theory is

---

health and safety. See County Sanitation Dist. No. 2 v. Los
Angeles County Employees Ass'n Local 660, 38 Cal. 3d 564, 586,
699 P.2d 835, 849, 214 Cal. Rptr. 424, 438 (1985).

[781] See Rockford v. International Ass'n of Firefighters, 98
Ill. App. 2d 36, 240 N.E.2d 705 (1968) (affirming lower court
order enjoining strike by firefighters because strike was threat
to safety of community); New York v. Tannihill, 59 Lab. Cas.
(CCH) ¶ 51,999 (N.Y. Sup. Ct. 1968) (finding that strike posed
unacceptable threat to safety of patients residing in mental
hospital); see also Pelton, Privatization of the Public Sector:
A Look at Which Labor Laws Should Apply to Private Firms
Contracted to Perform Public Services, 3 Det. C.L. Rev. 805, 818
(1986) (stating that the most compelling rationale for
prohibiting strikes by public employees is public safety).

Ten states have enacted statutes granting public employees
the right to strike. These states are Alaska, Hawaii, Idaho,
Illinois, Minnesota, Montana, Oregon, Pennsylvania, Vermont, and
Wisconsin. See Comment, Local Public Sanitation District v. Los
Angeles County Employees Association, 17 Pac. L.J. 533, 543
(1986). Even in those states that have authorized such strikes,
however, most limit or prohibit strikes by essential employees,
such as police and firefighters. Id. Alaska, for example,
expressly prohibits strikes by police, firefighters, hospital

commonly referred to as the "public safety rationale." Some

states, including Pennsylvania and Oregon, have adopted statutes

specifically prohibiting strikes by public prison employees.[782]

---

employees, and prison, jail, and other correctional employees.
Alaska Stat. §§ 23.40.200(a), (b) (1984); see Comment, supra, at
544 (reviewing provisions of other state statutes that give
public employees the right to strike). The Pennsylvania and
Oregon statutes also expressly prohibit strikes by prison
personnel. See infra note 782 (providing text of Pennsylvania
and Oregon statutes that prohibit strikes by prison personnel).

[782] 43 Pa. Cons. Stat. Ann. § 1101.1001 (Purdon Supp. 1988)
provides:

> Strikes by guards at prison or mental
> hospitals, or employes directly involved with and
> necessary to the functioning of the courts of this
> Commonwealth are prohibited at any time. If a
> strike occurs the public employer shall forthwith
> initiate in the court of common pleas of the
> jurisdiction where the strike occurs, an action for
> appropriate equitable relief including but not
> limited to injunctions. If the strike involves
> Commonwealth employes, the chief legal officer of
> the public employer or the Attorney General where
> required by law shall institute an action for
> equitable relief, either in the court of common
> pleas of the jurisdiction where the strike has
> occurred or the Commonwealth Court.

Id. Or. Rev. Stat. § 243.736(1) (1987) states:

> It shall be unlawful for any emergency
> telephone worker, police officer, firefighter or
> guard at a correctional institution or mental
> hospital to strike or recognize a picket line of a
> labor organization while in the performance of
> official duties.

Id. The Oregon law was applied in American Fed'n of State,
County & Mun. Employees v. Executive Dep't, 52 Or. App. 457, 628
P.2d 1228 (1981) (expanding scope of statute to prohibit strikes
by correctional employees who are not guards, but who are within
the same bargaining unit as guards). See also supra note 781
(noting that Pennsylvania and Oregon are among the states that
have adopted statutes allowing a limited right to strike for
public employees).

3. Private Facilities

a. The National Labor Relations Act

The National Labor Relations Act (NLRA)[783] is the primary body of federal law that controls labor-management relations in private industry.[784] The basic principle of the NLRA is stated in section 157,[785] granting employees the right to form, join, or assist labor organizations and to engage in other concerted activities for the purpose of collective bargaining. Courts have consistently held that collective bargaining, with the right to strike at its core, is the essence of the federal scheme concerning labor relations.[786]

---

[783] 29 U.S.C. §§ 151-169 (1982 & Supp. III 1985).

[784] The NLRA does not apply to public employers. See id. § 152(2) (excluding from the definition of "employer" all federal, state, and local government entities).

[785] Section 157 provides:

Employees shall have the right to self-organization, to form, join, or assist labor organizations, to bargain collectively through representatives of their own choosing, and to engage in other concerted activities for the purpose of collective bargaining or other mutual aid or protection, and shall also have the right to refrain from any or all of such activities except to the extent that such right may be affected by an agreement requiring membership in a labor organization as a condition of employment as authorized in section 158(a)(3) of this title.

Id. § 157.

[786] See, e.g., Division 1287 of the Amalgamated Ass'n of Street, Elec. Ry. & Motor Coach Employees v. Missouri, 374 U.S. 74, 82 (1963) (declaring that NLRA prohibits state attempt to

b. The Applicability of the National Labor Relations Act to Private Prison and Jail Employees

Private prison and jail employees, although they perform the same essential functions as do public prison and jail employees, may enjoy the right to strike under the NLRA.[787] Prior to 1979, the National Labor Relations Board (NLRB, or the Board) used the "intimate connection" test to determine whether it should assert jurisdiction over employers who provided services to government agencies.[788] Under the first part of this test, the NLRB determines whether the "employer retains sufficient control over its employees' terms and conditions of employment so as to be capable of effective bargaining with the employees' representative."[789] If it makes an affirmative finding on this question, it then examines the relationship between the functions that are performed by the employer and the purpose of the government agency. If the Board finds that there was an intimate

---

enjoin strike by employees of transit company); NLRB v. Erie Resistor Corp., 373 U.S. 221 (1963) (stating that nothing in NLRA, except as specifically provided, is to be construed to interfere with strike as means of redress); Kellogg Co. v. NLRB, 457 F.2d 519 (6th Cir.) (holding that employees have right to strike, whether for economic reasons, for purposes of improving work conditions, or for mutual aid or protection of employees who are members of another union), cert. denied, 409 U.S. 850 (1972).

[787] See supra notes 783-786 and accompanying text (discussing the applicability of provisions granting the right to strike to private employees).

[788] For a leading case in this area, see Rural Fire Protection Co., 216 N.L.R.B. 584 (1975).

[789] Id. at 586.

connection between the two, it will then decline to exercise jurisdiction over the employer.[790]

In _National Transportation Service_,[791] the Board expressly stated that it would no longer use the second part of the intimate-connection test and instead would look solely to the amount of control that an employer retained over the primary terms and conditions of employment.[792] The Board gave two reasons for this change. First, it concluded that the second part of the test was too vague and difficult to apply.[793] Second, it found no indication in the language or legislative history of the NLRA that Congress intended the Board to decline jurisdiction because an employer was performing a "public function."[794]

---

[790] _Id_.

[791] 240 N.L.R.B. 565 (1979).

[792] _Id_. at 565. _National Transportation Service_ involved a private bus company that provided, among other things, bus service to public schools. Two persons who were employed in that section of the company filed suit, alleging that they had been discharged in violation of the NLRA's nondiscrimination provisions. _Id_. The Board had previously held that the company was intimately connected to a public function and refused to assert jurisdiction over that portion of the company's operations. National Transportation Serv., 231 N.L.R.B. 980 (1977). In accordance with that decision, the administrative law judge below found that the two employees were not covered by the NLRA. The case was on appeal from that decision. 240 N.L.R.B. at 565.

[793] To determine whether there was an intimate connection between a private company and a government agency that is exempt from the NLRA, the NLRB looked to whether the company was performing a "governmental function." The Board cited numerous examples illustrating the difficulties that are inherent in deciding what constitutes a governmental function. 240 N.L.R.B. at 566 & n.7.

Subsequently, the Board has attempted to clarify the standard set forth in National Transportation Service. Two decisions, both issued on June 24, 1986, illustrate the difficulty in discerning how much control an employer must retain over labor-related matters before the Board will assert jurisdiction.[795] In Res-Care, Inc.,[796] the Board declined to assert jurisdiction over a private company that provided residential job-corps centers for the Department of Labor (DOL).[797] It stated that, to determine whether Res-Care could effectively bargain with its employees so as to bring it within the NLRA, it would "examine closely not only the control over essential terms and conditions of employment retained by the employer, but also the scope and degree of control exercised by the exempt entity over the employer's labor relations . . . ."[798]

The Board, after discussing in detail the extent of the DOL's involvement in Res-Care's operations,[799] focused

---

[794] Id. at 565. The Board exercised its discretion to decline jurisdiction under section 164(c)(1) of the NLRA, which allows the Board to "decline to assert jurisdiction over any labor dispute involving any class or category of employers, where, in the opinion of the Board, the effect of such labor dispute on commerce is not sufficiently substantial to warrant the exercise of its jurisdiction . . . ." 29 U.S.C. § 164(c)(1) (now codified in 1982 edition of the Code).

[795] Res-Care, Inc., 280 N.L.R.B. No. 78, slip op. (June 24, 1986); Long Stretch Youth Home, Inc., 280 N.L.R.B. No. 79, slip op. (June 24, 1986).

[796] 280 N.L.R.B. No. 78, slip op. (June 24, 1986).

[797] Id. at 2.

[798] Id. at 8.

[799] The Board noted that, as part of Res-Care's initial proposal, it was required to submit a line-item budget, including

specifically on the DOL's control over employee salary and benefit levels. As part of its initial proposal, Res-Care was required to submit minimum and maximum wage rates for each labor grade, fringe-benefit plans, and a line-item budget that included salaries and benefit plans.[800] When the DOL accepted Res-Care's proposal, these amounts became part of the contract. Res-Care could not deviate from these salary and benefit levels without prior approval from the DOL.[801] In addition, the level of compensation that Res-Care received from the DOL under the contract was tied directly to the approved maximum salary and benefit amounts. The DOL would not reimburse Res-Care for "disallowed costs," which were any amounts expended above the maximum salary and benefit levels in the approved budget.[802]

---

a Staff Manning Table listing job classifications, a Labor Grade Schedule, and a Salary Schedule indicating minimum and maximum salary levels for each grade. Id. at 3. Res-Care was also required to submit a statement of its personnel policies, including its policies regarding compensatory time, overtime, severance pay, holidays, vacation, probationary employment, sick leave, cost-of-living increases, and equal employment opportunities. Id. Moreover, the final contract set other standards regarding maximum wage levels that could be exceeded only be an express waiver from DOL. Id. at 4.

Res-Care retained control over hiring, firing, promotion, demotion, and transfer of employees under the contract, but it was required to submit its employee-selection criteria and hiring procedure to the DOL for approval. Id. DOL approval was also required for the job corps' director and other senior-staff positions. Id. The Board also noted that the contract required Res-Care to notify the DOL of any potential labor disputes at the facility. Id. at 6. Finally, the Board observed that the DOL maintained a high level of control through the operation-standards and monitoring portions of the contract. Id. at 6-7.

800 Id. at 3.

801 Id. at 3-4.

802 Id. at 5.

Thus, despite the fact that Res-Care actually formulated and submitted the proposed ranges for salaries and benefits, the NLRB concluded that the DOL retained ultimate control over these items.- The NLRB held, therefore, that Res-Care could not conduct meaningful bargaining with its employees.[803]

The second case, Long Stretch Youth Home, Inc.,[804] involved a private nonprofit corporation that was licensed by the Maryland Social Services Administration (MSSA).[805] Long Stretch provided room and board, social services, and medical treatment at its residential facility for teenaged boys, who were referred by the MSSA and the Maryland Department of Juvenile Services.[806] The NLRB held that, unlike Res-Care, Long Stretch "retain[ed] sufficient control over economic terms and conditions of employment essential to meaningful bargaining" to fall within the jurisdiction of the NLRB.[807]

Specifically, the Board found that Long Stretch, not MSSA, retained ultimate control of salary and benefit levels.[808] It

_____

[803] Id. at 10. The Board also stated that the level of control that the DOL retained over other labor-related issues was inapposite to this particular decision. Id. at 13; see supra note 799 (describing other areas over which the DOL retained varying degrees of authority).

[804] 280 N.L.R.B. No. 79, slip op. (June 24, 1986).

[805] Id. at 2.

[806] Id.

[807] Id. at 10.

[808] Id. at 11. The MSSA retained varying degrees of control over aspects of other labor-management issues. For example, MSSA regulations required Long Stretch to maintain certain staff positions, including child-care workers, social

acknowledged that there were, in fact, some constraints on Long Stretch's discretion with regard to employee compensation. Long Stretch was required, for example, to submit with its initial license application a statement of its personnel policies, a list of staff positions and qualifications, and a proposed budget for the current year.[809] Proposed salary ranges, hours, vacation time, sick leave, and retirement plans were included in this information. Once approved, these policies were reviewed only when Long Stretch renewed its license, which was necessary at least every five years.[810] MSSA did maintain guidelines for minimum and maximum salary ranges and for the percentage of total funds that should be allocated to salaries and benefits, but compliance with these guidelines was not mandatory.[811]

---

workers, housekeeping, food-service, and maintenance employees. Id. at 5-6. MSSA guidelines set forth suggested staff ratios. Id. at 6. These were not mandatory staffing requirements, but, if staffing were to drop to levels that were unacceptable to MSSA, then MSSA could suspend or revoke Long Stretch's license. Id. Long Stretch retained the authority to hire, fire, promote, or lay off workers as long as it remained within MSSA guidelines. Id. It also had flexibility in determining working conditions, subject to minimum MSSA requirements, such as amount of time off for child-care workers and amount of in-service training. Id.

Further, MSSA conducted a continuing review of Long Stretch's operations to ensure compliance with all licensing requirements and other regulations. Id. at 8. MSSA retained the authority to suspend or revoke Long Stretch's license should it not remedy any violation of MSSA standards. Id. at 7. The Board, however, did not find that any of these factors seriously limited Long Stretch's ability to engage in meaningful bargaining. Id. at 13-14.

[809] Id. at 3.

[810] Id. at 4.

[811] Id. at 3-4.

The Board concluded, however, that, despite these requirements, MSSA did not retain ultimate control over wage and benefit levels. It minimized the importance of MSSA's review of proposed personnel policies, noting that any substantive guidelines that MSSA maintained were not mandatory.[812] Moreover, the Board emphasized that, unlike Res-Care, Long Stretch did not need to obtain prior approval before making changes in its personnel policies.[813]

The Board also noted that, although Long Stretch was required to submit a proposed budget to MSSA annually, the amount of compensation that it received from MSSA was not directly linked to the salary and benefit amounts that were shown in the budget.[814] The Board contrasted this point with the facts of Res-Care, in which the DOL derived the appropriate amount of compensation from line items in the budget, including maximum salary and benefit amounts.[815] In Long Stretch, on the other hand, MSSA procedure was to combine the proposed budget with those from all other child-care institutions in the state. It

---

[812] Id. at 11. The Board noted, however, that an MSSA official had testified that the agency might intervene if it found that an employer's salaries were "grossly unfair." Id. at 4.

[813] Id. at 11. MSSA stated, however, that providers were required to submit annually for its approval any major changes in operations. Long Stretch would have to submit any major change in personnel policies to MSSA under this requirement. Id. at 5.

[814] Id. at 12.

[815] Id. at 11; see supra text accompanying notes 800-802 (describing method by which the DOL calculated employer's compensation).

then submitted its own proposed budget to the legislature. MSSA computed the amount that it would pay to Long Stretch on a per-resident basis after considering amounts that had actually been appropriated by the legislature.[816] Thus, Long Stretch was not absolutely required to allocate the allotted funds according to its proposed budget. Conceivably, it could pay its employees wages and benefits that were in excess of the maximum amounts, as long as its total expenditures were within the amounts that were received from MSSA. Therefore, Long Stretch could engage in meaningful bargaining on these issues.[817]

Thus, the important issue of National Transportation Service and its progeny is the relative amounts of control that are retained by the private employer and the exempt governmental entity over employee salary and benefit levels.[818] The exempt entity's authority to approve or deny salary ranges and benefit plans that are proposed by the employer does not necessarily deprive the employer of sufficient control over these areas.[819]

_____

[816] 280 N.L.R.B. No. 79, slip op. at 3.

[817] Id. at 12-13.

[818] See Res-Care, Inc., 280 N.L.R.B. No. 78, slip op. at 14 (holding that DOL control over salaries and benefits deprived Res-Care of control over primary terms and conditions of employment); Long Stretch Youth Home, Inc., 280 N.L.R.B. No. 79, slip op. at 10-11 (concluding that Long Stretch maintained sufficient control over economic terms and conditions of employment, based on its discretion to set salary and benefit levels); see also Locke, "Privatization" and Labor Relations: Some Welcome Guidance from the NLRB, 38 Lab. L.J. 166, 170-71 (1987).

[819] See Long Stretch Youth Home, Inc., 280 N.L.R.B. No. 79, slip op. at 11 (observing that Long Stretch was required to submit salary ranges and benefit plans to MSSA for approval).

Rather, the NLRB focuses on whether the employer actually has broad discretion in setting initial salary and benefit levels,[820] whether it retains the freedom to deviate from those levels without prior approval from the exempt entity,[821] and whether the employer's compensation is tied directly to salary and benefit amounts in its approved budget.[822]

It is not clear, however, whether control over other aspects of management could, in some circumstances, restrict the flexibility of an employer so as to remove it from NLRB's jurisdiction. In Res-Care and Long Stretch, the Board did not base its decisions on the amount of control that the exempt governmental entity maintained over other, non-economic aspects of the employer's labor relations. If an exempt government agency maintained extensive control over selection of employees, staffing levels, or other bargaining issues, however, the employer could argue that it was unable to engage in meaningful bargaining and should not be governed by the NLRA.[823]

---

[820] See id. (finding that, because MSSA did not maintain mandatory guidelines regarding personnel policies, Long Stretch ultimately determined the content of employee salaries and benefit plans).

[821] See id. (noting that Long Stretch could change its personnel policies without prior consultation with MSSA); Res-Care, Inc., 280 N.L.R.B. No. 78, at 3-4 (stating that Res-Care needed DOL approval before it deviated from minimum/maximum salary ranges or approved benefit plans).

[822] See Res-Care, Inc., 280 N.L.R.B. No. 78, slip op. at 10 (observing that Res-Care could not receive reimbursement for expenditures beyond specific budgetary limits); Long Stretch Youth Home, Inc., 280 N.L.R.B. No. 79, slip op. at 12 (finding that MSSA did not exert direct control over specific expenditures in budget, such as salaries and benefits).

The NLRB has not yet decided a case that addresses the NLRA's applicability to private-prison or private-jail employees. Several commentators have suggested that those employees would have the right to strike under the NLRA.[824] This broad conclusion does not seem warranted, however, in light of the NLRB's decisions. It is true that, under National Transportation Service, such employees will not be denied the right to strike merely because they perform a public function.[825] They may be denied protection under the NLRA, however, if the exempt government agency retains extensive control over the terms and conditions of their employment, precluding their employer from engaging in meaningful bargaining under the NLRA.

---

[823] Cf. Locke, supra note 818, at 171 (noting some commentators' views that the ability to bargain over non-economic labor issues can be an important indicator of whether the employer maintains discretion to engage in meaningful bargaining with its employees).

[824] See, e.g., CSG Report, supra note 533, at 26 (predicting that, under National Transportation Service, private prison guards will not be denied the right to strike); C. Ring, supra note 484, at 49 nn.2 & 3 (observing that the NLRA appears to extend to private prison employees); Hearings, supra note 375, at 156-60 (statements of Dave Kelly, President of the Council of Prison Locals, American Federation of Government Employees, and Norman A. Carlson, Director of the Federal Bureau of Prisons) (opining that private prison employees will enjoy the right to strike).

[825] See National Transportation Serv., 240 N.L.R.B. 565, 565 (1975) (stating that the Board would no longer use the intimate-connection test in deciding whether to assert jurisdiction over an employer who was under contract to an exempt government entity).

4. Recommendations

Because private correctional and detention employees may enjoy the right to strike under the NLRA, it is essential that certain provisions to prohibit such action be included in the contract. The contractor should be required, for example, to negotiate a "no strike" clause in the labor contract with its employees. This clause is an undertaking by the union that it will not resort to a strike during the duration of the contract.[826] Since 1970, an injunctive remedy has been available to management to halt a strike in violation of a no-strike clause.[827]

As a no-strike clause is enforceable only during the duration of a labor contract, the contract must provide for the periods in which the contractor and its employees negotiate a new contract, or an agreement is not in force for some other reason. Therefore, the contractor should be required to use its best efforts to reach an early and peaceful settlement to any labor dispute. In addition, the contractor should be required to

---

[826] Although private employees are guaranteed the right to strike by the NLRA, unions often agree to incorporate no-strike clauses into labor contracts. In return, management agrees to seek peaceful settlement of contract disputes through mutually administered grievance procedures culminating in third-party arbitration.

[827] See Boys Market, Inc. v. Retail Clerks Union, Local 770, 398 U.S. 235, 238 (1970) (holding that anti-injunction provisions of the Norris-LaGuardia Act, 29 U.S.C. § 104, do not deprive lower courts of authority to issue injunctions against work stoppages in violation of contractual agreements to settle disputes through arbitration).

notify the contracting agency at least sixty days prior to the termination of a labor agreement and immediately upon learning of a potential or impending dispute.[828] These provisions will give the contracting agency an opportunity to prepare to assume operation of the facility in the event of a strike and thereby avoid the serious consequences that accompany an unexpected labor disturbance. Costs that are incurred by the contracting agency during a strike or labor disturbance should be reimbursed by the contractor.

Model Contract Provision:

(1) The contractor shall include a no-strike provision in any labor agreement that it negotiates with a union that is formed or joined by its employees.

(2) The contractor shall use its best efforts to reach an early and peaceful settlement to any labor dispute. Such disputes include, but are not limited to, picketing, lockouts, and strikes.

(3) The contractor shall notify the contracting agency at least sixty (60) days prior to the termination of any labor agreement with its employees.

(4) The contractor shall notify the contracting agency immediately upon learning of a potential or impending strike or serious labor disturbance.

(5) In the event of a strike or serious labor disturbance, the contracting agency may call on the emergency resources of the [appropriate jurisdiction] to operate and/or control the facility or facilities until the strike or disturbance has

---

[828] See INS RFP at 67, § I(I) (incorporating by reference "Notice to Government of Labor Disputes" clause).

ended. In the event of such an emergency, the contractor shall cooperate fully with the contracting agency to ensure safe operations.

(6) The contractor shall reimburse the contracting agency [and/or the appropriate jurisdiction] for any costs incurred during or directly related to the strike or labor disturbance.

(7) The occurrence of a strike or a serious labor disturbance shall constitute grounds for cancellation, termination, or suspension of the contract by the contracting agency.

Section 5: Inmate Issues

Section 5(A): Inmate Management

Commentary:

There are four major categories of inmate management that must be addressed by the contracting parties: classification, transfer, discipline, and parole. Because these areas directly affect the nature or length of an inmate's confinement,[829] the Model Contract reserves final authority on all of these matters to the contracting agency. In appropriate cases, and with appropriate safeguards, provision has been made for participation by the contractor when such participation would not contravene constitutional rights or important policy considerations.

1. Classification

It is important from the outset of negotiations that the parties reach an understanding concerning the type(s) of prisoners that the contract will cover.[830] Unambiguous

---

[829] Of course, many aspects of prison operation affect the nature of confinement -- including food service, medical service, cell size, the provision of rudiments of personal hygiene, and the quality or existence of a law library. See Model Contract § 3(F)(1) (Operating Standards). The categories that are discussed in this section, however, affect individual inmates, rather than the inmate population as a whole.

[830] See CSG Report, supra note 533, at 65-67 (suggesting that contracting parties clearly specify the criteria for inmate

definitions are required to avoid any misunderstanding or confusion over whether a particular prisoner falls into a certain category or classification. If possible, the parties should use the contracting agency's existing classification scheme. Any modification or limitation of this scheme should be made in the contract.[831]

Precise language regarding classification is necessary to protect both parties to the contract. On the one hand, inmates whom the private contractor is unprepared or unable to care for should not be transferred to the private facility. On the other hand, the private contractor must not be permitted to refuse to accept certain types of inmates -- such as those who have contracted Acquired Immune Deficiency Syndrome or others whom it considers to be too difficult or too expensive to detain. Allowing the contractor to select its inmates in such a way could overwhelm the public corrections system with formidable and costly inmate detention and could compromise the contracting agency's ability to function in the public's best interest.[832] Furthermore, to the extent that the contractor can refuse to

---

selection in the contract). But cf. Tenn. Code Ann. § 41-24-103(d) (Cum. Supp. 1987) ("Any inmate sentenced to confinement in the department shall be legally eligible to be incarcerated in a facility in which a prison contractor is providing correctional services . . . .") (emphasis added).

[831] See id. at 66 (noting that overly restrictive classification scheme resulted in too few inmates to fill the contractual minimum number of beds at Kentucky's Marion Adjustment Center).

[832] See W. Collins, supra note 725, at 6 (noting that contract could be voided if found to be an excessive delegation of power, which arguably occurs when contracting agency is unable to function in public's best interest).

accept certain inmates, it would not be acting in its own long-term best interest. Although in the short term its cost figures and the relative absence of disturbances and escapes would be attractive, it would soon become clear that these gains resulted primarily from the inmate-selection process and not necessarily from the provision of exemplary services.

2.   Transfer

The danger that a private-prison company will act to further its own interests at the expense of those of the public and the inmates in its custody is particularly acute in the case of inmate transfers. Public prison officials consider the interests of the public and the inmates when making transfer decisions. In contrast, a private contractor's profit motive and concern for public relations may lead it to keep only well-behaved inmates, leaving the more difficult prisoners to the public prison system.[833] A contractor may, for example, institute a retaliatory transfer against an inmate who files a complaint or lawsuit against the private prison and/or its employees.[834]

_____

[833] See Note, supra note 9, at 1493. One contractor has negotiated successfully for the authority to require a governmental unit to take back unwanted inmates. 268 Center, Inc. Contract at 2, § C (providing that if, "in the opinion of the Center, [inmates] are disruptive by non-compliance to rules and regulations and the norms of operating the program, . . . upon notification to the County, the County will, forthwith, by means of County transportation and personnel, remove the person back to the Allegheny County Jail"). Such a provision is unacceptable because it subordinates the interests of the public and the inmate to those of the contractor.

Private-prison personnel might also transfer an inmate who exercises his first amendment rights, such as speaking critically of the private-prison company.[835] Finally, private-prison officials may transfer an inmate who formally requests services that the company is contractually or constitutionally required to provide.[836]

To avoid infirmity, the Model Contract expressly denies the private contractor the authority to transfer inmates.[837] Although private-prison personnel may make transfer recommendations, the Model Contract further provides that the contracting agency reserves the right to accept or reject any recommendation.[838]

---

[834] See Note, supra note 9, at 1492-93.

[835] Id. at 1492.

[836] See id.

[837] Public prison inmates do not have a procedural due process right to a pre-transfer hearing, even when the transferee institution is less desirable. See Olim v. Wakinekona, 461 U.S. 238 (1983); Montanye v. Haymes, 427 U.S. 236 (1976); Meachum v. Fano, 427 U.S. 21 (1976). Because of the private contractor's pecuniary and institutional biases, however, inmates in private facilities may be accorded heightened constitutional protection. Moreover, even public prisoners may not be transferred for having exercised their constitutional rights. See, e.g., Olim, 461 U.S. at 248 n.9; Baraldini v. Meese, No. 88-0764 (D.D.C. July 15, 1988) (memorandum opinion and order) (barring Federal Bureau of Prisons from "considering a prisoner's past political association or personal political beliefs" in deciding on transfers in federal prisons); Note, supra note 9, at 1492.

[838] See County of Atlantic Contract at 27, § 4.14.

3. Discipline

When a person is to be deprived of his or her rights, procedural due process requires a hearing before an impartial decisionmaker.[839] This is so because the delegation of adjudicative power to a private party poses the danger that the party will use that power to advance its own interests at the expense of those of both the public and the individual who is directly affected.[840]

In the private-incarceration context, the contractor and its employees will have two potential biases -- monetary and institutional. Regarding monetary bias, if the contractor's compensation is based on the number of inmates that it houses each day, then it has a pecuniary interest in increasing -- or, at least, not decreasing -- each inmate's stay.[841] Even if the

---

[839] See, e.g., Withrow v. Larkin, 421 U.S. 35, 47 (1975) ("Not only is a biased decisionmaker constitutionally unacceptable but 'our system of law has always endeavored to prevent even the probability of unfairness.'") (quoting In re Murchison, 349 U.S. 133, 136 (1955)); Murchison, 349 U.S. at 136 ("A fair [hearing] in a fair tribunal is a basic requirement of due process."); Redding v. Fairman, 717 F.2d 1105, 1112 (7th Cir. 1983) (stating that the requirement of a "neutral and detached" decisionmaker should not be impaired). See generally Jacob & Sharma, Disciplinary and Punitive Decisions and Due Process Values in the American Correctional System, 12 Stetson L. Rev 1, 91-99 (1982); Note, supra note 9, at 1485-89 (discussing procedural due process in private-prison context).

[840] See supra notes 170-208 and accompanying text (discussing concerns of courts that have invalidated adjudicative acts of private parties).

[841] See supra note 209 and accompanying text (discussing effect of compensation schemes on ability of private-prison personnel to render impartial decisions at disciplinary hearings); see also Note, supra note 9, at 1485-86 & nn.80-81 and

contractor's compensation does not depend on the length of an inmate's stay, the contractor will nevertheless have an institutional bias in favor of disciplining prisoners.[842]

The Model Contract takes the position that private-prison employees can never have the requisite impartiality that the Constitution requires. They cannot, therefore, adjudicate alleged institutional violations.[843] Thus, the contracting

---

accompanying text (discussing examples of practical effect of financial pressure to maintain high occupancy on private companies that provide services to inmates).

[842] See supra note 209 and accompanying text (discussing institutional factors that create private contractor's bias in favor of disciplining inmates).

[843] See Withrow, 421 U.S. at 47 ("[V]arious situations have been identified in which experience teaches that the probability of actual bias on the part of the judge or decisionmaker is too high to be constitutionally tolerable. Among these cases are those in which the adjudicator has a pecuniary interest in the outcome . . . ."); Wolff v. McDonnell, 418 U.S. 539, 556-70 (1974) (holding that disciplinary proceedings must be conducted according to the following procedural due process requirements: prison officials must give inmates at least 24-hours' written notice of the charges; inmates must have the opportunity to call witnesses and to present evidence in their defense, absent undue interference with security or institutional goals; the proceedings must be conducted by an impartial decisionmaker; and there must be a written record of the proceedings); Note, supra note 9, at 1486-87 & nn.85-86 (stating that impartial-decisionmaker requirement precludes private-prison personnel from sitting as hearing officers); see also supra notes 126-133 & 210 and accompanying text (providing examples of similar restrictions in this and other areas). Nevertheless, as one commentator has noted, "it is, for all practical purposes, probably impossible to completely eliminate private employee involvement in disciplinary proceedings," C. Ring, supra note 484, at 20, because private employees will inevitably be participants in such proceedings, whether as accusers or witnesses. See Mayer, supra note 76, at 320. See generally supra notes 170-208 (discussing constitutionality of delegation of adjudicative powers and concluding, based on DiLoreto case, that delegation is more likely to be upheld if judicial review is available; when prisoners' liberty interests are at stake, however, even provision of judicial review may not save delegation from finding of unconstitutionality).

agency must ensure that state or federal hearing officers perform all adjudicative functions and make all decisions that would tend to affect a prisoner's liberty interests.[844]

Because every state and the federal government already have disciplinary procedures that comport with the needs and administrative organization of their particular prison systems, it would serve no purpose for the Model Contract to suggest a procedure that incorporates approaches used by one or several of these systems. The Model Contract therefore requires that the contracting agency use the disciplinary procedures and rules

---

The contracting agency must be mindful that, by delegating the incarceration function, accountability is dispersed. As a CCA employee who was in charge of reviewing disciplinary cases at a privately run INS facility in Houston is reported to have said: "I'm the Supreme Court." Tolchin, Jails Run by Private Company Force It to Face Question of Accountability, N.Y. Times, Feb. 19, 1985, at A15, col. 1.

[844] For example, a hearing officer may refuse to honor an inmate's request to call a particular witness or to compel production of a particular document if he or she determines that it is "unduly hazardous to institutional safety or correctional goals." Wolff v. McDonnell, 418 U.S. 539, 566 (1974); accord Ponte v. Real, 471 U.S. 491, 495-500 (1985) (holding, inter alia, that due process requires that prison officials at some point state their reasons for refusing to call witnesses requested by an inmate at a disciplinary hearing); Baxter v. Palmigiano, 425 U.S. 308, 323-24 (1976); see Branham, Implementing and Ignoring the Dictates of the Supreme Court: A Comparative Study of Michigan and Illinois Prison Disciplinary Proceedings, 12 New Eng. J. on Crim. & Civ. Confinement 197, 202 (1986) (discussing factors to consider in making this determination). Other discretionary powers that prison hearing officers typically possess include approving restrictive detention in solitary confinement pending the hearing and deciding which sanctions to impose for rule violations. Because these discretionary powers are likely to affect the liberty interests of inmates, the Constitution requires that a neutral officer exercise them. Therefore, contracting agencies should pursue both statutory and contractual delineation of the functions that state or federal hearing officers must perform. Cf. Model Statute § 11 (Nondelegability of Contracting Agency's Authority).

currently in force in its public prison system for inmates serving time in privately operated facilities as well.

This approach is similar to that taken in the Council of State Governments' Report.[845] Both approaches recommend that the private contractor adopt the rules and procedures employed by the contracting agency. But, whereas the Council of State Governments' Report recommends only that public officers "participate in . . . disciplinary hearings concerning major rule infractions,"[846] the Model Contract requires that public officers actually conduct all hearings that will affect the prisoner's liberty interests.[847] This recommendation has two components: first, that the public officer conduct, and not merely participate in, the proceedings; and, second, that this involvement extend to all disciplinary hearings, and not just those that concern major rule infractions. Although the Council of State Governments' approach may be practical and convenient

_____

[845] CSG Report, supra note 533, at 31-33, 68-70.

[846] Id. at 70 (emphasis added); see also NIJ Report, supra note 546, at 4 ("Government staff should participate in all major disciplinary hearings."); cf. C. Ring, supra note 484, at 21 (suggesting that "disciplinary boards that hear and decide disciplinary matters could be made up, in whole or in part, of public employees") (emphasis added).

[847] See, e.g., Ariz. Rev. Stat. Ann. § 41-1609.01(P)(5) (Supp. 1987) ("No contract for correctional services may authorize, allow or imply a delegation of authority or responsibility to a prison contractor for any of the following: . . . taking any disciplinary actions."); Tenn. Code Ann. § 41-24-110(5) (Cum. Supp. 1987) (using essentially the same language). But see Federal Bureau of Prisons RFP at 28, § 2(5)(K)(m) (allowing private staff of halfway house to sit on committee that adjudicates disciplinary matters); Santa Fe RFP addendum 1, at 68, § III(3)(a) (permitting detention-center contractor to staff disciplinary panels).

for the contractor, the Model Contract's more stringent requirements safeguard the prisoner's constitutionally protected liberty interests.

For some of the same reasons that the delegation doctrine condemns delegation of adjudicative power to private parties, the doctrine also condemns delegation of rule-making power. This practice raises two major concerns: first, only legislatures are expressly authorized by the constitutions of their respective jurisdictions to wield rule-making power in the public interest; second, private entities might make rules that serve their own pecuniary or political interests, rather than those of the public or the inmates. The second concern is intensified because, unlike elected officials, private parties are insulated from the political process. Their accountability to the people is therefore suspect. In addition, once a rule has been privately promulgated, affected parties will be without recourse to urge its repeal or modification.

Thus, the contract should not grant the private entity discretion to formulate and implement its own disciplinary rules. Rather, the contract should incorporate the inmate disciplinary procedure utilized by the contracting agency at existing facilities. If the contractor wishes to participate in this process, the only constitutionally acceptable means is for it to propose rules that the government may then accept, reject, or modify.[848]

---

[848] CCA appears to be moving in this direction. In 1985, the Bay County Contract provided:

4. Parole

There is no constitutional deficiency in a practice that allows private-prison officials to recommend that a parole board either deny or grant parole.[849] As a policy matter, however, it would be unwise to permit a private-prison company routinely to make recommendations to parole boards concerning prisoners in its care. Apart from the financial interest that private contractors have in lengthening an inmate's incarceration[850] and the danger

> To the extent allowable by law, CCA is authorized to impose discipline and order throughout the County Detention Facilities through rules, regulations and orders, both verbal and written, and to punish violations in accordance with the disciplinary system meeting or exceeding such standards as may be from time to time promulgated by the American Correctional Association.

Bay County Contract at 16-17, § 5.3. One year later the Santa Fe Contract contained nearly identical language, but added a provision requiring that "[d]isciplinary rules and procedures . . . be submitted to the County Technical Representative within ten (10) working days of the effective date of this Contract." Santa Fe Contract at 5, § 3.2. It is unclear, however, whether this provision satisfies the constitutional requirement that a governmental entity accept, reject, or modify proposed disciplinary rules. See supra notes 136-169 and accompanying text (discussing constitutionality of delegation of rule-making authority).

[849] It must be emphasized that this statement is restricted to parole recommendations. Prisoners may well have a constitutional liberty interest in the parole decision, depending on the jurisdiction's statutory language. See, e.g., Board of Pardons v. Allen, 107 S. Ct. 2415, 2417-22 (1987); Greenholtz v. Inmates of the Neb. Penal and Correctional Complex, 442 U.S. 1, 11-12 (1979).

[850] See supra note 841 and accompanying text. In limited circumstances, the contractor would have a financial interest in decreasing, rather than increasing, the number of inmates it

that private-prison employees' parole recommendations will therefore not be objective,[851] the duration of one's confinement is simply not a private matter. Unlike recommendations regarding transfers, for example, which change only the place or the nature of confinement, parole decisions may end that confinement altogether.[852] Thus, they more clearly implicate a prisoner's liberty interest.[853]

To maintain the integrity of the parole system -- as well as the broader criminal-justice system -- and to avoid unfairness or the appearance of unfairness resulting from the contractor's inevitable bias, the Model Contract prohibits private-prison

_____

houses. This situation would arise if the contractor were guaranteed a minimum income. See Model Contract § 3(C) (Compensation). In such a case, the contractor might be biased in favor of recommending that parole be granted. This would be an infrequent occurrence, however, as the population level is largely within the control of the contracting agency. Moreover, since the concept of privatization of incarceration arose primarily in response to extreme overcrowding, it is unlikely that there would be too few inmates in any facility. Nevertheless, the contracting agency might want to consider this possibility in negotiating the contractor's minimum income.

[851] See Note, supra note 9, at 1490 & n.104 (citing Pennsylvania Legis. Budget & Finance Comm., Report on a Study of Issues Related to the Potential Operation of Private Prisons in Pennsylvania 30 (1985) (warning that private contractors may manipulate prisoners' records to interfere with parole eligibility); and UPI Wire Release, Aug. 5, 1986 (Commissioner of Nebraska Department of Corrections suggests that private-prison personnel may have a conflict of interest in making parole recommendations)).

[852] This statement is not meant to diminish the seriousness of different levels of confinement or conditions of confinement, but rather to emphasize that it is confinement nonetheless, rather than release.

[853] According to one source, Hamilton County, Tennessee has responded to this danger by having a public official make all parole recommendations for private-prison inmates. Note, supra note 9, at 1491 n.107.

employees from making parole recommendations.[854] Interposing a
neutral correctional officer between the private prison and the
parole board ensures that the interests of the public and the
inmate will be the focus of the parole hearing.[855]

For the parole board to make an informed decision, however,
it will need to have all relevant information, including some
that has been gathered or prepared by the contractor's
employees. In order to resolve the conflict between the parole
board's need for information and the contractor's unavoidable
bias, the Model Contract recommends that the contractor's
submissions be limited to written reports that have been prepared
in the ordinary course of business.

Model Contract Provisions:

(1) Classification

The contracting agency shall classify all
inmates, according to its own criteria. The
contractor shall be bound by the agency's
classifications.

---

[854] See CSG Report, supra note 533, at 69-70 (proposing
that, since "there may be some basis for legal challenge" if
private-prison personnel were to make recommendations to parole
authorities, "contribution to this process should be limited to a
presentation of the facts pertaining to the inmate's level of
adjustment during the period of confinement in the private
facility").

[855] See, e.g., Alaska Stat. § 33.16.030(a) (1986) ("The
governor shall appoint [parole] board members on the basis of
their qualifications to make decisions that are compatible with
the welfare of the community and of individual offenders."); N.M.
Stat. Ann. § 31-21-10(A)(3) (1987) ("the [parole] board shall
. . . make a finding that a parole is in the best interest of
society and the inmate").

(2) Transfer

The contractor shall have no authority to transfer an inmate. The contractor may, however, recommend in writing that the contracting agency transfer a particular inmate. The contracting agency shall have final authority with respect to any transfer decision.

(3) Discipline

The contractor shall have no authority to administer discipline to an inmate in its custody unless the discipline is ordered by a [state or federal] hearing officer, pursuant to [the jurisdiction's] disciplinary procedures. Rules that are formulated by the contractor shall be null and void except to the extent that they are accepted or modified by the contracting agency.

(4) Parole

No employee of the contractor shall have any authority to recommend that the parole board either deny or grant parole to any inmate in the contractor's custody. The contractor's submissions to the parole board shall be limited to written reports that have been prepared in the ordinary course of business.

Section 5(B): Use of Force

Commentary:

The contracting parties must address the issues of when, to what extent, and by whom force may be used against inmates of a privately operated facility. There are alternative ways of dealing with these issues and, because of the importance of the use-of-force provisions, an extended discussion of these alternatives follows.[856]

The eighth amendment to the United States Constitution prohibits cruel and unusual punishment.[857] The use of force against an inmate may result in a violation of his or her eighth amendment rights.[858] In narrow circumstances, however, the

---

[856] See, e.g., ACA Standard 2-4206:

> Written policy and procedure restricting the use of physical force to instances of justifiable self-defense, protection of others, protection of property, and prevention of escapes, as a last resort and in accordance with appropriate statutory authority. In no event is physical force justifiable as punishment. A written report is prepared following all uses of force and is submitted to the administrative staff for review.

See also ACA Standards 2-4186 to 2-4189 (policies and procedures concerning use of firearms). See generally Bay County Contract app. B at 22, § M; INS RFP at 31, § I(C)(10)(N); 1984 Kentucky RFP at 20, § e; Santa Fe Contract at 5-6, § 3.3.

[857] U.S. Const. amend. VIII; see also Note, supra note 9, at 1497 & n.154 (stating that guarantees of eighth amendment and due process prevent prison guards from using excessive force against inmates).

[858] See Note, supra note 9, at 1483 (noting that prisoners are subjected to cruel and unusual punishment if state fails to

-326-

government's use of force may be justified, particularly in light of the government's compelling interest in maintaining order and security within the facility.[859] In the privatization context, the question is whether a private contractor, which operates a facility and assumes the obligations of the government, may use physical force against inmates and, if so, to what extent. These issues should be addressed both in the contract between the parties and in a statute by each jurisdiction.

One alternative for dealing with use of force is to prohibit the private contractor from using any force at all against inmates by allowing the government to retain this power. This approach is impractical and unrealistic in a prison or jail environment, however, and could endanger both the inmates and the private contractor's employees. If private-prison guards were not allowed to use force, they would be defenseless against the inmates, who outnumber them, and they would be unable to offer

---

take reasonable steps to ensure prisoners' physical safety). The eighth amendment provides post-conviction protection against excessive force; in addition, however, "[m]ost courts consider police use of excessive force in both arrest and detention as violative of the guarantee of due process under the fourteenth amendment." Comment, Excessive Force Claims: Removing the Double Standard, 53 U. Chi. L. Rev. 1369, 1370 (1986).

[859] See Johnson v. Glick, 481 F.2d 1028, 1033 (2d Cir. 1973) (declaring standard to determine whether excessive force was justified during pretrial detention). In this case, Judge Henry Friendly stated that, to determine whether the pretrial detention force used was unconstitutional, a court must evaluate the "need for the application of force, the relationship between the need and the amount of force that was used, the extent of injury inflicted and whether force was applied in a good faith effort . . . or maliciously and sadistically for the very purpose of causing harm." Id. at 1371. See generally Note, Liability of State Officials and Prison Corporations for Excessive Use of Force Against Inmates of Private Prisons, 40 Vand. L. Rev. 983, 991-98 (1987).

protection to other inmates. Because of critical time considerations in the day-to-day situations that generally warrant the use of force, prison or jail personnel would be unable to maintain order and security if only designated government personnel were authorized to use force.

A second, and better, approach would permit private personnel to use non-deadly force in certain defined circumstances, but would reserve to the government the exclusive right to use deadly force in other limited circumstances. This system would function best under a contract that clearly designates the locations in which force can be used and specifically defines the circumstances that may require force. Under such an arrangement, the contracting agency's guards would be allowed to use deadly force when warranted, the private guards would provide better protection and be better protected, and the private contractor's use of force and the potential abuses that may arise from permitting it to exercise force would be restricted.

A third approach would permit the contractor to use both deadly and non-deadly force in limited circumstances, and thus remove the government entirely from the use of force at the facility. One could argue that private guards would be able to provide the best protection and maintain the greatest degree of control under this system because of their ability to respond immediately to any situation in the manner they deemed appropriate. Such open-ended use of force, however, may be abused unless certain safeguards and guidelines are specified in the contract.[860] Some of the important issues that the contract should address to limit the abuse of force include the adequate staffing of the facility, as well as the training of personnel on the distinction between deadly and non-deadly force, the circumstances and places in which force may be used, the reporting requirements when force is used, and the contractor's relationship with local law-enforcement agencies with respect to riots and searching for escapees.

Adequate staffing and proper training of prison personnel are two of the most effective methods to regulate the use of force.[861] Because it is generally feared that private contractors will cut costs by reducing training programs and staffing in the facility, these areas demand particular attention to protect inmates against arbitrary or excessive use of force. It is essential that the private contractor be required at least to meet ACA Standards and to staff facilities and train personnel to the same extent and in the same manner that the public facilities are staffed and the public personnel are trained.[862]

The contract must also provide definitions that distinguish

---

[860] The contractor obviously has significant incentives to minimize the use of force in its prison because of exposure to liability. See CSG Report, supra note 533, at 30 (noting effects of negative publicity as well). For an examination of liability issues the context of use of force, see Note, supra note 859.

[861] See Note, supra note 9, at 1497 & n.156 (observing that inmates are subject to greater risk of physical abuse in prisons that are understaffed or staffed with poorly trained personnel).

[862] See id. at 1499 & n.167 (recognizing that adequately trained guards are less likely to abuse inmates); Model Contract §§ 4(B) (Training Requirements), 4(D) (Staff Ratio).

between deadly and non-deadly force and identify when and where
it is appropriate for each to be used, regardless of which
approach the contracting parties elect to use. Most contracts
have adopted the ACA Standards, which generally state that
physical force should be restricted to instances of justifiable
self-defense, protection of others, protection of property,
prevention of escapes, and in accordance with appropriate
statutory authority.[863] This kind of general provision, however,
is not sufficiently detailed to protect inmates against cruel and
unusual punishment.[864]

In contrast, the Santa Fe Contract distinguishes between
deadly and non-deadly force and addresses where and when such
force may be used.[865] The contract designates the employees who
are entitled to use force and the locations in which they may use
it.[866] Deadly force is defined as "likely to cause death or
serious bodily injury," whereas non-deadly force normally does
not cause death or serious bodily injury.[867] In addition to
these differences, the specific circumstances in which deadly or

---

[863] ACA Standard 2-4206; see also supra note 856 (listing
contracts and RFP's).

[864] See Note, supra note 9, at 1482 (noting that eighth
amendment prohibition against cruel and unusual punishment has
played leading role in prisoners' rights litigation). See
generally Robbins & Buser, supra note 376.

[865] Santa Fe Contract at 5-6, § 3.3.

[866] Id. at 5, § 3.3(a). The employees entitled to use
force are designated "jailers" and may only use force on the
grounds of the facility, while in transport, or in pursuit of an
escapee. Id.

[867] Id. at 6, § 3.3(c).

non-deadly force may be used justifiably are set out.[868] Deadly

force may be used only as a last resort to prevent death or

serious bodily harm to the employee or another person. Non-

deadly force may be used to prevent the commission of a felony or

misdemeanor, to_defend against physical assault, to prevent

damage to property, to enforce institutional regulations and

orders, and to prevent or quell a riot.

The use of specific contract provisions such as those in the

Santa Fe Contract provides guidance to the contractor in

identifying what constitutes justifiable force and protects

inmates against arbitrary and excessive force. These provisions

may be modified, for example, to provide that only the

contracting agency may use deadly force and that private

employees may use only non-deadly force. In any event, to limit

abuse, the criteria for using force must be quite specific.

Another issue that should be addressed in the contract is

the reporting and documentation requirement following an incident

involving force. A contractor's use of force may be subject to

question, and perhaps litigation; therefore, reporting and

documentation of each such instance is imperative. This

requirement ensures that the contractor is accountable for its

actions and provides a record of the event for future

reference.[869] The ACA Standards, and all of the contracts that

---

868 Id.

869 See Walker, Controlling the Cops: A Legislative
Approach to Police Rulemaking, 63 U. Det. L. Rev. 361, 390 (1986)
(noting that rules with respect to use of force are more likely
to have effect where accompanied by mandatory reporting and

have adopted them, require the filing of a written report with the administrative staff, detailing the circumstances in which the force was used.[870]

A final issue, and one that no existing contract appears to address, is the relationship between the contractor and local law-enforcement agencies during escape and riot situations. The contracting agency typically will have either a formal or informal agreement with local law-enforcement agencies to aid facility personnel in these emergency situations. It is advisable for the private contractor to stand in the shoes of the contracting agency in this relationship, if possible, or to seek other arrangements to ensure the coordination of efforts and clarification of roles and responsibilities.[871]

In conclusion, the best provision for use of force, and the one that should be adopted both in the Model Contract and the Model Statute, is the provision used in the Santa Fe Contract. This provision is both restrictive and specific, in that it distinguishes between deadly and non-deadly force and offers sufficient detail regarding the circumstances in which force may be used. This provision must be supplemented, however, with language addressing training of prison and jail personnel in use of force and firearms, reporting and documentation requirements, and the contractor's relationship with local law-enforcement

_____

review mechanisms).

[870] ACA Standard 2-4206.

[871] But see CSG Report, supra note 533, at 30 (stating that "law enforcement officials should become the parties responsible for the ultimate capture and return of the escapee").

agencies in the event of riot or escape.

Model Contract Provision:

        (1)   The private contractor's employees serving
as "jailers" shall be allowed to use force only
while on the grounds of the facility, while
transporting inmates, and while pursuing escapees
from the facility.

        (2)   "Non-deadly force," which is force that
normally would cause neither death nor serious
bodily injury, and "deadly force," which is force
that is likely to cause death or serious bodily
injury, shall be used only as set forth herein.

        (3)   Non-Deadly Force. Any [contractor's name]
jailer shall be authorized to use only such non-
deadly force as the circumstances require in the
following situations: to prevent the commission of
a felony or misdemeanor, including escape; to defend
oneself or others against physical assault; to
prevent serious damage to property; to enforce
institutional regulations and orders; and to prevent
or quell a riot.

        (4)   Use of Firearms/Deadly Force.
[Contractor's name] jailers who have been appropriately certified as determined by the contracting
agency and trained pursuant to the provisions of
Subsection (5) shall have the right to carry and use
firearms and shall exercise such authority and use
deadly force only as a last resort, and then only to
prevent an act that could result in death or serious
bodily injury to oneself or to another person.

        (5)   Jailers shall be trained in accordance
with ACA Standards 2-4186 through 2-4189 and 2-4206,
concerning the use of force and the use of firearms,
and shall be trained, at the contractor's expense,
at the facilities that train public prison and jail
personnel for at least the minimum number of hours
that public personnel are currently trained.

        (6)   Within three (3) days following an
incident involving the use of force against an
inmate or another, the employee shall file a written
report with the administrative staff and contract
monitor describing the incident.

(7)   The contractor shall stand in the shoes of the contracting agency in any agreement, formal or informal, with local law-enforcement agencies concerning the latter's obligations in the event of emergency situations, such as riots or escapes.

Section 5(C): Inmate Transportation

Commentary:

Because inmates may need transportation in several different contexts, it is important that the parties provide for such needs in the contract.[872] For example, inmates must be transported to and from court, parole and disciplinary hearings, health services, rehabilitation programs, and work assignments, or to a new facility. The parties must also address who will be responsible for transporting the inmates in an emergency situation, such as a bomb threat.

No compelling public-policy reason necessitates that one party rather than the other be responsible for inmate transportation. This issue should be a matter of negotiation between the parties. If, on the one hand, the parties decide that the contracting agency will provide the transportation, a simple provision stating this arrangement would be sufficient. If, on the other hand, the parties decide that the private contractor will provide some or all of the transportation services, several safeguards must be addressed in the contract. The contract must delineate precisely the circumstances in which the contractor will provide for the inmate transportation and the

---

872 See CSG Report, supra note 533, at 85-86 (noting that "[t]he principal bone of contention between governments and contractors" is failure to provide specifically which party is responsible for costs related to transportation, medical care, and other services).

point at which responsibility shifts from the contractor to the contracting agency or to some other governmental representative or designee.

The contract must also specify that the Use of Force provision apply during transportation of inmates by the contractor[873] and that the contractor be required to comply with all applicable insurance, inspection, and motor-vehicle laws.

There are, of course, many possible hybrid arrangements in which both the governmental unit and the contractor provide transportation services.[874]

Model Contract Provisions:

If the parties decide that the contracting agency shall provide for all of the transportation needs of the inmates under the care of the private contractor, the following provision should be used:

> The contracting agency shall provide for all of the transportation needs of the inmates under the contractor's care without cost to the contractor.

---

[873]   See Model Contract § 5(B) (Use of Force).

[874]   See Bay County Contract at 17-18, § 5.6 (providing that contractor shall provide transportation to work site and to medical facilities when necessary or at request of county but that county shall provide for all other transportation needs of inmates).

If the parties decide that the contractor shall provide for all of the transportation needs of the inmates under its care, the following provision should be used:

> The contractor shall provide for all of the transportation needs of the inmates under its care, from the time that the prisoner is delivered to the facility by the contracting agency to his or her release or transfer by the contracting agency.
>
> The Use of Force provision in this contract shall apply during the time that the contractor is transporting inmates. The contractor shall comply with all relevant statutes, rules, and regulations regarding insurance, inspection, and motor vehicles while transporting the inmates.

Section 5(D): Inmate Labor

Commentary:

Perhaps not surprisingly, the current interest in prison privatization is occurring at the same time that federal and state governments are showing renewed interest in promoting private-sector involvement in the prison labor system.[875] There are many federal and state laws that prohibit or discourage private-sector involvement in the prison-labor system.[876] Most of this legislation grew out of public pressure during the 1920s and 1930s from trade unions and free laborers who feared unfair wage competition and businessmen who feared unfair price competition.[877] Much of this anti-inmate-labor sentiment has abated, however, following changing perceptions that prison labor does not necessarily pose a threat to labor and business interests and that imprisonment may serve important rehabilitative functions.[878] As a result, both federal and state governments have begun to experiment with some private-sector involvement in prison labor.[879]

---

[875] See supra notes 412-420 and accompanying text (discussing changes in private-sector involvement in prison-labor system since the 1970s).

[876] See supra notes 405-420 and accompanying text.

[877] See supra note 403 and accompanying text.

[878] See supra note 412 and accompanying text.

[879] See supra notes 412-420 and accompanying text.

Current privatization contracts indicate that parties are not using inmate labor for purposes other than facility operation and maintenance and contracting-agency work projects.[880] This may be the result of conflicting and changing laws on inmate labor. It may also stem from concerns that private contractors should not profit directly from inmate labor because of the potential inmate exploitation that could occur under such a system.[881] Undoubtedly, this issue will become increasingly important as governments continue to look for ways to reduce the cost of incarceration. The contracting parties should therefore be prepared to consider these issues.

The parties must negotiate the terms of inmate labor _inside_ the facility for purposes of facility upkeep and maintenance. The contracting agency must also consider whether inmates may be required to work on agency projects _outside_ the prison and, if so, who will be responsible for overseeing such projects. In addition to designating the type of work that will be permitted in the private facility, the agency must address whether inmates should receive any good-time credit or monetary compensation for their labor, who will be responsible for training and supervising the inmates, and who will be responsible for job designations, "hirings," and "firings."

---

880 _See, e.g.,_ Bay County Contract at 16, § 5.2; Santa Fe Contract at 26, § 9 & app. C.

881 _See, e.g.,_ Ark. Stat. Ann. § 12-50-106(e)(2) (Supp. 1987) ("the contractor shall not benefit financially from the labor of inmates").

Model Contract Provision:

The parties agree that all inmates shall be required to keep their living areas clean. In addition, inmates may, if they volunteer, work in the food service, laundry, or other areas of the facility. The contractor shall submit job descriptions for the contracting agency's approval before assigning inmates to those positions. Job assignments shall be made by the contractor. These assignments shall be subject to review by the contracting agency upon written request by the inmates, if they so elect. The contracting agency shall provide inmates with good-time credit or monetary compensation for labor performed. The contracting agency shall be responsible for establishing and administering this compensation program. The contractor shall make inmates available for contracting-agency work projects upon [number] (___) days' written notice to the contractor. The contracting agency shall be responsible for oversight, transportation, and security of the inmates during such work projects.[882]

---

[882] See Bay County Contract at 16, § 5.2; Santa Fe Contract at 26, § 9 & app. C.

Section 6: Monitoring

Commentary:

To what extent will the contract be monitored and what form
will these monitoring efforts take? The contracting agency's
monitoring of the contract will be extremely important both to
ensure that the private contractor is fulfilling its obligations
and to prevent managerial abuse.[883] Without an appropriate
monitoring device, the contracting agency will not be able to
supervise the quantity and quality of the services
delivered.[884] In addition, if private prisons become an

---

[883] See National Institute of Corrections, Private Sector
Operation of a Correctional Institution 77 (1985) (noting, in
evaluation of privately operated Florida School for Boys at
Okeechobee, that it is critical that contracting agency have
means of assuring that contractor is fulfilling obligations);
Durham, supra note 434, at 70 (stating that "[o]nly through
exacting monitoring and evaluation can a reasoned assessment of
the achievements of privatization be made"); Note, supra note
408, at 356 (noting that, if private prisons are not monitored,
forces that permit pecuniary savings will sacrifice prison
conditions and efficiency); Note, supra note 629, at 830 (stating
that monitors will reduce serious managerial abuse of private
prisons).

The contract monitor's role in ensuring compliance with
contractual obligations need not be limited to passive
observation of the contractor's performance. The Federal Bureau
of Prisons' RFP for halfway-house services defines the monitor's
duties to include in part "[giving d]irections to the Contractor
which re-direct the contract effort, shift work emphasis between
areas or tasks, require pursuit of certain lines of inquiry, fill
in details or otherwise serve to accomplish the contractual scope
of work" and "[supplying] information to the contractor which
assists in the interpretation of the technical portions of the
statement of work." Federal Bureau of Prisons RFP at 72, §§
I(G)(1)(a)(1), (2).

[884] See Note, supra note 408, at 356-57 (discussing market

entrenched industry, private corporations will be in a position to allow prison conditions and services to fall below contractual levels, leaving little recourse for the state.[885] Monitoring, therefore, will play a crucial role in detecting and preventing noncompliance with the contract at an early stage.[886]

Close and effective monitoring by the contracting agency is also necessary because the contracting agency retains ultimate responsibility for the care of inmates within the private prison despite its delegation of that function to the private corporation.[887] Thus, a contracting agency's inadequate monitoring could render the contract void upon charges of excessive delegation or increase the contracting agency's exposure to liability.[888] Therefore, the monitoring system recommended under the Model Contract is one that operates on a continual, current basis and reviews and evaluates the private contractor's performance at regular intervals.[889] A full-time

---

failure that occurs when consumer cannot monitor consumption and supplier exploits situation to increase profits).

[885] See id. at 357-58 (noting that corporation obtaining initial private contract is in optimal position due to its ability to own facilities, employ most persons with experience, and have least startup costs for future contracts).

[886] See W. Collins, supra note 725, at 17 (stating that conscientious monitoring provides early identification and correction of any corners cut by contractor in favor of enhancing profits); see also Note, supra note 408, at 358 (declaring that a monitoring system must be supplemented with a system to control economic power of the corporation).

[887] W. Collins, supra note 725, at 17.

[888] Id.; see CSG Report, supra note 533, at 26 (warning that contracting agency may be held liable for conditions resulting from inadequate monitoring).

monitoring system should keep the private corporation accountable
for fulfilling its contractual obligations at all times during
the term of the contract.

There are several alternative monitoring systems that may be
implemented.[890] One system, for example, provides that the
contracting agency appoint a full-time contract monitor with an
office at the facility.[891] Under this system, the monitor should
have access to all areas of the facility, including access to
inmates and staff at all times, whether announced or
unannounced. In addition, the contract should require the
contractor to make all books, records, and reports with respect
to the facility available to the contract monitor.[892] The

---

[889] Many public agencies have utilized a combination of
continuous on-site monitoring and periodic in-depth monitoring in
order to achieve the most effective monitoring system. CSG
Report, supra note 533, at 115.

[890] For examples of how some contracting agencies have
addressed the monitoring issue, see Bay County Contract at 17, §
5.5 (providing for county-appointed monitor with office space and
24-hour access to all areas of the facility as well as to all
necessary records and reports); 1984 Kentucky RFP at 5, § 8
(providing for periodic inspections of facility and sanctions for
violations uncovered during inspections); RCA Contract at 34, §
5.8 (providing for periodic on-site inspections and record
reviews to ensure compliance with all aspects of the contract);
Santa Fe Contract at 28, §§ 11.1, 11.2 (providing for county-
appointed liaison between county and private contractor who will
have office at facility as well as access to facility at all
times); see also CSG Report, supra note 533, at 113-21
(discussing possible methods of monitoring contract
performance). The alternatives discussed in this section are not
exclusive; several or all may be used in combination in order to
meet the contracting agency's monitoring needs.

[891] See Bay County Contract at 17, § 5.5; Santa Fe Contract
at 28, § 11.1.

[892] See CSG Report, supra note 533, at 102 (listing items
that should be included in contract to ensure effective
monitoring). Regular reports on all aspects of the contractor's

monitor will not be able to function effectively without this information.

The advantage of having an on-site contract monitor should be obvious -- monitoring is best achieved from the inside of the facility.[893] Larger facilities may require a monitoring staff to ensure that contractual obligations are fulfilled. Although this full-time monitoring system may be costly,[894] it is the best method for ensuring adequate supervision of the contract and facility. The more supervision there is over the implementation of the contract, the more likely it is that the contractor will comply with the terms of the contract.

An alternative to an on-site contract monitor is to have

---

performance are required as a part of many monitoring systems. Reports regarding extraordinary occurrences -- such as escapes, riots, or injuries to inmates -- are particularly crucial. The contracting agency should clearly specify all written reports and records that it expects the contractor to prepare in addition to those required by ACA Standards. This will ensure that the monitor has the information that he or she needs to monitor the contractor's performance adequately. Id. at 102-03; Eckerd Contract at 2, §§ K, M, and attach. I (specifically requiring various types of reports relating to maintenance, finance, health and safety, unusual incidents, and programs at the facility); CSG Report, supra note 533, at 102 (stating that Kentucky requires its Marion facility to report "extraordinary occurrences"). The contract should also state how often reports and records must be prepared, how long they should be maintained, and whether the contracting agency shall have possession of some or all of these materials upon termination of the contract.

[893] See Crane, supra note 433, at 39. Mr. Crane stated that, "[t]o make contractual obligations stick, the government should appoint a contract monitor with access, at all times, to the facility, inmates, employees and records. At larger institutions, this should be a full-time or even a round-the-clock position." Id.

[894] See CSG Report, supra note 533, at 117 (noting that, for a smaller facility, it may be more cost efficient to have a contracting-agency official visit the facility on a regular basis than to maintain a full-time monitor on site).

periodic inspections of the facility by persons designated by the contracting agency.[895] This monitoring system is less effective than an on-site monitor because deviations from the contract standards will be detected after the fact and the damage will already have been done.[896] Nevertheless, monitoring by inspection will impose some restrictions on the private contractor to make and keep it accountable, and will be less costly to implement.

Preserving public access to the facility has also been proposed as a supplemental method of monitoring the contract.[897] There is no constitutional guarantee of public access. To keep a private prison open to the public, therefore, the contract must include such a provision. Public access, particularly with respect to the media, offers an opportunity to monitor the private prison at virtually no cost to the government. If a very short notice period is required for access and the entire facility is accessible, public access may produce some satisfactory monitoring results.[898] Inmates can play a

---

[895]   See 1984 Kentucky RFP at 5, § 8.

[896]   See Note, supra note 408, at 364 (noting that effective monitoring system requires continuing long-term access to relevant information). But see CSG Report, supra note 533, at 113 (pointing out that periodic monitoring may provide for more in-depth review of a contractor's performance and may be particularly effective when used in conjunction with a continuous on-site monitoring program).

[897]   Note, supra note 408, at 363-67 (noting that a combination of fines, public access, and inmate interaction with the media will help to ensure compliance with the contract).

[898]   Id. at 365.

particularly significant role in alerting the public and the media to any problems within the facility.[899] This system used alone, however, cannot provide effective monitoring. The public is not aware of specific contractual obligations and will not be able to detect the more subtle deviations from the terms of the contract. In addition, in the interests of safety and security, certain limitations must be imposed on the public's access to private prisons.[900] These limitations undermine the effectiveness of public access as the sole monitoring device at a facility.

Finally, in addition to monitoring, a system imposing sanctions for detected abuses should be implemented to control the private firm's conduct effectively. A system of fines may provide the necessary incentives. As one commentator has noted, "[p]roperly set fines will operate to align private interest with public duty and will create market incentives to innovate in care and rehabilitation."[901] If a private firm continues to depart from its contractual obligations or violates the contract in many respects or repeatedly, the contractor may be considered in breach of the contract and the contracting agency must have contractual remedies to cure the breach.

In light of these various alternatives, the Model Contract

---

[899] _Id._ at 366-67.

[900] _Id._ at 365; _see also_ INS RFP at 34, § I(C)(13)(H) (stating that access may be denied where contractor has clear and convincing evidence that visits will jeopardize security of facility or safety of detainee or visitor).

[901] Note, _supra_ note 408, at 361 (footnotes omitted).

provides that the contracting agency should appoint a full-time, on-site contract monitor. This system of monitoring will most effectively detect abuses and deviations from the contract's provisions. The contract monitor should have access to inmates and staff, to all areas of the facility, and to all books, records, and reports of the facility on a twenty-four-hour basis. The contractor should be responsible for providing office space on-site for the contract monitor and his or her staff. The public, particularly the media, should be guaranteed access to the facility, and the procedure for gaining access on short-term notice should be described in the contract. Although a provision for public access is not critical, such a provision will provide additional control over the performance of the contract. In addition, the contractor should be fined for any noncompliance with the contract's provisions and, after repeated departures from the terms of the contract, the contractor may be deemed in breach of the contract.[902] Finally, the contract should specify that the contractor is responsible for all costs that are associated with monitoring the contract, except for the salaries of the contract monitor and his or her staff.[903]

---

[902] The Council of State Governments' Report makes similar recommendations regarding sanctions as a necessary component of a monitoring system. CSG Report, supra note 533, at 104-05. The Report also encourages the use of incentives to raise the level of contractor performance. Id. The Model Contract does not include an incentive clause. The level of compensation paid for services rendered under the contract should provide sufficient incentive for high-level contractor performance. Contracting agencies should not need to offer additional bonuses in order to secure a well-managed and well-operated private facility.

[903] Cf. McAfee, supra note 402, at 856 (noting that

Model Contract Provision:

(A) On or before thirty (30) days after the execution of this contract, the contracting agency shall appoint a contract monitor, who will be an employee of the contracting agency, to be the official liaison between the contracting agency and the contractor. The contract monitor [and his or her staff] shall be provided an office in the facility and shall have access at all times, with or without notice, to inmates and staff, to all areas of the facility, and to all books, records (including financial records), and reports kept by the contractor concerning the renovation, repair, construction, maintenance, and operation of the facility.[904]

The monitor [and his or her staff] will be responsible for monitoring compliance with all contractual obligations, including compliance with the incorporated ACA Standards. The contractor must maintain whatever documentation is necessary to prove that the contractor is meeting its obligations under the contract.[905] This includes, but is not limited to, all reports and other documentation required by ACA Standards, as well as the following reports: [list them]. The contractor shall be responsible for all costs associated with the monitoring of the facility, except for the salaries of the monitor [and his or her staff].

(B) Members of the public, including the media, must apply for access to the facility [number] (___) days before the date that such a visit is planned. An application for access shall include the date and time of the planned visit, the purpose of the visit, and any other relevant information that the contractor's representative requires. Access shall be granted, except where the contractor has clear and convincing evidence that such visits jeopardize the

---

Tennessee Private Prison Contracting Act of 1986 provides that contractor shall bear cost of monitoring).

[904] This provision is derived from Santa Fe Contract at 28, § 11.1.

[905] This provision is derived from Federal Bureau of Prisons RFP at 8, § II(1)(A).

security of the facility or the safety of the inmates or visitor.[906] The monitor shall have final review over all decisions regarding public access to the facility.

(C) The contractor shall be fined [number] (___) dollars for each instance of noncompliance with the contract.[907] The contractor will be given a reasonable time, as determined by the monitor, to rectify the noncompliance. If the noncompliance is not rectified in this period or if [number] (___) instances of noncompliance are detected in a [number] (___) month period,[908] the contractor shall be deemed to be in breach of the contract.

---

[906] This provision is derived from INS RFP at 34, § I(C)(13)(H).

[907] The contracting agency may want to set different levels of fines that are appropriate to the seriousness or the degree of the contractual violation. These levels should be specified in the contract.

[908] The contracting agency may want to vary the number of violations allowed before the contractor may be deemed in default, depending on the importance of the Standard violated. The contracting agency should specify such variations in the contract.

Section 7: Termination

Commentary:

The Model Contract provides the contracting agency with considerable latitude in determining what sanctions to impose when the private contractor fails to perform under the contract. Specifically, the contracting agency may terminate the contract for: contractor default;[909] the filing of a petition in bankruptcy, reorganization, or liquidation; unavailability of funds; or convenience.[910] Although the termination option should always be available at the discretion of the contracting agency,[911] it may not always be an effective means of dealing with performance deficiencies; thus, less drastic measures should

---

[909] Thus, for example, the contracting agency could terminate the contract in the event of a work stoppage.

[910] Also referred to as an "escape clause," this provision permits the contracting agency to terminate the contract for any reason whatsoever. This provision is necessary under the Supreme Court's decision in Fletcher v. Park, 10 U.S. (6 Cranch) 87 (1810), which interpreted article 1, section 10 of the Constitution as applying to contracts to which the state itself is a party. Thus, state contracts can be voided by the legislature only if the contract so provides. Id. at 135-39; see U.S. Const. art. 1, § 10 ("No State shall pass any . . . Law impairing the Obligation of Contracts"). See generally C. Ring, supra note 484, at 47-50 (discussing contract-termination provisions); McAfee, supra note 402, at 859-61 (discussing the necessity of an escape clause in privatization contracts).

[911] See, e.g., Mont. Code Ann. § 7-32-2232(2)(f) (1987) ("The agreement must include . . . a provision that the county may immediately terminate the contract for good cause."); Tex. Rev. Civ. Stat. Ann. art. 6166g-2, § 3(c)(5) (Vernon Supp. 1988) ("a proposal is not acceptable unless it . . . permits the state to terminate the contract for cause"). See generally W. Collins, supra note 725, at 18.

be available to cure the defective performance.[912]

The contracting agency must consider what steps it will take in the event that the contractor fails to perform under the contract, especially if the failure is abrupt and the contracting agency has no choice but to terminate the contract. Provision for who will assume the contractor's role and how prison or jail services will be immediately resumed must be clearly set forth in the contract. The wisest course is for the jurisdiction to enact a statute prohibiting the entering of a contract for the operation of an incarceration facility until a satisfactory plan has been developed and certified by the appropriate executive officer or legislative body, demonstrating the method by which the government would resume control of the facility upon contract termination.[913] Such a provision should also be included in an RFP.

The Model Contract's bankruptcy provision permits the contracting agency to act promptly by terminating the contract in the event that the private contractor files a petition for bankruptcy, reorganization, or liquidation. The contracting agency would therefore not be required to wait for actual bankruptcy proceedings. Assuming that the contract is deemed an executory contract under the Federal Bankruptcy Code, this

_____

[912] For example, the Model Contract permits the contracting agency to offset the contractor's default by deducting payments to the contractor. See Model Contract § 7(A) (Termination for Default).

[913] See Model Statute § 10 (Termination of Contract and Resumption of Government Control).

-351-

provision may be subject to challenge because the Code expressly prohibits termination or modification of a contract at any time after the filing for bankruptcy.[914] To avoid this potential conflict with the Code, the Model Contract, under the Termination for Convenience provision, requires the contractor to inform the contracting agency of its intention to file a petition for bankruptcy at least ten days prior to filing such a petition.[915]

The termination provisions help to ease the transition when control of the facility changes. These provisions also save the contracting agency time, resources, and money, including litigation expenses, by granting the contracting agency considerable latitude and flexibility in determining the appropriate measures to take in the event of a default or, as the Termination for Convenience clause provides, permitting termination of the contract simply when it is in the contracting agency's best interest.

_____

[914] 11 U.S.C. § 365(e)(1) (1982).

[915] Section 365(e)(1) applies only after bankruptcy has been filed, thus placing pre-petition termination action beyond the scope of the Code. For a thorough discussion of the implications of the Code on private prison contracts, see Note, Privatization of Corrections: Is the State Out on a Limb When the Company Goes Bankrupt?, 41 Vand. L. Rev. 317 (1988).

Model Contract Provisions:

This contract shall be subject to the following provisions:

(A) Termination for Default

The contracting agency may terminate this contract when it determines that (1) the private contractor has failed to meet the minimum standards of operations set forth in Subsection 3(F) of this contract, or (2) the contractor has failed to meet other contract provisions where such failure seriously affects the operation of the facility.

Thirty (30) days prior to termination by the contracting agency, it shall serve the contractor with written notice of default(s), by certified mail. If the contractor has failed to correct the default to the contracting agency's satisfaction within the period of time specified in the contracting-agency notice, the contractor shall be deemed to be in default of the contract and the contract shall be terminated immediately, or, at the option of the contracting agency, it may offset the default by deducting payments to the contractor or seek other equitable remedies.

If after Notice of Termination for Default it is determined by the contracting agency, the arbitrators, or a court that the contractor was in default because of causes beyond the control and without the error or negligence of the contractor, the termination shall be deemed to have been issued as a Termination for Convenience, with the parties' rights governed accordingly.

In the event of default, in full or in part as provided herein, the contracting agency may procure, on terms that it finds appropriate, goods or services similar to those to be provided hereunder, and the contractor shall be liable to the contracting agency for any excess costs for such similar goods and services. In addition, the contractor shall be liable to the contracting agency for administrative costs incurred by the contracting agency in procuring such similar goods or services. The performance bond required in Subsection 3(D) of this contract shall guarantee payment of such excess costs and the contractor shall be liable for any excess over and above said amount if the bond proceeds are insufficient to pay such costs.

In the event of Termination for Default, subject to the retainage provision, the contractor shall be paid in accordance with the contract price for each contracting-agency inmate held by the contractor until the date of termination.

The rights and remedies of the contracting agency provided in this Subsection shall not be exclusive and are in addition to any other rights and remedies provided by law or pursuant to the contract.

(B)   Termination for Contractor Bankruptcy

The contractor must inform the contracting agency of its intention to file a petition for bankruptcy at least ten (10) days prior to filing such a petition. The contractor's filing without conforming to this requirement shall be deemed a material pre-petition incurable breach.[916]

In the event of the filing of a petition in bankruptcy, reorganization, or liquidation pursuant to any chapter of the Bankruptcy Code, Title 11 U.S.C., the contracting agency shall have the right to terminate the contract under the same conditions as if it were a Termination for Default. In the event of termination for contractor bankruptcy, the contractor shall be required to cooperate and assist the contracting agency to the fullest extent possible to reestablish prison or jail services as quickly as possible.

(C)   Termination for Unavailability of Funds

In the event that the contracting agency's funds for the contract become unavailable, the contracting agency shall have the right to terminate the contract without penalty and on the same terms and conditions as if it were a Termination for

---

916   Note, supra note 915, at 338 (quoting Ruben, Legislative and Judicial Confusion Concerning Executory Contracts in Bankruptcy, 89 Dick. L. Rev. 1029, 1059 (1985)).

Convenience. Availability of funds will be
determined at the sole discretion of the contracting
agency.

(D) Termination for Convenience

The contracting agency may terminate
performance of work under the contract in whole or
in part whenever, for any reason, the contracting
agency determines that it is in its best interest to
do so. The contracting agency shall give the
contractor, without penalty to the state, ninety
(90) days' notice prior to termination of the
contract.

The contractor shall have no right to any
general, special, incidental, consequential, or any
damages whatsoever of any description or amount,
except that the contracting agency shall pay for all
supplies and equipment on order and not yet
delivered to the facility as of the date of
termination.

(E) Procedure on Termination

Upon delivery by certified mail to the
contractor of a Notice of Termination specifying the
nature of the termination, the extent to which
performance of work under the contract is
terminated, and the date on which such termination
becomes effective, the contractor shall:

(1) stop work under the contract on the
date and to the extent specified in the Notice
of Termination;

(2) place no further orders for materials,
services, or facilities, except as may be
necessary for completion of such portion of the
work under the contract as is not terminated;

(3) terminate all orders to the extent
that they relate to the performance of work
terminated by the Notice of Termination, except
as may be necessary to avoid the incurrence of
penalty assessments and the continuation of
which the contracting agency has approved;

(4) assign to the contracting agency in the manner and to the extent directed by the [contracting officer] all of the right, title, and interest of the contractor under the orders so terminated, in which case the contracting agency shall have the right, in its discretion, to settle or pay any or all claims arising out of the termination of such orders;

(5) with the approval or ratification of the [contracting officer], settle all outstanding liabilities and all claims arising out of such termination of orders, the cost of which would be reimbursable in whole or in part, in accordance with the provision of the contracts;

(6) transfer title to the contracting agency (to the extent that title has not already been transferred) and deliver in the manner, at the times, and to the extent directed by the [contracting officer] all files, processing systems, data manuals, or documentation, in any form, that relate to work terminated by the Notice of Termination;

(7) complete the performance of such part of the work as shall not have been terminated by the Notice of Termination; and

(8) take such action as may be necessary, or as the [contracting officer] may direct, for the protection and preservation of the property related to the contract that is in the possession of the contractor and in which the contracting agency has or may acquire an interest.

The contractor shall proceed immediately with the performance of the above obligations notwithstanding any delay in determining or adjusting the amount of any item of reimbursable price under this provision.

(F)   Resumption of Government Control

Notwithstanding any other provision of this contract to the contrary, prior to entering a contract for the private operation of any prison or jail, a plan shall be developed by the contracting agency and certified by the [Governor or appropriate executive officer or legislative body] demonstrating the method by which the government would resume control of the facility upon contract termination.

Section 8: Miscellaneous Provisions

Section 8(A): Entire Agreement

Commentary:

The entire-agreement provision is a standard contractual provision. Its purpose is to preclude a claim by either party that promises or statements made during the bidding or negotiation phases were meant to be part of the final contract, even though they were not expressly included in the contract itself. In this provision, the parties should identify all documents, schedules, attachments, appendices, exhibits, and other items that comprise the agreement.

Model Contract Provision:

> This contract constitutes the entire contract and supersedes all other prior agreements and understandings, both written and oral, between the parties with respect to the subject matter hereof. The term "contract" includes [list of Exhibits, Attachments, Appendices, etc.].

Section 8(B): Amendment

Commentary:

The amendment provision of the contract should conform to standard contract language. Thus, both parties should be required to sign any amendment to the contract.

Model Contract Provision:

This contract may be amended only in writing signed by the parties.

Section 8(C): Severability

Commentary:

The Model Contract includes a severability provision stating that, in the event that a court or legislature finds a provision of the agreement void, that provision shall be severed from the contract and the rest of the contract shall remain in force. If the contracting agency determines, however, that the severed provision is essential to the purpose or performance of the entire agreement, then it may terminate the contract. This action would be deemed a termination for convenience.[917]

The Model Contract provision ensures that an otherwise satisfactory contractual arrangement will not be disrupted or terminated by a judicial or legislative finding that a provision, not essential to the whole, is invalid. It also ensures, however, that a contracting agency will not be bound by a contract that no longer contains a provision that is essential to the private operation of the correctional facility. The provision is consistent with the general rule that a court may uphold as much of a contract as is valid, as long as the invalid provision is not essential to the purpose of the contract.[918]

----

[917] The Model Contract provision is patterned after the Santa Fe Contract's severability provision, which states that, should the county determine that the contract is "substantially impaired" by a finding of invalidity, the contract shall be terminated for the convenience of both parties. See Santa Fe Contract at 30, § 12.4. It further provides that the county need not observe the 90-day notice requirement that would otherwise apply to a termination for convenience under the contract. Id.

Model Contract Provision:

       If any term, provision, covenant, or
restriction of this contract is held by a court of
competent jurisdiction or the legislature to be
invalid, void, or unenforceable, the remainder of
the terms, provisions, covenants, and restrictions
of this contract shall remain in full force and
effect, and shall in no way be affected, impaired,
or invalidated.

       If, however, the contracting agency determines
that the invalid provision or provisions are
essential to the purpose or performance of the
contract, it may terminate the contract. Such a
termination shall be deemed a Termination for
Convenience as set forth in Section 7(D) of this
contract.

---

918   See S. Williston, A Treatise on the Law of Contracts §§
1630, 1779 (3d ed. 1972).

Section 8(D): Venue and Choice of Law

Commentary:

The contract should include a venue provision to select a forum that is convenient for the parties.[919] Further, a choice-of-law provision designating the internal law of the state in which the contract is entered should be included to aid in the resolution of any contract disputes. Such a provision avoids the problems that are encountered with the doctrine of renvoi.[920]

Model Contract Provision:

> Venue for the enforcement of this contract and all claims or disputes relating thereto shall be in the [select appropriate court and jurisdiction].
>
> This contract, the rights and obligations of the parties hereto, and any claims or disputes relating thereto shall be governed by and construed in accordance with the internal law of the State of [_____] in the resolution of all issues.[921]

---

[919] New Mexico requires a particular venue by statute. See 1988 N.M. Laws § 31-1-17(A)(5).

[920] Renvoi concerns whether, when one state is referred by its choice-of-law process to the law of another state, the referral is to the internal law of the other state only or to the whole law of the state, including its choice-of-law process. See generally E. Scoles & P. Hay, Conflict of Laws 67-72 (1982).

[921] This provision is derived from Hamilton County Contract app. B, at 3, art. V. The language "relating thereto," rather than "arising from this contract" or "arising on this contract," is recommended to avoid the problem of determining what law should be used for questions concerning modification of the contract. See, e.g., Siegelman v. Cunard White Star Ltd., 221 F.2d 189, 193-94 (2d Cir. 1955).

Section 8(E): Alternative Dispute Resolution

Commentary:

Although there is a variety of alternative dispute
resolution (ADR) techniques available,[922] most of the
privatization contracts that employ some form of ADR choose
arbitration.[923] These contracts require that the parties submit
to binding arbitration in accordance with the rules of the
American Arbitration Association if they are unable mutually to
resolve any contract-related controversy.[924] Although these
arbitration provisions are quite common in commercial
contracts,[925] the parties should carefully consider the need for
and suitability of binding arbitration in the privatization
setting.

Under an arbitration provision, the parties agree to submit
their dispute to neutral third parties (typically industry
experts) who will enter a decision that, depending on the
particular contract, will be either binding or nonbinding on the
parties.[926] Arbitration is "normally less formal, faster, and

---

[922] These techniques include negotiation, mediation, and
arbitration.

[923] E.g., Santa Fe Contract at 31-32, § 12.7; Bay County
Contract at 35-36, § 11.

[924] See supra note 923.

[925] See generally Riskin, The Special Place of Mediation in
Alternative Dispute Processing, 37 U. Fla. L. Rev. 19, 21 (1985)
(noting that "American Arbitration Association now handles close
to 10,000" commercial disputes each year).

less expensive than the judicial process"[927] and works well where there is a continuing relationship between the contracting parties.[928] The benefits of arbitration, however, must be weighed against the drawbacks -- including the use of an informal discovery process that might make it extremely difficult for the contracting agency to gain access to materials and evidence held by the private contractor, and decisions that are not fully developed. These features may hinder an appeal of the decision, if available. The parties should also consider the relationship between the contract's termination and arbitration provisions and determine whether an arbitration provision would be necessary or effective under a contract that allows termination at will. Finally, the parties must provide for the continued operation of the facility while the dispute is being arbitrated. Specifically, when the dispute involves an issue for which there is insufficient time to arbitrate, the parties must adopt interim measures that will allow them to arbitrate rather than terminate the contract.

Although commentators recommend some sort of ADR mechanism in general privatization contracts, there has been no substantive

---

926 "Binding decisions" are not truly binding on the parties because a dissatisfied party has the right to request a trial de novo, which is conducted without any reference to or consideration given to the prior arbitration process. Levin & Golash, Alternative Dispute Resolution in Federal District Courts, 37 U. Fla. L. Rev. 29, 32-33 (1985).

927 Riskin, supra note 925, at 21.

928 Sander, Alternative Methods of Dispute Resolution: An Overview, 37 U. Fla. L. Rev. 1, 5 (1985).

discussion of its appropriateness in the private-corrections context.[929] Before including an ADR provision in the contract, the parties should carefully consider the desirability of such a provision. The Model Contract provision is typical of those that parties have used in privatization contracts to date, although the discovery-process provision has been modified.[930]

Model Contract Provision:

> Any controversy regarding this contract that the parties are unable to resolve by mutual agreement may be submitted to binding arbitration in [location] in accordance with the rules of the American Arbitration Association.
>
> Any decision of the arbitrators shall be conclusive as to the matter submitted and may be enforced in any court of competent jurisdiction in the State of [_____]. Issues under arbitration shall be heard and decided by three arbitrators, one of whom shall be designated by the contracting agency, one of whom shall be designated by the contractor, and one of whom shall be designated by the court in [location], or, in the absence of such a designation, by the American Arbitration Association. Any factual decision on an issue being arbitrated, including the sharing of costs of arbitration, made by at least two of the arbitrators shall be the decision of the arbitrators and such decision shall be final, non-appealable, and binding on both parties.

---

[929] E.g., CSG Report, supra note 533, at 64 (stating that "[a] method for resolving any future contractual differences which may emerge should be agreed to before activation of the facility").

[930] This provision is derived from the Santa Fe Contract at 31-32, § 12.7, with the exception that Subsection (5) was added, Subsection (1) was deleted, and Subsection (2) was modified to require a written decision.

The following terms shall be binding on the parties:

(1) Either party may require that the hearing be recorded.

(2) After it is determined by either party that a dispute cannot be resolved without arbitration, it shall be submitted for arbitration within fifteen (15) business days. "Business days" shall mean Monday through Friday, excluding holidays. After submission, a written decision shall be rendered within ninety (90) days, unless an extension is agreed to by both parties.

(3) Neither party shall appoint an employee or agent as an arbitrator.

(4) Each party reserves the right to appeal any question of law.

(5) Discovery shall be conducted in accordance with the Federal Rules of Civil Procedure.

This Section shall operate only by mutual consent of the parties.

B. Summary of Model Contract Provisions

Section 1: Policy Statement -- Goals and Responsibilities of the Parties

This contract between the contracting agency and the contractor for the operation and maintenance of incarceration facilities, entered for the benefit of the public and inmates, is premised on the following goals of privatization:

(A) to provide the public with prison or jail services that are cost efficient and effective with respect to the purposes and goals of incarceration;

(B) to provide inmates with proper care, treatment, rehabilitation, and reformation; and

(C) to provide the public and inmates with prison or jail services that meet the requirements of the American Correctional Association and other such minimum standards that may be promulgated by the contracting agency.

This contract is entered in consideration of these goals of privatization.

Section 2: Private Financing and Physical Plant

Section 2(A): Private Financing

The private contractor will provide financing for the facility under this contract in accordance with the financing plan that has been approved by the contracting agency. Any financial obligation of the contracting agency under this plan is subject to the annual appropriation of funds by the legislature.

If this contract is terminated at any time under any of the termination clauses provided in Section 7, the contracting agency shall have the right to take possession of the facility immediately for the purpose of operating the facility. It shall

also have the option to repurchase the facility
within ninety (90) days of the termination of the
contract.

Section 2(B): Physical Plant

The contractor shall provide a facility in
accordance with the final architectural designs and
the final plans and specifications that have been
[will be] submitted by the contractor [by (date)]
and approved by the contracting agency. The
facility shall conform to all standards set forth in
the contract, including all applicable ACA Standards
regarding the physical plant. Compliance with all
applicable state and local building codes, including
[list, if desired], in accordance with ACA Standard
2-4153, is mandatory. In the event that there is a
conflict among state, local, and/or national codes,
the more stringent standard(s) shall apply.

Section 3: General Contract Terms

Section 3(A): Term

The term of this contract shall be for a period
of three (3) years commencing on [time and date] and
terminating on [time and date], subject to the
availability of funds and unless earlier terminated
in accordance with the relevant provisions of this
contract.

Section 3(B): Renewal

An option to renew this contract for an
additional [number] (___) year term shall be
exercisable by the contracting agency on like terms
and conditions except with respect to compensation
paid to the contractor. The contracting agency may

exercise its option to renew the contract [number] (___) times, after which the contracting agency will reopen the contract for competitive bidding.

Compensation shall be negotiated between the parties before each renewal period. The price shall not increase more than [number] (___) percent over any one renewal period, nor shall the price rise more than [number] (___) percent over the entire duration of the contract.

Should the private contractor desire to renew this contract, it shall notify the contracting agency in writing and submit a written price proposal at least [number] (___) days prior to the termination date of this contract. Should the private contractor not desire to renew this contract, it shall notify the contracting agency in writing no later than [number] (___) days prior to the termination date of this contract. Failure to so notify shall be a valid basis for forfeiture of the retainage account balance then held by the contracting agency and subsequent retainage amounts, until the termination of this contract.

Section 3(C): Compensation

(1) Per-Diem Rate

The contracting agency shall pay the contractor every [number] (___) days (payment period) a per-diem charge of [number] (___) dollars per inmate day (per-diem rate). For purposes of establishing an inmate day, the inmate's arrival and departure days will count as one inmate day. On or before [number] (___) days after the payment period, the contractor shall provide the contracting agency with a statement showing the number of inmate days charged for the prior payment period.

(2) Minimum and Maximum Inmate Population

The contracting agency shall pay the contractor a minimum of [number] (___) dollars per payment period, which shall be determined by multiplying the cost per inmate day times [number] (___) (guaranteed minimum inmate population). In no event shall the contracting agency pay the contractor in excess of

[number] (___) dollars, which shall be determined by
multiplying the cost per inmate day times [number]
(___) (maximum inmate population).

(3)   Annual Adjustments to Per-Diem Rate

The per-diem rate shall be adjusted at the
beginning of each fiscal year. The adjustment shall
be based on increases or decreases in the Consumer
Price Index. The adjustments, which are intended to
reflect changes in the purchasing power of a given
amount of money expressed in dollars, shall not be
greater than five percent (5%).

(4)   Unforeseen-Circumstances Adjustment

Although the parties intend to fix the per-diem
rate subject to annual adjustments, the parties
recognize that unforeseen circumstances may arise
during the term of this contract. Therefore, the
parties agree that within [number] (___) days after
the end of the [ordinal number] full fiscal year of
the term of this contract, either party may elect to
request in writing a change in the per-diem rate to
reflect any change in the cost of operating and
maintaining the facility. If there is an
irreconcilable breakdown in negotiations, the
parties should refer to Section 7 of this contract
for termination procedures.

Section 3(D):   Performance Bond

A performance bond in the amount of [number]
(___) dollars (or [number] (___) percent of the
contract price) is required to assure the
contractor's faithful performance of the
specifications and conditions of this contract. The
bond is required throughout the term of this
contract. The terms and conditions of the bond must
be approved by the contracting agency, and such
approval is a condition precedent to this contract
taking effect.

Section 3(E): Indemnification, Immunity, and Insurance

(1) Indemnification and Immunity

(A) The contractor assumes full responsibility
for and shall indemnify the contracting agency, its
officials, agents, employees, and representatives,
including attorneys, other public officials, and the
Superintendent/Warden, in their official or
individual capacities, and their respective legal
representatives, heirs and beneficiaries, and shall
pay all judgments rendered against any or all of
them for any and all loss or damage of whatever kind
and nature to any and all contracting-agency
property, real or personal, including but not
limited to any buildings, structures, fences,
equipment, supplies, accessories, inventory, or
parts furnished, while in the contractor's custody
and care for use or storage, resulting in whole or
in part from the acts, errors, or omissions of the
contractor or any officer, agent, representative,
employee, or subcontractor thereof for whatever
reason.

(B) The company shall save and hold harmless
and indemnify the contracting agency, its officials,
agents, employees, and representatives, including
attorneys, other public officials, and the
Superintendent/Warden, in their official or
individual capacities, and their respective legal
representatives, heirs, and beneficiaries, and shall
pay all judgments rendered against any or all of
them for any and all loss or damage of whatever kind
against any and all liability, claims, and cost, of
whatever kind and nature, for physical or personal
injury and any other kind of injury, including,
specifically, deprivation of civil rights, and for
loss or damage to any property or injury resulting
from a breach of the terms of this contract
occurring in connection with or in any way incident
to or arising out of the occupancy, use, service,
operation, or performance by the company, its
agents, employees, or representatives of any of the
provisions or agreements contained in this contract,
including any Appendices, for which the contracting
agency or any of the hereinabove-mentioned
indemnified parties, who may become legally liable
resulting in whole or in part from the acts, errors,
or omissions of the company, or any officer, agent,
representative, employee, or subcontractor thereof

for whatever reason.

(C) The company shall save and hold harmless and indemnify the contracting agency, its officials, agents, employees, and representatives, including attorneys, other public officials, and the Superintendent/Warden, in their official or individual capacities, and their respective legal representatives, heirs, and beneficiaries who may become legally liable resulting in whole or in part from any inmate who escapes from the facility.

(D) The company shall save and hold harmless and indemnify the contracting agency, its officials, agents, employees, and representatives, including attorneys, other public officials, and the Superintendent/Warden, in their official or individual capacities, and their respective legal representatives, heirs, and beneficiaries who may become legally liable resulting in whole or in part from damages to any person or firm injured or damaged by the company, its officers, agents, representatives, or employees, by the publication, translation, reproduction, delivery, performance, use, or disposition of any data processed under this contract in a manner not authorized by the contract or by federal or state statutes, rules, regulations, or case law.

(E) The company shall save and hold harmless and indemnify the contracting agency, its officials, agents, employees, and representatives, including attorneys, other public officials, and the Superintendent/Warden, in their official or individual capacities, and their respective legal representatives, heirs, and beneficiaries, for any failure of the company, its officers, agents, representatives, or employees to observe state and federal laws, including but not limited to labor, minimum-wage, and unfair-employment laws.

(F) The company agrees to pay losses, liabilities, and expenses under the following conditions:

(1) The parties who shall be entitled to enforce this indemnity of the contractor shall be the contracting agency, its officials, agents, employees, and representatives, including attorneys, other public officials, and the Superintendent/Warden, any successor in office to any of the foregoing individuals, and their respective legal representatives, heirs, and beneficiaries.

(2)   The losses, liabilities, and expenses that are indemnified shall include judgments, court costs, legal fees, the costs of expert testimony, amounts paid in settlement, and all other costs of any type whether or not litigation is commenced. Also covered are investigation expenses, including, but not limited to, the costs of utilizing the services of the contracting agency incurred in the defense and handling of said suits, claims, judgments, and the like, and in enforcing and obtaining compliance with the provisions of this paragraph whether or not litigation is commenced.

(3)   Nothing in this contract shall be considered to preclude an indemnified party from receiving the benefits of any insurance the contractor may carry that provides for indemnification for any loss, liability, or expense that is described in this contract.

(4)   The company shall do nothing to prejudice the contracting agency's right to recover against third parties for any loss, destruction of, or damage to the contracting agency's property. Upon the request of the contracting agency or its officials, the company shall furnish to the contracting agency all reasonable assistance and cooperation, including assistance in the prosecution of suits and the execution of instruments of assignment in favor of the contracting agency in obtaining recovery.

(5)   The settlement of any claim or action involving a monetary amount covered by insurance shall require the written consent of each indemnified party to this contract against whom a claim is made or action commenced. No such settlement shall be effective without such written consent. The indemnified party or parties shall not unreasonably withhold such consent.

(6)   The settlement of any claim or action involving a nonmonetary amount, or the settlement of an amount of damages in excess of or not otherwise covered by insurance, shall require the written consent of each indemnified party to this contract against whom a claim is made or action commenced. No such indemnified party shall be liable for any settlement of any

such claim or action effected without his, her, or its written consent.

(G) Nothing herein is intended to deprive the contracting agency of the benefits of any law limiting exposure to liability and/or setting a ceiling on damages, or any laws establishing defense(s) for the contracting agency.

(H) By entering this contract, the contracting agency does not waive any immunity that may extend to it by operation of law.

(I) By entering this agreement, the company expressly waives any immunity that may extend to it by operation of law.

(2) Insurance

(A) The contracting agency shall be named as an insured on any and all insurance policies taken by the contractor for the construction, operation, or management of a facility or facilities, and the coverage shall extend to its officials, agents, employees, and representatives, including attorneys, other public officials, and the Superintendent/ Warden, in their official or individual capacities, and their respective legal representatives, heirs, and beneficiaries.

(B)(1) All insurance or other certificates required under this contract must provide no less than thirty (30) days' advance notice to the contracting agency of any contemplated cancellation.

(B)(2) The company will not cancel, or allow to be canceled, any policy of insurance without contracting-agency approval. Each policy shall be approved by the contracting agency prior to the effective date of this contract. The contracting agency reserves the right, in its discretion, to reject any policy issued by an insurer that is deemed to be not fully reliable or otherwise deemed to be unsuitable.

(B)(3) The contracting agency shall have the right, but not the obligation, to advance an amount of money as required to prevent the insurance required herein from lapsing for nonpayment of premiums. If the contracting agency advances such amount, then the company shall be obligated to repay to the contracting agency the amount of any advances plus interest thereon at the maximum rate allowable by law, and the contracting agency shall be entitled to set off and deduct such amount from any amounts owed to the company pursuant to this contract. No election by the contracting agency to advance insurance premiums shall be deemed to cure a default by the company of its obligation to provide insurance.

(C) This contract shall not become effective until the contractor provides the contracting agency with policies of insurance of the following types, for the following purposes, and in the following amounts:

(1) Insurance protecting it under workers' compensation acts and from other claims for damages for physical or personal injury, including death, to inmates or prison employees, which may arise from operations performed by the contractor, by a subcontractor, or by a person directly or indirectly employed by either of them. Such insurance will cover, but is not limited to, claims arising out of personal-injury liability, professional liability (malpractice), and contractual liability.

(2) Insurance in an amount not less than current coverage as maintained by the contracting agency as of the effective date of this contract with a deductible not greater than ten-thousand dollars ($10,000), protecting the facility, and any other real or personal property described in or used pursuant to this contract, against loss by fire, theft, or any other hazard, including destruction in whole or in part. Future additional coverage shall be determined in accordance with reasonable valuation less the deductible stated above. In the event of a loss, the contractor shall pay all deductible amounts.

(3) General liability insurance, which shall specifically include civil-rights matters, in an amount not less than twenty-five-million dollars ($25,000,000) for each occurrence. Such insurance shall also include coverage for the cost of defense for all contracting-agency officials and others indemnified pursuant to this contract.

(4)- Automobile and other vehicle liability insurance in an amount not less than two-million dollars ($2,000,000) for each occurrence and ten-million dollars ($10,000,000) for all occurrences.

(5) Insurance in an amount not less than fifty-thousand dollars ($50,000) relating to instances of dishonesty.

(D) The contracting agency shall exercise its best efforts to allow the contractor to maintain insurance for the facility at the contractor's expense under the contracting agency's fire and property insurance. The contracting agency shall maintain fire and property insurance in accordance with state law.

(E)(1) The contractor shall assume the defense for any action for which there is insurance coverage with counsel selected by the contractor, but the contracting agency may participate in the defense if it chooses to do so.

(E)(2) Within ten (10) days after receipt by an indemnified party of written notice of the commencement of any action against him, her, or it, such party shall notify the contractor in writing of the commencement thereof. Failure to so notify the contractor within such period shall not relieve the contractor from any liability that it may have to the indemnified party otherwise hereunder unless a judgment shall have been entered against the contractor, or the contractor shall otherwise have suffered irreparable injury, on account of such failure. In case any such action shall be brought against an indemnified party, and if the indemnified party shall notify the contractor of the commencement thereof, the contractor shall be entitled to participate in and assume the defense thereof, with counsel selected by the company who is reasonably satisfactory to the contracting agency's counsel.

(F) The contracting agency shall remain solely responsible for any losses or costs resulting from claims or litigation pending at the time that this contract first becomes effective or arises thereafter from an occurrence prior to the time that this contract first became effective. The contractor agrees to cooperate with the contracting agency in the defense of these suits and conform its

operation of the facility or facilities to any court
orders or settlement agreements resulting from such
claims or litigation.

Section 3(F): Operating Standards

The contractor shall [construct,] operate and
maintain the facility in accordance with all
applicable constitutional standards, federal, state,
and local laws, rules, regulations, and ordinances,
and certification or licensing requirements that are
effective or become effective during the contract
term, as well as court orders rendered during the
contract term [including, but not limited
to, _____]. The contractor shall also comply
with one-hundred percent of the mandatory ACA
Standards and ninety percent of the nonmandatory ACA
Standards.

When the contract expressly provides that a
Standard is incorporated as mandatory, compliance
with that Standard is mandatory for purposes of the
contract despite the fact that it may be classified
as nonmandatory by the ACA.

If any provision of this contract is more
stringent than the applicable ACA Standard(s), the
contract provision shall govern and must be complied
with by the contractor.

If any applicable federal, state, or local law,
rule, or regulation is in conflict with the ACA
Standards, the more stringent requirement shall
govern and must be complied with by the contractor.

The contractor must maintain compliance with
the required percentages of mandatory and
nonmandatory ACA Standards, as well as all other
contractual provisions and standards, from the date
the contract commences to the date the contract
terminates [except that, when the contractor assumes
operation of an existing facility, it shall have
ninety (90) days from the date the contract
commences to achieve compliance with applicable ACA
Standards relating to the condition of the physical
plant]. In the event that the ACA Standards are
modified during the contract term, including any
renewal period, the contractor shall have [number]
(__) months to bring the facility into compliance

with the new Standards, provided that the new
Standards have been approved by the contracting
agency.

Section 3(G): Subcontracts and Assignments

The contractor shall not subcontract or assign
any or all of the services to be performed under
this contract without the consent, guidance, and
prior express written approval of the contracting
agency. In the event that approval is granted and
some or all of the services are subcontracted or
assigned, the contractor shall guarantee that the
subcontractor will comply with all of the provisions
of this contract, including the incorporated ACA
Standards. Employees of the subcontractor or
assignee shall have the same rights and obligations
under the contract as do employees of the
contractor.

[Optional Paragraph: The contractor shall be
required to provide a payment bond with a surety
company that is licensed to do business in [the
appropriate jurisdiction] and that is acceptable to
the contracting agency to insure the payment of all
subcontractors, material men, laborers, and taxes,
including but not limited to unemployment insurance
taxes.]

The contractor is ultimately responsible for
the performance of all work under the contract at
the contract price, regardless of whether some or
all of the work is subcontracted or assigned. In
the event that the contractor or subcontractor fails
to comply with the requirements of this or any other
contractual provision, the contracting agency may
fine the contractor [number] (___) dollars per
violation. Alternately [or in addition], the
contracting agency may hold the contractor in breach
of the contract and terminate the contract at the
contracting agency's option.

Section 3(H): Independent-Contractor Status

Nothing contained in this contract is intended or should be construed as creating the relationship of co-partners, joint-ventures, or an association between the contracting agency and the contractor. The contractor is an independent contractor and neither the contractor nor its employees, agents, or representatives shall be considered employees, agents, or representatives of the contracting agency. These parties shall not, therefore, be entitled to any benefits that accrue to employees, agents, or representatives of the contracting agency.

From any amount due the contractor, there will be no deductions for federal income tax or FICA payments, nor for any state income tax, nor for any other purposes that are associated with any employer-employee relationship, unless required by law. Payment of federal income tax, FICA, and any state income tax is the responsibility of the contractor.

Section 4: Employee Issues

Section 4(A): Hiring Criteria

(1) Employment Discrimination

The contractor shall not discriminate against any employee or applicant for employment because of race, color, religion, sex, national origin, age (except as provided by law), marital status, political affiliation, or handicap. The contractor must take affirmative action to ensure that employees, as well as applicants for employment, are treated without discrimination because of their race, color, religion, sex, national origin, age (except as provided by law), marital status, political affiliation, or handicap. Such action shall include, but is not limited to, the following: employment, promotion, demotion or transfer, recruitment or recruitment advertising, layoff or termination, rates of pay or other forms of compensation, and selection for training, including apprenticeship. The contractor agrees to post notices setting forth the provisions of this clause in conspicuous places, available to employees and applicants for employment.

The contractor shall, in all solicitations or advertisements for employees placed by or on behalf of the contractor, state that all qualified applicants will receive consideration for employment without regard to race, color, religion, sex, national origin, age (except as provided by law), marital status, political affiliation, or handicap, except where it relates to a bona fide occupational qualification. The contractor shall comply with the nondiscrimination clause contained in Federal Executive Order 11246, as amended by Federal Executive Order 11375, relative to Equal Employment Opportunity for all persons without regard to race, color, religion, sex, national origin, and the implementation of rules and regulations prescribed by the Secretary of Labor and with Title 41, Code of Federal Regulations, Chapter 60. The contractor shall comply with related [jurisdiction] laws and regulations.

The contractor shall comply with regulations issued by the Secretary of Labor of the United States in Title 20, Code of Federal Regulations, Part 741, pursuant to the provisions of Executive Order 11758 and the Federal Rehabilitation Act of 1973.

The contractor shall comply with the Civil Rights Act of 1964, and any amendments thereto, and the rules and regulations thereunder, and Section 504 of Title V of the Vocational Rehabilitation Act of 1973 as amended. This provision incorporates as mandatory ACA Standards 2-4054, 2-4055, 2-4057, and 2-4059. The contractor has a continuing obligation to comply with the Standards, as well as with revised or additional Standards to the extent that they are approved by the contracting agency.

In the event that the contractor fails to comply with these provisions, including the applicable ACA Standards, or with any other such rules, regulations, or orders, this contract may be cancelled, terminated, or suspended in whole or in part by the contracting agency and the contractor may be declared ineligible for further contracts.

(2) Employment Options for Correctional and
Detention Employees at Existing Facilities

Every correctional employee currently employed
by the contracting agency who desires to remain
employed at the facility shall be accepted as an
employee of the contractor if he or she
satisfactorily completes the training requirements
detailed in Subsection 4(B) of this contract and
meets all other requirements regarding employees set
forth in this contract. The contractor shall not be
required to hire otherwise qualified employees from
the existing facility if the contractor has met the
staffing levels required by this contract. The
contractor shall also have the discretion to hire a
new applicant over an existing employee if the
contractor determines that the new applicant is
better qualified for the position. Factors to be
considered may include, but are not limited to,
records and evaluations of the employee's past job
performance and his or her years of experience,
education, and/or training relevant to the position.

This provision supersedes ACA Standards 2-4054
and 2-4055 during the initial hiring period only.

Existing employees shall be entitled to
starting wages and benefits, including [list
benefits] that are equal to or greater than the
wages and benefits that an employee of comparable
qualifications would receive for the same position
from the contracting agency. The contractor shall
credit to each former contracting-agency employee
the amount of annual leave, compensatory leave time,
and personal leave time, including sick leave, that
the contracting agency certifies the employee has on
the day employment terminates with the contracting
agency.

(3) Employee Background Investigations

Prior to and as a condition of employment, a
background investigation shall be made of each
prospective employee. This investigation shall
include criminal (obtaining FBI or NCIC records),
medical, and employment histories. A prospective
employee may be denied employment if the background
investigation reveals information indicating that he
or she would not be an appropriate correctional
employee. The contractor shall maintain fingerprint
charts on every employee.

This provision incorporates as mandatory ACA
Standards 2-4061 through 2-4063. The contractor has

a continuing obligation to comply with these Standards, as well as with subsequent ACA Standards to the extent that they are approved by the contracting agency.

Section 4(B): Employee Training Requirements

All of the contractor's employees shall successfully complete a forty (40) hour new-employee orientation program, as required by ACA Standards, after being hired and prior to regular assignment. Thereafter, the contractor shall comply with all ACA Standards concerning training (or more stringent standards, should the law require) and shall ensure that the contractor's employees receive sufficient training to comply with ACA Standards 2-4079 through 2-4101. Standards 2-4079 through 2-4083, 2-4086 through 2-4095, and 2-4098 are incorporated as mandatory. [In addition, the contractor shall take all reasonable actions to help each correctional or detention employee retain his or her certification from the (appropriate authority and jurisdiction).]

The contractor shall provide to the contract monitor documentation of all completed employee training as soon as possible after its completion. Upon request, the monitor shall be permitted to review training curriculum and other training-related records that are maintained by the contractor. The monitor shall be permitted to audit training classes at any time.

The contractor shall be responsible for all training expenses.

Section 4(C): Personnel Policy

The contractor must implement and at all times maintain a personnel policy that includes:

(1) all of the elements and substantive guidelines that are set forth in ACA Standards 2-4060, 2-4064, 2-4065, 2-4067, 2-4070, 2-4076, 2-4077, and 2-4078, which are hereby incorporated as mandatory;

(2) all applicable federal, state, and local statutory and regulatory provisions, including [list provisions]; and

(3) the following additional standards: [list standards].

Section 4(D): Staff Ratio

The facility shall be staffed 24 hours per day, 7 days per week. The staffing pattern shall be adequate to ensure close inmate surveillance and maintenance of security within the facility. The contractor shall provide adequate staff to maintain an effective patrol of the perimeter of the facility during periods of darkness, times of emergency, and when inmates are not involved with supervised activities and/or programs.

The staffing pattern shall address transportation and security needs. The staffing pattern shall also consider the proximity of the facility to neighborhoods, schools, etc.

This provision incorporates as mandatory ACA Standards 2-4072 through 2-4075. The contractor has a continuing obligation to comply with the existing Standards, as well as with subsequent ACA Standards to the extent that they are approved by the contracting agency.

Section 4(E): Labor Disputes/Right to Strike

(1) The contractor shall include a no-strike provision in any labor agreement that it negotiates with a union that is formed or joined by its employees.

(2) The contractor shall use its best efforts to reach an early and peaceful settlement to any labor dispute. Such disputes include, but are not limited to, picketing, lockouts, and strikes.

(3) The contractor shall notify the contracting agency at least sixty (60) days prior to the termination of any labor agreement with its employees.

(4) The contractor shall notify the contracting agency immediately upon learning of a potential or impending strike or serious labor disturbance.

(5) In the event of a strike or serious labor disturbance, the contracting agency may call on the emergency resources of the [appropriate jurisdiction] to operate and/or control the facility or facilities until the strike or disturbance has ended. In the event of such an emergency, the contractor shall cooperate fully with the contracting agency to ensure safe operations.

(6) The contractor shall reimburse the contracting agency [and/or the appropriate jurisdiction] for any costs incurred during or directly related to the strike or labor disturbance.

(7) The occurrence of a strike or a serious labor disturbance shall constitute grounds for cancellation, termination, or suspension of the contract by the contracting agency.

Section 5: Inmate Issues

Section 5(A): Inmate Management

(1) Classification

The contracting agency shall classify all inmates, according to its own criteria. The contractor shall be bound by the agency's classifications.

(2) Transfer

The contractor shall have no authority to transfer an inmate. The contractor may, however, recommend in writing that the contracting agency transfer a particular inmate. The contracting agency shall have final authority with respect to any transfer decision.

(3) Discipline

The contractor shall have no authority to administer discipline to an inmate in its custody unless the discipline is ordered by a [state or federal] hearing officer, pursuant to [the jurisdiction's] disciplinary procedures. Rules that are formulated by the contractor shall be null and void except to the extent that they are accepted or modified by the contracting agency.

(4) Parole

No employee of the contractor shall have any authority to recommend that the parole board either deny or grant parole to any inmate in the contractor's custody. The contractor's submissions to the parole board shall be limited to written reports that have been prepared in the ordinary course of business.

Section 5(B): Use of Force

(1) The private contractor's employees serving as "jailers" shall be allowed to use force only while on the grounds of the facility, while transporting inmates, and while pursuing escapees from the facility.

(2) "Non-deadly force," which is force that normally would cause neither death nor serious bodily injury, and "deadly force," which is force that is likely to cause death or serious bodily injury, shall be used only as set forth herein.

(3) Non-Deadly Force. Any [contractor's name] jailer shall be authorized to use only such non-deadly force as the circumstances require in the following situations: to prevent the commission of a felony or misdemeanor, including escape; to defend oneself or others against physical assault; to prevent serious damage to property; to enforce institutional regulations and orders; and to prevent or quell a riot.

(4) Use of Firearms/Deadly Force. [Contractor's name] jailers who have been appropriately certified as determined by the contracting agency and trained pursuant to the provisions of

Subsection (5) shall have the right to carry and use firearms and shall exercise such authority and use deadly force only as a last resort, and then only to prevent an act that could result in death or serious bodily injury to oneself or to another person.

(5) Jailers shall be trained in accordance with ACA Standards 2-4186 through 2-4189 and 2-4206, concerning the use of force and the use of firearms, and shall be trained, at the contractor's expense, at the facilities that train public prison and jail personnel for at least the minimum number of hours that public personnel are currently trained.

(6) Within three (3) days following an incident involving the use of force against an inmate or another, the employee shall file a written report with the administrative staff and contract monitor describing the incident.

(7) The contractor shall stand in the shoes of the contracting agency in any agreement, formal or informal, with local law-enforcement agencies concerning the latter's obligations in the event of emergency situations, such as riots or escapes.

Section 5(C): Inmate Transportation

Either:

[The contracting agency shall provide for all of the transportation needs of the inmates under the contractor's care without cost to the contractor.]

or:

[The contractor shall provide for all of the transportation needs of the inmates under its care, from the time that the prisoner is delivered to the facility by the contracting agency to his or her release or transfer by the contracting agency.

The Use of Force provision in this contract shall apply during the time that the contractor is transporting inmates. The contractor shall comply with all relevant statutes, rules, and regulations regarding insurance, inspection, and motor vehicles while transporting the inmates.]

Section 5(D):   Inmate Labor

The parties agree that all inmates shall be required to keep their living areas clean. In addition, inmates may, if they volunteer, work in the food service, laundry, or other areas of the facility. The contractor shall submit job descriptions for the contracting agency's approval before assigning inmates to those positions. Job assignments shall be made by the contractor. These assignments shall be subject to review by the contracting agency upon written request by the inmates, if they so elect. The contracting agency shall provide inmates with good-time credit or monetary compensation for labor performed. The contracting agency shall be responsible for establishing and administering this compensation program. The contractor shall make inmates available for contracting-agency work projects upon [number] (___) days' written notice to the contractor. The contracting agency shall be responsible for oversight, transportation, and security of the inmates during such work projects.

Section 6:   Monitoring

(A) On or before thirty (30) days after the execution of this contract, the contracting agency shall appoint a contract monitor, who will be an employee of the contracting agency, to be the official liaison between the contracting agency and the contractor. The contract monitor [and his or her staff] shall be provided an office in the facility and shall have access at all times, with or without notice, to inmates and staff, to all areas of the facility, and to all books, records (including financial records), and reports kept by the contractor concerning the renovation, repair, construction, maintenance, and operation of the facility.

The monitor [and his or her staff] will be responsible for monitoring compliance with all contractual obligations, including compliance with the incorporated ACA Standards. The contractor must maintain whatever documentation is necessary to prove that the contractor is meeting its obligations under the contract. This includes, but is not

limited to, all reports and other documentation
required by ACA Standards, as well as the following
reports: [list them]. The contractor shall be
responsible for all costs associated with the
monitoring of the facility, except for the salaries
of the monitor [and his or her staff].

(B) Members of the public, including the
media, must apply for access to the facility
[number] (___) days before the date that such a
visit is planned. An application for access shall
include the date and time of the planned visit, the
purpose of the visit, and any other relevant
information that the contractor's representative
requires. Access shall be granted, except where the
contractor has clear and convincing evidence that
such visits jeopardize the security of the facility
or the safety of the inmates or visitor. The
monitor shall have final review over all decisions
regarding public access to the facility.

(C) The contractor shall be fined [number]
(___) dollars for each instance of noncompliance
with the contract. The contractor will be given a
reasonable time, as determined by the monitor, to
rectify the noncompliance. If the noncompliance is
not rectified in this period or if [number] (___)
instances of noncompliance are detected in a
[number] (___) month period, the contractor shall be
deemed to be in breach of the contract.

Section 7: Termination

This contract shall be subject to the following
provisions:

(A) Termination for Default

The contracting agency may terminate this
contract when it determines that (1) the private
contractor has failed to meet the minimum standards
of operations set forth in Subsection 3(F) of this
contract, or (2) the contractor has failed to meet
other contract provisions where such failure
seriously affects the operation of the facility.

Thirty (30) days prior to termination by the
contracting agency, it shall serve the contractor
with written notice of default(s), by certified
mail. If the contractor has failed to correct the

default to the contracting agency's satisfaction within the period of time specified in the contracting-agency notice, the contractor shall be deemed to be in default of the contract and the contract shall be terminated immediately, or, at the option of the contracting agency, it may offset the default by deducting payments to the contractor or seek other equitable remedies.

If after Notice of Termination for Default it is determined by the contracting agency, the arbitrators, or a court that the contractor was in default because of causes beyond the control and without the error or negligence of the contractor, the termination shall be deemed to have been issued as a Termination for Convenience, with the parties' rights governed accordingly.

In the event of default, in full or in part as provided herein, the contracting agency may procure, on terms that it finds appropriate, goods or services similar to those to be provided hereunder, and the contractor shall be liable to the contracting agency for any excess costs for such similar goods and services. In addition, the contractor shall be liable to the contracting agency for administrative costs incurred by the contracting agency in procuring such similar goods or services. The performance bond required in Subsection 3(D) of this contract shall guarantee payment of such excess costs and the contractor shall be liable for any excess over and above said amount if the bond proceeds are insufficient to pay such costs.

In the event of Termination for Default, subject to the retainage provision, the contractor shall be paid in accordance with the contract price for each contracting-agency inmate held by the contractor until the date of termination.

The rights and remedies of the contracting agency provided in this Subsection shall not be exclusive and are in addition to any other rights and remedies provided by law or pursuant to the contract.

(B)   Termination for Contractor Bankruptcy

The contractor must inform the contracting agency of its intention to file a petition for bankruptcy at least ten (10) days prior to filing such a petition. The contractor's filing without conforming to this requirement shall be deemed a material pre-petition incurable breach.

In the event of the filing of a petition in bankruptcy, reorganization, or liquidation pursuant to any chapter of the Bankruptcy Code, Title 11 U.S.C., the contracting agency shall have the right to terminate the contract under the same conditions as if it were a Termination for Default. In the event of termination for contractor bankruptcy, the contractor shall be required to cooperate and assist the contracting agency to the fullest extent possible to reestablish prison or jail services as quickly as possible.

(C)   Termination for Unavailability of Funds

In the event that the contracting agency's funds for the contract become unavailable, the contracting agency shall have the right to terminate the contract without penalty and on the same terms and conditions as if it were a Termination for Convenience. Availability of funds will be determined at the sole discretion of the contracting agency.

(D)   Termination for Convenience

The contracting agency may terminate performance of work under the contract in whole or in part whenever, for any reason, the contracting agency determines that it is in its best interest to do so. The contracting agency shall give the contractor, without penalty to the state, ninety (90) days' notice prior to termination of the contract.

The contractor shall have no right to any general, special, incidental, consequential, or any damages whatsoever of any description or amount, except that the contracting agency shall pay for all supplies and equipment on order and not yet delivered to the facility as of the date of termination.

(E) Procedure on Termination

Upon delivery by certified mail to the contractor of a Notice of Termination specifying the nature of the termination, the extent to which performance of work under the contract is terminated, and the date on which such termination becomes effective, the contractor shall:

(1) stop work under the contract on the date and to the extent specified in the Notice of Termination;

(2) place no further orders for materials, services, or facilities, except as may be necessary for completion of such portion of the work under the contract as is not terminated;

(3) terminate all orders to the extent that they relate to the performance of work terminated by the Notice of Termination, except as may be necessary to avoid the incurrence of penalty assessments and the continuation of which the contracting agency has approved;

(4) assign to the contracting agency in the manner and to the extent directed by the [contracting officer] all of the right, title, and interest of the contractor under the orders so terminated, in which case the contracting agency shall have the right, in its discretion, to settle or pay any or all claims arising out of the termination of such orders;

(5) with the approval or ratification of the [contracting officer], settle all outstanding liabilities and all claims arising out of such termination of orders, the cost of which would be reimbursable in whole or in part, in accordance with the provision of the contracts;

(6) transfer title to the contracting agency (to the extent that title has not already been transferred) and deliver in the manner, at the times, and to the extent directed by the [contracting officer] all files, processing systems, data manuals, or documentation, in any form, that relate to work terminated by the Notice of Termination;

(7) complete the performance of such part
of the work as shall not have been terminated
by the Notice of Termination; and

(8) take such action as may be necessary,
or as the [contracting officer] may direct, for
the protection and preservation of the property
related to the contract that is in the
possession of the contractor and in which the
contracting agency has or may acquire an
interest.

The contractor shall proceed immediately with
the performance of the above obligations
notwithstanding any delay in determining or
adjusting the amount of any item of reimbursable
price under this provision.

(F)   Resumption of Government Control

Notwithstanding any other provision of this
contract to the contrary, prior to entering a
contract for the private operation of any prison or
jail, a plan shall be developed by the contracting
agency and certified by the [Governor or appropriate
executive officer or legislative body] demonstrating
the method by which the government would resume
control of the facility upon contract termination.

Section 8:   Miscellaneous Provisions

Section 8(A):   Entire Agreement

This contract constitutes the entire contract
and supersedes all other prior agreements and
understandings, both written and oral, between the
parties with respect to the subject matter hereof.
The term "contract" includes [list of Exhibits,
Attachments, Appendices, etc.].

Section 8(B):   Amendment

This contract may be amended only in writing
signed by the parties.

Section 8(C): Severability

If any term, provision, covenant, or
restriction of this contract is held by a court of
competent jurisdiction or the legislature to be
invalid, void, or unenforceable, the remainder of
the terms, provisions, covenants, and restrictions
of this contract shall remain in full force and
effect, and shall in no way be affected, impaired,
or invalidated.

If, however, the contracting agency determines
that the invalid provision or provisions are
essential to the purpose or performance of the
contract, it may terminate the contract. Such a
termination shall be deemed a Termination for
Convenience as set forth in Section 7(D) of this
contract.

Section 8(D): Venue and Choice of Law

Venue for the enforcement of this contract and
all claims or disputes relating thereto shall be in
the [select appropriate court and jurisdiction].

This contract, the rights and obligations of
the parties hereto, and any claims or disputes
relating thereto shall be governed by and construed
in accordance with the internal law of the State of
[_____] in the resolution of all issues.

Section 8(E): Alternative Dispute Resolution

Any controversy regarding this contract that
the parties are unable to resolve by mutual
agreement may be submitted to binding arbitration in
[location] in accordance with the rules of the
American Arbitration Association.

Any decision of the arbitrators shall be
conclusive as to the matter submitted and may be
enforced in any court of competent jurisdiction in

the State of [_____]. Issues under arbitration
shall be heard and decided by three arbitrators, one
of whom shall be designated by the contracting
agency, one of whom shall be designated by the
contractor, and one of whom shall be designated by
the court in [location], or, in the absence of such
a designation, by the American Arbitration
Association. Any factual decision on an issue being
arbitrated, including the sharing of costs of
arbitration, made by at least two of the arbitrators
shall be the decision of the arbitrators and such
decision shall be final, non-appealable, and binding
on both parties.

The following terms shall be binding on the
parties:

     (1) Either party may require that the
hearing be recorded.

     (2) After it is determined by either
party that a dispute cannot be resolved without
arbitration, it shall be submitted for
arbitration within fifteen (15) business
days. "Business days" shall mean Monday
through Friday, excluding holidays. After
submission, a written decision shall be
rendered within ninety (90) days, unless an
extension is agreed to by both parties.

     (3) Neither party shall appoint an
employee or agent as an arbitrator.

     (4) Each party reserves the right to
appeal any question of law.

     (5) Discovery shall be conducted in
accordance with the Federal Rules of Civil
Procedure.

This Section shall operate only by mutual
consent of the parties.

IV. STATUTORY DIMENSIONS

This section of the paper is divided into two major parts.
The first part addresses the authority of the federal government
to contract for the private operation of its incarceration
facilities. Because the Federal Bureau of Prisons is required by
statute to "[p]rovide technical assistance to State and local
governments in the improvement of their correctional systems,"[931]
many state and local governments will likely look to the
authorization for and experience of federal prison and jail
privatization should they decide to consider privatization as an
option. This part concludes that there is federal authority to
contract out for the confinement of federal inmates only in
residential community-treatment centers. If the Bureau of
Prisons or any state or local government decides to privatize its
incarceration facilities, it should do so only after the
enactment of explicit and unambiguous legislation designed
specifically for that purpose. The public, through its elected
representatives, deserves a say in that decision.

The second part of this section presents a Model Statute and
accompanying commentary.

---

931 18 U.S.C. § 4042(4) (1982).

A. Federal Statutory Authorization to Designate Privately Operated Places of Confinement

1. Introduction

Any discussion concerning the federal government's authority to designate a privately operated facility as a place of confinement for adult federal prisoners must begin with 18 U.S.C. § 4082(b).[932] Section 4082(b) stated:

> The Attorney General may designate as a place of confinement any available, suitable, and appropriate institution or facility, whether maintained by the Federal Government or otherwise, and whether within or without the judicial district in which the person was convicted, and may at any time transfer a person from one place of confinement to another.[933]

The Comprehensive Crime Control Act of 1984[934] replaced section 4082(b) with 18 U.S.C. § 3621(b),[935] which provides:

> The Bureau of Prisons shall designate the place of the prisoner's imprisonment. The Bureau may designate any available penal or correctional facility that meets minimum standards of health and habitability established by the Bureau, whether maintained by the Federal Government or otherwise and whether within or without the judicial district

---

932 18 U.S.C. § 4082(b) (1982).

933 Id. (emphasis added).

934 Pub. L. No. 98-473, 98 Stat. 1837 (1984) (codified at scattered sections of 18 U.S.C. (Supp. IV 1986)).

935 18 U.S.C. § 3621(b) (Supp. IV 1986).

in which the person was convicted, that the Bureau determines to be appropriate and suitable . . . .[936]

The key words of section 4082(b) that have been used to support arguments in favor of federal authority to privatize prisons have not been altered by section 3621(b). As noted in Senate Report No. 225:

> Proposed 18 U.S.C. § 3621(b) follows existing law in providing that the authority to designate the place of confinement for Federal prisoners rests in the Bureau of Prisons. The designated penal or correctional facility need not be in the judicial district in which the prisoner was convicted and need not be maintained by the Federal Government. Existing law provides that the Bureau may designate a place of confinement that is available, appropriate, and suitable. Section 3621(b) continues that discretionary authority with a new requirement that the facility meet minimum standards of health and habitability established by the Bureau

---

[936] Id. (emphasis added). This section further provides that, in designating a place of confinement, the Bureau of Prisons should consider:

> (1) the resources of the facility contemplated;
> (2) the nature and circumstances of the offense;
> (3) the history and characteristics of the prisoner;
> (4) any statement by the court that imposed the sentence--
>
> > (A) concerning the purposes for which the sentence to imprisonment was determined to be warranted; or
> > (B) recommending a type of penal or correctional facility as appropriate; and
>
> (5) any pertinent policy statement issued by the Sentencing Commission pursuant to section 994(a)(2) of title 28. . . .

Id.

of Prisons.[937]

This language and the plain language of the statute indicate that Congress did not intend, through passage of section 3621(b), to expand the types of prison facilities in which federal prisoners could be placed. The critical phrase in section 4082(b) defining the types of eligible facilities -- those "maintained by the Federal Government or otherwise" -- remains intact in section 3621(b). Section 3621(b) merely sets forth certain additional factors that must be considered when the Bureau of Prisons selects a facility for a particular prisoner.[938] Consequently, one must examine the legislative history of section 4082(b) to determine whether the confinement of federal prisoners in private as well as in public facilities is authorized.

2.   18 U.S.C. § 4082(b)

18 U.S.C. § 4082(b) permitted the Attorney General to designate as a place of confinement for federal prisoners any "available, suitable, and appropriate institution or facility, whether maintained by the Federal Government or otherwise."[939]

---

[937] S. Rep. No. 225, 98th Cong., 2d Sess. 141-42 (1985) (emphasis added), reprinted in 1985 U.S. Code Cong. & Admin. News 3182, 3324-25.

[938] See supra note 936.

[939] 18 U.S.C. § 4082(b) (1982) (emphasis added).

-398-

The meaning of "or otherwise" is unclear on its face and is therefore subject to alternative interpretations.

The legislative history of section 4082 is silent, however, with respect to the meaning of this language. The former Director of the Federal Bureau of Prisons, Norman A. Carlson, suggested at one point that the "or otherwise" language authorized the Attorney General to contract with private corporations for the confinement of federal prisoners in all situations -- i.e., in both secured and unsecured contexts.[940] This phrase, however, has also been interpreted as referring to other public facilities only -- i.e., facilities operated by a state or territory or some political subdivision thereof.[941] With respect to prisoners in the secured-confinement context, the

_____

940 Hearings, supra note 375, at 141 (statement of Norman A. Carlson, Director, Federal Bureau of Prisons). In 1985, however, Mr. Carlson testified to the contrary, stating that the Bureau of Prisons lacked the necessary statutory authority to contract with the private sector for the confinement of adult federal prisoners in both the secured and unsecured contexts. Director Carlson stated:

> My gut reaction would be that [the Bureau of Prisons] would not be able to privatize one of the existing 45 institutions. . . . I do not think we have the authority and, as Director, I would not contemplate contracting out to the private sector for the operation of one of our regular institutions.

Bureau of Prisons and the United States Parole Commission: Hearings Before the Subcomm. on Courts, Civil Liberties, and the Administration of Justice of the House Comm. on the Judiciary, 98th Cong., 2d Sess. 16-17 (1985) (testimony of Norman A. Carlson, Director, Federal Bureau of Prisons).

941 Hearings, supra note 375, at 106 (statement of Ira P. Robbins, Barnard T. Welsh Scholar and Professor of Law and Justice, The American University, Washington College of Law).

latter interpretation is correct. This construction of the "or otherwise" language is supported by the current contracting provisions of 18 U.S.C. § 4002,[942] as well as by Congress's purposes in enacting section 4082(b) and the Act of which it was originally a part.[943] Subsequent amendments to section 4082(b) have modified these purposes. Consequently, the meaning of the phrase "or otherwise" has changed, but only to the rather limited extent of permitting the Attorney General to contract with private corporations for the confinement of federal prisoners in certain special facilities, such as residential community-treatment centers.

a. Legislative Intent of 18 U.S.C. § 4082(b)

18 U.S.C. § 4082(b) is derived from 18 U.S.C. § 753f, enacted in 1940,[944] which provided in pertinent part that the

---

[942] 18 U.S.C. § 4002 (1982). Section 4002 provides:

> For the purpose of providing suitable quarters for the safekeeping, care, and subsistence of all persons held under authority of any enactment of Congress, the Attorney General may contract, for a period not exceeding three years, with the proper authorities of any State, Territory, or political subdivision thereof, for the imprisonment, subsistence, care, and proper employment of such persons.

Id.; see infra notes 964-967 and accompanying text (discussing impact of section 4002 on section 4082(b)).

[943] "Act to Reorganize the Administration of Federal Prisons, to authorize the Attorney General to contract for the care of United States prisoners, to establish Federal jails, and for other purposes." H.R. 7832, 71st Cong., 2d Sess. (1930), reprinted in 1930 U.S. Code Cong. & Admin. News 325.

Attorney General "may designate any available, suitable, and appropriate institutions, whether maintained by the Federal Government or otherwise," for the confinement of federal prisoners.[945] Section 753f was passed in conjunction with several other statutes under an "Act to Reorganize the Administration of Federal prisons, to authorize the Attorney General to contract for the care of United States prisoners, to establish Federal jails, and for other purposes."[946] Thus, section 753f must be interpreted in relationship to both the entire Act of which it was a part and the congressional purpose behind passage of the Act.[947] In particular, sections 753a through 753c establish the necessary context for interpreting section 753f.[948]

In large part, the Act was passed in response to a shortage of prison space for federal prisoners.[949] Not only were the

_____

[944] 18 U.S.C. § 753f (1940) (recodified at 18 U.S.C. § 4082(b) (1982)).

[945] Id.

[946] H.R. 7832, 71st Cong., 2d Sess. (1930), reprinted in 1930 U.S. Code Cong. & Admin. News 325.

[947] See, e.g., Philbrook v. Glodgett, 421 U.S. 707, 713 (1974) ("In expounding a statute, we must not be guided by a single sentence or member of a sentence, but look to the provisions of the whole law, and to its object and policy.") (quoting United States v. Heirs of Boisdore, 8 How. 113, 122 (1849), and citing Chemehuevi Tribe of Indians v. FPC, 420 U.S. 395, 402-03 (1975); Richards v. United States, 369 U.S. 1, 11 (1962)).

[948] See infra notes 957-963 and accompanying text (discussing text of section 753a through section 753c and their relationship to section 753f).

[949] See Federal Prisoners and Penitentiaries: Hearings on

federal institutions severely overcrowded, but the state and local institutions on which the federal government heavily relied for providing additional prison space were overcrowded as well.[950] The conditions of confinement in the state and local prisons that did accept federal inmates were generally far below federal standards.[951] Under existing law, the federal government was "powerless to remedy the deplorable conditions of filth, contamination, and idleness which [were] present in most of the antiquated jails of the country, for it [was] wholly dependent upon the charity of the States" with respect to whether and on what terms a state would accept federal prisoners.[952]

These problems were exacerbated by the lack of a central administrative organization that was empowered to remedy this

---

H.R. 7832 Before the House Comm. on the Judiciary, 71st Cong., 2d Sess. 13-15 (1929) [hereinafter Hearings on H.R. 7832] (statement of William DeWitt Mitchell, U.S. Attorney General, remarking that existing federal institutions were grossly inadequate with respect to the burgeoning numbers of federal prisoners); id. at 21-22 (comments of Rep. John G. Cooper, stating that a serious crisis confronted those who administered the federal penal system, due in part to the tremendous increase in the number of federal prisoners); S. Rep. No. 533, 71st Cong., 2d Sess. 1 (1930) (Senate Judiciary Committee noting that congestion in federal penal institutions constituted emergency situation requiring passage of Act); H.R. Rep. No. 106, 71st Cong., 2d Sess. 2 (1930) (letter from William DeWitt Mitchell, stating that both federal and state penal institutions were overcrowded).

[950] See H.R. Rep. No. 106, 71st Cong., 2d Sess. 2 (1930) (letter from William DeWitt Mitchell, stating that both federal and state penal institutions were overcrowded).

[951] See Hearings on H.R. 7832, supra note 949, at 21-22 (letter from William DeWitt Mitchell, remarking that conditions in nonfederal institutions, especially city and county jails, were deplorable).

[952] S. Rep. No. 533, 71st Cong., 2d Sess. 2 (1930) (letter from William DeWitt Mitchell), quoted in H.R. Rep. No. 106, 71st Cong., 2d Sess. 2 (1930).

situation.[953] Congress considered and ultimately adopted the view of United States Attorney General William DeWitt Mitchell, who called upon the legislature to establish a "bureau which is definitely charged with a duty of supervising the care and treatment of Federal prisoners."[954] Mitchell noted that it was "doubtful if the Federal Government ought ever to have a complete system of jails paralleling similar institutions now found in the political subdivisions of the various states. It is possible, however, for the central government to improve conditions by certain administrative revisions of its present practices."[955] Express authorization under the Act to designate the institution

---

[953] S. Rep. No. 533, 71st Cong., 2d Sess. 1 (1930) (letter from William DeWitt Mitchell, stating that existing organizational system was altogether inadequate); Hearings on H.R. 7832, supra note 949, at 21-22 (letter from William DeWitt Mitchell, stating that those administering the federal penal system faced a very serious crisis due, in part, to the lack of a proper program to deal with federal prisoners).

[954] S. Rep. No. 533, 71st Cong., 2d Sess. 2 (1930) (letter from William DeWitt Mitchell), quoted in H.R. Rep. No. 106, 71st Cong., 2d Sess. 2 (1930). Prior to the enactment of section 753f, federal prisoners had been confined in various institutions pursuant to 18 U.S.C. §§ 691 and 692. Section 691, entitled "Temporary jails for confinement of United States prisoners," provided that "[i]n a State where the use of jails, penitentiaries, or other houses is not allowed for the imprisonment of [federal prisoners,] any marshal in such state . . . may hire, or otherwise procure . . . a convenient place to serve as a temporary jail." 18 U.S.C. § 691 (1926). Section 692 authorized the marshal to make "such other provisions as he may deem expedient or necessary for the safe-keeping of the prisoners." Id. § 692. A plain reading of these statutes would suggest that a marshal could contract with both public and private entities for the temporary confinement of federal prisoners. Sections 691 and 692 were repealed, however, by the 1948 recodification of Title 18.

[955] S. Rep. No. 533, 71st Cong., 2d Sess. 2 (1930) (letter from William DeWitt Mitchell), quoted in H.R. Rep. No. 106, 71st Cong., 2d Sess. 2 (1930).

to which a prisoner should be sent and the power to transfer prisoners from one institution to another were also considered to be necessary for the efficient administration of the federal prison system.[956]

Section 753 was a broad provision placing the Bureau of Prisons in charge of all federal penal and correctional institutions, as well as "the safekeeping, care, protection, instruction, and discipline" of all federal offenders.[957] This section empowered the federal government to contract with the "proper authorities of any State or Territory or political subdivision thereof" for a period not to exceed three years.[958]

---

[956] See S. Rep. No. 533, 71st Cong., 2d Sess. 3 (1930) (letter from William DeWitt Mitchell, stating that "proper administration and regulation of [federal] penal institutions makes it necessary for some central coordinating agency to exercise authority of designating prisoners' place of confinement and prison transfers"), quoted in H.R. Rep. No. 106, 71st Cong., 2d Sess. 3 (1930); S. Rep. No. 533, 71st Cong., 2d Sess. 1 (1930) (letter from William DeWitt Mitchell, remarking that Act "will enable the Bureau of Prisons to act immediately with respect to certain classes of prisoners and thus alleviate the present congestion and unsafe conditions without waiting for the completion [of construction of other federal facilities provided for in companion bill,]" as well as "provide an adequate system for dealing with certain great masses of Federal prisoners held in local jails and workhouses"); Hearings on H.R. 7832, supra note 949, at 21-22 (comments of Sanford Bates, Superintendent of Prisons, U.S. Dep't of Justice, remarking that the Act would remedy conflicting statutes regarding placement of federal prisoners in federal, state, and county institutions).

[957] 18 U.S.C. § 753a (1940) (now codified at 18 U.S.C. § 4002 (1982)).

[958] Id. § 753b (now codified at 18 U.S.C. § 4002 (1982)). Section 753b provided that "[i]t shall be the duty of the [Bureau of Prisons] to provide suitable quarters for the safe-keeping, care, and subsistence of all persons convicted of offenses against the United States, [or] charged with offenses against the United States . . . . For this purpose the Director of the -[Bureau of Prisons] may contract for a period not exceeding three

If these other jurisdictions were unable or refused to enter into a contract, or if existing facilities were not available at a reasonable cost for the imprisonment of federal prisoners, then section 753c authorized the Attorney General to build a federal "house of detention, workhouse, jail, prison-industries project or camp or other place of confinement."[959]

In the context of sections 753b and 753c, the "or otherwise" phrase of section 753f can only be interpreted as referring to institutions belonging to a state, territory, or political subdivision thereof.[960] The Act authorized only three

_____

years with the proper authorities of any State or Territory or political subdivision therof for the imprisonment, subsistence, care and proper employment of any person held under authority of any United States statute." Id. (emphasis added); see infra notes 964-967 and accompanying text (discussing importance of section 4002's restrictions on section 4082(b)).

[959] 18 U.S.C. § 753c (1940) (now codified at 18 U.S.C. § 4003 (1982)). Section 753c provided that:

> If by reason of the refusal or inability of the authorities having control of any jail, workhouse, penal, correctional, or other suitable institution of any State or Territory, or political subdivision thereof, to enter into a contract for the imprisonment, subsistence, care, or proper employment of United States prisoners, or if there are no suitable or sufficient facilities available at reasonable cost, the Attorney General is authorized to select a site either within or convenient to the State, Territory, or judicial district concerned and cause to be erected thereon a house of detention, workhouse, jail, prison-industries project, or camp, or other place of confinement.

Id. (emphasis added). Notably, Congress authorized only one course of action in situations in which nonfederal public institutions were unavailable: construction of a federal facility. Congress made no mention whatsoever of using the private sector to fill this need.

[960] See S. Rep. No. 533, 71st Cong., 2d Sess. (1930); H.R.

alternatives for confining federal prisoners: an existing federal institution;[961] a new federal institution;[962] or a state, territorial, or other public institution.[963] Thus, there is no statutory authority under section 753f -- the precursor to sections 4082(b) and 3621(b) -- or any other section of the original Act, either express or implied, that enables the federal government to contract with private entities for the confinement of federal prisoners.

b. 18 U.S.C. § 4002's Restrictions on 18 U.S.C. § 4082(b)

18 U.S.C. § 4002, based on 18 U.S.C. § 753b, is the only provision that authorizes the Attorney General to contract for the confinement of adult federal prisoners.[964] Section 4002 permits the federal government to contract for the confinement of federal prisoners in state institutions.[965] Title 18 of the United States Code is silent concerning contracts with private entities for the confinement of adult federal prisoners. In view of section 4002's explicit terms, the fairest reading of the "or otherwise" language in section 4082(b) is that it does not

---

Rep. No. 106, 71st Cong., 2d Sess. (1930); Hearings on H.R. 7832, supra note 949; see also supra note 959.

[961] 18 U.S.C. § 753f (1940).

[962] Id. § 753c.

[963] Id. § 753b.

[964] See supra note 942 (quoting provisions of 18 U.S.C. § 4002 (1982)).

[965] 18 U.S.C. § 4002 (1982).

encompass private institutions.[966]   Any other reading of section

4082(b) would contradict the plain meaning of this phrase as it

is established in section 4002.[967]

---

[966]   An interesting question is whether, after the federal
government contracts with a state to house a federal prisoner
pursuant to section 4002, the state may then place the federal
inmate in a facility that is operated by a private contractor.
Obviously, Congress has not addressed this question. Such a
situation may create an assignor-assignee relationship, so that
the assignee (the state) will stand in the shoes of the assignor
(the federal government). If so, then the state will not have
the authority because the federal government cannot confer more
power than it has.

[967]   But see Hearings, supra note 375, at 150 (letter from
Clair Cripe, General Counsel, Federal Bureau of Prisons). Mr.
Cripe concluded that "there is authority to contract with private
facilities . . . based both on the legislative history to Section
4082, and on the need to read Section 4002 so as to make
meaningful the language of Section 4082, which allows designation
to non-federal facilities, including private facilities." Id.
This 18-sentence opinion letter lacks comprehensive support for
this conclusion. See also infra note 979.

Nevertheless, the President's Commission on Privatization,
in its March 1988 Report, gave great weight to this letter in
determining that the federal government was authorized to
contract for the private operation of correctional and detention
facilities, see Report of the President's Commission on
Privatization, supra note 9, at 147, and recommended that the
Federal Bureau of Prisons, "as an experiment, . . . contract for
the private operation of one new facility comparable to at least
one government-run facility, and cooperate with outside
researchers in an evaluation of the results." Id. at 153. In
its "Management Improvement Program," the Reagan Administration
also proposed pilot projects to "test private sector management
and operation at a minimum security prison." Executive Office of
the President, Office of Management and Budget, Management of the
United States Government -- Fiscal Year 1989, at 103 (1988). So
far Congress has refused to fund the proposal, H.R. 4782, 100th
Cong., 2d Sess. (1988). See S. Rep. No. 388, 100th Cong., 2d
Sess. 48 (1988) ("The Committee notes that utilizing private
sector detention firms for specialized inmate populations may be
appropriate but feels the budget proposal affecting a Federal
minimum security facility signals the first step in the
privatization of the Federal Prison System and opposes such a
move."); H. Rep. No. 688, 100th Cong., 2d Sess. 17 (1988)
(recommending "no new budget . . . authority for fiscal year 1989
for those Department of Justice programs and activities for which

no authorization of appropriations has been enacted.").

Along with section 4002, which provides for housing federal prisoners in state or other public institutions or facilities, one might try to find support in 18 U.S.C. § 5003 for federal authority to privatize prisons. Such an effort would also be futile. Section 5003, entitled "Custody of State offenders," provides in pertinent part:

(a)(1) The Director of the Bureau of Prisons when proper and adequate facilities and personnel are available may contract with proper officials of a State or territory, for the custody, care, subsistence, education, treatment, and training of persons convicted of criminal offenses in the courts of such State or territory.

(2) Any such contract shall provide--

(A) for reimbursing the United States in full for all costs or expenses involved;

(B) for receiving in exchange persons convicted of criminal offenses in the courts of the United States, to serve their sentence in appropriate institutions or facilities of the State or territory by designation as provided in section 4082(b) [now 3621(b)] of this title, this exchange to be made according to formulas or conditions which may be negotiated in the contract; or

(C) for compensating the United States by means of a combination of monetary payment and of receipt of persons convicted of criminal offenses in the courts of the United States, according to formulas or conditions which may be negotiated in the contract.

(3) No such contract shall provide for the receipt of more State or territory prisoners by the United States than are transferred to that State or territory by such contract.

18 U.S.C. § 5003(a) (Supp. IV 1986).

Although the term "facilities" is not defined in the statute, it should be interpreted as referring only to those institutions that are available for the confinement of federal prisoners under 18 U.S.C. § 4082(b) -- i.e., public facilities or, only in the special case of residential community-treatment

c. 1965 Amendment to Section 4082(b) Expanding Scope of Attorney General's Authority to Designate Places of Confinement

In 1948, section 753f was recodified at section 4082(b), with changes in phraseology that did not affect the substance of the provision.[968] Section 4082(b) was amended in 1965 to add the

_____

centers, private facilities. The legislative history of section 5003 supports this interpretation. The House Committee on the Judiciary, for example, reported the following:

> Frequently, State officials request the Bureau of Prisons to undertake the custody, treatment, and training of State prisoners where specialized types of institutions and training programs are indicated but are not available in the States. These requests are usually related to juveniles and drug addicts, concerning whom many of the States are without satisfactory institutions and training programs. The Bureau of Prisons points out that it now has Federal facilities available, including medical and administrative personnel, to accommodate those State offenders that are in need of the various types of treatment that Federal institutions are providing. In this respect, the Bureau states that the accommodation of State prisoners will materially help to reduce the overhead expenses of maintaining and running these Federal prison institutions.

H.R. Rep. No. 1663, 82d Cong., 2d Sess. (1952) (emphasis added), reprinted in 1952 U.S. Code Cong. & Admin. News 1420, 1420-21 (uniformly referring to the facilities in section 5003 as federal institutions).

Thus, section 5003 provides absolutely no support for federal authority to privatize institutions or facilities for the confinement of federal prisoners. To contend otherwise would be to create no more than a bootstrap argument.

968 H.R. 3190, 80th Cong., 2d Sess. (1948), 93 Cong. Rec. 4012 (1948). Only minor changes in phraseology were made. Compare 18 U.S.C. § 4082 (1964) with 18 U.S.C. § 753f (1940) (illustrating differences between statute before and after recodification). See also H.R. Rep. No. 304, 80th Cong., 2d Sess. (1948) (discussing changes resulting from recodification). Prior to 1948, there had been other amendments

term "facility,"[969] in order to expand the Attorney General's authority to designate places of confinement for federal prisoners.[970] Specifically, the amendment gave the Attorney General the "additional authority to commit or transfer prisoners to residential community treatment centers."[971] The purpose of the amendment was to facilitate the rehabilitation of federal prisoners by providing "prerelease assistance in obtaining jobs and shelter and thus reduc[ing] the likelihood of further conflicts with the law."[972] However, this privilege was intended

---

to 18 U.S.C. § 753f that made substantive changes in the statute; these changes, however, did not affect the "or otherwise" phrase. See S.R. 1698, 77th Cong., lst Sess., 87 Cong. Rec. 9897 (1939); H.R. 1831, 77th Cong., lst Sess., 87 Cong. Rec. 122 (1941); H.R. Rep. No. 172, 77th Cong., lst Sess. (1941); S. Rep. No. 369, 77th Cong., lst Sess. (1941); S. Rep. No. 593, 77th Cong., lst Sess. (1941); H.R. Rep. No. 1606, 76th Cong., 2d Sess. (1940).

[969] S. Rep. No. 613, 89th Cong., lst Sess. (1965), reprinted in 1965 U.S. Code Cong. & Admin. News 3076, 3078.

[970] The 1965 amendment

designated as subsec. (b) the former second and third unnumbered paragraphs of the section, added "or facility" following "appropriate institution", substituted "may at any time transfer a person from one place of confinement to another" for "may order any inmate transferred from one institution to another", and made minor changes in language.

18 U.S.C. § 4082 amendments (1976); see H.R. 6964, 89th Cong., lst Sess., 111 Cong. Rec. 6452 (1965); S. Rep. No. 613, 89th Cong., lst Sess., reprinted in 1965 U.S. Code Cong. & Admin. News 3076; H.R. Rep. No. 694, 89th Cong., lst Sess. (1965); infra notes 971-979 and accompanying text (discussing scope of changes incurred with addition of term "facility").

[971] S. Rep. No. 613, 89th Cong., lst Sess., reprinted in 1965 U.S. Code Cong. & Admin. News 3077.

[972] H.R. Rep. No. 694, 89th Cong., lst Sess. 3 (1965); see S. Rep. No. 613, 89th Cong., lst Sess. (1965), reprinted in 1965 U.S. Code Cong. & Admin. News 3077 (stating that the "residential

to extend only to prisoners who were "considered to be salvageable and amenable to such programs. Those prisoners who remain[ed] a distinct threat to the community [would] be retained in secure institutions."[973]

In amending the statute, Congress referred to the existing residential community-treatment centers and halfway houses that had been operated for youthful and juvenile offenders under the Youth Corrections Act[974] and the Juvenile Delinquency Act,[975] and expressed the view that a similar variety of facilities was contemplated for adult federal prisoners.[976] Because both the YCA and the JDA explicitly authorized the Attorney General to contract with public and private entities for the provision of

---

community treatment centers, the so-called halfway houses, would make it possible to reintroduce prisoners to the community in a gradual and controlled way").

[973] S. Rep. No. 613, 89th Cong., 1st Sess. (1965) (letter from Nicholas Katzenbach, United States Attorney General), reprinted in 1965 U.S. Code Cong. & Admin. News 3082; see also H.R. Rep. No. 694, 89th Cong., 1st Sess. 2-3 (1965) (stating that "only prisoners who are considered good material for such treatment will be committed to [residential community-treatment centers]").

[974] Federal Youth Corrections Act, Pub. L. No. 93-415, tit. V, § 501 (1974) (later codified as amended at 18 U.S.C. §§ 5001-5025 (1982)), repealed by Comprehensive Crime Control Act of 1984, Pub. L. No. 98-473, tit. II, § 218(g).

[975] Act of June 16, 1938, ch. 486, 52 Stat. 764 (later codified as amended at 18 U.S.C. §§ 5031-5042 (1982 & Supp. IV 1986)).

[976] S. Rep. No. 613, 89th Cong., 1st Sess. (1965), reprinted in 1965 U.S. Code Cong. & Admin. News 3078; see also H.R. Rep. No. 694, 89th Cong., 1st Sess. 2 (1965) (stating that the amendment "would authorize commitment of adult prisoners to similar treatment centers" -- i.e., similar to the centers that were being operated at the time that the amendment was considered).

residential community-treatment centers, the amendment has been interpreted by the Bureau of Prisons as granting the Attorney General the same power to contract for adult residential community-treatment centers.[977] This interpretation has not been contested. Since 1981, the federal government has relied solely on contract community-treatment centers; some seventy percent of those contracts are now with private entities.[978]

Thus, although section 4082(b) was expanded to allow the Attorney General to confine adult federal prisoners in privately run facilities, Congress contemplated such action only with respect to qualified pre-release prisoners in residential community-treatment centers.[979] Congress did not intend the

---

[977] See Hearings, supra note 375, at 168-69 (Bureau of Prisons staff paper entitled "Privatization in Federal Corrections"); see also supra note 940 and accompanying text; supra note 967.

[978] See Hearings, supra note 375, at 168 (Bureau of Prisons staff paper entitled "Privatization in Federal Corrections").

[979] In this regard, the conclusions that were reached by the Bureau of Prisons' General Counsel are incorrect. See Hearings, supra note 375, at 149-50. Mr. Cripe stated that the 1965 amendment "broaden[ed] the scope of both § 4082 and § 4002." Id. at 149. In his view, the legislative history of the 1965 amendment to section 4082(b) "makes it clear that the legislation was meant to extend to adult inmates the kind of authority which the Attorney General already had in Sections 4082, 5013 and 5039. This prior authority allowed the Attorney General to commit and transfer juveniles . . . to halfway houses . . . ." Id. at 149-50. The logic of this statement is unclear: If section 4082(b) already authorized such designations of confinement, why would an amendment be necessary? Furthermore, Mr. Cripe concluded that there is "nothing in Section 4082 or its legislative history [that] would restrict [contracting with] private halfway houses." Id. at 150. The analysis set forth elsewhere in this paper, however, concludes that contracting with private entities for the confinement of adult federal prisoners was not allowed until the 1965 amendment, and then only for facilities such as residential community-

amendment to be a broad grant of authority to place adult federal prisoners in all types of privately run facilities.

3.   Conclusion

18 U.S.C. § 4082(b), now section 3621(b), authorized the Attorney General to confine adult federal prisoners in institutions or facilities run by the federal government or by any state, territory, or political subdivision thereof. This interpretation of the statute is supported by its language and legislative history, as well as by 18 U.S.C. § 4002. An exception arises only with respect to the confinement of federal prisoners in residential community-treatment centers. Section 3621(b) permits the Bureau of Prisons to contract with a private entity for the confinement of qualified pre-release prisoners in such facilities. Thus, section 3621(b) should not be construed as authorizing the Bureau to contract with private entities for the confinement of adult federal prisoners in any other context.

If Congress determines that such authorization is necessary or desirable, then it should so provide explicitly and unambiguously. And if the Bureau of Prisons privatizes confinement for adult federal prisoners in the absence of such legislation, then it will be setting an inappropriate example for the states.

_____

treatment centers. See supra notes 970-978 and accompanying text.

B. Model Statute and Commentary

There are many similarities between the Model Statute and the Model Contract. Like the Model Contract, for example, the Model Statute responds to the concerns of the constitutional-delegation section[980] by having accountability as its dominant theme. Also like the Model Contract, the best provisions from current statutes were incorporated or adapted. Further, like the Model Contract, the Model Statute does not purport to be exhaustive. Some jurisdictions may already have general legislation that adequately addresses various features and concerns of private incarceration (such as the need to avoid conflicts of interest in the contracting process); others may not. If a legislature decides to privatize an incarceration facility, it must enact legislation that comports with the existing body of law.

There is one significant difference between the Model Statute and the Model Contract: the provisions of the Model Statute must not be compromised. They set a mandatory minimum level for private-incarceration contracts and the private-incarceration process.[981] As such, the content of the statute is a matter for the legislature and the contracting agency, and not

---

[980] See supra notes 11-213 and accompanying text (analyzing constitutionality of delegating incarceration function).

[981] A legislature should, of course, consider building on this bedrock with more stringent, but not less stringent, requirements if that would be appropriate to circumstances within the jurisdiction.

for the private contractor.[982]

The following statutes were considered in drafting the Model

Statute:

• Alaska Stat. § 33.30.031 (1986) (authorizing
corrections commissioner to contract with private
entities, inter alia, for the provision of halfway
houses, group homes, and facilities for misdemeanor
offenders).

• Ariz. Rev. Stat. Ann. §§ 41-1609 & 41-1609.01 (1985 &
Supp. 1987) (authorizing corrections department to
contract with private entities for the confinement of
adult and youth offenders and the provision of various
related services enumerated in the statute).

• Ark. Stat. Ann. §§ 12-50-100 to 12-50-110 (Supp. 1987)
(authorizing state, regional, and local corrections
agencies to contract with private entities for the
financing, acquisition, construction, and operation of
correctional facilities).

• Colo. Rev. Stat. §§ 17-27-101 to 17-27-115 (1986 &
Supp. 1987) (authorizing local corrections boards to
utilize community correctional facilities and programs
operated by private organizations); Colo. Rev. Stat. §§
30-11-104.1 & 30-11-104.2 (1986) (authorizing counties
to finance jails and other buildings through lease-
purchase agreements).

• Fla. Stat. Ann. §§ 944.105 & 944.1053 (West Cum. Supp.
1988) (authorizing state corrections department to
contract with private entities for the provision,
operation, and maintenance of correctional facilities);
Fla. Stat. Ann. §§ 951.062 & 951.063 (West Cum. Supp.
1988) (authorizing counties to contract with private
entities for operation and maintenance of county
detention facilities).

---

[982] See supra note 424 (defining terms). Also unlike the
section on the Model Contract, this section on the Model Statute
presents the commentary after the statutory provision, rather
than before. This is done because the statutory commentary is
necessarily shorter than is the contractual commentary -- first,
because the statutory provisions should not be negotiable, and
second, because the statutory commentary avoids repetition by
drawing on and cross-referencing the contractual commentary.

- Haw. Rev. Stat. §§ 352-3, 353-1.1 & 353-1.2 (1985) (authorizing director of social services to contract for private residential youth facilities, community correctional centers, and high-security correctional facilities); Haw. Rev. Stat. § 353-3(7) (Supp. 1987) (authorizing director of corrections to contract with private entities for "the treatment, training, education, and work of committed persons").

- Ind. Code Ann. § 11-8-3-1 (Burns 1981) (authorizing corrections department to contract with private entities for the custody and care of committed persons and for related services).

- Kan. Stat. Ann. § 75-5210 (1984 & Cum. Supp. 1987) (authorizing secretary of corrections to contract with private entities for the provision of facilities and various rehabilitation programs for inmates in the secretary's custody).

- 1988 Ky. Rev. Stat. & R. Serv. §§ 197.500 to 197.525 (Baldwin) (authorizing state to contract with private entities to establish, operate, and manage adult correctional facilities).

- La. Rev. Stat. Ann. §§ 39:1780 to 39:1795 (West Cum. Supp. 1988) (inter alia, providing for private ownership and lease-purchase financing of correctional facilities).

- Minn. Stat. Ann. § 241.32 (West 1972 & Cum. Supp. 1988) (authorizing commissioner of corrections to contract with private entities for separate custody or specialized care and treatment of inmates).

- Mo. Ann. Stat. § 217.138 (Vernon Cum. Supp. 1988) (authorizing state department of corrections, cities, and counties to contract with private entities for the construction of corrections facilities).

- Mont. Code Ann. § 7-32-2201 (1987) (authorizing contracts with private parties for the provision, maintenance, and operation of county jails); Mont. Code Ann. § 7-32-2231 (1987) (authorizing construction of county jails by private industry and the lease back of such facilities for operation by the county); Mont. Code Ann. §§ 7-32-2232 to 7-32-2234 (1987) (providing statutory requirements for privately operated county jails); Mont. Code Ann. § 53-30-106 (1987) (authorizing state department of corrections to enter contract with private entities to house "selected inmates").

- Nev. Rev. Stat. Ann. § 209.141 (Michie 1987) (general grant of authority to state department of prisons to

contract with private entities to carry out
corrections-related functions).

- 1988 N.M. Laws § 33-1-17 (amending N.M Stat. Ann.
  § 33-1-17 (1987)) (authorizing state department of
  corrections to contract for the operation of "any adult
  female facility" and the renovation or construction of
  such facilities); N.M. Stat. Ann. §§ 33-3-26 & 33-3-27
  (1987) (authorizing two projects for private operation,
  or private provision and operation, of county jails).

- Okla. Stat. Ann. tit. 57, §§ 561, 563 & 563.1 (West
  Cum. Supp. 1988) (authorizing department of corrections
  to contract with private entities for operation of the
  department's correctional facilities and to use other
  non-departmental facilities for the incarceration and
  treatment of persons under the custody of the
  department).

- Pa. Stat. Ann. tit. 61, §§ 1081 to 1085 (Purdon Cum.
  Supp. 1988) (instituting one-year moratorium on the
  private operation of correctional facilities in the
  state, through June 30, 1987).

- 1987 S.C. Acts § 55.7 (authorizing department of
  corrections to contract for "any and all services").

- Tenn. Code Ann. §§ 41-24-101 to 41-24-115 (Cum. Supp.
  1987) (authorizing commissioner of corrections to
  contract with private entities for the provision of
  correctional services).

- Tex. Rev. Civ. Stat. Ann. art. 6166g-2 (Vernon Supp.
  1988) (authorizing board of corrections to contract
  with private entities for the financing, construction,
  operation, maintenance, and management of secure
  correctional facilities).

- Utah Code Ann. § 64-13-26 (1986 & Supp. 1987)
  (authorizing department of corrections to contract with
  private entities for the care, treatment, and
  supervision of offenders in its custody).

- Va. Code Ann. §§ 53.1-180 to 53.1-185 (1982 & Cum.
  Supp. 1987) (authorizing director of department of
  corrections and localities to contract with private
  nonprofit entities for residential and nonresidential
  community-diversion programs and services).

- Wyo. Stat. §§ 7-18-101 to 7-18-114 (1987) (authorizing
  contracts with private profit organizations for the
  establishment, maintenance, and operation of community
  correctional facilities and programs).

Section 1: Enabling Legislation

The contracting agency may contract with
private entities for the construction, lease,
acquisition, improvement, operation, and management
of correctional facilities and services only as
provided in this Act.

No contract shall be entered or renewed unless
it offers substantial cost savings to the
contracting agency and at least the same quality of
services as that offered by the contracting agency.

The intended beneficiaries of any contract
entered pursuant to this Act shall include inmates
incarcerated at the affected facility or facilities
and members of the public.

Commentary:

Enabling legislation authorizing the contracting agency to
contract with a private entity will most likely be necessary in a
jurisdiction that decides to privatize its prisons.[983] The
proposed enabling legislation grants the contracting agency broad
authority to contract with a private entity for "construction,
lease, acquisition, improvement, operation, and management of
correctional facilities and services." The jurisdiction may
choose to limit its grant of authority to tailor the legislation
more closely to its actual needs and thereby restrict private
contracts to the construction of a facility, for example, or
permit such contracts at minimum-security facilities only.[984]

---

[983] See supra pp. 415-17 (listing private-incarceration
statutes).

[984] See, e.g., Mo. Ann. Stat. § 217.133 (Vernon Cum. Supp.

Advocates of prison privatization have cited two primary

benefits that will result from privatization: less cost to the

public, and proper treatment and care for inmates. Consequently,

the proposed enabling legislation seeks to hold the private

entity strictly accountable for these results by requiring it to

show that the contract will offer substantial cost savings to the

contracting agency and by expressly creating third-party-

beneficiary status under the contract for inmates and the public.

Several jurisdictions have incorporated the requirement of

cost savings into their prison-privatization laws. Tennessee,

for example, requires that proposals for correctional-services

contracts offer "substantial cost savings"[985] to the state, a

requirement that is met if the proposer's annual cost projection

is "at least 5% less than the likely full cost to the state of

providing the same services."[986] Texas requires at least a 10%

cost savings from private facilities, which must offer "a level

and quality of programs at least equal to those provided by

state-operated facilities that house similar types of

inmates."[987] Arizona permits the renewal of a private contract

---

1988) (permitting private contracts for construction of
correctional facility); Mont. Code Ann. § 53-30-106 (1987)
(authorizing private contracts for confinement of "selected
inmates where suitable programs have been established"); 1987
S.C. Acts § 55.7 (permitting private contracts "for any and all
services" related to construction of a new facility); Tex. Rev.
Civ. Stat. Ann. art. 6166g-2, §§ 1(b)(1), 2 (Vernon Supp. 1988)
(restricting private contracts to facilities with up to 500
inmates, and minimum- and medium-security inmates).

[985] Tenn. Code Ann. § 41-24-104(c)(1) (Cum. Supp. 1987).

[986] Id. § 41-24-104 (c)(1)(E).

[987] Tex. Rev. Civ. Stat. Ann. art. 6166g-2, § 3(c)(4)

"only if the contractor is providing at least the same quality of services as [the] state at a lower cost or if the contractor is providing services superior in quality to those provided by [the] state at essentially the same cost."[988]   South Carolina authorizes private contracting for the construction of a facility, but requires that such services "(1) demonstrate reasonably comparable, cost-effectiveness to traditional methods of construction, (2) result in long-term operational cost-savings, and (3) result in the provision of a new facility of sufficient bed, program, and support space more expeditiously than traditional methods . . . ."[989]

(Vernon Supp. 1988).

[988]   Ariz. Rev. Stat. Ann. § 41-1609.01(L) (Supp. 1987).   In determining the quality of services provided by the contractor, the statute requires consideration of the following factors:

1.   The nature of inmates in the facilities.
2.   Whether the facilities meet professional standards.
3.   The level of training provided to the staff and the level of training accomplished by the staff.
4.   The number and nature of complaints against the staff.
5.   The number and nature of violent or other disruptive incidents among inmates or against the staff.
6.   The number of escapes and attempted escapes.
7.   The number and nature of disciplinary actions against inmates and the staff.
8.   The number of inmates productively active, the level of production and the nature of the activity provided to inmates.
9.   The rate at which inmates complete programs successfully.
10.   Other matters related to the quality of services provided.

Id. § 41.1609.01(M).

[989]   1987 S.C. Acts § 55.7.

The proposed enabling legislation requires "substantial" cost savings to the jurisdiction and the provision of services of at least the same quality as services that are provided by the government. Substantial cost savings, rather than reasonable cost savings, was the term chosen for the proposed statute, for several reasons. First, considering the oft-stated claim by proponents of prison and jail privatization that they can reduce costs substantially, they should be held to their promise to the taxpayers and government officials. Second, considering the arguably unsuitable message that privatization of corrections conveys,[990] the government should be reluctant to compromise its obligations to the public without showing substantial benefits in return. Third, considering the constitutional risk that the government undertakes by delegating the incarceration function,[991] its potential economic gain should be maximized in return.

As a practical matter, of course, it must be recognized that the difference between substantial and reasonable cost savings is one of degree only. The legislature, therefore, can statutorily specify a formula for evaluating cost savings, as Tennessee has done.[992] Alternatively, or in addition, the contracting parties can particularize the method for assessing costs. Moreover, the

---

990   See supra notes 211-213 and accompanying text (discussing question of symbolism).

991   See supra notes 11-213 and accompanying text (discussing constitutionality of private-prison delegation).

992   Tenn. Code Ann. § 41-24-104(c)(1) (Cum. Supp. 1987).

cost-saving formula will necessarily incorporate a complex set of factors -- including cost projections and subjective criteria measuring the quality of services and conditions of confinement -- that will be difficult to quantify. For example, a five-percent or greater cost savings to the state under Tennessee's "substantial cost savings" provision would be deceptive if the contractor were to provide lower quality services. Hence, the proposed standard should be understood to require at the very least that the contractor provide the same quality of services at substantially less cost or substantially better services at the same or less cost than that which the contracting agency would have to pay.[993] This requirement applies both to the initial contract and to contract renewals.

No jurisdiction has explicitly designated the public or inmates as third-party beneficiaries in its privatization contracts. Arguably, third-party-beneficiary status may be implied from statutory language requiring the private contractor to assume all liability for any breach of contract.[994] The

_____

[993] See id. § 41-24-104(c)(2) ("No proposal shall be accepted unless such proposal offers a level and quality of services which are at least equal to those which would be provided by the state."); cf. supra note 749 (discussing California correctional officers' contention that cost savings do not justify circumventing civil-service system).

[994] For example, section 944.105(3) of the Florida statutes provides:

Any private entity entering into a contract with the department pursuant to this section shall be liable in tort with respect to the care and custody of inmates under its supervision and for any breach of contract with the department.

proposed enabling legislation expressly designates inmates and the public as third-party beneficiaries in private contracts. The reasons for including this provision, such as increased contractor accountability, are thoroughly explored in the Model Contract.[995]

_____

Fla. Stat. Ann. § 944.105(3) (West Cum. Supp. 1988).

[995] See Model Contract § 1 (Policy Statement -- Goals and Responsibilities of the Parties).

Section 2: Site Selection

Before the contracting agency may award a contract for the private construction and/or operation of a correctional or detention facility, the agency must approve the site for the proposed facility. Approval shall be based on the following:

(A) criteria formulated by the contracting agency, including:

(1) availability of qualified personnel within the local labor market;

(2) total usable and developable acreage of various sites considering the use and purpose of the facility;

(3) accessibility of each site to existing utility, transportation, educational, law enforcement, health care, social, fire protection, refuse collection, water, and sewage disposal services;

(4) susceptibility of each site to natural and man-made environmental hazards;

(5) patterns of residential growth and projected population growth;

(6) community opinion as determined at a public hearing or hearings of record; and

(7) any other criteria that the contracting agency, in conjunction with local governments, deems appropriate; and

(B) a report prepared by the governing body of the jurisdiction in which the proposed site is located, stating whether the site is in compliance with local-government comprehensive plans, land-use ordinances, zoning ordinances or regulations, and other local ordinances that are in effect at the time the report is submitted.

After the contracting agency has approved a site, the agency must then seek approval from the legislature, which shall consider all of the information that was reviewed by the contracting agency, as well as any other criteria that it deems appropriate. Construction and/or operation of a private facility may not commence until the legislature has approved the selected site.[996]

Commentary:

The Model Statute addresses basic concerns that may arise with respect to the siting of a privately owned and/or operated prison or jail. There are several ways in which to choose such a site. The contracting agency may select the site itself, for example, or the site may already be owned by the government and designated for the purpose of incarceration. In these cases, additional legislation may not be necessary. Alternatively, the private contractor might select the site, with the RFP merely setting general geographical guidelines. In that case, additional legislation may be necessary to ensure that the site

---

[996] Some of these provisions are derived from Fla. Stat. Ann. § 944.095 (West Cum. Supp. 1988), which addresses the citing of correctional facilities generally. See also ACA Standard 2-4161: "The institution [should be] located within 50 miles of a civilian population center of at least 10,000 people, or minimally within one hour driving time of a hospital, fire protection, and public transportation." The note that accompanies Standard 2-4161 provides:

> Proximity to a civilian population center is essential in order to augment the services provided directly by the institution, to provide greater recruitment and training opportunities for staff, to accommodate visitors, and to provide educational and employment opportunities for inmates on work or study release. Nearby social agencies, schools, colleges, universities, and hospitals are potentially valuable resources for a correctional institution.

ACA Standard 2-4161 discussion. At least one state requires legislative approval of the site of each private correctional or detention facility. Ariz. Rev. Stat. Ann. § 41-1609.01(3) (Supp. 1987).

will be selected not only on the basis of factors that are important to the contractor -- such as the price of the property -- but also on the basis of factors that protect the interests of the the contracting agency, the surrounding community, and the inmates.

The Model Statute requires that the contracting agency make an initial evaluation of each proposed site according to the criteria that are set forth in the statute and any other criteria deemed important by the contracting agency.[997] Many jurisdictions may already have established criteria for the selection of sites for public facilities; these criteria may be adaptable for use in the evaluation of sites for private facilities as well.[998]

The requirement that a public hearing be held for each proposed site is intended to ensure that the public will have meaningful input in the site-selection process. Although it may be administratively cumbersome to hold public hearings concerning several proposed sites, community opinion -- which is an essential component -- will have little effect on the selection of a site unless it is considered during the initial phase of the process.

----

[997] Consideration of these factors in the early stages should prevent situations such as the one that arose in Pennsylvania, where a private interstate protective-custody facility was proposed to be built on a toxic-waste dump. See supra note 467.

[998] See supra note 996.

The initial contract for the operation of a
facility or for incarceration of prisoners or
inmates therein shall be for a period of not more
than three (3) years with an option to renew for an
additional period of two (2) years.[999]   Contracts
for construction, purchase, or lease of a facility
shall not exceed a term of fifteen (15) years.[1000]
Any contract for the construction or operation of a
facility shall be subject to annual appropriation by
the [appropriate legislative body].[1001]

---

[999]   See Ariz. Rev. Stat. Ann. §§ 41-1609.01(I), (J) (Supp.
1987) ("the initial contract term shall be for a period of three
years in order to allow the contractor sufficient time to
demonstrate its performance and to provide sufficient information
to allow a comparison of the performance of the contractor to the
performance of this state in operating similar facilities";
"[t]he initial contract may include an option to renew for an
additional period of two years"); Tenn. Code Ann. §§ 41-24-
105(a), (b) (Cum. Supp. 1987) ("the initial contract term shall
be for a period of three (3) years in order to allow the
contractor sufficient time to demonstrate its performance and to
provide sufficient information to allow a comparison of the
performance of the contractor to the performance of the state in
operating similar facilities"; "[t]he initial contract may
include an option to renew for an additional period of two (2)
years"); see also N.M. Stat. Ann. § 33-3-27(A) (1987) ("No
agreement . . . for the operation of a jail or for incarceration
of prisoners therein shall be made for a period of more than
three years."); Tex. Rev. Civ. Stat. Ann. art. 6166g-2, § 3(c)(7)
(Vernon Supp. 1988) ("for an initial contract term of not more
than three years, with an option to renew for additional periods
of two years").   But see Fla. Stat. Ann. § 944.105(2) (West Cum.
Supp. 1988) ("The contract term shall be determined by the
negotiating parties and shall be contingent upon annual
appropriations."); Okla. Stat. Ann. tit. 57, § 561(L) (West Cum.
Supp. 1988) ("Contracts awarded . . . shall be entered into for a
period of one (1) year, subject to renewal at the option of the
State of Oklahoma for a cumulative period not to exceed fifty
(50) years.").

[1000]   See N.M. Stat. Ann. § 33-3-27(A) (1987) ("Agreements
binding on future governing bodies for construction, purchase, or
lease of a jail facility for not more than fifteen years are
hereby authorized.").

[1001]   See, e.g., Ark. Stat. Ann. § 12-50-106(d) (Supp. 1987)
("subject to the requirement for annual appropriation of funds by

Commentary:

As discussed in the Model Contract sections on Term and Renewal,[1002] the overall contract term must be long enough for the contractor to become established in its new role and to develop a track record on which the contracting agency can base a comparison of public and private performance. However, the contract term must also be short enough to prevent market entrenchment and to provide the parties with sufficient flexibility to deal with changing needs and priorities. The Model Statute adopts a term provision that reflects an accommodation of these conflicting concerns, and one that the majority of states employ: an initial three-year term with an option to renew for one two-year period.[1003] Thus, the Model Statute limits the total initial contract term to five years, requiring a competitive rebidding process within that period to benefit the contracting parties as well as other private companies that may want to compete for access to the market.

---

each political subdivision and subject to the requirement of biennial appropriations by the state"); Fla. Stat. Ann. § 944.105(2) (West Cum. Supp. 1988) ("The contract term . . . shall be contingent upon annual appropriations."); 1988 N.M. Laws § 33-1-17(A)(6) ("continuation of the contract is subject to the availability of funds"); 1987 S.C. Acts § 55.7(4) ("services must . . . be subject to the year-to-year appropriation process of the General Assembly and the state procurement procedures"); Tex. Rev. Civ. Stat. Ann. art. 6166g-2, § 3(c)(2) (Vernon Supp. 1988) ("payment by the state is subject to the availability of appropriations").

[1002]   See Model Contract §§ 3(A) (Term), 3(B) (Renewal).

[1003]   See supra note 999.

The Model Statute also recognizes the potential need for longer contract terms when the contract involves more than just the operation of a facility -- for example, when construction, purchase, or lease of a facility is involved. Thus, the Model Statute authorizes terms of up to fifteen years for such contracts.

The Model Statute offers a workable compromise in the long-term versus short-term debate by offering the contractor the possibility of a five-year, stable, and ongoing arrangement if its performance meets the standards established by the contracting agency.[1004] This Term and Renewal Provision creates an environment in which there is sufficient incentive for the contractor to risk the undertaking. There is also sufficient security for the contracting agency. If the contractor does not perform as required, the contract will not be renewed.

Finally, many of the statutes that authorize multi-year contracts for the ownership or operation of a correctional or detention facility provide that payments due under the contract are subject to annual or biennial appropriation by the legislature.[1005] Such a limitation ensures that the contract will be viewed as a current expense, and not a long-term debt of the jurisdiction.[1006] Although this provision places some limitation on the contracting agency's obligation to perform for

---

[1004] See Model Statute § 1 (Enabling Legislation).

[1005] See supra note 1001; see also Model Contract §§ 2(A) (Private Financing), 3(A) (Term).

[1006] See Model Contract § 2(A) (Private Financing).

the full contract term, the risk that it poses to the private
contractor is minimal, for it is unlikely that a jurisdiction
would in fact fail to appropriate the necessary funds for such an
essential governmental function as the operation of a prison or
jail facility.

Section 4: Standards of Operation

All facilities that are governed by this Act shall be designed, constructed, and at all times maintained and operated in accordance with the American Correctional Association Standards in force at the time of contracting, as well as with subsequent ACA Standards to the extent that they are approved by the contracting agency. The facility shall meet the percentage of Standards required for accreditation by the American Correctional Association, except where the contract requires compliance with a higher percentage of nonmandatory standards. The contract may allow the contractor an extension of time in which to meet a lower percentage of nonmandatory Standards only when the contract is for the renovation of an existing facility, in which case the contractor shall have not longer than three (3) months to meet those Standards that are applicable to the physical plant.

In addition, all facilities shall at all times comply with all federal and state constitutional standards, federal, state, and local laws, and all court orders.

Commentary:

The Model Statute requires that all private correctional facilities meet at least the percentage of ACA Standards necessary to receive accreditation by the ACA and the Commission on Accreditation for Corrections. The ACA Standards are widely regarded in the industry as comprehensive and demanding.[1007] Thus, the Standards provide a respected, uniform measure of the quality of service that the contractor is providing.

The statutory language requires that the contractor meet at

[1007] See Model Contract § 3(F)(1) (Operating Standards).

least the percentage of nonmandatory Standards required for accreditation. It allows the contracting agency to require compliance with a higher level of nonmandatory Standards under the contract, however. The contracting agency should review the Standards closely to determine whether some or all of the nonmandatory Standards are so vital to the operation of a private facility that compliance should be required in the contract. Likewise, legislators should review the Standards to determine whether there are any that should be made mandatory by statute as well as by contract. Further, to avoid the possible finding of an unconstitutional delegation in this area to the extent possible,[1008] ACA Standards that are developed subsequent to the contract date shall bind the contractor only to the extent that they are approved by the contracting agency.

The Model Statute requires the contractor to bring the facility into compliance immediately and to maintain compliance throughout the contract term. An exception is made for contracts that include renovation of an existing structure as part of an operations and management contract because of the special problems that a contractor may encounter in bringing such a facility into compliance.[1009] The Model Statute, therefore, allows the contracting agency to give the contractor a short extension of time to meet nonmandatory Standards when the

---

[1008] See *supra* notes 136-169 and accompanying text (discussing constitutional requirements for delegation of rule-making authority).

[1009] See Model Contract § 3(F)(1) (Operating Standards).

contracting agency feels that an extension is necessary and justified.

Several jurisdictions require accreditation by statute and/or by contract as a supplemental means of monitoring compliance with ACA Standards.[1010] The Model Statute does not make accreditation a statutory requirement, however. The accreditation process can in no way replace on-site monitoring by the state, and its usefulness as a supplemental means of monitoring is limited by the questions that have been raised concerning its effectiveness.[1011] Thus, it is an issue that is best left to negotiation between the contractor and the contracting agency.

In addition to requiring compliance with ACA Standards, the Model Statute also expressly requires that the facility conform to all federal and state constitutional standards, applicable laws, and court orders. This language, derived from the Texas statute,[1012] places prospective contractors on notice that all applicable legal standards are necessarily incorporated in a valid contract for the private ownership and/or operation of a

---

[1010] Okla. Stat. Ann. tit. 57, § 561(R)(2) (West Supp. 1988) (requiring contractor to receive accreditation within three years); Tex. Rev. Civ. Stat. Ann. art. 6166g-2, § 1(b)(3) (Vernon Supp. 1988) (stating that facility must receive and retain accreditation, but not specifying time period); cf. 1988 Ky. Rev. Stat. & R. Serv. § 197.510 (Baldwin) (requiring private adult correctional facility to submit plan for achieving compliance with ACA Standards within five years).

[1011] See Model Contract § 3(F)(1) (Operating Standards).

[1012] Tex. Rev. Civ. Stat. Ann. art. 6166g-2, § 1(b)(2) (Vernon Supp. 1988) (requiring compliance with court orders and federal constitutional standards).

correctional or detention facility, even if they are not expressly stated in the contract.

Section 5: Use of Force

(A) A private contractor's employees serving as "jailers" shall be allowed to use force only while on the grounds of a facility, while transporting inmates, and while pursuing escapees from a facility.

(B) "Non-deadly force," which is force that normally would cause neither death nor serious bodily injury, and "deadly force," which is force that is likely to cause death or serious bodily injury, shall be used only as set forth herein.

(C) Non-Deadly Force. A private-company jailer shall be authorized to use only such non-deadly force as the circumstances require in the following situations: to prevent the commission of a felony or misdemeanor, including escape; to defend oneself or others against physical assault; to prevent serious damage to property; to enforce institutional regulations and orders; and to prevent or quell a riot.

(D) Use of Firearms/Deadly Force. Private-company jailers who have been appropriately certified as determined by the contracting agency and trained pursuant to the provisions of Subsection (E) shall have the right to carry and use firearms and shall exercise such authority and use deadly force only as a last resort, and then only to prevent an act that could result in death or serious bodily injury to oneself or to another person.

(F) Private-company jailers shall be trained in the use of force and the use of firearms, in accordance with ACA Standards 2-4186 through 2-4189 and 2-4206, and shall be trained, at the contractor's expense, at the facilities that train public prison and jail personnel for at least the minimum number of hours that public personnel are currently trained.

(G) Within three (3) days following an incident involving the use of force against an inmate or another, the employee shall file a written report with the administrative staff and contract monitor describing the incident.

(H) A private contractor shall stand in the shoes of the contracting agency in any agreement, formal or informal, with local law-enforcement agencies concerning the latter's obligations in the event of an emergency situations, such as a riots or escapes.

Commentary:

Given the paramount importance of and concerns regarding the use of force in a prison or jail setting, especially by private personnel, it is surprising that so few jurisdictions have statutes that govern use of force.[1013] Even the few states that do have use-of-force provisions do not address the issue with any specificity. As discussed in the Model Contract section on Use of Force, comprehensiveness is not only desirable in such a provision, but also essential to ensure the safety of facility personnel and inmates alike. With only phraseological changes, the Model Statute adopts the provision recommended in the Model Contract.

[1013] See, e.g., Ark. Stat. Ann. § 12-50-107 (Supp. 1987); 1988 Ky. Rev. Stat. & R. Serv. § 197.510(20) (Baldwin); Mont. Code Ann. § 7-32-2234 (1987); Okla. Stat. Ann. tit. 57, § 561(O) (West Cum. Supp. 1988).

Section 6: Employee Training Requirements

All employees of a facility operated pursuant to this Act must receive, at a minimum, the same quality and quantity of training as that required by federal, state, and/or local statutes, rules, and regulations for employees of public correctional and detention facilities. If any or all of the applicable American Correctional Association Standards relating to training are more stringent than are governmental standards, training shall be provided in accordance with the more stringent Standard(s). All training expenses shall be the responsibility of the contractor.

Commentary:

It is essential that minimum employee-training requirements be set by statute as well as in the contract. A correctional or detention facility cannot be operated safely and according to constitutional, statutory, and contractual standards without an adequately trained staff. Training is expensive, however. Incarceration is a labor-intensive industry, with labor costs comprising approximately eighty to ninety percent of total costs.[1014] Training is one area in which prospective contractors may attempt to reduce costs in order to ensure that they make a profit.[1015] Minimum training levels, therefore, should not be subject to negotiation, but rather should be set by statute.[1016]

[1014] See Note, supra note 9, at 1498 n.158.

[1015] See Model Contract § 4(A)(2) (Employment Options for Correctional or Detention Employees at Existing Facilities).

[1016] But see Mont. Code Ann. § 7-32-2232(2)(e) (1987) (stating that "[t]he agreement must include . . . minimum

Despite the importance of this issue, many jurisdictions have failed to address it in statutes that authorize privately operated correctional or detention facilities. Of those that have addressed the issue, only one -- Florida -- requires private employees to meet the same training requirements that government employees must meet.[1017] The Model Statute expressly provides that private employees must, at a minimum, receive the same amount of training that their counterparts in the public sector receive. The training must not only equal the number of _hours_ provided for by law, but the _quality_ of coverage of the required subject areas must also be equivalent. If ACA Standards are higher than the contracting jurisdiction's minimum requirements, however, ACA Standards should govern. This language ensures that the private contractor's employees will be adequately trained to operate the facility in accordance with constitutional, statutory, and contractual standards. Finally, the Model Statute requires that the contractor be responsible for all training expenses.[1018]

---

standards for the training of jailers"); N.M. Stat. Ann. § 33-3-27(C) (1987) (allowing for "minimum training standards [to be] specified in the contract").

[1017] _See_ Fla. Stat. Ann. § 944.105(6) (West Cum. Supp. 1988).

[1018] _See_, _e.g._, _id._ § 951.062(6) (requiring private contractor to pay training expenses for employees who supervise inmates); N.M. Stat. Ann. § 33-3-27(C) (1987) (requiring contractor to pay expenses for jailers to meet minimum training standards).

Section 7: Monitoring

An individual who is responsible for monitoring all aspects of the private contractor's performance under the contract shall be appointed and employed by the contracting agency. The monitor shall appoint a staff to assist in monitoring at the facility, as the monitor determines to be necessary. The monitor shall be provided an on-site work area, shall be on-site on a daily basis, and shall have access to all areas of the facility and to inmates and staff at all times. The contractor shall provide any and all data, reports, and other materials that the monitor determines are necessary to carry out monitoring responsibilities under this Section.

The monitor or his designee shall report to the [_____] committee of the legislature at least annually on the contractor's performance.

Members of the public shall have the same right of access to private facilities as they do to public facilities.

Commentary:

It is essential that any statute authorizing the private operation of correctional or detention facilities contain a provision directing the contracting agency to monitor all aspects of the contractor's performance on the contract, and granting it broad authority to carry out its monitoring responsibilities. Although the contracting agency may be able to delegate some of the governmental functions that are associated with the operation of a facility, it cannot delegate its responsibility to see that those functions are carried out in accordance with constitutional and legislative standards, as well as with other standards that are mandated by public policy.[1019] Without an effective monitoring system, contractor abuses will go undetected and the contracting agency will not be able to ensure the safety of prisoners, staff, and the surrounding community. Nor will it be able to ensure the integrity of other aspects of the private contractor's operations, such as its use of contract funds.

The Model Statute is designed to give the contracting agency maximum access to all of the information that it will need to carry out its oversight responsibilities. It provides that the contracting agency must appoint a monitor for the facility who will be on-site on a daily basis.[1020] It also expressly provides that the contracting agency shall have access to any other information that it deems necessary to oversee the facility effectively.[1021] The information that can be obtained through daily first-hand observation and contact with staff and inmates is crucial to the effectiveness of any monitoring system. Periodic in-depth inspections and written reports, while valuable sources of additional information, cannot by themselves be relied on to provide adequate evaluation of a prison or jail

---

[1019] See supra notes 11-213 and accompanying text (discussing constitutionality of delegating incarceration function).

[1020] Currently, only one state statute expressly requires on-site monitoring. See Tex. Rev. Civ. Stat. Ann. art. 6166g-2, § 3(c)(1) (Vernon Supp. 1988) (requiring that every proposal provide for "regular, on-site monitoring by the Texas Department of Corrections"). Several contracts also provide for on-site monitoring. See Bay County Contract at 17, § 5.5; Santa Fe Contract at 28, § 11.1.

[1021] See Model Contract § 6 (Monitoring) (noting importance of access to all areas of the facility, to inmates and staff, and to all records and reports maintained by the contractor).

facility.[1022]

Members of the public and the media who visit a facility may prove to be another helpful source of information for the monitor.[1023] Therefore, the Model Statute provides that the public shall have access to a private correctional or detention facility, subject only to the limitations that are placed on access to an equivalent public facility. Jurisdictions may want to consider other means of involving the public in the monitoring process, such as placing members of the public on the monitoring team. The Model Statute stops short of requiring such steps, however.

Finally, the Model Statute provides that the monitor shall report at least annually to an appropriate committee of the legislature on the contractor's performance.[1024] This requirement will ensure that the legislature is kept up-to-date on the condition of private facilities. It will also allow the legislature to determine whether further action is necessary or, in fact, whether private operators should be allowed to continue operating correctional or detention facilities at all.

[1022] See Model Contract § 6 (Monitoring) (discussing alternative methods of monitoring).

[1023] See Model Contract § 6 (Monitoring).

[1024] This portion of the monitoring provision is derived from the Tennessee statute. See Tenn. Code Ann. § 41-24-109 (Cum. Supp. 1987) (stating that the monitor "shall report at least annually or as requested to the select oversight committee on corrections or any other legislative committee on the performance of the contractor").

Section 8: Liability and Sovereign Immunity

(A) The contractor shall assume all liability arising under the contract.

(B) The sovereign immunity of the contracting agency shall not extend to the contractor. Neither the contractor nor the insurer of the contractor may plead the defense of sovereign immunity in any action arising out of the performance of the contract.

Commentary:

As discussed in the Model Contract section on Immunity, the private contractor should be required to assume all liability arising under the contract and should be prohibited from using the state or federal government's sovereign-immunity defense to limit such liability.[1025] Arizona,[1026] Tennessee,[1027] and Texas,[1028] for example, have adopted this statutory scheme in their prison-privatization legislation. Under these provisions,

---

[1025] See Model Contract § 3(E)(1) (Indemnification and Immunity). The contracting agency may want to consider language that specifically states that the private contractor is not deprived of the "benefit of any law limiting exposure to liability, setting a limit on damages, or establishing defenses to liability." Tex. Rev. Civ. Stat. Ann. art. 6166g-2, § 4 (Vernon Supp. 1988). Such language would seem unnecessary, however, to the extent that the provision merely affirmatively states what is already available to the private contractor.

[1026] Ariz. Rev. Stat. Ann. § 41.1609.01(0) (1985 & Supp. 1987).

[1027] Tenn. Code Ann. § 41-24-107(b) (Cum. Supp. 1987).

[1028] Tex. Rev. Civ. Stat. Ann. art. 6166g-2, § 4 (Vernon Supp. 1988).

there is an economic incentive compelling the private contractor to provide proper inmate care and treatment. In other words, it creates a self-enforcing accountability system in which the private contractor is required, without constant governmental oversight and supervision, to exercise the necessary degree of care to ensure compliance with the contract.

To preserve the level of accountability established under the liability statute, the second part of the proposed statutory scheme recommends that the contractor be denied use of the contracting agency's sovereign-immunity defense, which serves to limit liability.[1029] Under this arrangement, the private contractor will be more accountable because it is required to assume all liability arising under the contract. Permitting the contractor to escape liability through the use of a sovereign-immunity defense would undermine the goal of accountability. Prohibiting the use of this defense acts as an additional safeguard against noncompliance with the contract because it eliminates a significant escape device and places full responsibility on the contractor for its failure to provide the type of inmate care and treatment with which it has been entrusted.

[1029] The courts have not yet addressed the question of whether a private contractor can assert a sovereign-immunity defense. See Model Contract § 3(E)(1) (Indemnification and Immunity).

Section 9: Insurance

The contractor shall provide an adequate plan of insurance, specifically including insurance for civil-rights claims, as determined by an independent risk-management or actuarial firm with demonstrated experience in public liability for [state/county] governments. In determining the adequacy of the plan, the firm shall determine whether:

(A) the insurance is adequate to protect the contracting agency from actions by a third party against the contractor or contracting agency as a result of the contract;

(B) the insurance is adequate to assure the contractor's ability to fulfill its contract with the contracting agency in all respects and to assure that the contractor is not limited in this ability due to financial liability that results from judgments;

(C) the insurance is adequate to protect the contracting agency against claims arising as a result of any occurrence during the term of the contract on an occurrence basis; and

(D) the insurance is adequate to satisfy other requirements specified by the independent risk-management or actuarial firm.[1030]

Insurance accepted under this statute may not be provided by the contractor.

Commentary:

As discussed in the Model Contract section on Insurance, the contracting agency _must_ require that the private contractor be adequately insured to avoid becoming liable itself for the

---

1030   This statute is derived from Ariz. Rev. Stat. Ann. § 41-1609.01(N)(2) (Supp. 1987) and Tenn. Code Ann. § 41-24-107(a)(2) (Cum. Supp. 1987).

contractor's mistakes and breaches of contract.[1031] To
accomplish this goal, both Arizona[1032] and Tennessee[1033] have
adopted statutory provisions that require an expert in the area
of risk management to evaluate the adequacy of the private
contractor's proposed insurance plan. Specifically, an
experienced independent risk-management or actuarial firm will be
required to evaluate the overall adequacy of a proposed plan by
considering, among other things, whether the insurance applies to
third-party actions, whether it is adequate to assure completion
of and compliance with the contract, and whether it is issued on
an occurrence basis.

The statute expressly prohibits self-insurance by the
contractor to protect the contracting agency against the
possibility that the contractor will be unable to absorb the
financial losses that are associated with prisoner litigation.
Self-insurance adds further risk in an area in which the
contracting agency will want to ensure, to the greatest extent
possible, that it will not be held financially accountable for
the contractor's wrongdoing. This goal can be accomplished by
shifting the risk to an independent insurance company. Taken
together with other factors considered by the risk-management or
actuarial firm to be necessary for eliminating the contracting
agency's exposure, this statute provides the necessary steps for

---

[1031]   See Model Contract §§ 3(E)(2) (Insurance).

[1032]   Ariz. Rev. Stat. Ann. § 41-1609.01(N)(2) (Supp. 1987).

[1033]   Tenn. Code Ann. § 41-24-107(a)(2) (Cum. Supp. 1987).

ensuring that the private contractor obtain an adequate plan of
insurance.

Section 10: Termination of Contract
and Resumption of Government Control

The contracting agency may cancel the contract without cause at any time after the first year of operation, without penalty to the contracting agency, on giving ninety (90) days' written notice.

Notwithstanding any other provision in this Act to the contrary, prior to entering a contract for the private operation of a prison or jail, a plan shall be developed by the contracting agency and certified by the [Governor or appropriate executive officer or legislative body] demonstrating the method by which the government will resume control of the facility upon contract termination.

Commentary:

Both Arizona[1034] and Tennessee[1035] have enacted no-cause termination statutes that permit the contracting agency to terminate the contract, with ninety days' written notice, for convenience or without cause.[1036] It is imperative that the

---

[1034] Ariz. Rev. Stat. Ann. § 41-1609.01(C) (Supp. 1987) (contract "[p]roposer must agree that this state may cancel the contract at any time after the first year of operation, without penalty to this state, on giving ninety days' written notice").

[1035] Tenn. Code Ann. § 41-24-104(4) (Cum. Supp. 1987) (containing language nearly identical to Arizona's).

[1036] For states that provide for termination for cause, see, e.g., N.M. Stat. Ann. § 33-3-27(F) (1987) ("All agreements with private independent contractors for the operation, or provision and operation, of jails shall provide for termination for cause by the local public body parties upon ninety days' notice to the independent contractor."); Tex. Rev. Civ. Stat. Ann. art. 6166g-2, § (3)(b)(5) (Vernon Supp. 1988) (contract must permit "the state to terminate the contract for cause, including as cause the failure of the private vendor or county to meet the conditions required by this article and other conditions required by the contract").

contracting agency be granted such authority, because the provision enables the agency to respond quickly and effectively to problems arising under the contract or, alternatively, to internal problems, such as appropriation of funds. Because the need for such action is unlikely during the early stages of the contract term, the contracting agency should be prohibited from exercising this authority during the first year of the contract. Of course, the contracting agency may terminate _for cause_ at _any_ time, including within the first year of the contract.[1037]

Further, to anticipate abrupt contract termination, such as from bankruptcy, strike, or judicial finding of unconstitutionality, each jurisdiction must develop a comprehensive plan -- in advance of entering a contract -- for reassuming control of a facility immediately.[1038]

[1037] For the Model Contract's language on "cause," see Model Contract § 7 (Termination).

[1038] _See_ Tenn. Code Ann. § 41-24-106(1) (Cum. Supp. 1987).

Section 11: Nondelegability of Contracting Agency's Authority

No contract for private correctional or detention services shall authorize, allow, or imply a delegation of the authority or responsibility of the contracting agency to a prison or jail contractor to:

(A) classify inmates or place inmates in less restrictive custody or more restrictive custody;

(B) transfer an inmate, although the contractor may recommend in writing that the contracting agency transfer a particular inmate;

(C) formulate rules of inmate behavior, violations of which may subject inmates to sanctions, except to the extent that they are accepted or modified by the contracting agency;

(D) take any disciplinary action;

(E) grant, deny, or revoke sentence credits;

(F) recommend that the parole board either deny or grant parole, although the contractor may submit written reports that have been prepared in the ordinary course of business;

(G) develop and implement procedures for calculating sentence credits or inmate-release and parole-eligibility dates;

(H) require an inmate to work, except on contracting-agency projects; approve the type of work that inmates may perform; or award or withhold wages or sentence credits based on the manner in which individual inmates perform such work; or

(I) determine inmate eligibility for furlough and work release.

Commentary:

To the greatest extent possible, this section is designed to accommodate constitutional concerns involving delegation. As discussed in the Model Contract section on Inmate Management, the contracting agency is much more likely than the contractor is to take into consideration the interests of the public and the inmates in formulating and implementing incarceration rules and policies -- i.e., to be accountable.[1039] Therefore, all of the important questions concerning the nature and length of inmate confinement are reserved exclusively to the contracting agency. Many of the states that authorize privatization have enacted similar statutes.[1040]

[1039] See Model Contract § 5(A) (Inmate Management); see also supra notes 11-213 and accompanying text (discussing constitutionality of delegating incarceration function).

[1040] See, e.g., Ariz. Rev. Stat. Ann. § 41-1609.01(P) (Supp. 1987); Ark. Stat. Ann. § 12-50-108 (Supp. 1987); Tenn. Code Ann. § 41-24-110 (Cum. Supp. 1987); Tex. Rev. Civ. Stat. Ann. art. 6166g-2, § 3(e) (Vernon Supp. 1988).

Section 12: Conflict of Interest

(A) The following individuals shall not solicit or accept, directly or indirectly, any personal benefit or promise of a benefit from a private correctional or detention company negotiating, doing business with, or planning (within the individual's knowledge) to negotiate or do business with the contracting agency:

(1) a member of, or any other person or entity under contract with, any governmental body that exercises any functions or responsibilities in the review or approval of the undertaking or carrying out of the project,[1041] including but not limited to any employee of the contracting agency, any person serving as the monitor of a private corrections or detention facility, and any person on the staff of such a monitor; and

(2) a member of the immediate family of any of the above-named individuals.

None of the above-named individuals shall use his or her position, influence, or information concerning such negotiations, business, or plans to benefit himself, herself, or another.

(B) A private prison or jail contractor shall agree that, at the time of contracting, it has no interest and shall not acquire any interest, direct or indirect, that would conflict in any manner or degree with the performance of its services. The contractor shall further covenant that, in the performance of the contract, it shall not employ any person having any such known interests.[1042]

(C) Any violation of this Section shall be governed by Section [___] of this Code.

1041   This provision is derived from 1984 Kentucky RFP at 6, § 14.

1042   This provision is derived from 1984 Kentucky RFP at 6, § 14.

Commentary:

As is the case with contracting for other goods and services,[1043] contracting with the private sector for the construction and operation of incarceration facilities carries with it the danger that government officials, employees, and contractors will have actual or apparent conflicts of interest in the course of their mutual dealings.[1044] All jurisdictions already have conflict-of-interest statutes that govern the procurement process. Because these statutes are quite detailed and complex, they can generally be applied in the private-incarceration context. To supplement existing law, if necessary, jurisdictions should include a conflict-of-interest provision in legislation authorizing the private construction, ownership, or operation of prison and jail facilities.[1045]

[1043] See, e.g., Wines, Conflict-of-Interest Rules Ignored, Pentagon Aides Tell House Panel, N.Y. Times, July 7, 1988, at B5, col. 1 (stating that "Defense Department officials and private consultants have widely ignored some regulations intended to prevent conflicts of interest in weapons purchases," according to testimony of the Pentagon's inspector general).

[1044] See, e.g., 2 "Model" Prisons, supra note 433. This article reported, inter alia, that Corrections Corporation of America Chairman Thomas Beasley "gave three contracts directly to sitting commissioners" of Hamilton County while CCA's proposal was before the county's Board of Commissioners. Id. Also, "[w]hen Beasley was negotiating with the commission, he gave a contract for local public relations to the woman who had managed [the election campaign of one of the commissioners]." Id. That commissioner has since been voted out of office in an election in which CCA was an issue. Id.; see also Pennsylvania Joint State Gov't Comm'n, Report of the Private Prison Task Force 34 (1987) (stating that "[p]rivate prison entrepreneurs who invest in lobbying efforts which support tougher sentences and mandatory imprisonment may be able to increase the demand for their service").

The Model Statute's language is broad. Some of its restrictions apply to any person whose interests may conflict with those of the contracting agency, the community, and the inmates of a private facility. Specifically, it extends to any member of any governmental body that is charged with the initial decision to privatize facilities, the selection of a contractor, or any other responsibilities in connection with the private construction and/or operation of a facility. Also included are any official or employee of the contracting agency, regardless of his or her rank or function, as well as the monitor of the private facility and his or her staff. The statute also reaches the contractor and its employees.

No amount of legislation can completely deter illegal or unethical behavior in the contracting process. The Model Statute, therefore, expresses the jurisdiction's commitment to fairness in the competitive-bidding process and provides notice to individuals who conceivably might run afoul of the law. Appropriate state or federal officials must be vigilant in detecting and punishing violations in accordance with other relevant laws of the jurisdiction.

1045 Cf. ACA Standard 2-4070 ("The institution makes available to all employees a written code of ethics that prohibits employees from using their official position to secure privileges for themselves or others and from engaging in activities that constitute a conflict of interest.").

C. Summary of Model Statutory Provisions

Section 1: Enabling Legislation

The contracting agency may contract with private entities for the construction, lease, acquisition, improvement, operation, and management of correctional facilities and services only as provided in this Act.

No contract shall be entered or renewed unless it offers substantial cost savings to the contracting agency and at least the same quality of services as that offered by the contracting agency.

The intended beneficiaries of any contract entered pursuant to this Act shall include inmates incarcerated at the affected facility or facilities and members of the public.

Section 2: Site Selection

Before the contracting agency may award a contract for the private construction and/or operation of a correctional or detention facility, the agency must approve the site for the proposed facility. Approval shall be based on the following:

(A) criteria formulated by the contracting agency, including:

(1) availability of qualified personnel within the local labor market;

(2) total usable and developable acreage of various sites considering the use and purpose of the facility;

(3) accessibility of each site to existing utility, transportation, educational, law enforcement, health care, social, fire protection, refuse collection, water, and sewage disposal services;

(4) susceptibility of each site to natural and man-made environmental hazards;

(5) patterns of residential growth and projected population growth;

(6) community opinion as determined at a public hearing or hearings of record; and

(7) any other criteria that the contracting agency, in conjunction with local governments, deems appropriate; and

(B) a report prepared by the governing body of the jurisdiction in which the proposed site is located, stating whether the site is in compliance with local-government comprehensive plans, land-use ordinances, zoning ordinances or regulations, and other local ordinances that are in effect at the time the report is submitted.

After the contracting agency has approved a site, the agency must then seek approval from the legislature, which shall consider all of the information that was reviewed by the contracting agency, as well as any other criteria that it deems appropriate. Construction and/or operation of a private facility may not commence until the legislature has approved the selected site.

Section 3: Contract Term and Renewal

The initial contract for the operation of a facility or for incarceration of prisoners or inmates therein shall be for a period of not more than three (3) years with an option to renew for an additional period of two (2) years. Contracts for construction, purchase, or lease of a facility shall not exceed a term of fifteen (15) years. Any contract for the construction or operation of a facility shall be subject to annual appropriation by the [appropriate legislative body].

Section 4: Standards of Operation

All facilities that are governed by this Act shall be designed, constructed, and at all times maintained and operated in accordance with the

American Correctional Association Standards in force
at the time of contracting, as well as with
subsequent ACA Standards to the extent that they are
approved by the contracting agency. The facility
shall meet the percentage of Standards required for
accreditation by the American Correctional
Association, except where the contract requires
compliance with a higher percentage of nonmandatory
standards. The contract may allow the contractor an
extension of time in which to meet a lower
percentage of nonmandatory Standards only when the
contract is for the renovation of an existing
facility, in which case the contractor shall have
not longer than three (3) months to meet those
Standards that are applicable to the physical plant.

In addition, all facilities shall at all times
comply with all federal and state constitutional
standards, federal, state, and local laws, and all
court orders.

Section 5: Use of Force

(A) A private contractor's employees serving
as "jailers" shall be allowed to use force only
while on the grounds of a facility, while
transporting inmates, and while pursuing escapees
from a facility.

(B) "Non-deadly force," which is force that
normally would cause neither death nor serious
bodily injury, and "deadly force," which is force
that is likely to cause death or serious bodily
injury, shall be used only as set forth herein.

(C) Non-Deadly Force. A private-company
jailer shall be authorized to use only such non-
deadly force as the circumstances require in the
following situations: to prevent the commission of
a felony or misdemeanor, including escape; to defend
oneself or others against physical assault; to
prevent serious damage to property; to enforce
institutional regulations and orders; and to prevent
or quell a riot.

(D) Use of Firearms/Deadly Force. Private-
company jailers who have been appropriately
certified as determined by the contracting agency
and trained pursuant to the provisions of Subsection
(E) shall have the right to carry and use firearms

and shall exercise such authority and use deadly force only as a last resort, and then only to prevent an act that could result in death or serious bodily injury to oneself or to another person.

(F)   Private-company jailers shall be trained in the use of force and the use of firearms, in accordance with ACA Standards 2-4186 through 2-4189 and 2-4206, and shall be trained, at the contractor's expense, at the facilities that train public prison and jail personnel for at least the minimum number of hours that public personnel are currently trained.

(G)   Within three (3) days following an incident involving the use of force against an inmate or another, the employee shall file a written report with the administrative staff and contract monitor describing the incident.

(H)   A private contractor shall stand in the shoes of the contracting agency in any agreement, formal or informal, with local law-enforcement agencies concerning the latter's obligations in the event of an emergency situations, such as a riots or escapes.

Section 6:   Employee Training Requirements

All employees of a facility operated pursuant to this Act must receive, at a minimum, the same quality and quantity of training as that required by federal, state, and/or local statutes, rules, and regulations for employees of public correctional and detention facilities. If any or all of the applicable American Correctional Association Standards relating to training are more stringent than are governmental standards, training shall be provided in accordance with the more stringent Standard(s). All training expenses shall be the responsibility of the contractor.

Section 7: Monitoring

An individual who is responsible for monitoring
all aspects of the private contractor's performance
under the contract shall be appointed and employed
by the contracting agency. The monitor shall
appoint a staff to assist in monitoring at the
facility, as the monitor determines to be
necessary. The monitor shall be provided an on-site
work area, shall be on-site on a daily basis, and
shall have access to all areas of the facility and
to inmates and staff at all times. The contractor
shall provide any and all data, reports, and other
materials that the monitor determines are necessary
to carry out monitoring responsibilities under this
Section.

The monitor or his designee shall report to the
[_____] committee of the legislature at least
annually on the contractor's performance.

Members of the public shall have the same right
of access to private facilities as they do to public
facilities.

Section 8: Liability and Sovereign Immunity

(A) The contractor shall assume all liability
arising under the contract.

(B) The sovereign immunity of the contracting
agency shall not extend to the contractor. Neither
the contractor nor the insurer of the contractor may
plead the defense of sovereign immunity in any
action arising out of the performance of the
contract.

Section 9: Insurance

The contractor shall provide an adequate plan
of insurance, specifically including insurance for
civil-rights claims, as determined by an independent
risk-management or actuarial firm with demonstrated
experience in public liability for [state/county]

governments. In determining the adequacy of the plan, the firm shall determine whether:

(A) the insurance is adequate to protect the contracting agency from actions by a third party against the contractor or contracting agency as a result of the contract;

(B) the insurance is adequate to assure the contractor's ability to fulfill its contract with the contracting agency in all respects and to assure that the contractor is not limited in this ability due to financial liability that results from judgments;

(C) the insurance is adequate to protect the contracting agency against claims arising as a result of any occurrence during the term of the contract on an occurrence basis; and

(D) the insurance is adequate to satisfy other requirements specified by the independent risk-management or actuarial firm.

Insurance accepted under this statute may not be provided by the contractor.

Section 10: Termination of Contract and Resumption of Government Control

The contracting agency may cancel the contract without cause at any time after the first year of operation, without penalty to the contracting agency, on giving ninety (90) days' written notice.

Notwithstanding any other provision in this Act to the contrary, prior to entering a contract for the private operation of a prison or jail, a plan shall be developed by the contracting agency and certified by the [Governor or appropriate executive officer or legislative body] demonstrating the method by which the government will resume control of the facility upon contract termination.

Section 11: Nondelegability of Contracting Agency's Authority

No contract for private correctional or detention services shall authorize, allow, or imply a delegation of the authority or responsibility of the contracting agency to a prison or jail contractor to:

(A) classify inmates or place inmates in less restrictive custody or more restrictive custody;

(B) transfer an inmate, although the contractor may recommend in writing that the contracting agency transfer a particular inmate;

(C) formulate rules of inmate behavior, violations of which may subject inmates to sanctions, except to the extent that they are accepted or modified by the contracting agency;

(D) take any disciplinary action;

(E) grant, deny, or revoke sentence credits;

(F) recommend that the parole board either deny or grant parole, although the contractor may submit written reports that have been prepared in the ordinary course of business;

(G) develop and implement procedures for calculating sentence credits or inmate-release and parole-eligibility dates;

(H) require an inmate to work, except on contracting-agency projects; approve the type of work that inmates may perform; or award or withhold wages or sentence credits based on the manner in which individual inmates perform such work; or

(I) determine inmate eligibility for furlough and work release.

Section 12: Conflict of Interest

(A) The following individuals shall not solicit or accept, directly or indirectly, any personal benefit or promise of a benefit from a private correctional or detention company negotiating, doing business with, or planning (within the individual's knowledge) to negotiate or do business with the contracting agency:

(1) a member of, or any other person or entity under contract with, any governmental body that exercises any functions or responsibilities in the review or approval of the undertaking or carrying out of the project, including but not limited to any employee of the contracting agency, any person serving as the monitor of a private corrections or detention facility, and any person on the staff of such a monitor; and

(2) a member of the immediate family of any of the above-named individuals.

None of the above-named individuals shall use his or her position, influence, or information concerning such negotiations, business, or plans to benefit himself, herself, or another.

(B) A private prison or jail contractor shall agree that, at the time of contracting, it has no interest and shall not acquire any interest, direct or indirect, that would conflict in any manner or degree with the performance of its services. The contractor shall further covenant that, in the performance of the contract, it shall not employ any person having any such known interests.

(C) Any violation of this Section shall be governed by Section [___] of this Code.

V. CONCLUSION

The problems that face our nation's prisons and jails will not be resolved in the foreseeable future. One idea that has been suggested, at least as a partial solution, is privatization. If a jurisdiction that is endeavoring to manage the incarceration crisis finds privatization of one or more facilities to be attractive, it will then unavoidably confront some extremely difficult choices.

On the one hand stand the risks of private incarceration, including: voter alienation; improper and inadequate inmate care; a failed experiment costing many millions of dollars and depleting the government's expertise and work force; creation of additional liability; and a symbol that, as a matter of principle, may be imprudent to embrace. On the other hand stand the perceived benefits of privatization: better care at reduced cost. Because these benefits are as yet only promised and, in the adult secure-confinement context, unfulfilled, a government that is considering prison or jail privatization should do so only with utmost caution. It is toward that end that this paper has been written.

The constitutional, contractual, and statutory analyses contained in this paper are designed to assist jurisdictions in their evaluation of the critical legal issues of private incarceration, so that they may anticipate and avoid later problems to the greatest extent possible. One aim of the Model Contract and Model Statute is to emphasize that, before financial benefits to the private-incarceration industry are considered, the rights, interests, and concerns of the public, the government, and the inmates must be addressed satisfactorily.

One must realize that, although this paper is comprehensive, it is not complete, for the extent of adoption of the relevant documents will necessarily vary from one jurisdiction to another. Further, in such a new area as this, issues and ideas will need to be developed and explored further. Thus, although there may be agreement that something _must_ be done about the sordid state of our nation's prisons and jails, the urgency of the need should not interfere with the circumspection that must accompany a decision to delegate to private companies one of government's most basic responsibilities: controlling the lives and living conditions of those whose freedom has been taken in the name of the government and the people.

Perhaps the privatization experiment will fail. If so, at least the recent privatization debate will have provided an incentive and, perhaps, an example for the government to perform its incarceration function better. Alternatively, perhaps the experiment will succeed. If it is to do so, however, the debate must be an ongoing one, with all of the interested parties at all times recognizing the need for the government's continual involvement, the need to consider alternatives to incarceration, the need to consider incarceration in its broader criminal-justice context, and the admonition that privatization will not relieve the government of its obligations or the private provider of its corresponding responsibilities.

It bears repeating that privatization of prisons and jails
may be neither constitutional nor wise. If the concept is going
to be implemented, however, it is clear that, to have any chance
of succeeding in the long run, it must be accomplished with total
accountability. With incarceration, as with all areas of the
justice system, we must remain eternally vigilant.

VI. SELECTED BIBLIOGRAPHY

ABC News, "Nightline." "Who Should Run Our Prisons?" Transcript
    from ABC News, Nightline, July 11, 1986, show #1340.

Abolitionist 23. "Private Prisons -- By Appointment to H.M. The
    Queen: Purveyors of Incarceration, Solitary Confinement and
    Body Belts." London: 1987.

ACJS Today. "Corporation Plans Security Facility." (September
    1983): 14.

Adami, Kenneth. "Pros, Cons of Private Prisons." Pennsylvania
    Law Journal-Reporter (April 1, 1985): 2.

Adamson, Christopher. "The Breakdown of Canadian Prison
    Administration: Evidence from Three Commissions of
    Inquiry." Canadian Journal of Criminology 25 (October
    1983): 433-46.

Adkins, Lynn. "If the Taxpayers Won't Build New Prisons,
    Business Will Fill the Gap." Dun's Business Month (June
    1984): 66.

Advisory Commission on Intergovernmental Relations. Jails:
    Intergovernmental Dimensions of a Local Problem.
    Washington, D.C.: 1984.

Ahern, Don. "Private Bids Sought for Ramsey Jail." St. Paul
    Pioneer Press/Dispatch (June 26, 1984): 1A.

Aigtoro, Adjure A. "Privatization: An Inappropriate Response to
    Prison and Jail Overcrowding." Monograph presented at
    Criminal Justice Braintrust, Congressional Black Caucus
    Legislative Weekend, September 27, 1985.

Albuquerque Journal. "Counties Call on Anaya to Introduce
    Private-Jail Legislation." (January 14, 1984): 2B.

Alexander, Laurence E., ed. Privatization Strategies and Tactics
    in Privatization and Contracting Out. New York: Alexander
    Research and Communications, 1987.

Allen, Francis A. The Borderland of Criminal Justice. Chicago:
    University of Chicago Press, 1964.

American Bar Association. Private Prisons. Washington, D.C.:
    1984.

American Bar Association. The Model Procurement Code for State
    and Local Governments: Recommended Regulations.
    Washington, D.C.: 1986.

American Bar Association. Section of Criminal Justice. Report to the House of Delegates, December 10, 1985. (Amended then Approved as ABA Policy by the ABA House of Delegates, February 1986).

American Bar Association. "Privatization Project Launched." ABA Journal (February 1, 1987): 124.

American Civil Liberties Union of Southern California. "Board Debates Cal Fed Case, Votes Down Private Management of Prisons." Open Forum (April 1986).

American Correctional Association. Standards for Adult Correctional Institutions. College Park, Md: 1981.

American Correctional Association. National Correctional Policy on Private Sector Involvement in Corrections Policy Statement. College Park, Md: 1985.

American Correctional Association. Standards for Adult Local Detention Facilities. 2d ed. 1981. Reprint, College Park, Md: 1985.

American Correctional Association. Correctional Standards Supplement. College Park, Md: 1986.

American Correctional Association. Public Policy for Corrections. College Park, Md: 1986.

American Federation of State, County and Municipal Employees, AFL-CIO. Passing the Buck: The Contracting Out of Private Services. Washington, D.C.: 1983.

American Federation of State, County and Municipal Employees. "Prisons for Profit?: Fighting the Rush to Contracting Out." Public Employee 50 (December 1985): 11-15.

American Federation of State, County and Municipal Employees, AFL-CIO. Does Crime Pay? An Examination of Prisons for Profit. Washington, D.C.: 1985.

American Federation of State, County and Municipal Employees. Policy Position on the Privatization of Correctional Facilities. Washington, D.C.: 1985.

American Federation of State, County and Municipal Employees. Position on Contracting Out Correctional Facilities. Washington, D.C.: 1985.

American Friends Service Committee. Struggle for Justice. New York: Hill & Wang, 1971.

American Legislative Exchange Council. "Privatizing the Public

Sector: An Initiative for Service and Savings." The State
    Factor (January 1986): 1.

Anders, Marjorie. "Jails for Profit: Penology's New Wave."
    Trenton Times (August 4, 1985).

Anders, Marjorie. "Profiting from Prisons." The State
    (Columbia, South Carolina) (August 11, 1985): 1B.

Anderson, Curt. "Local Officials on Houston Jail Tour." Daily
    News Journal (Rutherford County, Tennessee) (April 24,
    1984): 1.

Anderson, Curt. "Officials Pleased at Jail in Houston." Daily
    News Journal (Rutherford County, Tennessee) (April 25,
    1984).

Anderson, Curt. "New Jail Proposal on Hold." Daily News Journal
    (Rutherford County, Tennessee) (May 15, 1984): 1.

Anderson, John Ward, and Nancy Lewis. "Pennsylvania Bars D.C.
    Inmates. D.C. Judge Blocks Use of NE Facility for at Least
    a Week." Washington Post (March 15, 1986): A1.

Anderson, John Ward, and Nancy Lewis. "D.C. Inmates Permitted in
    Pa. Prison Tuesday. Ruling May Bring Reprieve in Jail
    Crisis." Washington Post (March 16, 1986): B1.

Anderson, Patrick, Charles R. Davoli, and Laura Moriochy.
    "Private Corrections: Feast or Fiasco?" Prison Journal 65
    (Autumn-Winter 1985): 32-41.

Angrist, Stanley W. "Justice at a Price." Forbes (March 12,
    1984): 190-91.

Appleton, Charles. "Operating Private Prisons." Venture (August
    1983).

Aranson, Peter, Ernest Gellhorn, and Glen O. Robinson. "A Theory
    of Legislative Delegation." Cornell Law Review 68 (1982):
    1-67.

Armington, R.Q., and William D. Ellis, eds. This Way Up: The
    Local Officials Handbook for Privatization and Contracting
    Out. Chicago: Regency Gateway, 1984.

Ashby, Alan. "Congress May Halt State Plan to Fund Prisons
    Privately." Los Angeles Daily Journal (February 6, 1984):
    1.

Ashford, Philip. "Private Prisons Opposed." Memphis Commercial
    Appeal (February 25, 1986): B1.

Atlanta Constitution. "Prisons-for-Profit: A Siren Song."

(September 16, 1985): 12-A.

Augustus. "Prison Privatization Past and Present: How Privatization Failed at San Quentin." (March 1987): 21.

Babington, Charles. "Privately Run Prisons Raise Thorny Issues of Profit, Propriety." Raleigh News and Observer (August 25, 1985): 1.

Bacas, Harvey. "When Prisons and Profits Go Together." Nation's Business (October 1984): 62-63.

Baker, Bill. "For-Profit Companies Could Save State Money, According to Report." Greenville News (August 20, 1985).

Ballantyne, Aileen. "MPs Say Private US Gaols Show Way for Britain." Guardian (October 28, 1986): 5.

Ballantyne, Aileen. "US Private Gaols 'Shock' UK Officers." Guardian (February 12, 1987): 6.

Barber, Ben. "Inmates Shipped Out After Riot." USA Today (May 30, 1986): 3A.

Barbieri, L., and S. Haller. "Examination of a Shared Public/Private Sector Responsibility for Community Corrections Policy and Programs in the State of Connecticut." Proceedings of the One Hundred and Ninth Annual Congress of Corrections, 101-116, Washington, D.C.: American Correctional Association, 1980.

Barker, Mayerene. "Supervisors OK Prison Operated by Private Firm." Los Angeles Times (May 7, 1986): CC II.

Barnes, John. "The Failure of Privatization." National Review (July 18, 1986): 38.

Barron, James. "New York Prisons Find New Work for Inmates." New York Times (February 8, 1988): B3.

Barry, Rick. "Corporate-Run Jail is Locking Out Doubts." Tampa Tribune (March 12, 1987): 1A.

Bartlett, Kay. "They Call It the Holiday Inn of Jails." The State (Columbia, South Carolina) (August 1, 1985).

Bass, Stephanie. "Community Punishment." Raleigh News and Observer (December 4, 1985): 16A.

Bast, Diane Carol. "In Defense of Private Prisons." A Heartland Perspective. Chicago: The Heartland Institute, (March 4, 1986).

Baton Rouge Morning Advocate. "The Coming Trend Toward

Privatizing Public Sector." (August 24, 1984).

Battle, Bob. "Nashville Firm to Run Alabama Prison Center." _Nashville Banner_ (August 8, 1986).

Bazelon, David. "The Accreditation Debate: Two Views." _Corrections Magazine_ 8 (December 1982): 20.

Beach, Bennett. "Doing Business Behind Bars." _Time_ (September 1, 1980): 62.

Bean, Ed. "Private Jail in Bay County, Fla., Makes Inroads for Corrections Firms, But the Jury is Still Out." _Wall Street Journal_ (August 29, 1986): 38.

Bear, Stearns and Voinovich Companies. _Turnkey Services for Criminal Justice Facilities_. Boston: Bear, Stearns and Voinovich Companies, 1983.

Beasley, Thomas W. "Give Private Enterprise a Chance." _USA Today_ (November 18, 1985): 10A.

Beasley, Thomas W. "CCA Chief Responds to Newspaper Series." _Tennessean_ (May 29, 1988): 1D.

Becker, Craig. "With Whose Hands: Privatization, Public Employment, and Democracy." _Yale Law & Policy Review_ 6 (1988): 88-108.

Becker, Craig, and Amy Dru Stanley. "Incarceration Inc.: The Downside of Private Prisons." _The Nation_ (June 15, 1985): 728-30.

Becker, Gary S. "Why Public Enterprises Belong in Private Hands." _Business Week_ (February 24, 1986): 20.

Behar, Richard. "Partners in Crime." _Forbes_ (February 11, 1985): 112-18.

Benenson, Robert. "Privatizing Public Services." _Editorial Research Reports_ 2 (July 26, 1985): 559-76.

Bennett, James T., and Manuel H. Johnson. _Better Government at Half the Price: Private Production of Public Services_. Ottawa, Ill.: Caroline House Publishers, 1981.

Bennett, James T., and Thomas J. DiLorenzo. "Public Employee Unions and the Privatization of 'Public' Services." _Journal of Labor Research_ 4 (Winter 1983): 33-45.

Berger, Joseph. "D'Amato Calling for Private Ownership of Prisons." _New York Times_ (August 9, 1984): 3.

Bergman, Carol. "Our Prison System is a Failure." _USA Today_

(November 18, 1985): 10A.

Bernstein, Dennis, and Connie Blitt. "Central American Refugees for Profit." In These Times (March 19-25, 1986).

Bernstein, Paul. "El Derecho y El Hecho: Law and Reality in the Mexican Criminal Justice System." Chicano Law Review 8 (1985): 40-60.

Bernstein, Peter W., et al. "Will Uncle Sam Go Private?" Fortune (January 9, 1984): 33-34.

Betts, Paul. "France Aims to Build 60 Private Prisons." Financial Times (October 28, 1986): 3.

Bilek, Arthur J., John C. Klotter, and R. Keegan Federal. Legal Aspects of Private Security. Cincinnati: Anderson Publishing Co., 1981.

Biner, Steven D. "An Exciting New Way to Finance Jails: An Alternative to General Obligation Financing." Denver: E.F. Hutton and Company, 1983.

Bivens, Terry. "Can Prisons for Profit Work?" Philadelphia Inquirer Magazine (August 3, 1986): 14.

Blau, Peter M. Exchange and Power in Social Life. New York: John Wiley & Sons, 1967.

Bleiberg, Robert M. "From Public to Private Hands." Barron's (January 20, 1986): 9.

Blitt, Connie. "Profiting from Refugee Loss." In These Times (March 19-25, 1986).

Blumstein, Alfred. "'Free Enterprise Corrections': Using Industry to Make Offenders Economically Viable." Prison Journal 48 (1986): 26-28.

Blumstein, Alfred, Jacqueline Cohen, and William Gooding. "The Influence of Capacity on Prison Population: A Critical Review of Some Recent Evidence." Crime and Delinquency 29 (January 1983): 1-51.

Blustein, Paul. "Panel Urges 'Privatization' of Many Federal Services." Washington Post (March 18, 1988): A9.

Bornhoft, Steve. "Injunction Denied: Group Loses Bid to Stop CCA Takeover of Bay Jail." Panama City News-Herald (September 28, 1985): 1A-2A.

Bortz, Bruce. "Is Maryland Business Looking to 'Get Into Jail?'" Maryland Daily Record (June 17, 1985): 1.

Bosarge, Betty. "Sen. D'Amatc Introduces Bill For Private
      Funding/Leaseback of Jail, Prison Facilities." Corrections
      Digest (September 26, 1984): 7-9.

Bosarge, Betty B. "Privatization Commission Recommends
      Contracting Out U.S., State, Local Corrections: Says
      Liability, Accountability Not 'Insurmountable Obstacles.'"
      Corrections Digest (March 23, 1988): 1.

Bosarge, Betty B. "Prison-for-Profit Concept Has Serious
      Drawbacks, New Study Concludes: What Happens When
      Governments Shut Down Corrections Agencies?" Corrections
      Digest (March 23, 1988): 2.

Bosarge, Betty B. "Michigan Sheriffs Fighting 16 Bills Which
      Would Allow Privatization of Jail/Lockups: Focusing on New
      Potential for Future 'Economic Blackmail.'" Correction
      Digest (April 20, 1988): 1.

Bostick, Alan. "Effort to Halt Private-Run Prison Fails."
      Tennessean (November 22, 1986): 14A.

Boston Globe. "Privately Run Jails Would Not Result in Job Loss,
      Legislative Study Says." (August 17, 1986): 73.

Brakel, Samuel J. "Legal Problems of People in Mental and Penal
      Institutions: An Exploratory Study." ABF Research Journal
      (1978): 565-645.

Brakel, Samuel J. "Special Masters in Institutional
      Litigation." ABF Research Journal (1979): 543-69.

Brakel, Samuel J. "Administrative Justice in the Penitentiary:
      A Report on Inmate Grievance Procedures." ABF Research
      Journal (1982): 111-40.

Brakel, Samuel J. "Ruling on Prisoners' Grievances." ABF
      Research Journal (1983): 393-425.

Brakel, Samuel J. "'Mastering' the Legal Access Rights of Prison
      Inmates." New England Journal on Criminal and Civil
      Confinement 12 (1986): 1-69.

Brakel, Samuel J. "Prison Reform Litigation: Has the Revolution
      Gone Too Far?" Judicature 70 (June-July 1986): 5.

Brakel, Samuel J. "Prison Management, Private Enterprise
      Style: The Inmates' Evaluation." American Bar Foundation:
      1988.

Brakel, Samuel J. "'Privatization' in Corrections: Radical
      Prison Chic or Mainstream Americana?" New England Journal
      on Criminal and Civil Confinement 14 (1988): 1-39.

Brettler-Berenyi, Eileen. "Public and Private Sector Interaction Patterns in the Delivery of Local Public Services." Government Finance 9 (March 1980): 3-9.

Breuer, Daniel D., and Daniel W. Fitzpatrick. "An Experience in Contracting Out for Services." Government Finance 9 (March 1980): 11-13.

Broad, William. "Shuttle Panelist Urges Private Takeover of Fleet." New York Times (July 2, 1986): A14.

Broder, David. "Some Give Great Gifts and Some Seek to Privatize." Akron Beacon Journal (August 17, 1986): D3.

Bronstein, Alvin J. "The Legal Implications of Privatization." National Prison Project Journal (Winter 1984): 1-2.

Brown, Aaron. National Institute of Corrections, Prison Division. Interview with author. July 1984.

Brown, Andrew C. "For Sale: Pieces of the Public Sector." Fortune (October 31, 1983): 78-84.

Brown, George. "Whither Thiboutot? Section 1983, Private Enforcement, and the Damages Dilemma." DePaul Law Review 33 (1983): 31-74.

Brown, Mick. "Sweden's Progressive Prisons." World Press Review (February 1980): 60.

Bruff, Harold H. "Legislative Formality, Administrative Rationality." Texas Law Review 63 (1984): 207-50.

Brunelli, Richard. "Merits of Privately Run Prison Industry Debated." Chicago Daily J. Bulletin (November 19, 1985): 1.

Buchwald, Art. "The Big House, A Great Place to Shelter Taxes." Washington Post (April 7, 1985): H1.

Buckingham Security. Private Prison Management First Year Report, 1985-86. Butler County, Pa.: Buckingham Security, 1986.

Burden, Ordway. "Private Relief for the Public's Prison Problem." Law Enforcement News (July 9, 1984): 9.

Burger, Warren E. Remarks at the Safer Foundation Banquet, Chicago, January 26, 1984.

Burger, Warren E. "Keynote Address. National Conference on 'Factories with Fences': The Prison Industries Approach to Correctional Dilemmas." (June 18, 1984). Reprinted in Prisoners and the Law, ed. Ira P. Robbins. New York: Clark Boardman, 1985.

Burger, Warren E. Remarks at the Osgoode Hall Law School, Toronto, Canada, September 20, 1985.

Burke, Robert K. Financing for Jails. Denver: Colorado Division of Criminal Justice, June 1982.

Bush, Evelyn J. "Privatization May Foster Corruption." The State (Columbia, South Carolina) (November 9, 1985): 16A.

Butler, Stuart M. The Privatization Option: A Strategy to Shrink the Size of Government. Washington, D.C.: Heritage Foundation, 1985.

Butler, Stuart M. Privatizing Federal Spending: A Strategy to Reduce the Deficit. New York: Universe Books, 1985.

Butler, Stuart M. "Why It Pays to Privatize Public Services." New York Times (January 19, 1986): 2 (Business).

Butler, Stuart M. "Privatizing Federal Services: A Primer." Backgrounder. Heritage Foundation: Washington, D.C., February 20, 1986.

California. Department of Corrections. Report to the Legislature: Alternative Financing of California Prisons. Sacramento: January 1, 1984.

California. Legislative Analyst. The Use or Lease or Lease-Purchase Arrangements to Acquire State Prisons. Sacramento: April 1984.

California. Department of Corrections. Financial Management Handbook for Private Return-to-Custody Facilities. July 1985.

Camp, Camille, and George Camp. Private Sector Involvement in Prison Services and Operations. Report to National Institute of Corrections. Washington, D.C.: National Institute of Corrections, 1984.

Camp, Camille, and George Camp. "Correctional Privatization in Perspective." Prison Journal 65 (Autumn-Winter 1985): 14-31.

Camp, George M. "Private Sector Involvement in Prison Services and Operations." In Does Crime Pay? An Examination of Prisons for Profit. Washington, D.C.: American Federation of State, County and Municipal Employees, AFL-CIO, 1985.

Camp, George, and Camille Camp. The Corrections Yearbook: Instant Answers to Key Questions in Correction. Pound Ridge, N.Y.: Criminal Justice Institute, 1982.

Camp, George, and Camille Camp. The Real Cost of Corrections: A Research Report. South Salem, N.Y.: Criminal Justice Institute, 1985.

Camp, George, and Camille Camp. "Stopping Escapes: Perimeter Security." Construction Bulletin. Washington, D.C.: National Institute of Justice, August 1987.

Cannon, Amanda. "Experiences and Issues in Private Sector Management Contracting in Corrections." 1986.

Cannon, Lou. "Reagan Picks Privatization Panelists." Washington Post (September 4, 1987): A23.

Caring. "Privatization: Yea or Nay?" (Winter 1987): 18.

Carlsbad Current Argus. "Jail Proposals Require Study." (August 30, 1983).

Carlsen, Christopher. "Opinion of Paul Bardacke, Attorney General." Santa Fe, N.M.: Department of Justice, November 29, 1983.

Carlson, Norman A. "The Need for Private Involvement in Corrections." American Journal of Corrections 40 (March-April 1978): 30.

Carlson, Norman A. Testimony before the Subcommittee on Courts, Civil Liberties, and the Administration of Justice of the House Judiciary Committee, March 18, 1986.

Carroll, Barry J., Ralph W. Conant, and Thomas A. Easton, eds. Private Means-Public Ends: Private Business in Social Service Delivery. New York: Praeger, 1986.

Carter, Stephen A., and Ann Chadwell Humphries. "Inmates Build Prisons in South Carolina." Construction Bulletin. Washington, D.C.: National Institute of Justice, December 1987.

Casebolt, Barry J. "Commissioners Consider New Jail Proposal." Carlsbad Current Argus (August 4, 1983).

Casebolt, Barry J. "Mayor Suggests Referendum on New Jail." Carlsbad Current Argus (August 31, 1983).

Cason, Albert. "CCA Warns Losses May Continue." Tennessean (September 24, 1986): 5B.

Cason, Albert, and Dwight Lewis. "Corrections Field Firm Formed Here." Tennessean (May 29, 1983): A1, A6.

Castro, Janice. "Public Service, Private Profits." Time (February 10, 1986): 64.

Cazales, Mike, and Art Surber. "Inmates Say They Like CCA's Way of Doing Things." News Herald (June 15, 1986): E1.

CBS News, "60 Minutes." "Crime Pays." Transcript from CBS News, 60 Minutes, June 30, 1985, Volume XVII, Number 42.

Chabotar, Kent John. "Financing Alternatives for Prison and Jail Construction." Government Finance Review 1 (August 1985): 7-13.

Chakin, Jan, and Stephen Meunemeyer. Lease-Purchase Financing of Prison and Jail Construction. Washington, D.C.: National Institute of Justice, August 1986.

Chambers, Marcia. "California's Swift, Costly Private Judicial System." New York Times (February 24, 1986): B7.

Charlotte Observer. "Joint Committee Bars Private Prison Plan." (June 27, 1986): 2D.

Chausseborg, Anne. "In the Senate: Privatization of Prisons: Intermission." Le Monde (December 26, 1986): 5L3.

Chevalier, Fred. "The Privatization of Prisons." Business Report (September 1985).

Chi, Keon S. "Private Contractor Work Release Center: The Illinois Experience." Innovations, The Council of State Governments (July 1982).

Chi, Keon S. "Privatization: A Public Option?" State Government News 28 (June 1985): 4-12.

Chi, Keon S. Alternative Service Delivery and Management Improvement in State Government: A Bibliography. Lexington, Ky.: Council of State Governments, 1987.

Chicago Sun-Times. "Private Jail Bankrupt, Prisoners Bused Out." (March 19, 1986): 7.

Cikins, Warren I. "Privatization of the American Prison System: An Idea Whose Time Has Come?" Notre Dame Journal of Law, Ethics & Public Policy 2 (1986): 445-64.

Citizens Commission on Alternatives to Incarceration. Citizens Commission on Alternatives to Incarceration Report. Durham, N.C.: 1982.

Ciuros, William, Jr. "Privatization." CAYSA Journal (August 11, 1985).

Clear, Todd R., Patricia M. Harris, and Albert L. Record. "Managing the Cost of Corrections." Prison Journal (Spring-

Summer 1982).

Clendinen, Dudley. "Officials of Counties Debate Private Jail
    Operation." New York Times (November 19, 1985): A27.

Clendinen, Dudley. "Crowded Prisons in South Lead to Tests of
    Other Punishments." New York Times (December 18, 1985):
    A18.

Clifford, Mark. "Free Enterprise: The Jail Builders."
    Financial World (May 30-June 12, 1984): 20.

Clovis News Journal. "Joint Jail Facility Eyed." (November 14,
    1983).

Coalition for a Moratorium on Private Prisons. Memorandum.
    Philadelphia: Pennsylvania Prison Society, September 25,
    1985.

Coalition for a Moratorium on Private Prisons. Privatization of
    Correctional Facilities. Philadelphia: Pennsylvania Prison
    Society, 1985.

Coalition for Prisoners' Rights. "Jails for Profit Hurt Us
    All." Coalition for Prisoners' Rights Newsletter (March
    1984): 8.

Coalition for Prisoners' Rights. "Private Jails Too
    Expensive." Coalition for Prisoners' Rights Newsletter
    (October 1985): 1-2.

Coase, R.H. "The Regulated Industries-Discussion." American
    Economic Review 54 (1964): 194.

Codden, Eve, and David Sherman. "Private Prisons: Legal Issues
    and Concerns." Paper prepared at San Diego School of Law,
    July 1984.

Cody, W.J. Michael, and Andy D. Bennett. "The Privatization of
    Correctional Institutions: The Tennessee Experience."
    Vanderbilt Law Review 40 (1987): 829-49.

Cole, L. "Tax-Exempt Leasing: A Financing Option." Current
    Municipal Problems 12 (1985): 439-43.

Coleman, Michelle. "Corrections and the Private Sector: Fad or
    Future?" MoCAI: Newsletter of the Missouri Coalition for
    Alternatives to Imprisonment 14 (January 1986): 6-7.

Collins, William C. "Contracting for Correctional Services:
    Some Legal Considerations." Washington, D.C.: National
    Institute of Corrections, 1985.

Colorado. Colorado General Assembly, Legislative Council.

Privately-Operated Prisons: Legal Issues -- Report to the Members of the Colorado General Assembly, January 1987.

Comment. "State Action After Jackson v. Metropolitan Edison Co.: Analytical Framework for a Restrictive Doctrine." Dickinson Law Review 81 (1977): 315-46.

Comment. "The Fourth Branch: Reviving the Nondelegation Doctrine." Brigham Young University Law Review (1984): 619-45.

Comment. "Excessive Force Claims: Removing the Double Standard." University of Chicago Law Review 53 (1986): 1369-98.

Comment. "Prison Industries: A Case for Partial Privatization." Notre Dame Journal of Law, Ethics & Public Policy 2 (1986): 479-501.

Comment. "Prisons for Profit." Hamline Journal of Public Law and Policy 7 (1986): 123-41.

Comment. "Private Prisons." Emory Law Journal 36 (1987): 253-83.

Commonwealth of Kentucky. History of Corrections in Kentucky. Commonwealth of Kentucky, Corrections Cabinet, Office of Corrections Training, 1987.

Commonwealth of Massachusetts. Legislative Research Council. Legislative Research Bureau. Report Relative to Prisons for Profit, 1986.

Commonwealth of Pennsylvania. Pennsylvania General Assembly. Legislative Budget and Finance Committee. Report on a Study of Issues Related to the Potential Operation of Private Prisons in Pennsylvania, October 1985.

Commonwealth of Pennsylvania. General Assembly. Joint State Government Commission. Report of the Private Prison Task Force, March 1987.

Congressional Record. Statement of Senator D'Amato introducing §2903, the "Prison Construction Privatization Act of 1984." August 2, 1984: §9682.

Contracting State Government Functions Policy Research Project. Contracting Selected State Government Functions: Issues and Next Steps. Policy Research Project Report No. 75. University of Texas, 1986.

Copulos, Milton R. "Cutting the Deficit By Selling Federal Power Marketing Administrations." Backgrounder. Heritage Foundation: Washington, D.C., February 13, 1986.

Corrections Compendium. "Privatization Falls Flat in South Carolina." (July 1986): 15.

Corrections Compendium. "1986 Jail Survey Finds Crowding, Litigation." (November 1986): 7.

Corrections Corporation of America. 1985 Executive Report.

Corrections Corporation of America. Corporate Profile.

Corrections Corporation of America. "Adult Corrections Plan for the State of Tennessee." Nashville, November 1985.

Corrections Development Corporation. "Proposal To the State of South Carolina to Construct and Operate Correctional Institutions for Non-Violent Inmates Who are Now Serving or will be Sentenced from 90 Day to 2 Year Terms." Columbia, S.C.: 1986.

Corrections Digest. "Legal Issues Arise in Private Operation of Jails." (January 2, 1985): 9.

Corrections Digest. "Privatization of Corrections Conference Hosted by National Institute of Justice." (February 27, 1985): 1.

Corrections Digest. "National Sheriff's Association Opposes Privatization of Jails, Detention Facilities." (April 10, 1985): 2.

Corrections Digest. "Private Corporation Seeking 99-year Contract to Run Entire Tennessee State Prison System." (September 25, 1985): 5-7.

Corrections Digest. "Prison Construction in 1986 Costing over $3 Billion." (July 2, 1986): 5.

Corrections Digest. "Prisons For Profit: Is This a Viable Concept For Adult Correctional Systems?" (October 9, 1985): 1.

Corrections Digest. "Congress Studies Privatization: FBOP Director and Employers' President Present Their Views." (March 26, 1986): 1.

Corrections Digest. "Pennsylvania Bars D.C. Inmates From Private Prison; Governor Signs Law Curbing Privatization." (March 26, 1986): 5.

Corrections Digest. "Prison Construction in 1986 Costing over $3 Billion." (July 2, 1986): 5.

Corrections Digest. "Corrections Corp. Selling Stock." (October

8, 1986): 6.

Corrections Digest. "Privately Owned Juvenile Corrections
    Facility to Provide Sex Offender Therapy." (March 18,
    1987): 2.

Corrections Digest. "Texas Governor Backs Study of Contracts for
    Private Prisons." (April 29, 1987): 6.

Corrections Digest. "Private Prisons for Adults Becoming a
    Reality, NIJ Says." (May 13, 1987): 7.

Corrections Digest. "Supreme Court To Hear Case Involving Prison
    Doctors." (October 28, 1987): 10.

Corrections Digest. "Deportee Sues Private Jail." (November 11,
    1987): 4.

Corrections Digest. "Privatization Commission Calls for Greater
    Use of Private Contractors for Prisons." (January 13,
    1988): 9.

Cory, Bruce. "From Rhetoric to Reality: Privatization Put to the
    Test." Corrections Compendium 10 (May 1986): 1.

Cory, Bruce, and Stephen Gettinger. Time to Build? The
    Realities of Prison Construction. New York: Edna McConnell
    Clark Foundation, 1984.

Coughlin, Thomas. "The New York Experience." In Does Crime
    Pay? An Examination of Prisons for Profit. Washington,
    D.C.: American Federation of State, County and Municipal
    Employees, AFL-CIO, 1985.

Council of State Governments and the Urban Institute. Issues in
    Contracting for the Private Operation of Prisons and
    Jails. Washington, D.C.: National Institute of Justice,
    1987.

Cox, Gail D. "Firms Ask L.A. County to Send Some Jail Business
    Their Way." Los Angeles Daily Journal (January 30, 1986):
    B1.

Cox, Gail D. "The Best Judges Money Can Buy." National Law
    Journal (December 21, 1987): 1.

Crane, Richard. Testimony on Privatization of Corrections before
    House Subcommittee on Courts, Civil Liberties, and the
    Administration of Justice of the House Judiciary Committee,
    November 6, 1985.

Crane, Richard. "Should Prisons Be Privately Run?: A Business
    Like Any Other." ABA Journal (April 1, 1987): 39.

Crime Control Digest. "National Sheriff's Association Opposes
    Privatization of Jails, Detention Facilities." (April 1,
    1985): 1.

Criminal Justice Associates. Research Report -- Private Sector
    Involvement in Prison-Based Businesses: A National
    Assessment. Washington, D.C.: National Institute of
    Justice, 1986.

Criminal Justice Newsletter. "Private Business Plans to Run
    Prisons." (June 20, 1983): 3.

Criminal Justice Newsletter. "Controversial ACA Policy Calls for
    Further Privatization." (February 1, 1985): 1-3.

Criminal Justice Newsletter. "Privatization a Hot Topic:
    Governors Endorse the Concept." (March 15, 1985): 5.

Criminal Justice Newsletter. "Private Company Makes Bid on
    Entire Tennessee Prison System." (October 1, 1985): 3.

Criminal Justice Newsletter. "Privatization Does Not Ease
    State's Liability, Panel Told." (December 2, 1985): 3.

Criminal Justice Newsletter. "Pennsylvania Legislature Moves to
    Slow Privatization." (January 2, 1986): 3.

Criminal Justice Newsletter. "Overcrowding Crisis Forcing
    Extreme Measures in D.C." (April 1, 1986): 3.

Criminal Justice Newsletter. "Federal Prisons Director Appears
    Cool to Privatization." (April 15, 1986): 5.

Criminal Justice Newsletter. "California's First Privately
    Operated Prison Established." (June 16, 1986): 6.

Criminal Justice Newsletter. "ABA Launches Study of Prison
    Privatization." (January 2, 1987): 4.

Criminal Justice Newsletter. "Privatization Saves Time, Not
    Necessarily Money, Study Finds." (June 1, 1987): 6.

Criminal Justice Newsletter. "Presidential Commission Urges
    Privatization of Corrections." (January 18, 1988): 4.

Criminal Justice Newletter. "Bureau of Prisons Announces
    Privatization Campaign." (March 1, 1988): 3-4.

Criminal Justice Report. "Corrections and Institutional
    Confinement Seminar." (May 1985): 1.

Criminal Law Reporter. "Use of Private Prosecutors Involved in
    Civil Case Upheld." (December 11, 1985): 2209.

<u>Criminal Law Reporter</u>. "Anti-Drug Abuse Act of 1986, Public Law
    99-570 -- Selected Section -- Study on the Use of Existing
    Federal Buildings as Prisons." (November 19, 1986): 3119.

Cromer, Ed. "McCullough Set to Enter Prison Field: Refuses to
    Comment About Joining Firm." <u>Tennessean</u> (August 2, 1985):
    A1.

Cromer, Ed. "CCA Tells Prison Plan: No Tax Increase in 'Best
    Ever Written.'" <u>Tennessean</u> (November 12, 1985): A1.

Cromer, Ed. "Lobbyists Fail to File Disclosures." <u>Tennessean</u>
    (December 10, 1985): 1B.

Cromer, Ed. "Bill to Let Private Firm Run Prisons All But
    Dead." <u>Tennessean</u> (March 12, 1986): 1A.

Cromer, Ed. "Democrats Oppose Bill's New Life: Vote to Keep
    Private Prison Move Tabled." <u>Tennessean</u> (March 13, 1986):
    B5.

Cromer, Ed. "Privately-Run Prison Bill Revived." <u>Tennessean</u>
    (April 2, 1986): 1A.

Cromer, Ed, and Jim O'Hara. "Committee Passes Private Prison
    Bill." <u>Tennessean</u> (April 9, 1986):1A.

Cullen, Francis T. "The Privatization of Treatment: Prison
    Reform in the 1980's." <u>Federal Probation</u> 50 (March 1986):
    8-16.

Cunniff, Mark A. "Justice for Profit." <u>News Update</u>.
    Washington, D.C.: National Association of Criminal Justice
    Planners, August 1, 1984.

Cunniff, Mark A. "Breaking Up Government's Monopoly on Prison
    Cells." <u>New York Times</u> (March 3, 1985): 22E.

Cunniff, Mark A. "Privatization of Corrections." In <u>Does Crime
    Pay? An Examination of Prisons for Profit</u>. Washington,
    D.C.: American Federation of State, County and Municipal
    Employees, AFL-CIO, 1985.

Cunningham, William C., and Todd H. Taylor. "The Growing Role of
    Private Security." <u>Research in Brief</u>. Washington, D.C.:
    National Institute of Justice, October 1984.

Cusick, Frederick. "House Passes Moratorium on Private Prisons
    in Pa." <u>Philadelphia Inquirer</u> (April 17, 1985): 1B.

<u>Daily Record</u>. (Rochester, NY) "New ABA Project: Private
    Prisons?" (December 23, 1986): 4.

D'Amato, Anthony. "Surrogate Motherhood Should Be Privatized."

New York Times (March 2, 1987): A2.

Daniel, Leon. "Do Profits Have Place in the Justice System?" _Trenton Times_ (May 19, 1985): B1.

Davis, Deborah. "2 'Model' Prisons Cast Doubt on CCA Claims." _Tennessean_ (May 15, 1988): 1D.

Davis, Deborah. "5-Year-Old CCA Has Yet to Make a Profit." _Tennessean_ (May 15, 1988): 5D.

Davis, Deborah. "CCA Falls Short on Accreditation, Insurance Vows." _Tennessean_ (May 16, 1988): 4E.

Davis, R.A. "Work In Prison." _Prison Journal_ 62 (Autumn-Winter, 1982).

Davis, S.L. _Seduction of the Private Sector - Privatization In Ontario Corrections_. Washington, D.C.: National Institute of Justice, 1980.

Decker, Cathleen. "Firm to Close Besieged Alien Holding Center." _Los Angeles Times_ (November 27, 1986): CC I,II.

DeConcini, Dennis, and Robert Faucher. "The Legislative Veto: A Constitutional Amendment." _Harvard Journal on Legislation_ 21 (1984): 29-59.

Dedman, Bill. "Is Silverdale Penal Farm Ready to Go the Route of Private Ownership?" _Chattanooga Times_ (August 27, 1984): A1.

Dedman, Bill. "Tom Beasley's Firm is Prison Equivalent of a Fast Food Chain." _Chattanooga Times_ (August 28, 1984): A1.

Dedman, Bill. "Attorney's Memos on Workhouse Plan Analyze Contract." _Chattanooga Times_ (August 29, 1984): A1.

Dedman, Bill. "Roberts Says CCA Could Be Cure for Silverdale Headache." _Chattanooga Times_ (August 30, 1984): A1.

Dedman, Bill. "Plan to Lease Silverdale on Hold." _Chattanooga Times_ (August 31, 1984): A1.

Dedman, Bill. "Criminal Justice Experts Raising Questions About Leasing Penal Farm." _Chattanooga Times_ (September 5, 1984): B2.

Dedman, Bill. "Robinson Joins CCA in Talks with Judges." _Chattanooga Times_ (September 7, 1984): B2.

Dedman, Bill. "CCA Locks up Commission Vote for Lease of Silverdale Penal Farm." _Chattanooga Times_ (September 19, 1984): B1.

Dedman, Bill. "County Inmates Now 'Residents' Behind CCA Bars." Chattanooga Times (October 15, 1984): B1.

Dedman, Bill. "CCA Assigns Escape Risks to Road Crews." Chattanooga Times (March 8, 1985): A1.

Dedman, Bill. "Corrections Firm Terminates Plan Putting Escape-Risks on Road Crews." Chattanooga Times (April 6, 1985): A1.

Dedman, Bill. "Despite Private Warden, DUI Arrests Send Silverdale Cost Over the Fence." Chattanooga Times (April 8, 1985): A1.

Dedman, Bill. "CCA Unveils Architect's Renderings for Silverdale." Chattanooga Times (April 12, 1985): B1.

Dedman, Bill. "The Whole World Watches the Silverdale Experiment." Chattanooga Times (June 29, 1985): B1.

Dedman, Bill. "Using Excessive Force Gets Silverdale Guard Suspended for 10 Days." Chattanooga Times (July 18, 1985): B1.

Dedman, Bill. "Prisoner Smuggles Gun Into Silverdale: Goes Undetected for 24 Hours." Chattanooga Times (August 5, 1985): A1.

Dedman, Bill. "Private Management of Silverdale Has Not Worked Out, Commissioner Says." Chattanooga Times (September 30, 1985): A1.

DeGroot, B. Private Re-Entry Work Furlough Facility Component Rate Study. Sacramento: California Youth and Adult Correction Agency, 1982.

DeHoog, Ruth Hoogland. Contracting Out For Human Services: Economic, Political, and Organizational Perspectives. Albany: State University of New York Press, 1984.

Demsetz, Harold. "Why Regulate Utilities?" Journal of Law and Economics 11 (1968): 55-65.

Deseret News. "Triad Studies Possibility of Building, Operating a Jail in Missoula County." (June 20-21, 1985): B7.

DeWitt, Charles B. "Florida Sets Example with use of Concrete Modules." Construction Bulletin. Washington, D.C.: National Institute of Justice, March 1986.

DeWitt, Charles B. "New Construction Methods for Correctional Facilities." Construction Bulletin. Washington, D.C.: National Institute of Justice, March 1986.

DeWitt, Charles B. "California Tests New Construction Concepts." Construction Bulletin. Washington, D.C.: National Institute of Justice, June 1986.

DeWitt, Charles B. "Ohio's New Approach to Prison and Jail Financing." Construction Bulletin. Washington, D.C.: National Institute of Justice, July 1986.

DeWitt, Charles B., and Cindie Unger. "Oklahoma Prison Expansion Saves Time and Money." Construction Bulletin. Washington, D.C.: National Institute of Justice, July 1987.

DeYoung, Karen. "Britain Plans to Privatize Electricity Industry." Washington Post (February 26, 1988): F3.

DiIulio, John J., Jr. Prisons, Profits and the Public Good: The Privatization of Corrections. Paper presented at the 1985 Interagency Workshop, College of Criminal Justice, Sam Houston University, 1986. Reprinted in Research Bulletin, Criminal Justice Center, Sam Houston State University, 1986.

DiIulio, John J., Jr. Governing Prisons: A Comparative Study of Correctional Management. New York: Free Press, 1987.

DiIulio, John J., Jr. "What's Wrong with Private Prisons." Public Interest 92 (Summer 1988): 66-83.

DiIulio, John, Bob Britton, George Beto, and Rolando v. del Carmen. Panel on Privatization: The Corrections Alternative, Twentieth Annual Interagency Workshop, Criminal Justice Center, Sam Houston State University, Huntsville, Texas, May 20, 1985.

DiPaolo, Joseph R. "Private Sector: Breaking the Shackles of Tradition." Corrections Today 48 (April 1986): 144.

Dobbs, James C. "Rebuilding America: Legal Issues Confronting Privatization." Privatization Review 1 (Summer 1985): 28-38.

Dobie, Bruce. "McWherter Leaving Door Open for CCA." Nashville Banner (February 25, 1985): A1.

Dobie, Bruce. "Prison Design Firm Blasts State Corrections Policy." Nashville Banner (May 27, 1985): C2.

Dobie, Bruce. "Alexander Concerned Favoritism Not Mar Proposals on Prisons." Nashville Banner (September 11, 1985).

Dobie, Bruce. "Company to Let Public Purchase Prison Stock." Nashville Banner (September 12, 1985): A1.

Dobie, Bruce. "CCA in Houston Running Smoothly After Rough

Start." <u>Nashville Banner</u> (September 19, 1985): A1.

Dobie, Bruce. "250 Million Offered by CCA for Prisons."
    <u>Nashville Banner</u> (September 22, 1985): 1F.

Dobie, Bruce. "Cody Says State Could Hire Prison Firm."
    <u>Nashville Banner</u> (October 22, 1985).

Dobie, Bruce. "Bill Allowing CCA Contract Filed with
    Lawmakers." <u>Nashville Banner</u> (November 15, 1985): C1.

Dobie, Bruce. "CCA Officials Meet to Discuss Strategy Following
    Defeat." <u>Nashville Banner</u> (March 12, 1986): C14.

Dobie, Bruce, and Patricia Templeton. "Exec Praises Lawmakers
    for Prison Firm Vote." <u>Nashville Banner</u> (April 18, 1986).

Donahue, John D. <u>Prisons for Profit: Public Justice, Private
    Interests</u>. Washington, D.C.: Economic Policy Institute,
    1988.

Drucker, Peter F. <u>Management: Tasks, Responsibilities,
    Practices</u>. New York: Harper & Row, 1973.

Dudek, Donna. "Privatization is Samoa's Answer to U.S. Budget
    Constraints." <u>Wall Street Journal</u> (July 7, 1986): 13.

Duerlinger, Jean. "Private Jail Nearer Reality." <u>Albuquerque
    Journal</u> (May 3, 1985).

Duffy, Susan. "Breaking Into Jail: The Private Sector Starts to
    Build and Run Prisons." <u>Barron's</u> (May 14, 1984): 20-22.

Dugger, Ronnie. "On Capitalist Punishment." <u>Texas Observer</u>
    (September 16, 1985).

Duncan, Jeanine. <u>Report on Corrections and the Private Sector</u>.
    Salt Lake City: Commission on Criminal and Juvenile
    Justice, June 18, 1986.

Durham, Alexis M. III. "Evaluating Privatized Correctional
    Institutions: Obstacles to Effective Assessment." <u>Federal
    Probation</u> 52 (June 1988): 65-71.

Durkeim, Emile. <u>The Division of Labor in Society</u>. New York:
    Free Press, 1933.

Eaton, Leslie. "Jail Financing is Unpopular But Necessary so
    Counties Look for New Financing Methods." <u>Credit Market</u>
    (October 22, 1984): 1.

<u>Economist</u>. "Prisons: No Admittance." (January 11, 1986): 24.

<u>Economist</u>. "Going Private." (March 16, 1985): 40-43.

E.F. Hutton. <u>Innovative Alternatives to Traditional Jail Financing</u>. New York: E.F. Hutton, 1983.

Egler, Daniel, and Hank Gratteau. "Thompson Plans 2 More Prisons by 1990." <u>Chicago Tribune</u> (April 3, 1986): C1.

Egler, Daniel, and Hank Gratteau. "Crowding Forces State to Plan 3 New Prisons." <u>Chicago Tribune</u> (April 4, 1986): C1.

Ellison, W. James. "Privatization of Corrections: A Critique and Analysis of Contemporary Views." <u>Cumberland Law Review</u> 17 (1987): 683-729.

Elvin, Jan. "Private Firms Cash In On Crime." <u>National Prison Project Journal</u> (Fall 1984): 6-7.

Elvin, Jan. "A Civil Liberties View of Private Prisons." <u>Prison Journal</u> (Autumn-Winter 1985): 48-50.

Elvin, Jan. "Private Prison Plans Dropped by Buckingham." <u>National Prison Project</u> 6 (Winter 1985): 11.

<u>Engineering News Record</u>. "Privatization Spreads to American Prisons." (April 5, 1984).

Engler, R.D., and W.G. Gay. <u>Contract Law Enforcement: A Practical Guide to Program Development</u>. Washington, D.C.: Department of Justice, 1978.

<u>Environmental Law Reporter</u>. "Panel Discussion: Private Facilitating and Adjudicative Functions." (July 1987): 10263-72.

Evans, Dwight. "Prisons For Profit? Pennsylvania Senate Rushes In." <u>Philadelphia Daily News</u> (January 29, 1986).

Fair, Kathy. "Prison Privatization: Cheaper, But Better?" <u>Huntsville News</u> (May 21, 1985): 1.

Fairchild, Mary. "States Aren't Ready for Privately Owned Prisons -- Yet." <u>State Legislatures</u> 12 (April 1986): 7-8.

Farkas, Gerald. "Prison Industries: Working with the Private Sector." <u>Corrections Today</u> (June 1985): 102-03.

Farrell, Kevin. "Public Business in Private Hands." <u>Venture</u> (July 1984): 34.

<u>Fayetteville Observer</u>. "Private Prisons." (May 27, 1985): 4A.

<u>Fayetteville Observer</u>. "Leasing Prison?" (September 19, 1985).

Federal Bureau of Prisons. Statement of the General Counsel of the Federal Bureau of Prisons, "Authority to Contract with Private Institutions for Placement of Federal Prisoners." June 10, 1983.

Fedo, Michael. "Private Industry and the Prisons." America (October 21, 1978): 267-68.

Fedo, Michael. "Free Enterprise Goes to Prison." Corrections Magazine 7 (April 1981): 5-13.

Feldman, Dan. "Longer Sentences Do Not Deter Crime." New York Times (October 3, 1987): 27.

Feldman, Roger D., Carlos J. Berrocal, and Howard L. Sharfsten. "Public Finance Through Privatization: Providing Infrastructure for the Future." Stetson Law Review 16 (1987): 705-34.

Feldstein, Martin. "The Job of Controlling Public Sector Pay." Wall Street Journal (October 1, 1981): 26.

Fenton, Joseph. "A Private Alternative to Public Prisons." Prison Journal 65 (Autumn-Winter 1985): 42-47.

Fenton, Joseph. "Pro: No Moratorium for Private Prisons." Privatization Review 1 (Fall 1985): 21-24.

Ferrara, Peter J. "Medicare and the Private Sector." Yale Law & Policy Review 6 (1988): 61-87.

Financial World. "Prisons: Are We Ready For This Growth Industry?" (November 12, 1985): 26.

Finckenauer, James O. Juvenile Delinquency and Corrections: The Gap Between Theory and Practice. Orlando, Fla.: Academic Press, 1984.

Finder, Alan. "New York Hopes to Learn From Rink Trump Fixed." New York Times (November 21, 1986): B1.

Finger, Bill. "Can the Private Sector Do It Better?" Business: North Carolina (February 1986).

Fitzgerald, Randy. "Free-Enterprise Jails: Key to Our Prison Dilemma?" Reader's Digest 128 (March 1986): 85-88.

Fixler, Philip. "Privatization Hits Britain." Fiscal Watchdog 57 (July 1981).

Fixler, Philip. "Privatization In Europe." Fiscal Watchdog 58 (August 1981).

Fixler, Philip. "Privatization: How Widespread?" Fiscal Watchdog 75 (January 1983).

Fixler, Philip E.   "Can Privatization Solve the Prison Crisis?"
     Fiscal Watchdog 90 (April 1984).

Fixler, Philip.   "Germany's Privatization Push."   Fiscal Watchdog
     95 (September 1984).

Fixler, Philip E.   "Behind Bars We Find An Enterprise Zone."
     Wall Street Journal (November 29, 1984): 34.

Fixler, Philip.   "Private Corrections Breakout."   Fiscal Watchdog
     101 (March 1985): 4-5.

Fixler, Philip.   "Britain Leads Way in Privatization."   Fiscal
     Watchdog 103 (May 1985).

Fixler, Philip.   "Privatization Wrap-up -- An International
     Perspective."   Fiscal Watchdog 110 (December 1985).

Fladung, Thom.   "Legislatures Struggle with Whether Private Firm
     Should Run Prison."   The State (Columbia, South Carolina)
     (November 27, 1985).

Fleishman, Jeffrey.   "Lehigh Officials 'Get Serious' Over New
     Prison."   Morning Call (June 11, 1986): A1.

Flicker, Barbara.   Reducing Overcrowding in Juvenile
     Institutions.   New York: Institute of Judicial
     Administration, 1983.

Florida Bar News.   "ABA Launches Prison Privatization Study."
     (January 15, 1987): 10.

Florida State Senate.   Committee on Corrections, Probation, and
     Parole.   Experience and Issues in Private Sector Management
     Contracting in Corrections, August, 1985.

Foltz, Kim.   "The Corporate Warden."   Newsweek (May 7, 1984): 80

Forbes.   "No Prison Break."   (February 24, 1986): 12.

Fortune.   "Second Thoughts on Private Slammers."   (March 17,
     1986): 10.

Foster, J. Todd.   "1.5 Million Silverdale Facelift By CCA
     Suggested to County."   Chattanooga News-Free Press (July 3,
     1985): B5.

Foucalt, Michael.   Discipline & Punish -- The Birth of the
     Prison.   New York: Pantheon Books, 1977.

Fox, Ken.   "Should Private, Profit-Making Firms Operate County
     Jails?: Yes."   County News (November 4, 1985): 6.

Franklin, Ben. "Inmate's Complaint Puts 2 Agencies at Odds." New York Times (February 16, 1987): 11.

Freedman, James O. "Delegation of Power and Institutional Competence." Chicago Law Review 43 (1976): 307-36.

Freyermuth, R. Wilson. "Rethinking Excessive Force." Duke Law Journal (1987): 692-711.

Fried, Joseph. "Queens Cleric's Panel Gives Offenders 2d Chance." New York Times (September 22, 1978): 51.

Friedman, David. The Machinery of Freedom: Guide to a Radical Capitalism. New York: Harper & Row, 1973.

Friel, H. Operational and Resource Management, Review No. 7: Privatization, Phase I. Canada: Correctional Service of Canada, September 1985.

Friends Committee on Legislation (FCL) of California. "Privatization of Prisons." FCL Newsletter (February 1986): 3,7.

Funke, Gail S. "Who's Buried in Grant's Tomb?" Economics and Corrections for the Eighties and Beyond. Alexandria, Va.: Institute for Economic and Policy Studies, 1983.

Funke, Gail S. "Is Privatization Cheaper?" Summary of Remarks to the National Conference of State Legislatures, Alexandria, Va.: Institute for Economic and Policy Studies, (September 9, 1984).

Funke, Gail S. "The Economics of Prison Crowding." The Annals of the American Academy of Political and Social Science (March 1985): 90-93.

Funke, Gail S., Billy L. Wayson, and Neal Miller. Assets and Liabilities of Correctional Industries. Lexington, Mass.: Lexington Books, 1981.

Funke, Gail S., Robert C. Grieser, and Neal Miller. Guidelines for Prison Industries. National Institute of Corrections, National Institute of Justice, Washington, D.C.: January 1984.

Gage, Theodore. "Cops, Inc." Reason (November 1982): 23-28.

Galanter, Marc. "Why the 'Haves' Come Out Ahead: Speculations On the Limits of Legal Change." Law & Society Review 9 (1974): 95-151.

Gallagher, Patrick J. "The Real Cost of Liability and What Must Be Done to Reduce It." Corrections Digest (July 30, 1986): 2.

Garaventa, Eugene. "The Privatization of Prisons: An Overview." <u>Journal of Private Enterprise</u> 2 (Fall 1986): 127.

Garner, Joe. "Denver Officials Reject Proposal for Private Jail." <u>Rocky Mountain News</u> (January 10, 1984): 32.

Gaylin, Willard, Ira Glasser, Steven Marcus, and David J. Rothman. <u>Doing Good: The Limits of Benevolence</u>. New York: Pantheon Books, 1981.

Geedon, Frank. "Government Contract Law." <u>Case & Comment</u> (July-August 1986): 27.

Geis, Gilbert. "The Privatization of Prisons: Panacea or Placebo?" In <u>Private Means-Public Ends: Private Business in Social Service Delivery</u>. New York: Praeger, 1986.

Gelfand, M. David. <u>State and Local Government Debt Financing</u>. Wilmette, Ill.: Callaghan & Company, 1986.

General Counsel, Federal Bureau of Prisons. "Authority to Contract with Private Institutions for Placement of Federal Prisoners." June 10, 1983.

Gest, Ted. "Bulging Prisons." <u>U.S. News & World Report</u> (April 23, 1984): 42.

Gest, Ted. "Prisons for Profit: A Growing Business." <u>U.S. News & World Report</u> (July 2, 1984): 45-46.

Gettinger, Stephen. "Accreditation on Trial." <u>Corrections Magazine</u> (February 1982): 7.

Gettinger, Stephen. <u>Assessing Criminal Justice Needs</u>. National Institute of Justice Research in Brief. Washington, D.C.: Department of Justice, 1984.

Gewirtz, Paul. "The Courts, Congress, and Executive Policy-Making: Notes on Three Doctrines." <u>Law and Contemporary Problems</u> 40 (Summer 1976): 46-85.

Giancinti, Thomas A. "Dealing with the Private Sector in Corrections (or 'A Bureaucrat Makes a Pact With the Devil.')" <u>News Update</u>. Washington, D.C.: National Association of Criminal Justice Institute Planners, February 19, 1985.

Gianoli, L. "Jails for Profit." <u>National Sheriff</u> (February-March 1985).

Gillespie, John W. "Lease Purchase -- A Financial Alternative." <u>Corrections Today</u> (April 1986): 32-34.

Goldman, Harvey, and Sandra Mokuvos.   The Privatization Book.
     New York: Arthur Young, 1984.

Goldman, Harvey, and Sandra Mokuvos.   "Financing: Privatization
     From a Banker's Perspective." Privatization Review 1
     (Summer 1985): 39-47.

Goodman, Ellen. "Privatizating War." Washington Post (March 26,
     1985): A17.

Goodsell, Charles T. "In Defense of Bureaucracy: Perspectives
     on Privatization." State Government News (July 1986): 20-
     21.

Gordon, Paul. "Justice Goes Private." Reason (September 1985):
     23-30.

Greenberg, David. "A Voucher System for Corrections." Crime and
     Delinquency 19 (1973): 212-17.

Greengard, Samuel. "Making Crime Pay." Barrister (Winter 1986):
     12-16.

Greenville News. "Private Enterprise and Public Good." (August
     9, 1985).

Greenwood, Peter. "Let Private Enterprise Run the Prisons."
     Criminal Justice Newsletter (July 6, 1981): 4.

Greenwood, Peter. Private Enterprise Prisons. Why Not? The Job
     Would Be Done Better and at Less Cost. Santa Monica,
     Cal.: Rand Corporation, 1981.

Greenwood, Peter. "Private Prisons: Are They Worth a Try?"
     California Lawyer (July-August 1982): 41-42.

Gregory, David L. "The Congressional Response to NLRB v.
     Bildisco and the Constitutional Subtleties of the
     Nondelegation Doctrine." University of Detroit Law Review
     62 (1985): 245-73.

Gruber, Lloyd. Private Sector Involvement in the Financing and
     Management of Correctional Facilities: Policy Issues in
     Perspective. Washington, D.C.: National Criminal Justice
     Association, 1986.

Gustafson, Paul. "Women's Jail Is First Run By Private
     Concern." Minneapolis Star and Tribune (November 20, 1984):
     1B.

Hackett, Judith C., Harry P. Hatry, Robert B. Levinson, Joan
     Allen, Keon Chi, and Edward D. Feigenbaum. "Contracting for
     the Operation of Prisons and Jails." Research in Brief.

Washington, D.C.: National Institute of Justice, June 1987.

Halbert, Marvin. "A Private Prison Advocate Speaks His Mind." Pennsylvania Law Journal-Reporter (December 10, 1985): 10.

Hale, Robert L. "Our Equivocal Constitutional Guaranties." Columbia Law Review 39 (1939): 563-78.

Hall, Andy. "Systemwide Strategies to Alleviate Jail Crowding." Research in Brief. Washington, D.C.: National Institute of Justice, January 1987.

Hammett, Theodore. AIDS in Correctional Facilities: Issues and Options. 3d ed. Washington, D.C.: National Institute of Justice, April 1988.

Hanke, Steve H., ed. Prospects for Privatization. New York: Academy of Political Science, 1987.

Hanrahan, John D. Government for Sale: Contracting Out the New Patronage. Washington, D.C.: American Federation of State, County and Municipal Employees, 1980.

Hanrahan, John D. Passing the Buck: The Contracting Out of Public Services. Washington, D.C.: American Federation of State, County and Municipal Employees, AFL-CIO, 1982.

Hanrahan, John D. Government By Contract. New York: W.W. Norton, 1983.

Hanrahan, John D. "Why Public Services Should Stay Public." Des Moines Register (March 31, 1983): 11A.

Hansmann, Henry B. "The Role of Nonprofit Enterprise." Yale Law Journal 89 (1980): 835-901.

Haq, Kathy. "County Hires Private Jail Operator." Albuquerque Journal (June 21, 1986): B1.

Harrel, Rhett, Jr. "Governmental Leasing Techniques." Governmental Finance (March 1980): 15-18.

Harrison, E.W., and M.G. Gosse. "In My Opinion...Privatization: A Restraint Initiative." Canadian Journal of Criminology 28 (April 1986): 185-93.

Harriston, Keith. "'New Generation' California Jail Comes to Prince George's." Washington Post (March 22, 1987): A1.

Hartis, Nancy. "$25 Million Coverage Asked for Penal Farm." Chattanooga Times (June 26, 1984): B1.

Hatry, Harry P. A Review of Private Approaches for Delivery of Public Services. Washington, D.C.: The Urban Institute

Press, 1983.

Hatry, Harry P., and Eugene Durman. Issues in Competitive Contracting for Social Services. Falls Church, Va.: National Institute of Government Purchasing, August 1985.

Havemann, Judith. "Postal Chief Denounces Privatization Advocates." Washington Post (April 8, 1988): A19.

Hazard, Geoffrey C., Jr., and Paul D. Scott. "The Public Nature of Private Adjudication." Yale Law & Policy Review 6 (1988): 42-60.

Hazard, Katherine. Evaluation of Privately Operated Prisons. Juneau, Ala.: Alaska State Legislature Research Agency, 1986.

Heller, Matthew. "Crime Pays for U.S. Prisons." Management Today (June 1985): 21.

Hemming, Richard, and Ali M. Mansoor. Privatization and Public Enterprises -- IMF Working Paper. Washington, D.C.: International Monetary Fund, February 25, 1987.

Herman, Susan N. "The New Liberty: The Procedural Due Process Rights of Prisoners and Others Under the Burger Court." New York University Law Review 59 (1984): 482-585.

Herzlinger, Regina, and William Krasker. "Who Profits from Nonprofits?" Harvard Business Review (January-February 1987): 93.

Hirsch, James. "What's New In Private Prisons." New York Times (April 26, 1987): F17.

Hirschkop, Philip J., and Michael A. Millemann. "The Unconstitutionality of Prison Life." Virginia Law Review 55 (1969): 795-839.

Hirsley, Michael. "Tennessee Tempted By Prison Plan." Chicago Tribune (November 17, 1985): C3.

Hoelter, Herbert. "The Private Pre-sentence Report: Issues For Consideration." Prison Journal (Autumn-Winter 1985): 53.

Holmes, John. "Wide Open Industry Goes Private." Insight (May 16, 1988): 50-51.

Holmes, Peter A. "Taking Public Services Private." Nation's Business (August 1985): 18-24.

Horan, James D. The Pinkertons. New York: Crown Publishers, 1967.

Hornblum, Allen. "Are We Ready for the Privatization of America's Prisons?" Privatization Review (Fall 1985): 25-29.

Hornblum, Allen. "Grass Roots Organizing Stifles Private Prison Proponents." Jericho 41 (Winter 1986): 2.

Houk, Wade B. "Acquiring New Prison Sites: The Federal Experience." Construction Bulletin. Washington, D.C.: National Institute of Justice, December 1987.

Hudgins, Bill. "CCA Prison Management Expected to Quadruple." Nashville Banner (September 12, 1985): A16.

Hudgins, Bill. "Prison Firm Shied Away From State." Nashville Banner (September 12, 1985): A16.

Hudgins, Bill. "CCA Believes Businesslike Approach Can Save the Day." Nashville Banner (September 13, 1985).

Hudson, Kathryn. "Private Industry's Ventures Working Inside Prison Walls." Insight (March 21, 1988): 42-43.

Huggins, M. Wayne. Testimony Before Subcommittee on Courts, Civil Liberties and the Administration of Justice, House Judiciary Committee, November 13, 1985.

Humphrey, Tom. "Prison Overcrowding in Tennessee Forces Emergency Legislative Session." Christian Science Monitor (November 6, 1985): 3.

Huntly, Helen. "Reform School Much Improved, But It's Too Soon to Tell Whether It Can Turn Boys Away From Crime." St. Petersburg Times (March 26, 1984): 1B.

Hunzeker, Donna. "Norris Deals With Overcrowding." Corrections Compendium 10 (January 1986): 8-10.

Hutto, T. Don, and Gary E. Vick. "Designing the Private Correctional Facility." Corrections Today 46 (April 1984): 78.

Immarigeon, Russ. "Private Prisons, Private Programs, and Their Implications for Reducing Reliance on Imprisonment in the United States." Prison Journal 65 (Autumn-Winter 1985): 60-74.

Immarigeon, Russ. "The Trend Toward Privatization: Update." Jericho 40 (Fall 1985): 1.

Institute for Court Management/National Center for State Courts. "Workshop on the Private Sector in the Juvenile Justice System: Program Scope, Contracting, and Accountability." Denver, April 28-May 1, 1985.

Institutional Investor. "Alfonse D'Amato into the Breach."
(March 1986): 147-49.

Institutions Etc. "If You Think This Sounds Good, Wait'll You
Hear About Discount Gas Chambers." (November 1983): 6-8.

Institutions Etc. "Corrections and the Land of Opportunity."
(October 1984): 2-9.

International City Management Association. Alternative
Approaches for Delivering Public Services. Washington,
D.C.: Urban Data Service Report, 1982.

Irwin, John, and James Austin. It's About Time: Solving
America's Prison Crowding Crisis. San Francisco: National
Council on Crime and Delinquency, 1987.

Jacob, Bruce R., and K.M. Sharma. "Disciplinary and Punitive
Transfer Decisions and Due Process Values in the American
Correctional System." Stetson Law Review 12 (1982): 1-134.

Jacoby, Sidney B. "Delegation of Powers and Judicial Review: A
Study in Comparative Law." Columbia Law Review 36 (1936):
871-907.

Jaffe, Louis L. "Law Making by Private Groups." Harvard Law
Review 51 (1937): 201-53.

Jaffe, Louis L. "An Essay on Delegation of Legislative Power:
II." Columbia Law Review 47 (1947): 561-93.

Jaffe, Louis L. Judicial Control of Administrative Action.
Boston: Little, Brown, 1965.

Janus, Michael, Jerome Mabli, and J.D. Williams. "Security and
Custody." Federal Probation (March 1986): 35.

Jayewardene, C.H.S., T.J. Juliani, and C.K. Talbot. "Supply Side
Corrections or Human Resource Management -- A New Strategy
for Parole and Probation." International Journal of
Comparative and Applied Criminal Justice 7 (Spring 1983):
99-108.

Jayewardene, C.H.S., and C.K. Talbot. "Entrusting Corrections to
the Private Sector." International Journal of Offender
Therapy and Comparative Criminology 26 (1982): 177-87.

Jenkins, John. "Prisons for Profit." TWA/Ambassador (November
1985): 26.

Jensen, Meckling. "Theory of the Firm: Managerial Behavior,
Agency Cost and Ownership Structure." Journal of Financial
Economics 3 (1976): 305.

Jensen, Walker, Jr., Edward M. Mazze, and Neal Miller. "Legal
    Reform of Prison Industries: New Opportunities for
    Marketing Managers." American Business Law Journal 12
    (1974-75): 173-80.

Joel, Dana. "A Guide to Prison Privatization." Backgrounder.
    Washington, D.C.: Heritage Foundation, May 24, 1988.

Johnson, Aaron J. "How to Uncrowd N.C. Prisons: Let Private
    Firm Run Minimum Security Prison." Charlotte Observer
    (April 4, 1986): 21A.

Johnson, D. "Corporate-Run Prisons a 'Growth Industry': Some
    Businessmen Claim They Can Do The Job Cheaper.... and
    Better." Los Angeles Times (March 29, 1985): V1.

Johnson, Judith. "Should Adult Correctional Facilities Be
    Privately Managed?" National Sheriff (April-May 1985).

Johnson, Judith. "Should Private, Profit Making Firms Operate
    County Jails?: No." County News (November 4, 1986).

Johnson, Kirk. "Debate Is Sharpening over Alternatives to
    Prison." New York Times (March 13, 1987): B3.

Johnson, Paul B. "What Are the Legal Problems Involved in the
    Privatization of State/Local Corrections?" Corrections
    Digest (April 9, 1986): 1-7.

Johnson, Thomas, A. "Policy Implications of Private Sector
    Involvement in Correctional Services and Programs." Journal
    of Forensic Sciences (1985): 221.

Johnston, David. "Stockbroker Is Investing in Prisoners." Los
    Angeles Times (March 29, 1985): 26.

Judges' Journal. "Private Prison Declares Bankruptcy." (Winter
    1986): 1-2.

Jurik, Phil. "Brushy Guards Warn Against Letting Company Run
    Prisons." Knoxville Journal (February 25, 1986): C2.

Kakalik, James S., and Sorrel Wildhorn. Private Police in the
    United States: Findings and Recommendations Vol. 1.
    Washington, D.C.: U.S. Department of Justice, 1971.

Kakalik, James S., and Sorrel Wildhorn. The Private Police. New
    York: Crane Russak, 1977.

Karmin, Monroe W. "Hanging a 'For Sale' Sign on Government."
    U.S. News & World Report (January 13, 1986): 18-19.

Kassenbaum, G. Contracting for Correctional Services in the

Community: Vol. 1, Summary. Washington, D.C.: U.S. Department of Justice, 1978.

Kassouf, George. "Involuntary Servitude In Modern Times: Searching For A Definition." Preview of United States Supreme Court Cases 9 (February 26, 1988): 262-64.

Kaufer, L. Privately Managed Alternative Correctional System. Portland, Ore.: Job Therapy of Oregon, 1976.

Kay, Susan L. "The Implications of Prison Privatization on the Conduct of Prisoner Litigation Under 42 U.S.C. Section 1983." Vanderbilt Law Review 40 (1987): 867-88.

Keating, J. Michael, Jr. "Some Thoughts on Prisons for Profit." National Association of Criminal Justice Planners, Contracting for Justice Functions (1985): 8.

Keating, J. Michael, Jr. "Thoughts about Prisons for Profit." In Does Crime Pay? An Examination of Prisons for Profit. Washington, D.C.: American Federation of State, County and Municipal Employees, AFL-CIO, 1985.

Keating, J. Michael, Jr. Public Ends and Private Means: Accountability Among Private Providers of Public Social Services. Washington, D.C.: National Institute for Dispute Resolution, 1986.

Keating, J. Michael, Jr. Seeking Profit in Punishment: The Private Management of Correctional Institutions. Washington. D.C.: American Federation of State, County, and Municipal Employees, AFL-CIO, 1985.

Keller, Dorthea A. "Prisons for Profit Arrive in New Jersey." New Jersey Corrections Quarterly 2 (December 1986): 1.

Kelley, Dave. Statement before the Subcommittee on Courts, Civil Liberties, and the Administration of Justice of the House Judiciary Committee, November 13, 1985, March 18, 1986.

Kelley, Dave. The Privatization of Corrections. Washington, D.C.: American Federation of Government Employees (March 18, 1986).

Kelley, Dave. "The Privatization of Corrections." Corrections Digest 17 (March 26, 1986): 4-6.

Kent, Calvin A. "Privatization of Public Functions: Promises and Problems." Heartland Policy Study No. 8. Chicago: The Heartland Institute, February 18, 1986.

Kilborn, Peter T. "Panel Urging Public-to-Private Shift." New York Times (March 7, 1987): A12.

Kilborn, Peter T. "Reagan Plan to Privatize Government Is Gaining Support From Democrats." New York Times (February 15, 1988): A10.

King, Bob. "Prison Profits: Making Crime Pay." Tennessee Business (September-October 1985): 19.

King, Wayne. "Contracts for Detention Raise Legal Questions." New York Times (March 6, 1984): A10.

Kirschner, Richard, Craig Becker, and John J. Sullivan. "'Punishment for Profit:' The Contracting Out of Corrections." Paper prepared for the American Federation of State, County and Municipal Employees, AFL-CIO, 1986.

Klucina, John. "Bills Target Non-Profit Prison Organizations." Knickerbocker News (May 28, 1986): 4B.

Knapp, Frank, Jr. "The Privatization of Corrections." Business and Economic Review (January 1986).

Knickerbocker News. "Prison Business Plan Proposed." (May 13, 1986): 5A.

Knight, Robin. "Britain Sells and Sells and Sells." U.S. News & World Report (January 13, 1986): 18-19.

Knobelsdorff, Kerry Elizabeth. "The Move to Hand Prison Over to Private Businesses Draws Flak." Christian Science Monitor (July 27, 1987): 17.

Koenig, Richard. "More Firms Turn to Private Courts to Avoid Expensive Legal Fights." Wall Street Journal (January 4, 1984): 25.

Kolderie, Ted. "The Two Different Concepts of Privatization." Public Administration Review 46 (July-August 1986): 285-91.

Kopper, Dick. "County Eyes Leasing the Penal Farm Rather Than Selling It To Company." Chattanooga Times (June 13, 1984): B2.

Kopper, Dick. "County, CCA Begin Drawing up Contract to Lease Penal Farm." Chattanooga Times (June 21, 1984): B1.

Koren, Edward I. "Legal Implications of Privatization." Summary of Remarks to the NIJ's Conference on Corrections and the Private Sector, Washington, D.C.: National Jail Project. 1985.

Koren, Edward I. Statement before the Subcommittee on Courts, Civil Liberties, and the Administration of Justice of the House Judiciary Committee, November 13, 1985.

Kraakman, Reinier H. "Corporate Liability Strategies and the Costs of Legal Controls." Yale Law Journal 93 (1984): 857-98.

Krajick, Kevin. "Supply-Side Punishment." Mother Jones (February-March 1984): 12.

Krajick, Kevin. "Punishment for Profit." Across the Board (March 1984): 20-27.

Krajick, Kevin. "Prisons for Profit: The Private Alternative." State Legislatures 10 (April 1984): 9-14.

Krajick, Kevin. "Private, For-Profit Prisons Take Hold in Some States." Christian Science Monitor (April 11, 1984): 27.

Krajick, Kevin. "Private Financing and Management of Prisons and Jails." New York: Edna McConnell Clark Foundation, May 1984.

Krajick, Kevin, and Steve Gettinger. Overcrowded Time: Why Prisons Are So Crowded and What Can Be Done. New York: Edna McConnell Clark Foundation, 1982.

Krasner, Jeffrey. "Hub Fund Invests $9.7M in Prison." Boston Herald (February 19, 1986): 25.

Krause, Rheinhardt. "The Private Sector's Growing Role in Corrections." Law Enforcement Technology (May 1985): 14-16.

Kravitz, Lee. "Tough Times for Private Prisons." Venture (May 1986): 56-60.

Kroll, Michael. "Prisons for Profit." Progressive 48 (September 1984): 18-22.

Kulis, Chester J. "Profit in the Private Presentence Report." Federal Probation 47 (December 1983): 11-16.

Kurtz, Howard. "Inmates as 'Federal Employes.'" Washington Post (February 12, 1987): A25.

Kuttner, Robert. "When Ambulance Service Goes Private." Boston Globe (January 5, 1985): 15.

Kuttner, Robert. "The Private Market Can't Always Solve Public Problems." Business Week (March 10, 1986): 14.

LaFraniere, Sharon. "Private Pa. Prison Seeks to Keep 55 Inmates." Washington Post (March 18, 1986): A1.

LaFraniere, Sharon. "D.C. Prisoners' Brief Visit Stirs Up Long-Simmering Debate in PA. Town." Washington Post (March 19, 1986): A12.

Lambert, Bruce. "City's Prison Boat Is Late and Costly." New York Times (March 24, 1987): B8.

Lang, Tony R. "Financing Construction of Prisons and Jails: How Much Justice Can States Afford?" Eleventh Annual Meeting, National Conference of State Legislatures, Seattle, August 5, 1985.

Las Vegas Optic. "Jail Plan Gets OK." (November 21, 1983).

Latessa, Edward J., Jr., and Lawrence F. Travis III. "The Role of Private Enterprise in Institutional Corrections: A Call For Caution." Urban Resources (Summer 1985): 25.

Latimer, Leah. "Accord Reached in Suit By Paraplegic Inmate." Washington Post (November 22, 1984): A20.

Lauter, David. "The Plunge into 'Private Justice.'" National Law Journal 1 (March 11, 1985): 1.

Laven, Roger. "Using Private Sector Providers for Public Sector Mandates." Paper presented at National Association of Public Administration Conference, Indianapolis, March 1985.

Law Enforcement News. "Private Prison Is Nonprofit Affair." (May 24, 1986): 4.

Lawrence, David M. "Private Exercise of Governmental Power." Indiana Law Journal 61 (1986): 647-95.

Leban, Janet. "The Pennsylvania Prison Debate: Introduction." Privatization Review 1 (Fall 1985): 20-21.

Leder, Philip. "Privatizing N.I.H. Is an 'Idiotic Idea.'" New York Times (January 12, 1988): A27.

Lee, Roger J., and Laurin Wollan, Jr. "The Libertarian Prison: Principles of Laissez-Faire Incarceration." Prison Journal 65 (Autumn-Winter 1985): 108-21.

Lee, Wayne. "Private Businesses Begin Managing Detention Centers." Washington Times (November 20, 1984): 1A.

Lee, Wayne. "Accountability Issues Arise On Private Jails." Washington Times (November 21, 1984): 1A.

Leftridge, Mary. "Privatization of Prisons." Maryland Bar Journal 20 (July 1986): 8.

Legal Intelligencer. "Examining Private Prison Issues." (December 19, 1986): 1.

Le Gendre, Bertrand. "Une Seule Solution, la Privatisation des

Prisons." Le Monde (November 20, 1986): 26.

Le Gendre, Bertrand. "Prisons Privées: Les 'Pour' et les 'Contre.'" Le Monde (December 19, 1986).

LeKachman, Robert. "Privatization: Personal Perspective." Christianity and Crisis (April 29, 1985): 150-51.

Leverson, Leonard G. "Constitutional Limits on the Power to Restrict Access to Prisons: An Historical Re-Examination." Harvard Civil Rights-Civil Liberties Law Review 18 (1983): 409.

Levin, Blair, and Clyde Medworth. "Locking Up a New Real Estate Market." Wall Street Journal (July 7, 1986).

Levine, Jody. "Private Prison Planned on Toxic Waste Site." National Prison Project Journal 5 (Fall 1985): 8-9.

Levinson, Marc R. "In South Carolina Community Corrections Means the Alston Wilkes Society." Corrections Magazine 9 (September 1983): 41-46.

Levinson, Robert B. "The Private Sector and Corrections." Corrections Today 46 (August 1984): 42.

Levinson, Robert B. "Okeechobee: An Evaluation of Privatization in Corrections." Prison Journal 65 (Autumn-Winter 1985): 75-93.

Levinson, Robert B. Private Operation of a Correctional Institution. Report to National Institute of Corrections. Washington, D.C.: National Institute of Corrections, 1985.

Lewis, Anthony. "A Public Right to Know About Public Institutions: The First Amendment as a Sword." Supreme Court Review (1980): 1-25.

Lewis, D.E. "Plan for Private Prisons Debated." Asheville Times (June 30, 1986).

Lewis, Nancy, and John Ward Anderson. "Study Warns of Major Disturbance at Overcrowded Lorton Facilities." Washington Post (July 9, 1986): A1.

Lewis, Paul. "France Begins Privatization." New York Times (November 24, 1986): D10.

Liebmann, George W. "Delegation to Private Parties in American Constitutional Law." Indiana Law Journal 50 (1975): 650-719.

Lightman, Ernie. "The Private Employer and the Prison Industry." British Journal of Criminology 22 (January

1982): 36-48.

Lindquist, Charles A. "The Private Sector in Corrections: Contracting Probation Services from Community Organizations." Federal Probation 44 (March 1980): 58-64.

Lippold, Robert A. Corrections and the Private Sector. Olympia, Wash.: Washington State Department of Corrections, February 1985.

Locke, John. Second Treatise on Civil Government (1689), Excerpted in Political Man and Social Man; Readings in Political Philosophy, ed. Robert Paul Wolff. New York: Random House, 1966.

Locke, Keltnor W. "'Privatization' and Labor Relations: Some Welcome Guidance from the NLRB." Labor Law Journal 38 (March 1987): 166-72.

Locker, Richard. "Prison Bill Given OK By Senate." Memphis Commercial Appeal (April 12, 1986): B1.

Logan, Charles H. "Competition in the Prison Business." The Freeman (August 1985): 470-78.

Logan, Charles H. "Should States Opt for Private Prisons? Yes." Hartford Courant (January 12, 1986): E1.

Logan, Charles H. "Commercial Institutions Are Significant Alternatives." Nashville Banner (January 21, 1986).

Logan, Charles H. "Incarceration Inc.: Competition in the Prison Business." USA Today (March 1986): 58.

Logan, Charles H. "Private Prisons, Part I: A Yardstick for System." Law Enforcement News (May 5, 1986): 8.

Logan, Charles H. "Proprietary Prisons." In The American Prison: Issues in Research and Policy, eds. Lynne Goodstein and Doris L. MacKenzie. New York: Plenum, 1988.

Logan, Charles H. "The Propriety of Proprietary Prisons." Federal Probation 51 (September 1987): 35-40.

Logan, Charles H., and Sharla P. Rausch. "Incarceration Inc.: The Privatization of Prisons." Paper presented at the Annual Meeting of the Society for Study of Social Problems, Washington, D.C., August 1985.

Logan, Charles H., and Sharla P. Rausch. "Punish and Profit: The Emergence of Private Enterprise Prisons." Justice Quarterly 2 (September 1985): 303-18.

Lohmann, Bill. "Can Private Enterprise Operate U.S. Prisons?"

The Daily Record (September 28, 1985): 1.

Lohmann, Bill. "Can Private Enterprise Run the Prisons System." Los Angeles Daily Journal (October 4, 1985): 4.

Louisiana. Commission on Law Enforcement and Administration of Criminal Justice. Governor's Prison Overcrowding Policy Task Force. Report on Privatization to the 1986 Legislature, July 1986.

Louisiana. Governor's Prison Overcrowding Policy Task Force. "Interim Report of the Privatization and Corrections Committee to the Governor's Prison Overcrowding Policy Task Force." Commission on Law Enforcement and Administration of Criminal Justice, 1985.

Louisiana. Governor's Prison Overcrowding Policy Task Force. "Report on Privatization of Corrections." In Governor's Prison Overcrowding Policy Task Force Report. Louisiana Commission on Law Enforcement and Administration of Criminal Justice, March 1, 1986.

Lunner, Chet. "Private Prisons Warning Given By State Official." Tennessean (December 3, 1986): 1.

Lyndon B. Johnson School of Public Affairs, The University of Texas at Austin. Policy Research Project Report No. 75. Contracting Selected State Government Functions: Issues and Next Steps. University of Texas, 1986.

Lyons, William, and Michael Fitzgerald. "Alternative Service Delivery In Local Government -- Conceptual Issues and Current Trends." In Research in Urban Policy. Greenwich, Conn.: JAI Press. Forthcoming.

McAfee, Ward M. "Tennessee's Private Prison Act of 1986: An Historical Perspective With Special Attention to California's Experience." Vanderbilt Law Review 40 (1987): 851-65.

McAllister, Bill. "A Privatization Chief From the Private Sector." Washington Post (September 3, 1987): A2.

McCarthy, Colman. "The Answer is Not More Jails." The Washington Post (May 6, 1984): C11.

McCarthy, John J. "Contract Medical Care: Prescription For Change." Corrections Magazine 8 (April 1982): 6-17.

McClelland, Mike, and Ron Wiginton. "Opinion Clouds CCA Certification: Employees May Be In Violation." Panama City News-Herald (October 25, 1986): 1A-2A.

McConkie, M.L. Management By Objectives -- A Corrections

Perspective. Washington, D.C.: U.S. Department of Justice, 1979.

McDonald, Janice. "State Privatization Headaches." Beach-Bay News (Panama City, Florida) (March 19, 1986).

McEntee, Gerald W. "Contracting Out Prisons." In Does Crime Pay? An Examination of Prisons for Profit. Washington, D.C.: American Federation of State, County and Municipal Employees, AFL-CIO, 1985.

McEntee, Gerald W. "Easy Answer Has Serious Shortcomings." Memphis Commercial Appeal (October 13, 1985): E3.

McEntee, Gerald W. "The Case Against Privatization." Privatization Review (Fall 1985): 6-9.

McEntee, Gerald W. "Prisons for Profit?" Public Employee 50 (December 1985): 2.

McGowan, Carl. "Congress, Court, and Control of Delegated Power." Columbia Law Review 77 (1977): 1119-74.

McHugh, T. Privately Owned and Operated Prisons. Salem, Ore.: Oregon Legislative Research, State Capitol: 1985.

McSparron, James. "Community Correction and Diversion." Crime and Delinquency 26 (1980): 226-47.

Machlowitz, David. "Should Criminal Contempt of Court Be Prosecutable by Private Counsel?" Natural Law Journal (January 19, 1987): 24.

Madden, Thomas J. "Legal Issues in Privatization of Core Correctional Functions." Washington, D.C.: Howard & Civiletti, 1985.

Maghan, Jess, and Edward Sagorin. "Private Prisons, II: A History of Failures." Law Enforcement News (May 26, 1986): 8.

Magnusson, Paul. "Selling Uncle Sam's Assets: Why Reagan Has a Real Shot Now." Business Week (September 23, 1987): 41.

Main, Jeremy. "When Public Services Go Private." Fortune (May 27, 1985): 92-102.

Mangold, Tom. "Profiting from Crime: Private Sector Prisons." Institutions Etc. (November 1985): 27-29.

Marlin, John Tepper. Contracting Municipal Services - A Guide for Purchase from the Private Sector. New York: John Wiley & Sons, 1984.

Marlin, John T., and Karyn Feidan. "To Avoid Private Firms' Public Scandals." New York Times (February 15, 1986): A27.

Mashaw, Jerry L. "Prodelegation: Why Administrators Should Make Political Decisions." Journal of Law, Economics, and Organizations 1 (1985): 81-100.

Massoth, Lisa. "Firm Suggests Project to Rent Prison Space." Kansas City Times (May 14, 1986): B4.

Mathews, Jay. "Freedom Means Having to Say You're Sorry." Washington Post (November 9, 1983): A5.

Mathias, Robert, and Diane Steelman. "Controlling Prison Populations: An Assessment of Current Mechanisms." National Council on Crime and Delinquency, 1982.

Mausteler, Twedt. "Judge Orders 55 Inmates Out of Private Jail by Tuesday." Pittsburgh Press (March 16, 1986): A10.

May, Edgar. "Maine: Was Inmate Capitalism Out of Control?" Corrections Magazine (February 1981): 17.

Mayer, Connie. "Legal Issues Surrounding Private Operation of Prisons." Criminal Law Bulletin 22 (1986): 309-25.

Meese, Edwin III. Address before The National Conference on Correctional Policy, Washington, D.C., June 1986.

Mercer, James L. "Growing Opportunities in Public Service Contracting." Harvard Business Review (March-April 1983): 178.

Merina, Victor. "INS Defends Conversion of Motel in Residential Area to Detention Site." Los Angeles Times (January 16, 1986): CC II.

Merina, Victor. "INS' Aliens Motel Cited Over Zoning, Building Violations." Los Angeles Times (January 18, 1986).

Merrill, Maurice H. "Standards-A Safeguard For the Exercise of Delegated Power." Nebraska Law Review 47 (1968): 469-91.

Merry, George. "Private Firms Enter the Business of Operating Government Prisons." Christian Science Monitor (August 3, 1984): 6.

Merry, George. "Private Firms Operate Government Prisons." L.A. Daily Journal (August 16, 1984): D5.

Metaxas, John. "Symposium Brouhaha." National Law Journal (March 2, 1987): 4.

Meyer, Jack A. Meeting Human Needs: Toward a New Public

Philosophy. Washington, D.C.: American Enterprise Institute for Public Policy Research, 1982.

Michigan Department of Corrections. "Corrections and the Private Sector." Memorandum prepared by Marjorie Van Ochten, October 8, 1985.

Michigan. Opinion Letter of the Michigan Attorney General. No. 6474 (October 21, 1987).

Miller, Jerome G. "The Private Prison Industry: Dilemmas and Proposals." Notre Dame Journal of Law, Ethics & Public Policy (1986): 465-77.

Miller, Neal, Gail S. Funke, and Robert C. Grieser. "Prison Industries in Transition: Private Sector or Multistate Involvements." Federal Probation 47 (December 1983): 24-31.

Miller, Rod, and Bill Clark. "Maine Jails: Progress Through Partnerships." Construction Bulletin. Washington, D.C.: National Institute of Justice, May 1987.

Mills, Nicolaus. "The March Toward Privatization: The White House Goes Condo." Commonweal 113 (March 14, 1986): 142-43.

Minnesota Citizen's Council on Crime and Justice. Adult Incarceration: The Cost to Minnesota Taxpayers. Minneapolis, 1983.

Minnesota Public Employee. "Correctional Members Approach Privatization Head On at AFSCME Conference." (February 1985).

Mitford, Jessica. "An Update on the 'Prison Business.'" Nation (October 30, 1982): 424-26.

Mondelker, D., D. Netsch, and P. Saldich. State and Local Government in a Federal System. 22d ed. Charlottesville, Va.: Michie Company, 1983.

Money. "Dividends of Crime." (November 1985): 14.

Money. "Getting a Lock on the Private-Prison Business." (May 1986): 32.

Montgomery, Jim. "Corrections Corp. Seeks Lease to Run Tennessee's Prisons." Wall Street Journal (September 13, 1985): 45.

Montilla, M. Robert. Prison Employee Unionism: Management Guide for Correctional Administrators. Washington, D.C.: U.S. Department of Justice, 1978.

Moore, Stephen. "How to Privatize Federal Services By

'Contracting Out.'" Backgrounder No. 494. Washington,
D.C.: The Heritage Foundation, March 13, 1986.

Morgan, Barney. "Hamilton Officials, CCA Head Say Author Twisted
Information." Chattanooga Times (May 21, 1988): B2.

Morgan, Kim E. "Three Escape From Silverdale Workhouse."
Chattanooga Times (August 31, 1985): B3.

Morganthau, Tom. "For Sale: Uncle Sam." Newsweek (December 30,
1985): 18.

Morning Call. "Private Jail Shut Temporarily." (January 31,
1986): A4.

Morning Call. "Judge Orders Inmates From Private Prison."
(March 16, 1986): A4.

Morning Call. "Bill Would Ban Private Prisons." (March 20,
1986): A6.

Morning Call. "Private Prison Moratorium Becomes Law." (March
22, 1986): A19.

Morning Call. "Private Prison Sues State Over Law's
Restrictions." (April 4, 1986): A4.

Morris, David. "Letters to the Editor: Privatization Concept
Works Well Where Used." The State (Columbia, South
Carolina) (November 10, 1985): 16A.

Mullen, Joan. "Corrections and the Private Sector." Research in
Brief. Washington, D.C.: National Institute of Justice,
March 1985.

Mullen, Joan. "Prison Crowding and the Evolution of Public
Policy." The Annals of the American Academy of Political
and Social Science. (March 1985).

Mullen, Joan. "Corrections and the Private Sector." Prison
Journal (Autumn-Winter 1985): 1.

Mullen, J., K.J. Chabotar, and D.M. Carrow. Privatization of
Corrections. Washington, D.C.: National Institute of
Justice, 1985.

Myler, Kathleen. "Captive Market Proves Attractive To a
Developer." Washington Post (September 17, 1983): E54.

NAPA Register. "Private Prisons Are Working." (December 26,
1984): 3.

Narvaez, Alfonso. "Panel Gives Newark 693 Suggestions." New York
Times (November 26, 1986): B2.

Nashville Banner. "Prison Issue Deserves Full Debate." (March 13, 1986).

Nathanson, Nathaniel L. "Separation of Powers and Administrative Law: Delegation, the Legislative Veto, and the 'Independent' Agencies." Northwestern University Law Review 75 (1981): 1064-1111.

National Advisory Committee on Criminal Justice Standards and Goals. Private Security: Report of the Task Force on Private Security. Washington, D.C.: U.S. Government Printing Office, 1976.

National Center for Policy Analysis. Privatization in the U.S.: Cities and Countries (NCPA Policy Report 116). Dallas: June 1985.

National Clearinghouse for Criminal Justice Planning and Architecture. The High Cost of Building Unconstitutional Jails. Urbana, Ill.: University of Illinois, 1977.

National Coalition for Jail Reform. "Jails Operated by Private Companies." In Covering the Jail: Resources for the Media. Washington, D.C.: 1984.

National Criminal Justice Association. Private Sector Involvement In Financing and Managing Correctional Facilities. Washington, D.C.: April 1987.

National Institute of Corrections. Evaluation of Pre-Manufactured Housing for Correctional Purposes. Columbia, S.C.: Carter-Goble Associates, February 1985.

National Institute of Corrections. "Our Crowded Prisons." Annals of the American Academy of Political and Social Science 478. Washington, D.C.: March 1985.

National Institute of Corrections. Private Sector Operation of a Correctional Institution. Washington, D.C.: 1985.

National Institute for Corrections. Resources for Prison Design. Boulder: Library Information Specialists, 1985.

National Institute of Justice Reports. "Corrections and the Private Sector-Fad or Future?" (Videotape) (January 1986).

National Institute of Justice. Correctional Facility Design and Construction Management. Washington, D.C.: February 1985.

National Institute of Justice. Returning to Prison. Washington, D.C.: 1984.

National Institute of Justice. "Private Sector Involvement in

Corrections." <u>Topical Search</u>. Washington, D.C.: 1985.

National Institute of Justice. <u>The Privatization of Corrections</u>. Washington, D.C.: 1985.

National Institute of Justice. <u>Briefing Book: The Justice System and the Private Sector: Traditional Practice and Emerging Trends in the Private Delivery of Police, Court and Correction Services</u>. Washington, D.C.: 1987.

National Institute of Justice. "Fast Findings -- The Privatization of Corrections." Washington, D.C.

<u>National Sheriff</u>. "National Sheriffs' Association Position on Privatization of Adult Local Detention Facilities." (May-June 1985): 38.

<u>National Sheriff</u>. "Privatization of Adult Local Detention Facilities." (June-July 1985): 38.

National Sheriffs' Association. Resolution -- Disapproval of the Private Operation of Jails. Adopted at General Session, June 20, 1984.

Nederhoff, Dale. "Jail Architecture: Planning & Design Concepts for Current & Future Needs." <u>National Sheriff</u> (April-May 1984): 33-43.

Neikirk, Bill. "Going Private Can Jar the Public." <u>Chicago Tribune</u> (March 24, 1986): Cl.

Nesbary, Dale. "Leasing - An Infrastructure Financing Alternative." <u>State Legislatures</u> (February 1986): 7-8.

<u>New Mexican</u>. "Private Jail Applauded." (June 22, 1986): A4.

New Mexico. Opinion Letter of the New Mexico Attorney General. No. 83-5 (November 29, 1983).

<u>New York Times</u>. "Plan by Tennessee Governor Is Aimed at Prison Crowding." (September 18, 1985): A22.

<u>New York Times</u>. "2d Tennessee Plan on Prisons Urged." (November 7, 1985): A33.

<u>New York Times</u>. "Opposition is Vowed on Plan for the Sale of Housing Agency." (December 15, 1985): 38.

<u>New York Times</u>. "The Rush to Privatize." (January 13, 1986): A14.

<u>New York Times</u>. "Judge's Order Removes Inmates From A Bankrupt Private Prison." (March 19, 1986): A31.

New York Times. "Curb on Private Jails Voted By Pennsylvania Lawmakers." (March 20, 1986): A22.

New York Times. "Private-Prison Bill is Signed." (March 23, 1986): 16.

New York Times. "Jails Crowded Too, Study Says." (May 26, 1986): 7.

New York Times. "Privatizing Arms Control." (June 30, 1986): A18.

New York Times. "Private Concern to Staff U.S. Missions in Soviet Union." (November 7, 1986): All.

New York Times. "Delaware Prisoners Finding Careers at 50¢ a Day." (March 1, 1987): A34.

New York Times. "I.M.F. Studies Privatization." (April 18, 1987): 30.

New York Times. "Carpets and Courses for $100 a Day." (April 26, 1987): F17.

New York Times. "Do Profitable Jails Serve a Social Good?" (April 26, 1987): F17.

New York Times. "Can Social Responsibility Be 'Privatized'?" (May 3, 1987): 4.

New York Times. "Tennessee Prisons Calm as Building Goes On." (November 17, 1987): A25.

New York Times. "Many Cruise Ships Fail U.S. Health Standards." (January 24, 1988): 27.

New York Times. "Going Private." (March 18, 1988): A16.

New York Times. "Panel Urges Privatizing of U.S. Services." (March 19, 1988): 54.

News-Herald. "CCA's Handling of Bay Jail Proves Privatization Works." (March 7, 1986): 5A.

Niederberger, Mary, and P.J. Boyle. "8 County Prisoners Sent to Private Jail." Pittsburgh Press (August 12, 1985).

Nissen, Theodore. "Free-Market Prisons." Nation (September 14, 1985): 194.

Nix, Crystal. "City Criticized for Way It Selects Shelter Guards." New York Times (November 1, 1986): 33.

North Carolina Prison and Jail Project. "Prisons and the Private

Sector." Alternatives to Incarceration Bulletin (June-July 1985).

North Carolina Department of Corrections. "Privatization." In Corrections at the Crossroads: Plan for the Future. Raleigh: 1986.

Note. "Delegation of Power to Private Parties." Columbia Law Review 37 (1937): 447-61.

Note. "The State Courts and Delegation of Public Authority to Private Groups." Harvard Law Review 67 (1954): 1398-1408.

Note. "Florida's Adherence to the Doctrine of Nondelegation of Legislative Power." Florida State University Law Review 7 (1979): 541-57.

Note. "Rethinking Regulation: Negotiation as an Alternative to Traditional Rulemaking." Harvard Law Review 94 (1981): 1871.

Note. "Rethinking the Nondelegation Doctrine." Boston University Law Review 62 (1982): 257.

Note. "Private Judging: An Effective and Efficient Alternative to the Traditional Court System." Valparaiso University Law Review 21 (1987): 681-718.

Note. "Regulating Fraud in Military Procurement: A Legal Process Model." Yale Law Journal 95 (1985): 390-413.

Note. "Section 1983 and the Independent Contractor." Georgetown Law Journal 74 (1985): 457-80.

Note. "Third Party Beneficiary and Implied Right of Action Analysis: The Fiction of One Governmental Intent." Yale Law Journal 94 (1985): 875-94.

Note. "Inmates' Rights and the Privatization of Prisons." Columbia Law Review 86 (1986): 1475-1504.

Note. "The Panopticon Revisited: The Problem of Monitoring Private Prisons." Yale Law Journal 96 (1986): 353-75.

Note. "Breaking the Code of Deference: Judicial Review of Private Prisons." Yale Law Journal 96 (1987): 815-37.

Note. "Liability of State Officials and Prison Corporations for Excessive Use of Force Against Inmates of Private Prisons." Vanderbilt Law Review 40 (1987): 983-1021.

Note. "Making Prisons Private: An Improper Delegation of Governmental Power." Hofstra Law Review 15 (1987): 649-75.

Note. "Privatization of Corrections: Is the State Out on a Limb When the Company Goes Bankrupt?" Vanderbilt Law Review 41 (1988): 317-41.

Novey, Donald. "Privatization in Prisons: A Potential Forest Fire Across the USA." U.S. News & World Report (February 1985): 8.

Nozick, Robert. Anarchy, State, and Utopia. New York: Basic Books, 1974.

O'Conner, Paul. "Private Prisons Gain Favor." Hickory (NC) Daily Record (October 12, 1984).

O'Hara, Jim. "Cody Warns of Prison 'Quick Fix.'" Tennessean (August 13, 1985): B1.

O'Hara, Jim. "Private Prison Building Suggested." Tennessean (August 15, 1985): B1.

O'Hara, Jim. "Norris Terms Prison Plan 'Starting Point.'" Tennessean (September 26, 1985): A1.

O'Hara, Jim. "Elevation Eyed for Prison Management Offer: State Check of Financial Benefits." Tennessean (October 2, 1985): B1.

O'Hara, Jim. "'Privatization' of State Prisons: Tennessee's Attempt in 1800's a Far Cry from Successful." Tennessean (October 6, 1985): H1.

O'Hara, Jim. "Cody Says State Must Keep Inmate Control." Tennessean (November 30, 1985): B1.

O'Hara, Jim. "No Need to Make Prison Report Public: Aide." Tennessean (January 18, 1986): 1A.

O'Hara, Jim. "Groups Squabble at Prison Operation." Tennessean (February 25, 1986): B1.

O'Hara, Jim. "Push for Prison Privatization Called Political By Union Official." Tennessean (August 23, 1986): 3B.

O'Hara, Jim. "Prison Pact Must Cut State's Costs 5%." Tennessean (September 5, 1986): B1.

O'Hearn, Jim. "Jail Builder Expects Unfavorable Ruling." Carlsbad Current Argus (August 29, 1983).

Ohio. Opinion Letter of the Ohio Attorney General. No. 85-008 (April 9, 1985).

Orsund, G.A. "Profits vs. Nonprofits-Is It Really a Debate?" Caring (Winter 1987): 22.

Osborne, Diana Taylor, and Jack Brammer. "Private Firm Wins Contract to Run Prison." Lexington Herald-Leader (Lexington, Kentucky)(October 5, 1985).

Ostrow, Ronald. "U.S. Official Urges Study of Private Penal Institutions." Los Angeles Times (February 18, 1985): 4.

O'Toole, George. The Private Sector. New York: W.W. Norton & Co., 1978.

Palumbo, Dennis J. "Privatization and Corrections Policy." Policy Studies Review 5 (1986): 598-605.

Pascour, E.C., Jr. "Privatization: Is It the Answer?" The Freeman (August 1983): 462-69.

Patrick, Allen. "Profit Motive vs. Quality." Corrections Today 48 (April 1986): 68.

Pear, Robert. "U.S. Expanding Use of Private Groups to Collect Debts." New York Times (March 26, 1987): A1.

Pearce, Fred B. "Remarks to the National Institute of Justice's National Forum on Corrections and the Private Sector." Portland, Oregon, Multnomah County Sheriff's Office, February 21, 1985.

Peirce, Neal. "Can Entrepreneurs Cash in on the Prison Crisis?" Charlotte Observer (November 2, 1985): 18A.

Peirce, Neal. "Privatization New Trend in Prison Operations." Nation's Cities Weekly (November 11, 1985): 10.

Pelton, Eric J. "Privatization of the Public Sector: A Look at Which Labor Laws Should Apply to Private Firms Contracted to Perform Public Sevices." Detroit College of Law Review 3 (1986): 805-23.

Pennsylvania Prison Society. "Information on Private Prisons." September 1985.

Pennsylvania Prison Society. "Fact Sheet: Private Prisons." January 1986.

Philadelphia Inquirer. "Prisons Run for Profit: Studying the Bottom Line." (April 11, 1985): 22A.

Philadelphia Inquirer. "Put Private Prisons on Hold." (April 18, 1985): 20A.

Philadelphia Inquirer. "Don't Rush Into Profit Prisons." (June 19, 1985): 10A.

Philadelphia Inquirer. "Private Jails' Phony Promise."
    (February 18, 1986): A10.

Phillips, Jim. "Companies Selected to Operate 2 Prisons."
    Austin American-Statesman (October 20, 1987): B2.

Phillips Swager Associates. Lease Purchasing a County Jail
    Facility. Peoria, Ill.: 1983.

Pietila, Antero. "Soviet Aide Asks Privatization of Service
    Industry." Baltimore Sun (March 6, 1986): 1A.

Pifer, Alan, and Forrest Chisman. "Putting Out a Contract on the
    Government." Wall Street Journal (October 15, 1985): 28.

Pirie, Madsen. "The Privatization Option: The British
    Experience." The Heritage Lectures. Washington, D.C.:
    Heritage Foundation, May 25, 1984.

Pirie, Madsen. Dismantling the State: The Theory and Practice
    of Privatization. Santa Barbara: Local Government Center,
    1985.

Pirie, Madsen. "Sale of the Century: Britain's Privatization
    Bonanza." Policy Review 31 (Winter 1985): 79-80.

Pittsburgh Post-Gazette. "Legislature Reseachers to Study
    Private Prisons." (May 2, 1985): 16.

Pittsburgh Post-Gazette. "Private Jail Opens, May Ease
    Crowding." (May 15, 1985): 4.

Pittsburgh Post-Gazette. "Free Enterprise? Private Facility
    Developer Will Take Over Butler Prisons." (August 31,
    1985): 5.

Pollack, Martin D. "Sale-Leaseback Transactions Adversely
    Affected by a Variety of Recent Developments." Journal of
    Taxation 64 (March 1986): 151.

Poole, Robert W., Jr. "Objections to Privatization." Policy
    Review 24 (1983): 105-19.

Poole, Robert W., Jr. "Privatization: An Option that Local
    Officials Have Yet to Consider." American City and County
    (March 1983): 47-52.

Poole, Robert W., Jr. Municipal Services: The Privatization
    Option (Backgrounder). Washington, D.C.: Heritage
    Foundation, January 1985.

Poole, Robert. Cutting Back City Hall. New York: Universe
    Books, 1980.

Portales News Journal. "The Jail." (September 2, 1983): 1.

Portales News Tribune. "County to Explore Jail, Hospital
     Issues." (August 2, 1983): 1.

Posner, Richard A. "Natural Monopoly and Its Regulation."
     Stanford Law Review 21 (1969): 548-643.

President's Commission on Privatization. Report.
     Privatization: Toward More Effective Government.
     Washington, D.C.: 1988.

Press, Aric. "Bursting at the Seams." Newsweek (November 11,
     1985): 85.

Press, Aric, and David L. Gonzalez. "A Person, Not a Number."
     Newsweek (June 29, 1987): 63.

Pretrial Reporter. "ACA, NGA, NSA Stands on Privatization."
     (April 1985).

Price, Julie. "Utah Firm Picked to Run Prison Camp." Daily News
     of Los Angeles (May 8, 1986): 6.

Price, Julie. "Visitation Limits Might Prompt ACLU to Protest
     Prison Opening." Daily News of Los Angeles (May 14, 1986):
     5.

Priest, George L. "Introduction: The Aims of Privatization."
     Yale Law & Policy Review 6 (1988): 1-5.

Prison Journal. "Corrections and Privatization: An Overview."
     (Autumn-Winter 1985).

Prison Officers' Association. "America's Private Prisons:
     'Penal Institutions as Potential Moneyspinners.'" Jericho
     44 (Fall 1987): 10-11.

Privatization Council. Compendium of Privatization Laws. New
     York: Privatization Council, April 1986 & November 1986
     Supplement.

Privatization: Strategies and Tactics in Privatization and
     Contracting Out. New York: Alexander Research &
     Communications, 1986--.

Prudential-Bache Securities. Correctional Facility Financing.
     New York: Prudential-Bache Securities, 1983.

Quade, Vicki. "Jail Business: Private Firm Breaks In." ABA
     Journal (November 1983): 1611-12.

Quinn, Kevin G. "Privatization." Virginia Town and Country 20
     (1985): 8-10.

Quinn, Kevin G., and Myron A. Olsten. "Privatization: Public-Private Partnerships Providing Essential Services." Municipal Finance Journal 5 (1984): 247-65.

Rafter, Nicole Hahn. "Left Out by the Left: Crime and Crime Control." Socialist Review 89 (1986): 7-23.

Raia, J.N. Issues In Contracting for Probation Services. Albany: New York State Division of Probation, n.d.

Raines, Howell. "Privatization Faces Test in Britain." New York Times (February 29, 1988): D13.

Rains, Lon. "U.S. Program to Test Privately Run Centers for Juvenile Offenders." Washington Post (December 9, 1983): B3.

Raleigh News and Observer. "New Warning on Private Prisons." (February 14, 1986): 22A.

Raleigh News and Observer. "No Rush for Private Prisons." (May 19, 1986): 8A.

Raton Daily Range. "Jail Talks Proceed." (November 15, 1983).

Reason Foundation. "Private Prisons Begin to Establish Track Record." Fiscal Watchdog (June 1986): 1.

A Report on the Regulation of Public Security Guard Services. Washington, D.C.: U.S. Government Printing Office, 1976.

Richard, Sherry. "County's First Private Prison a 'Holiday Inn' Environment." Des Moines Register (March 6, 1985): M1.

Richburg, Keith B. "ACLU Asks for Justice, Literally." Washington Post (December 19, 1985): A21.

Richey, Warren. "Penal Authorities Debate Prisons for Profit." Christian Science Monitor (September 23, 1985): 3.

Richter, Paul. "Going Private Hiring-Out of Public Services on the Rise Along with Foe's Misgivings." Raleigh Times (May 25, 1985).

Riker, Ali. "Prison Lease-Purchasing: Innovation or Evasion?" California Prisoner 15 (1986): 1.

Ring, Charles R. Contracting for the Operation of Private Prisons: Pros and Cons. College Park, Md.: American Correctional Association, 1987.

Ring, Charles. "Private Prisons Need a Fair Trial." Wall Street Journal (May 8, 1987): 22.

Rips, Geoffrey. "Credit-Card Prisons." Texas Observer (March 22, 1985).

Robbins, Ira P., and Michael B. Buser. "Punitive Conditions of Prison Confinement: An Analysis of Pugh v. Locke and Federal Court Supervision of State Penal Administration Under the Eighth Amendment." Stanford Law Review 29 (1977): 893-930.

Robbins, Ira P. "Federalism, State Prison Reform, and Evolving Standards of Human Decency: On Guessing, Stressing, and Redressing Constitutional Rights." University of Kansas Law Review 26 (1978): 551-69.

Robbins, Ira P. Prisoners' Rights Sourcebook: Theory, Litigation, Practice. New York: Clark Boardman, 1980.

Robbins, Ira P. "Should Private Firms Run Prisons for Profit?" Newsday (March 31, 1985): 5.

Robbins, Ira P. Testimony before the Subcommittee on Courts, Civil Liberties, and the Administration of Justice of the House Judiciary Committee, November 13, 1985.

Robbins, Ira P. "Privatization of Corrections: Defining the Issues." Judicature 69 (April-May 1986): 324-31.

Robbins, Ira P. "Privatization of Corrections: Defining the Issues." Federal Probation 50 (September 1986): 24-30.

Robbins, Ira P. "Privatization of Corrections: Defining the Issues." Los Angeles Daily Journal (September 12, 1986): 3.

Robbins, Ira P. "Privatization of Corrections: Defining the Issues." Vanderbilt Law Review 40 (1987): 813-28.

Robbins, Ira P. Prisoners and the Law. New York: Clark Boardman, 1987.

Robbins, Ira P. "Possible Bars to Private Prisons." Wall Street Journal (February 23, 1987): 25.

Robbins, Ira P. "Should Prisons Be Privately Run?: No Quick Fixes." ABA Journal (April 1, 1987): 38.

Robbins, Ira P. "The Impact of the Delegation Doctrine on Prison Privatization." UCLA Law Review 35 (1988): 911-52.

Robbins, Marvin. "Prison Grievance Mechanisms." Maryland Bar Journal (July 1986): 4.

Robbins, Mary Alice. "Prison Proposal Referred to Committee." Lubbock Avalanche-Journal (February 12, 1987): B1.

Roberts, Albert R., and Gerald T. Powers. "The Privatization of Corrections: Methodological Issues and Dilemmas Involved in Evaluative Research." Prison Journal 65 (Autumn-Winter 1985): 95-107.

Roberts, Charley. "Officials Not Eager to Join Trend Toward Privately Run Prisons." L.A. Daily Journal (December 17, 1985): 2.

Roberts, Karen. "New Management Improves Center." Johnson City, Tennessee Press (June 8, 1986).

Roberts, Linda. "Ault Prison Backers Stay Confident." The Coloradoan (March 1, 1987).

Rogers, John M., and Michael H. Sims. "Administrative Law." Kentucky Law Journal 69 (1981): 489-516.

Roome, Frank. "Investing In Prisoners Is Good Business." Corrections Magazine 7 (April 1981): 13-15.

Roper, Brian. "Market Forces, Privatization and Prisons: A Polar Case for Government Policy." The Social Economist on Nuclear Arms: Crime and Prisons: Health Care (1986): 77-92.

Rosenberg, Jean. "Private Prisons: Who Says Crime Doesn't Pay?" Jericho 35 (Spring 1984): 1.

Ross, Bruce. "Privatization, Prisons and the Public." American City and County 99 (December, 1984): 46.

Roswell Daily Record. "Bardacke Vetoes Private Jail Plan." (November 30, 1983).

Rothman, David J. The Discovery of the Asylum. Boston: Little, Brown, 1971.

Rothman, David J. Conscience and Convenience: The Asylum and Its Alternatives in Progressive America. Boston: Litte, Brown, 1980.

Rowlands, David D., ed. The Privatization Option: A Strategy to Shrink the Size of Government. Washington, D.C.: Heritage Foundation Lectures, No. 42, 1985.

Rudolph, Wallace, and Janet Rudolph. "Free Government and the Doctrine of Non-Delegation of Legislative Power." New England Law Review 19 (1984): 551-73.

Russakoff, Dale. "Deficit Worries Bolster New Push for 'Privatization.'" Washington Post (January 13, 1986): All.

Ryan, Mick, and Tony Ward. "Politics and Prison Privatization in Britain." 1988.

Sagarin, Edward, and Jess Maghan. "Should States Opt for Private Prisons? No." Hartford Courant (January 12, 1986): E1.

Sagarin, Edward, and Jess Maghan. "New Privatization Movement Offers Even Less Than the Old." Nashville Banner (January 21, 1986).

Salamon, Lester M. "Rethinking Public Management: Third-Party Government and the Changing Forms of Government Action." Public Policy 29 (1981): 255-75.

Samuel, Peter. "Battling the Budget -- Gracefully." Reason 16 (1984): 34-39.

Savas, E.S. "Municipal Monopoly." Harper's Magazine 243 (December 1971): 55-60.

Savas, E.S. "Municipal Monopolies vs. Competition In Delivering Urban Services." Urban Affairs Annual Reviews 8 (1974): 473-500.

Savas, E.S., ed. Alternatives For Delivering Public Services: Toward Improved Performance. Boulder: Westview Press, 1977.

Savas, E.S. Privatizing the Private Sector: How to Shrink Government. Chatham, N.J.: Chatham House, 1982.

Savas, E.S. "Privatization: A Powerful New Tool For Government." Privatization Review 1 (Summer 1985): 4-6.

Savas, E.S. "Privatization and Prisons." Vanderbilt Law Review 40 (1987): 889-99.

Savas, E.S. Privatization: The Key to Better Government. Chatham, N.J.: Chatham House, 1987.

Savas, E.S. "Private Enterprise Is Profitable Enterprise." New York Times (February 14, 1988): B2.

Sawyer, Kathy. "Prison-Crowding Crisis Deepens in Tennessee." Washington Post (November 6, 1985): A3.

Schlesinger, Mark, and Robert Dorwart. "Ownership and Mental Health Services: A Reappraisal of the Shift Toward Privately Owned Facilities." New England Journal of Medicine 311 (October 11, 1984): 959-65.

Schneider, Ronna G. "The 1982 State Action Trilogy: Doctrinal Contraction, Confusion, and a Proposal for Change." Notre Dame Law Review 60 (1985): 1150-86.

Schneider, Ronna G. "State Action -- Making Sense Out of Chaos
     -- An Historical Approach." University of Florida Law
     Review 37 (1985): 737-84.

Schoen, Kenneth. "Private Prison Operators." New York Times
     (March 28, 1985): A31.

Schoenbrod, David. "The Delegation Doctrine: Could the Court
     Give It Substance?" Michigan Law Review 83 (1985): 1223-90.

Scholz, John T. "Cooperation, Deterrence, and the Ecology of
     Regulatory Enforcement." Law and Society Review 18 (1984):
     179-224.

Schulze, Cathy. "CCA Expected to Sign Contract for New Mexico
     Jail." Nashville Banner (August 4, 1986).

Sechrest, Dale K., Nick Pappas, and Shelley J. Price. "Building
     Prisons: Pre-Manufactured, Prefabricated, and Prototype."
     Federal Probation 51 (March 1987): 35-41.

Security Letter. "Prisons, Correctional Facilities Continuing
     Trend to More Technology, Private Services." (October 1,
     1985): 2.

Seelmyer, John. "Private Business Goes to Jail; Growing Numbers
     of Companies Are Trying to Turn a Profit While Helping to
     Solve America's Prison Problem." Dun's Business Month (June
     1984): 64-67.

Seligman, Daniel. "Incarceration Unlimited." Fortune (July 25,
     1983): 31-32.

Sexton, George E., Barbara J. Auerbach, Franklin C. Farrow,
     Robert H. Lawson, John M. Schaller, and Merily B.
     McFadden. Private Sector Involvement In Prison-Based
     Businesses: A National Assessment. Washington, D.C.:
     National Institute of Justice, 1985.

Sexton, George E., Franklin C. Farrow, and Barbara J. Auerbach.
     "The Private Sector and Prison Industries." Research in
     Brief. Washington, D.C.: National Institute of Justice,
     August 1985.

Seymour, William. "San Joaquin Valley Town Gears Up For New
     State Prison -- and Business." Los Angeles Daily Journal
     (December 28, 1984): 2.

Sharkansky, Ira. "Government Contracting." State Government 53
     (Winter 1980): 22-27.

Shearson Lehman/American Express Inc. Financing Alternatives For
     State and Local Correctional Facilities, n.d.

Shen, Fern. "Investors Hope to Spring Profit from Private Prison." Hartford Courant (April 1, 1984): A1.

Shenkman, Richard. "Rescue By the Private Sector." National Review (May 30, 1980): 652.

Sher, Andy. "Three Flee Silverdale; Two Caught Hailing Cab." Chattanooga Times (April 8, 1985): B1.

Sher, Andy. "Roberts Recommends State Take CCA up on Offer to Run Prisons." Chattanooga Times (September 19, 1985): B1.

Sherman, Michael, and Gordon Hankins. Imprisonment In America: Choosing the Future. Chicago: University of Chicago Press, 1981.

Shipp, E.R. "Group Aiding Ex-Convicts Begins Running A Jail." New York Times (February 17, 1985): 28.

Shuler, Marsha. "Private Financing for Prisons Considered By Corrections Dept." Baton Rouge Morning Advocate (July 12, 1985).

Shuler, Marsha. "Task Force Against Privatizing Prisons." Baton Rouge Morning Advocate (February 21, 1986).

Siegal, Randy. "For Rent: Tiny Room, No View." USA Today (November 18, 1985): 10A.

Simons, Marlise. "Brazil Inmates Find Meditation a Calm Island." New York Times (March 14, 1986): 8.

Skoler, Daniel L. "Private Sector Delivery of Criminal Justice Services -- The Hidden Impact." Criminal Justice Digest 4 (1976): 1-3.

Slind-Flor, Victoria. "Criminal Bar Told to Watch Private Prisons." Daily Journal (January 2, 1987).

Smith, Bruce. The New Political Economy: The Public Use of the Private Sector. New York: John Wiley & Sons, 1975.

Smith, George. "States Should Ignore Prison Overcrowding." USA Today (November 18, 1985): 10A.

Smith, James. "Reform Prisons; Don't Sell Them." Tennessean (March 12, 1986): 8A.

Smith, Lee. "Reagan's Budget: Selling Off the Government." Fortune (March 3, 1986): 70-74.

Snedeker, Michael. "Private Prisons -- A Bankrupt Idea." California Prisoner 15 (1986): 5.

Sontheimer, Henry G. "The Privatization of Corrections in the Juvenile and Adult Systems of Pennsylvania." Paper presented to the Annual Meeting of the American Society of Criminology (Atlanta, GA). Shippensburg, Pennsylvania: Center for Juvenile Justice Training and Research, 1986.

South Carolina Board of Corrections. "Position of the Board of Corrections Regarding Privatization of Corrections." Columbia, S.C.: 1985.

South Carolina Department of Corrections. "Cost Surveying Document for a Privately-Managed 600 Bed Medium/Maximum Facility." Columbia, S.C.: 1985.

South Carolina. State Reorganization Commission. "Draft of Suggested Items to be in RFP for Private Contracting Services to Operate a Med/Max Prison." Columbia, S.C.: 1985.

Spitzer, Steven, and Andrew Scull. "Social Control In Historical Perspective: From Private to Public Responses to Crime." In Corrections and Punishment, ed. D. Greenberg. Beverly Hills: Sage, 1977.

Starr, Paul. "The Meaning of Privatization." Yale Law & Policy Review 6 (1988): 6-41.

Starr, Paul. The Limits of Privatization. Washington, D.C.: Economic Policy Institute, 1987.

Steelman, Diane. Overcrowding in New Jersey. Hackensack, N.J.: National Council on Crime and Delinquency, 1981.

Stein, Mark. "California's First 'Private Prison' is Open For Business." Los Angeles Times (May 29, 1986): 3.

Steinberg, Sheldon S., J. Michael Keating, and James J. Dahl. Potential For Contracted Management In Local Correctional Facilities. Washington, D.C.: Center for Human Services for the National Institute of Corrections, 1981.

Steinhardt, Barry. "Problems with Private Prisons." Pittsburgh Post-Gazette (June 8, 1985): 6.

Steptoe, Sonja. "Inmates Claim Prisons Are Failing to Provide Adequate Medical Care." Wall Street Journal (May 15, 1986): 1.

Stevens, Catherine. "Are We Ready for this Growth Industry?" Financial World (October 30, 1985): 26.

Stewart, James K. "Opening Remarks to the National Forum on Corrections and the Private Sector." Washington, D.C.: National Institute of Justice, February 20, 1985.

Stewart, James K. "Breaking Up Government's Monopoly on Prison Cells." New York Times (March 3, 1985): E22.

Stewart, James K. "Part I . . . The Private Sector and Corrections: Some Factors to Consider in Your Planning." Corrections Digest (May 22, 1985): 1.

Stewart, James K. "Part II . . . The Private Sector and Corrections: Some Factors to Consider in Your Planning." Corrections Digest (June 5, 1985): 4-5.

Stewart, James K. "Public Safety and Private Police." Public Administration Review 45 (November 1985): 758-65.

Stewart, James K. Statement before the President's Commission on Privatization, December 22, 1987.

Stewart, Richard B. "The Reformation of American Administrative Law." Harvard Law Review 88 (1975): 1669.

Stigler, George J. "The Theory of Economic Regulation." Bell Journal of Economics & Management Science 2 (1971): 3-21.

Strauss, Peter L. "The Place of Agencies in Government: Separation of Powers and the Fourth Branch." Columbia Law Review 84 (1984): 573-669.

Stromberg, Amy. "D.C. Officials Consider Private Prison in Pa. to House City Inmates." Washington Times (March 13, 1986): 6B.

Stromberg, Amy. "D.C. Flirts With Idea of Private, Showy Jail." Washington Times (April 1, 1986): 1A.

Sullivan, Ronald. "Surge in AIDS Cases Leading to Crisis in Prisons." New York Times (March 5, 1987): B1.

Surber, Art. "CCA Takes Keys: Private Firm Encounters Minor Problems, Flooding in First Day." Panama City News-Herald (October 2, 1985): 1A.

Swallow, Wendy. "Freddie Mac Conversion to Private Firm Opposed." Washington Post (February 12, 1987): D12.

Swart, Stanley L. "Private Sector Corrections in the 1980's: Some Notes." Journal of Offender Counseling, Services & Rehabilitation (Fall 1982): 79-82.

Tafoya, Fernando. "The Trend to Privatization: Analysis." Jericho 40 (Fall 1985): 1.

Taft, P.B., Jr. "Private Vendors, Part 1 -- The Fiscal Crisis in Private Corrections." Corrections Magazine 8 (December

1982): 27-32.

Taft, P.B., Jr. "Private Vendors, Part 2 -- Survival of the Fittest." Corrections Magazine 9 (February 1983): 36.

Talbot, Charles K., ed. Privatization In Canadian Corrections: A More Economical and Humane Solution? Ottawa: University of Ottawa, 1981.

Taylor, Paul. "Should Private Firms Build, Run Prisons?" Washington Post (May 7, 1985): A15.

Taylor, Paul. "States Showing Growing Interest in Privately-Run Prisons." Albuquerque Journal (May 10, 1985): B2.

Taylor-Weeks, Grier. "The Trend to Privatization: Behind the Scenes." Jericho 40 (Fall 1985): 7.

Telser, L.G. "On the Regulation of Industry: A Note." Journal of Political Economy 77 (1969): 937-52.

Teltsch, Kathleen. "Cost Bringing Punishments Out of Prison." New York Times (July 19, 1987): 1.

Templeton, Patricia. "Bill Lets Norris Decide on CCA." Nashville Banner (November 12, 1985): A1.

Templeton, Patricia. "Senate Panel Tables Private Prison Plan." Nashville Banner (March 11, 1986): A1.

Templeton, Patricia. "CCA Asks to Manage One Prison." Nashville Banner (April 1, 1986): A1.

Templeton, Patricia, and Mike Pigott. "Senate Panel Passes Private Prison Bill After Intense Debate." Nashville Banner (April 8, 1986).

Tennessean. "Bar Wants Prison Privatization Stayed." (February 12, 1986): 1.

Tennessee. "Private Companies Will Bid on CCWC." The Corrections Courier, Tennessee Department of Corrections (Spring 1986): 6.

Tennessee. Opinion Letter of the Tennessee Attorney General. No. 85-286 (November 27, 1985).

Tennessee House of Representatives. Finance, Ways and Means Committee. Hearings on House Bill No. 1334 and Private Prisons. Statement of Craig Becker, Associate General Counsel, American Federation of State, County and Municipal Employees, AFL-CIO. February 24, 1986.

Tennessee House of Representatives. Finance, Ways & Means

Committee. Hearings on House Bill No. 1334 and Private Prisons. Statement of Ira P. Robbins, Professor of Law and Justice, The American University, Washington College of Law, February 24, 1986.

Tennessee House of Representatives. Finance, Ways & Means Committee. Hearings on House Bill No. 1334 and Private Prisons. Statement of Hedy Weinberg, Executive Director, American Civil Liberties Union of Tennessee, February 24, 1986.

Terrell, Paul, and Ralph M. Kramer. "Contracting With NonProfits." Public Welfare 42 (Winter 1984): 31-37.

Thomas, Charles, and Linda Calvert-Hanson. "Evaluating Civil Liability Risks In 'Privatized' Correctional Facilities." Paper presented at the 32nd Annual Southern Conference on Corrections, Tallahassee, February 26-27, 1987.

Thomas, Pierre. "Private Jail Is Urged in Pr. William." Washington Post (February 24, 1988): B5.

Thompson, Mark. "Controversial ACA Policy Calls for Further Privatization." Criminal Justice Newsletter 16 (February 1, 1985): 1.

Thompson, Mark. "Who's Minding the Store?" Student Lawyer (February 1986): 24.

Tillet, Debbie C. Private Jails: Contracting Out Public Service. Lexington, Ky.: Council of State Government, 1985.

Timberlake, Mary Gael. "Finance Subcommittee Considers Prison Construction Privatization Act." Tax Notes 24 (September 24, 1984): 1220-21.

Time. "Public Service, Private Profits." (February 10, 1986): 64.

Times Union. "Privatization of Prison Industries Assailed." (May 13, 1986): B1.

Tofani, Loretta. "More Correctional Facilities Operated by Private Firms." Washington Post (February 18, 1985): A6.

Tolchin, Martin. "As Privately Owned Prisons Increase, So Do Their Critics." New York Times (February 11, 1985): A1.

Tolchin, Martin. "Operation of Prisons by Private Groups on the Increase, Causing Concern." Los Angeles Daily Journal (February 15, 1985): 18.

Tolchin, Martin. "Companies Easing Crowded Prisons." New York Times (February 17, 1985): A29.

Tolchin, Martin. "Jails Run by Private Company Force It to Face Question of Accountability." New York Times (February 19, 1985): A15.

Tolchin, Martin. "New Studies Are Planned on Trend Toward Privately Operated Jails." New York Times (February 25, 1985): A18.

Tolchin, Martin. "Breaking up Government's Monopoly on Prison Cells." New York Times (March 3, 1985): 22E.

Tolchin, Martin. "Governors Cautious in Endorsing the Private Operation of Prisons." New York Times (April 3, 1985): 26.

Tolchin, Martin. "Privately Operated Prison in Tennessee Reports $200,000 in Cost Overruns." New York Times (May 21, 1985): A14.

Tolchin, Martin. "More Cities Paying Industry to Provide Public Services." New York Times (May 28, 1985): A1.

Tolchin, Martin. "When the Justice System is Put Under Contract." New York Times (August 4, 1985): E5.

Tolchin, Martin. "Private Concern Makes Offer to Run Tennessee's Prisons." New York Times (September 13, 1985): A14.

Tolchin, Martin. "Experts Foresee Adverse Effects from Private Control of Prisons." New York Times (September 17, 1985): A17.

Tolchin, Martin. "Disputing the President on Privatization." New York Times (November 10, 1985): 64.

Tolchin, Martin. "Private Guards Get New Role in Public Law Enforcement." New York Times (November 29, 1985): A1.

Tolchin, Martin. "Off-Duty Officers Doubling as Private Guards, But System Draws Criticism." New York Times (December 1, 1985): 5A.

Tolchin, Martin. "Prospects of Privately Run Prisons Divides Pennsylvania Legislators." New York Times (December 15, 1985): 78.

Tolchin, Martin. "Bar Groups Urge Halt in Use of Privately Run Jails." New York Times (February 12, 1986): A28.

Tolchin, Martin. "U.S. Links Some Foreign Aid to Privatization." New York Times (February 20, 1986): A13.

Tolchin, Martin. "Governors' Interest in Private Prisons Rising." New York Times (March 2, 1986): 35L.

Travis, Lawrence F. III, and Edward J. Latessa, Jr. "The Role of Private Enterprise In Institutional Corrections." Paper presented at the ASPA/ICMA Joint Conference on Privatization and Alternative Service Delivery, Cincinnati, November 1984.

Travis, Lawrence F. III, Edward J. Latessa, and Gennaro F. Vito. "Private Enterprise and Institutional Corrections: A Call for Caution." Federal Probation 49 (December 1985): 11-16.

Travisono, Anthony P. "A Rose By Any Other Name . . . ." Corrections Today 46 (April 1984): 4.

Tribe, Laurence. "The Legislative Veto Decision: A Law By Any Other Name?" Harvard Journal on Legislation 21 (1984): 1-59.

Tully, Shawn. "Europe Goes Wild Over Privatization." Fortune (March 2, 1987): G8.

Uchitelle, Louis. "Public Services Found Better If Private Agencies Compete." New York Times (April 26, 1988): A1.

Uehlein, Julius. "Prisons: No Place for Private Enterprise." Pennsylvania AFL-CIO News (May 1985).

Uhlfelder, Mark N., and Sally Hanlon. "The New Face of Privatization Under Tax Reform." Tax Notes 33 (October 13, 1986): 135-37.

Unger, Harry. "Private Firm Has Alternative to Jail." San Gabriel Valley Tribune (May 11, 1986).

United Kingdom. House of Commons. Third Report from the Home Affairs Committee: State and Use of Prisons. April 23, 1987.

United Kingdom. House of Commons. Fourth Report from the Home Affairs Committee: Contract Provision of Prisons. May 6, 1987.

United Nations Centre on Transnational Corporations. Features and Issues in Turnkey Contracts in Developing Countries: A Technical Paper. New York: United Nations, 1983.

USA Today. "Private Investing." (November 30, 1984).

USA Today. "States Must Act to Ease Overcrowding." (November 18, 1985): 10A.

U.S. Congress. House Committee on the Judiciary. Subcommittee on Courts, Civil Liberties, and the Administration of Justice. Hearings on Privatization of Corrections. 99th

Cong., 1st and 2d sess., November 13, 1985, and March 18, 1986. G.P.O. Serial No. 40.

U.S. Congress. House Committee on Appropriations. Subcommittee on Commerce, Justice, State, the Judiciary and Related Agencies. Departments of Commerce, Justice and State, the Judiciary, and Related Agencies Appropriations for 1986: Hearings on FY 1986 Appropriations. 98th Cong., 1st sess., 1985: 464-73 (statement of David Kelley).

U.S. Congress. Senate. Prison Construction Privatization Act of 1984: S.2933. 98th Cong., 2d sess., 1984.

U.S. Congress. Senate Committee on Appropriations. Subcommittee on the District of Columbia. District of Columbia Appropriations FY 1986 -- Prison Privatization. 99th Cong., 1st sess., May 14, 1985.

U.S. Congress. Senate Joint Economic Committee. Hearing and Privatization of Prison Construction in New York. 98th Cong., 2d sess., 1984. S.Hrg. 98-1279.

U.S. Department of Justice. Bureau of Justice Statistics. Justice Expenditures and Employment. Washington, D.C.: 1983.

U.S. Department of Justice. Bureau of Justice Statistics. Children in Custody: 1982/83 Census of Juvenile Detention and Correctional Facilities. Washington, D.C.: 1983.

U.S. Department of Justice. Alternative Financing of Jail Construction. Boulder: Information Center, National Institute of Corrections, December 1983.

U.S. Department of Justice. National Institute of Justice. Professional Conference Series: "Corrections and the Private Sector: A National Forum." February 20-22, 1985.

U.S. Department of Justice. Office of Juvenile Justice and Delinquency Prevention. Private Sector Corrections Initiative for the Chronic Serious Juvenile Offender: Notice of Issuance of Guidelines for New Program Initiative. April 4, 1984.

U.S. Department of Justice. Prisoners in 1987. Bulletin. Washington, D.C.: Bureau of Justice Statistics, 1988.

U.S. Department of Justice. Report to the Nation on Crime and Justice: The Data. 2d ed. Washington, D.C.: Bureau of Justice Statistics, 1988.

U.S. Department of Justice. National Institute of Law Enforcement and Criminal Justice. The National Manpower Survey of the Criminal Justice System: An Executive

Summary. Washington, D.C.: GPO, 1975.

U.S. General Accounting Office. Federal Productivity: Potential Savings From Private Sector Cost Comparisons. Washington, D.C.: GAO, December 1986.

United States Law Week. "City's Vehicle `Booting' Program Violates Due Process." (December 24, 1985): 1097.

U.S. News & World Report. "When Uncle Sam Goes Into Business for Himself." (July 27, 1981): 61.

U.S. News & World Report. "'No Vacancy' Signs Go Up at Nation's Jails." (December 23, 1985): 39.

U.S. Private Security Advisory Council. A Report on the Regulation of Private Security Guard Services. Washington, D.C.: U.S. Government Printing Office, 1976.

Utah Foundation. "Contracting for Corrections." Research Report No. 469. Salt Lake City: 1985.

Vilinsky, A., G.S. Funke, and B.L. Wayson. Cost-Effectiveness Analysis of Community Corrections in Connecticut. Alexandria, Va.: Institute for Economic and Policy Studies, 1980.

Vise, David. "Private Company Asks for Control of Tenn. Prisons." Washington Post (September 22, 1985): F1.

Vogel, Todd. "Jails Could Be Texas' Next Ten-Gallon Business." Business Week (April 20, 1987): 33.

Voisin, Elizabeth. "Privatization and Prisons." City and State (April 1985): 1.

Von Hoffman, Nicholas. "Penal System -- Public or Private?" Baton Rouge Morning Advocate (October 28, 1985).

Wackenhut Corporation. 1986 Annual Report.

Wald, Matthew. "AIDS Cases Found Rising Slowly in Jails." New York Times (March 12, 1987): A18.

Walker, David. "Prisons: Must Britain Be a Slave to Tradition?" The Times (April 24, 1984): 12.

Wall Street Journal. "Seeking to Aid Society, Control Data Takes on Many Novel Ventures." (December 22, 1982): 1.

Wall Street Journal. "Prison for Profit." (February 5, 1987): 20.

Walzer, Michael. "At McPrison and Burglar King, It's . . . Hold the Justice." New Republic 192 (April 8, 1985): 10-12.

Ward, Joe. "Prison Business Captures Interest of Entrepreneurs from Kentucky." Courier-Journal (Louisville, Kentucky) (May 19, 1986).

Warren, David. "Leases and Service Contracts with Tax-Exempt Entities After the DRA." Tax Adviser (April 1985): 230-34.

Washington Post. "Private Firms Operate Jails: Legality Challenged." (December 20, 1984): E1.

Washington Post. "Private Prisons Suggested." (December 31, 1984): B7.

Washington Post. "Judges Close Prison's Doors." (October 24, 1985): A14.

Washington Post. "At Last, a Prison Site . . . and a Prison Worry." (March 23, 1986): F6.

Washington Post. "Suing Civil Servants." (March 5, 1987): A26.

Washington Post. "Firm to Build, Run Texas Prison Centers." (April 21, 1988): A24.

Waters, Alan Rufus, and Gayle R. Avant. "Privatization: Calculating Costs and Making Hard Choices." Paper presented at the 48th Annual National Conference of the American Society for Public Administration, Boston, March 28-April 1, 1987.

Watkin, Tom. "TM Group in Vt. Wants to Build Jail." National Law Journal (August 15, 1983): 3.

Wedel, Kenneth, Arthur Katz, and Ann Weick. Social Services by Government Contracts: A Policy Analysis. New York: Praeger, 1979.

Weinberg, Hedy. "Privatization of Prisons." In ACLU of Tennessee -- 1985 Bill of Rights Report. 1985.

Weinberg, Hedy. ACLU Position Paper of Prison Privatization in Tennessee. Nashville: American Civil Liberties Union of Tennessee, March 11, 1986.

Weisheit, Ralph A. "Trends in Programs for Female Offenders: The Use of Private Agencies as Service Providers." International Journal of Offender Therapy and Comparative Criminology 29 (1985): 35-42.

Wengard, Al. Prisons for Profit: A Moral Dilemma. Elkhart, Ind.: Mennonite Central Committee, Office of Criminal Justice, March 1986.

Wengard, Al.   "Privatization of Prisons."   JSAC Update Criminal Justice 8 (Winter 1986): 6-7.

Werkman, Dirk.   "Private Prison Operation Opposed."   Daily News of Los Angeles (December 17, 1985): 9.

Werkman, Dirk.   "Two-House Panel Passes Prison Bill."   Daily News of Los Angeles (August 26, 1986): 3.

Wesner, David.   "Crowding, Lack of Funds Have Counties Considering Privately Operated Jails."   Albuquerque Journal (November 6, 1983): C3.

West, Jude P.   The Role of Correctional Industries -- A Summary Report.   Washington, D.C.: U.S. Department of Justice, Law Enforcement Assistance Administration, 1972.

Westbrook, James E.   "The Use of the Nondelegation Doctrine in Public Sector Labor Law: Lessons from Cases That Have Perpetuated an Anachronism."   Saint Louis University Law Journal 30 (1986): 331-84.

White, Katherine.   "N.C. May Use Private Firm: Results Mixed in Other States Trying Out Private Facilities."   Charlotte Observer (March 31, 1986): B1.

Whitfield, Robert.   "Partnership: Private and Public Agencies."   Caring (Winter 1987): 23.

Widner, Jamie.   "Denver Firm Offers Lease Proposal."   Clovis News Journal (August 2, 1983).

Wiginton, Ron.   "County to Ink Contract with CCA on Tuesday."   Panama City News-Herald (August 20, 1985): 1A.

Wiginton, Ron.   "County Gives CCA Vote of Confidence."   Panama City News-Herald (August 21, 1985): 1A.

Wiginton, Ron.   "County Still Seeks CCA Jail Monitor."   Panama City News-Herald (September 24, 1985): 4B.

Wiginton, Ron.   "Watchdog Picked: County Emergency Management Director Named CCA Jail Monitor."   Panama City News-Herald (September 25, 1985): 1E.

Wiginton, Ron.   "Smith Considers CCA Certification."   Panama City News-Herald (September 27, 1985): 1A.

Wiginton, Ron.   "CCA Takes Over: Keys to County Jail Handed to Private Firm This Morning."   Panama City News-Herald (October 1, 1985): 1A.

Wiginton, Ron.   "CCA: Chairman of Board Visits the Facility."

Panama City News-Herald (October 3, 1985): 1D.

Wiginton, Ron. "Judge to Rule on CCA Contract with County." Panama City News-Herald (October 4, 1985): 1A.

Wiginton, Ron. "Ruling Expected: Simons to Hear CCA Case; Inmates Like Jail Takeover." Panama City News-Herald (October 9, 1985): 1A.

Wiginton, Ron. "Request Denied: Simons Blocks Injunction to Stop CCA Jail Takeover." Panama City News-Herald (October 10, 1985): 1A.

Wiginton, Ron. "County Rebuts Opinion on CCA." Panama City News-Herald (October 26, 1985): 1A.

Wiginton, Ron. "Bay to Pay Jailers: Commission to Decide Later Which Fund Will Foot the Bill." Panama City News-Herald (November 20, 1985): 1E.

Wiginton, Ron. "Jail Bill is Baited: Information Committee Has Turns Out to be Misleading." Panama City News-Herald (January 9, 1986): 1B.

Wiginton, Ron. "Lying is Denied: Attorney: Information On Jail is 'Misunderstood.'" Panama City News-Herald (January 10, 1986): 1A.

Wiginton, Ron. "CCA Jail Facility is Subject of Reviews and National News." Panama City News-Herald (February 20, 1986): 1A.

Wildstrom, Stephen H., and Richard Hoppe. "The OMB's Latest Hat Trick: Trying to Sell Government Assets." Business Week (December 23, 1985): 37.

Williams, Karrie. "Interim Jail Plan Discussed." Las Vegas Optic (October 21, 1983).

Williams, Karrie. "New Jail Plan Being Studied." Las Vegas Optic (October 21, 1983).

Williams, Karrie. "Guadalupe Votes Against Regional Jail." Las Vegas Optic (November 28, 1983).

Wilson, John. "Proposal Ready on Transfer of Workhouse to Private Firm." Chattanooga News-Free Press (August 24, 1984): A1.

Wilson, John. "Mahn Wary of Penal Transfer; Urges Careful Scrutiny of Corrections Corp. Contract." Chattanooga News-Free Press (August 26, 1984): A1.

Winter, Steven. "Tennessee v. Garner and the Democratic Practice of Judicial Review." Review of Law and Social Change (1986): 679.

Wise, Stuart M. "There's No Business Like Jail Business." National Law Journal 5 (June 20, 1983): 43.

Wittenauer, Cheryl, and Harrison Fletcher. "County Selects Firm to Operate Jail." New Mexican (June 21, 1986): C1.

Woestendiek, John. "Case Against Private Jails Is Aired." Philadelphia Inquirer (February 1, 1986): 1-B.

Wolf, Don. "Private Jail Ban Wanted for a Year." Beaver County Times (May 30, 1985).

Wolfgang, Marvin E. Prisons: Present and Possible. Lexington, Mass.: Lexington Books, 1979.

Woolley, Mary. "Prisons for Profit: Policy Considerations for Government Officials." Dickinson Law Review 90 (1985): 307-31.

Woolley, Mary. Private Prisons: Policy Considerations for Public Officials. Harrisburg, Pa.: House Judiciary Committee, December 1985.

Workman, Bill. "How a Private Firm Runs a San Mateo Prison." San Francisco Chronicle (April 13, 1985): 6.

Wortzel, Lawrence H. "'Privatizing' Does Not Always Work." New York Times (February 14, 1988): B2.

Wray, Harmon L. "Prisons for Profit." Comin' Out: The Project Return Newsletter. (Winter 1985): 11-15.

Wray, Harmon L. "Cells for Sale?" Southern Neighborhoods 9 (May-June 1986): 3-5.

Wray, Harmon L. "Cells for Sale." Southern Changes 8 (September 1986): 3-6.

Wynne, John M., Jr. Prison Employee Unionism: The Impact on Correctional Administration and Programs. Washington, D.C.: U.S. Department of Justice, 1978.

Wyoming Eagle. "Karpen Comments on Prison." (April 4, 1987).

Yondorf, Barbara. "Innovative Approaches to Prison Finance." The Fiscal Letter: An Information Service of the National Conference of State Legislatures 8 (1986): 1.

Young, Peter. The Prison Cell. London: ASI (Research) Ltd., 1987.

Yozwiak, Steve. "Bill to Let Private Firms Construct, Run
    Arizona Prisons O.K.'d by Panel." Arizona Republic (January
    20, 1987): A4.

Zedlewski, Edwin W. The Economics of Disincarceration. NIJ
    Reports. Washington, D.C.: National Institute of Justice,
    1984.

Zedlewski, Edwin W. "Making Confinement Decisions." Research in
    Brief. Washington, D.C.: National Institute of Justice,
    June 1987.

Zeitoun, Louis. "Contract Services -- The Canadian Experience."
    Corrections Today (August 1984).

Ziegler, Edward H., Jr. "Legitimizing the Administrative
    State: The Judicial Development of the Nondelegation
    Doctrine in Kentucky." Northern Kentucky Law Review 4
    (1977): 87-120.

Zoley, George C. "Contracting Correctional Facilities to the
    Private Sector." Proceedings of the 29th Annual Southern
    Conference on Corrections, March 1985, Florida State
    Conference Center, Tallahassee.

Zuesse, Eric. "Prison Run as Business Could Well Profit the
    Taxpayer, the Victim, the Inmates." Moneysworth 10 (March
    1980): 12.